Designing Embedded Hardware

Other resources from O'Reilly

Related titles
Building Embedded Linux Systems

Home Hacking Projects for Geeks

Hardware Hacking Projects for Geeks

PC Hardware Buyer's Guide

Programming Embedded Systems in C and C++

Car PC Hacks

Smart Home Hacks

oreilly.com
oreilly.com is more than a complete catalog of O'Reilly books. You'll also find links to news, events, articles, weblogs, sample chapters, and code examples.

oreillynet.com is the essential portal for developers interested in open and emerging technologies, including new platforms, programming languages, and operating systems.

Conferences
O'Reilly brings diverse innovators together to nurture the ideas that spark revolutionary industries. We specialize in documenting the latest tools and systems, translating the innovator's knowledge into useful skills for those in the trenches. Visit *conferences.oreilly.com* for our upcoming events.

Safari Bookshelf (*safari.oreilly.com*) is the premier online reference library for programmers and IT professionals. Search across thousands of electronic books simultaneously and zero in on the information you need in seconds. Read the books on your Bookshelf from cover to cover or simply flip to the page you need. Try it today for free.

SECOND EDITION

Designing Embedded Hardware

John Catsoulis

O'REILLY®

Beijing · Cambridge · Farnham · Köln · Paris · Sebastopol · Taipei · Tokyo

Designing Embedded Hardware, Second Edition
by John Catsoulis

Published by O'Reilly Media, Inc., 1005 Gravenstein Highway North, Sebastopol, CA 95472.

O'Reilly books may be purchased for educational, business, or sales promotional use. Online editions are also available for most titles (*safari.oreilly.com*). For more information, contact our corporate/institutional sales department: (800) 998-9938 or *corporate@oreilly.com*.

Editor:	Andy Oram
Production Editor:	Sanders Kleinfeld
Cover Designer:	Emma Colby
Interior Designer:	David Futato

Printing History:

November 2002:	First Edition.
May 2005:	Second Edition.

 This book uses RepKover™, a durable and flexible lay-flat binding.

ISBN: 0-596-00755-8

[M]

This book is dedicated to my uncle,
Vince Catsoulis

Table of Contents

Preface

[Enlightenment] resides as comfortably in the circuits
of a digital computer ... as at the top of a mountain or
in the petals of a flower.
—Robert M. Pirsig
Zen and the Art of Motorcycle Maintenance

Welcome to the second edition of *Designing Embedded Hardware*. In these pages, I hope to give you an understanding of the design process for creating computer hardware. Just as there is beauty in well-written software, there is beauty in well-designed hardware. With embedded computers, you get to understand the machine at all levels, at once aware of currents flowing through circuit traces and software executing complex algorithms. In fact, it is not possible to write embedded software without understanding the hardware, nor is it possible to design hardware without understanding software. You become involved with the machine to a degree beyond that which is possible with desktop computers. Best of all, it's a lot of fun.

In selecting chips and designs for this book, I have tried to choose, where possible, parts that are both trivial to use yet exceptionally useful. I have no connection, financial or otherwise, with any of the companies or businesses mentioned in this book, and I receive no benefits from them. Every component or product included in this book is there based on its own merits. You may notice a prevalence of components from certain manufacturers. This simply reflects my personal preference for using their chips, based on my experience. Such companies produce chips that are easy to use, are reliable and robust, have great technical support, and provide thorough and comprehensive technical data. In other words, they meet all the necessary requirements for inclusion in a book for beginners.

When the first edition of *Designing Embedded Hardware* was published, I deliberately left out software. There were two reasons for this. First, there are many good books already written on C programming, embedded firmware development in C, porting Linux to embedded systems, coding in Python, writing Java software, and so on. (And of course, the best of these are naturally published by O'Reilly.) The second reason is that assembly language, that most basic of programming tools, is so different from processor to processor that it would not have been possible to cover all the instruction sets of the processors in the book, let alone do them justice. However, I have decided to include some software in this edition. I won't even attempt to cover the instructions of each processor in this book. What I will do is show some simple assembly language techniques. While the instructions may be wildly different between architectures, the basic concepts are the same.

Also new to this book is a chapter on the Forth programming language. Forth is a relatively old language that has faded from the forefront of software development, and as such, it's rare to find a book giving the language good coverage. Forth is a very useful tool for embedded system development to which many engineers have yet to be exposed. The language is the basis of the Open Firmware standard and is used by design engineers at Apple, Sun, and many other manufacturers. It's a useful language to know, and it is worth taking the time to learn.

Many of the designs in this book look easy, and they are. They are intended as simple building blocks, allowing you to mix and match to achieve the embedded systems you need. I hope you will find this book useful. Once you've finished reading it, go and build something!

—John Catsoulis
Brisbane, Australia
January 2005
jtc@embedded.com.au
http://www.embedded.com.au

Organization of This Book

This book is informally divided into four sections. The first covers fundamental concepts and introductory material. The second section gives an overview of assembly language and Forth. From there, we'll look at peripherals and how to add functionality to your embedded systems. Finally, we'll look at a variety of processors widely used in embedded systems, and look at the design process for integrating them into computers.

Chapter 1 gives an overview of computer architectures and explains what constitutes an embedded system. Chapters 2 and 3 explore software with assembly language and Forth.

Chapter 4 provides some background electronics theory and introduces some important concepts. If you're already electronics-savvy, then you can skip on to Chapter 5, where we'll look at providing power for your embedded system. We'll also look at how to protect your embedded computer against electrical interference and other gremlins that can cause it grief. In Chapter 6, you'll see how to physically produce and debug an embedded computer system.

Chapters 7 and 8 cover SPI and I²C, two protocols that allow a wide range of small peripherals to be added to microcontrollers. Chapters 9, 10, and 11 cover serial interfaces. These give our embedded system access to host computers and to external peripherals such as modems. We'll look at RS-232C, RS-422, Infrared communication, and USB.

Networks are covered in Chapter 12, where we'll see how to add a low-cost industrial network (CAN) to our embedded computer. Also in Chapter 12, we learn how to add an Ethernet port to our embedded system, by which we can connect to other computers, servers, and gateways and, through them, to the wider Internet.

In Chapter 13, we'll look at real-world interfacing. We'll see how to convert analog signals into digital values for processing and, conversely, how to convert digital values back into analog voltages. We'll also see how to interface sensors to our embedded system, whereby we can measure temperature, light, pressure, acceleration and magnetic fields. Also in Chapter 13, we'll look at Pulse Width Modulation and motor control. We'll see how to use an embedded computer to control small electric motors.

Chapter 14 begins the microprocessor section of the book, where we'll look at the first of our embedded processor architectures, the Microchip PIC. In subsequent chapters, we'll meet a variety of processors, from tiny standalone, 8-bit microcontrollers to 32-bit, bus-based chips with some computing grunt. While it is not possible to cover every embedded processor (as there are literally many hundreds), the chips chosen are representative of various classes of processor. The skills you learn will be adaptable to whatever processor you choose for your application.

Using Code Examples

This book is here to help you get your job done. In general, you may use the code in this book in your programs and documentation. You do not need to contact O'Reilly for permission unless you're reproducing a significant portion of the code. For example, writing a program that uses several chunks of code from this book does not require permission. Selling or distributing a CD-ROM of examples from O'Reilly books does require permission. Answering a question by citing this book and quoting example code does not require permission. Incorporating a significant amount of example code from this book into your product's documentation does require permission.

We appreciate, but do not require, attribution. An attribution usually includes the title, author, publisher, and ISBN. For example: "*Designing Embedded Hardware*, by John Catsoulis. Copyright 2005 O'Reilly Media, Inc., 0-596-00755-8."

If you feel your use of code examples falls outside fair use or the permission given above, feel free to contact the publisher at *permissions@oreilly.com*.

Conventions

The conventions used in this book are as follows:

Main text

    Source Code

Signal (active high)

S̄īḡnal (active low)

Hexadecimal numbers are denoted with the prefix *0x*, and sometimes with the prefix *$*, where appropriate for certain processors.

Binary numbers are denoted by the prefix %.

K is 1,024, while k is 1,000.

 This icon indicates a tip, suggestion, or general note.

 This icon indicates a warning or caution.

Safari® Enabled

 When you see a Safari® Enabled icon on the cover of your favorite technology book, it means the book is available online through the O'Reilly Network Safari Bookshelf.

Safari offers a solution that's better than e-books. It's a virtual library that lets you easily search thousands of top technology books, cut and paste code samples, download chapters, and find quick answers when you need the most accurate, current information. Try it for free at *http://safari.oreilly.com*.

How to Contact Us

Please address comments and questions concerning this book to the publisher:

O'Reilly Media, Inc.
1005 Gravenstein Highway North
Sebastopol, CA 95472
(800) 998-9938 (in the United States or Canada)
(707) 829-0515 (international/local)
(707) 829-0104 (fax)

There is a web page for this book, which lists errata, examples, and any additional information. You can access this page at:

http://www.oreilly.com/catalog/dbhardware2/

To comment or ask technical questions about this book, send email to:

bookquestions@oreilly.com

To contact the author directly with comments or questions, send email to:

jtc@embedded.com.au

For more information about books, conferences, Resource Centers, and the O'Reilly Network, see our web site at:

http://www.oreilly.com

Acknowledgments

I'd like to give a special thank you to my editors, Andy Oram and Mike Hendrickson. I'd also like to thank Jon Orwant, editor of the first edition. In the past, I have often read in prefaces how authors thank their editors for the help they gave. It is only now that I understand the depth and significance of this help.

As you have no doubt already noticed, O'Reilly publishes beautifully presented books. I would like to thank the production team, especially Sanders Kleinfeld, for their hard work. This book is as much the result of their efforts as it is mine. I'd also like to thank David Chu for all his help.

Thank you to Dallas Semiconductor, Kathy Vehorn, Don Loomis, Mike Quarles, and Moe Rubenzahl for their assistance and for allowing me access to pre-release versions of the MAXQ processor. Thank you to Peter Paine, Donna Mack and Cooper Tools, Karen Rolan and Fluke Corporation, and Tektronix for allowing me to use their images in the book. Thank you also to Rupert Baines of Picochip for his assistance.

Geoff McDonald has been a great friend and has made many helpful suggestions regarding the content of this book. He also proofread the book, and I thank him for all his help.

Thanks to Michael, Mary, Renee, and Mitchell Lees. Michael did significant proofreading and offered many helpful comments.

I'd like to thank Dr. Jeff O'Keefe for his long friendship and support over the years. He's been a good friend ever since we were undergrads together, blowing up integrated circuits and irradiating lecturers in second-year lab!

Thank you to Prof. Neil Bergmann, Dr. John Williams, Keith Ball, Denis Bill, Barry Bettridge, and the staff of the School of ITEE at the University of Queensland for their help and support.

I'd like to thank my friends and colleagues David Nicholls, Peter Stewart, Mark Gentile, Professor John Devlin, Richard Wiltshire, Michelle and Robert Salier, Addy and Derek Clark, Kam Tam, Phil McDonald, and Vamsi Madasu.

Finally and most importantly, I'd like to thank my extended family for their love and support. Most especially, I'd like to thank my sister Kris, and my two nephews, Andrew and James, whose love and good humor have made life worth living. I'd also like to thank Chris and Jeff Goopy for always being there, and my cousins Theo and Maree; David and Jenevieve; Michael, Andrew and Karen; Antony; and Fiona, Drew, Ashley, and Max for their care and support. A special thank you to my uncles, Vince and Dave Catsoulis, who have shown me the meaning of love, honor, and strength of character. I owe them much.

An Introduction to Computer Architecture

*Each machine has its own, unique personality which
probably could be defined as the intuitive sum total of
everything you know and feel about it. This
personality constantly changes, usually for the worse,
but sometimes surprisingly for the better...*

—Robert M. Pirsig
Zen and the Art of Motorcycle Maintenance

This book is about designing and building specialized computers. We all know what
a computer is. It's that box that sits on your desk, quietly purring away (or rattling if
the fan is shot), running your programs and regularly crashing (if you're not running
some variety of Unix). Inside that box is the electronics that runs your software,
stores your information, and connects you to the world. It's all about processing
information. Designing a computer, therefore, is about designing a machine that
holds and manipulates data.

Computer systems fall into essentially two separate categories. The first, and most
obvious, is that of the desktop computer. When you say "computer" to someone,
this is the machine that usually comes to her mind. The second type of computer is
the embedded computer, a computer that is integrated into another system for the
purposes of control and/or monitoring. Embedded computers are far more numerous than desktop systems, but far less obvious. Ask the average person how many
computers he has in his home, and he might reply that he has one or two. In fact, he
may have 30 or more, hidden inside his TVs, VCRs, DVD players, remote controls,
washing machines, cell phones, air conditioners, game consoles, ovens, toys, and a
host of other devices.

In this chapter, we'll look at computer architecture in general. This is applicable to
both embedded and desktop computers, because the primary difference between an
embedded machine and a general-purpose computer is its application. The basic
principles of operation and the underlying architectures are fundamentally the same.

Both have a processor, memory, and often several forms of input and output. The primary difference lies in their intended use, and this is reflected in the system design and their software. Desktop computers can run a variety of application programs, with system resources orchestrated by an operating system. By running different application programs, the functionality of the desktop computer is changed. One moment, it may be used as a word processor; the next it is an MP3 player or a database client. Which software is loaded and run is under user control.

In contrast, the embedded computer is normally dedicated to a specific task. In many cases, an embedded system is used to replace application-specific electronics. The advantage of using an embedded microprocessor over dedicated electronics is that the functionality of the system is determined by the software, not the hardware. This makes the embedded system easier to produce, and much easier to evolve, than a complicated circuit.

The embedded system typically has one application and one application only, which is permanently running. The embedded computer may or may not have an operating system, and rarely does it provide the user with the ability to arbitrarily install new software. The software is normally contained in the system's nonvolatile memory, unlike a desktop computer where the nonvolatile memory contains boot software and (maybe) low-level drivers only.

Embedded hardware is often much simpler than a desktop system, but it can also be far more complex too. An embedded computer may be implemented in a single chip with just a few support components, and its purpose may be as crude as a controller for a garden-watering system. Alternatively, the embedded computer may be a 150-processor, distributed parallel machine responsible for all the flight and control systems of a commercial jet. As diverse as embedded hardware may be, the underlying principles of design are the same.

This chapter introduces some important concepts relating to computer architecture, with specific emphasis on those topics relevant to embedded systems. Its purpose is to give you grounding before moving on to the more hands-on information that begins in Chapter 2. In this chapter, you'll learn about the basics of processors, interrupts, the difference between RISC and CISC, parallel systems, memory, and I/O.

Concepts

Let's start at the beginning.

In essence, a computer is a machine designed to process, store, and retrieve data. Data may be numbers in a spreadsheet, characters of text in a document, dots of color in an image, waveforms of sound, or the state of some system, such as an air conditioner or a CD player. *All data is stored in the computer as numbers*. It's easy to forget this when we're deep in C code, contemplating complex algorithms and data structures.

The computer manipulates the data by performing operations on the numbers. Displaying an image on a screen is accomplished by moving an array of numbers to the video memory, each number representing a pixel of color. To play an MP3 audio file, the computer reads an array of numbers from disk and into memory, manipulates those numbers to convert the compressed audio data into raw audio data, and then outputs the new set of numbers (the raw audio data) to the audio chip.

Everything that a computer does, from web browsing to printing, involves moving and processing numbers. The electronics of a computer is nothing more than a system designed to hold, move, and change numbers.

A computer system is composed of many parts, both hardware and software. At the heart of the computer is the processor, the hardware that executes the computer programs. The computer also has memory, often several different types in one system. The memory is used to store programs while the processor is running them, as well as store the data that the programs are manipulating. The computer also has devices for storing data, or exchanging data with the outside world. These may allow the input of text via a keyboard, the display of information on a screen, or the movement of programs and data to or from a disk drive.

The software controls the operation and functionality of the computer. There are many "layers" of software in the computer (Figure 1-1). Typically, a given layer will only interact with the layers immediately above or below it.

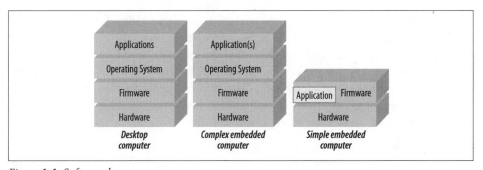

Figure 1-1. Software layers

At the lowest level, there are programs that are run by the processor when the computer first powers up. These programs initialize the other hardware subsystems to a known state and configure the computer for correct operation. This software, because it is permanently stored in the computer's memory, is known as *firmware*.

The *bootloader* is located in the firmware. The bootloader is a special program run by the processor that reads the operating system from disk (or nonvolatile memory or network interface) and places it in memory so that the processor may then run it. The bootloader is present in desktop computers and workstations, and may be present in some embedded computers.

Above the firmware, the operating system controls the operation of the computer. It organizes the use of memory and controls devices such as the keyboard, mouse, screen, disk drives, and so on. It is also the software that often provides an interface to the user, enabling her to run application programs and access her files on disk. The operating system typically provides a set of software tools for application programs, providing a mechanism by which they too can access the screen, disk drives, and so on. Not all embedded systems use or even need an operating system. Often, an embedded system will simply run code dedicated to its task, and the presence of an operating system is overkill. In other instances, such as network routers, an operating system provides necessary software integration and greatly simplifies the development process. Whether an operating system is needed and useful really depends on the intended purpose of the embedded computer and, to a lesser degree, on the preference of the designer.

At the highest level, the *application software* constitutes the programs that provide the functionality of the computer. Everything below the application is considered *system software*. For embedded computers, the boundary between application and system software is often blurred. This reflects the underlying principle in embedded design that a system should be designed to achieve its objective in as simple and straightforward a manner as possible.

Processors

The processor is the most important part of a computer, the component around which everything else is centered. In essence, the processor is the computing part of the computer. A processor is an electronic device capable of manipulating data (information) in a way specified by a sequence of instructions. The instructions are also known as *opcodes* or *machine code*. This sequence of instructions may be altered to suit the application, and, hence, computers are programmable. A sequence of instructions is what constitutes a program.

Instructions in a computer are numbers, just like data. Different numbers, when read and executed by a processor, cause different things to happen. A good analogy is the mechanism of a music box. A music box has a rotating drum with little bumps, and a row of prongs. As the drum rotates, different prongs in turn are activated by the bumps, and music is produced. In a similar way, the bit patterns of instructions feed into the execution unit of the processor. Different bit patterns activate or deactivate different parts of the processing core. Thus, the bit pattern of a given instruction may activate an addition operation, while another bit pattern may cause a byte to be stored to memory.

A sequence of instructions is a machine-code program. Each type of processor has a different *instruction set*, meaning that the functionality of the instructions (and the bit patterns that activate them) varies. Processor instructions are often quite simple, such as "add two numbers" or "call this function." In some processors, however, they can be as complex and sophisticated as "if the result of the last operation was zero, then use this particular number to reference another number in memory, and then increment the first number once you've finished." This will be covered in more detail in the section on CISC and RISC processors, later in this chapter.

Basic System Architecture

The processor alone is incapable of successfully performing any tasks. It requires memory (for program and data storage), support logic, and at least one I/O device ("input/output device") used to transfer data between the computer and the outside world. The basic computer system is shown in Figure 1-2.

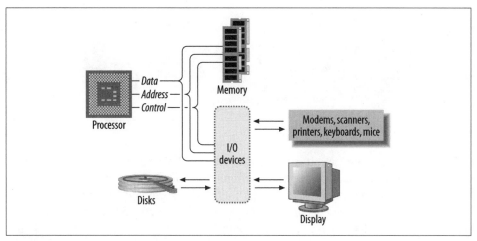

Figure 1-2. Basic computer system

A *microprocessor* is a processor implemented (usually) on a single, integrated circuit. With the exception of those found in some large supercomputers, nearly all modern processors are microprocessors, and the two terms are often used interchangeably. Common microprocessors in use today are the Intel Pentium series, Freescale/IBM PowerPC, MIPS, ARM, and the Sun SPARC, among others. A microprocessor is sometimes also known as a *CPU* (*Central Processing Unit*).

A *microcontroller* is a processor, memory, and some I/O devices contained within a single, integrated circuit, and intended for use in embedded systems. The buses that interconnect the processor with its I/O exist within the same integrated circuit. The range of available microcontrollers is very broad. They range from the tiny PICs and AVRs (to be covered in this book) to PowerPC processors with inbuilt I/O, intended for embedded applications. In this book, we will look at both microprocessors and microcontrollers.

Microcontrollers are very similar to *System-on-Chip* (*SoC*) processors, intended for use in conventional computers such as PCs and workstations. SoC processors have a different suite of I/O, reflecting their intended application, and are designed to be interfaced to large banks of external memory. Microcontrollers usually have all their memory on-chip and may provide only limited support for external memory devices.

The memory of the computer system contains both the instructions that the processor will execute and the data it will manipulate. The memory of a computer system is never empty. It always contains something, whether it be instructions, meaningful data, or just the random garbage that appeared in the memory when the system powered up.

Instructions are read (fetched) from memory, while data is both read from and written to memory, as shown in Figure 1-3.

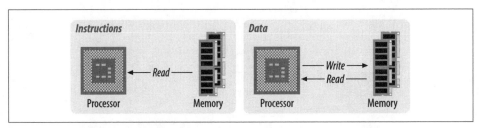

Figure 1-3. Data flow

This form of computer architecture is known as a *Von Neumann machine*, named after John Von Neumann, one of the originators of the concept. With very few exceptions, nearly all modern computers follow this form. Von Neumann computers are what can be termed control-flow computers. The steps taken by the computer are governed by the sequential control of a program. In other words, the computer follows a step-by-step program that governs its operation.

 There are some interesting non–Von Neumann architectures, such as the massively parallel Connection Machine and the nascent efforts at building biological and quantum computers, or neural networks.

A classical Von Neumann machine has several distinguishing characteristics:

There is no real difference between data and instructions. A processor can be directed to begin execution at a given point in memory, and it has no way of knowing whether the sequence of numbers beginning at that point is data or instructions. The instruction 0x4143 may also be data (the number 0x4143, or the ASCII characters "A" and "C"). The processor has no way of telling what is data or what is an instruction. If a number is to be executed by the processor, it is an instruction; if it is to be manipulated, it is data.

Because of this lack of distinction, the processor is capable of changing its instructions (treating them as data) under program control. And because the processor has no way of distinguishing between data and instruction, it will blindly execute anything that it is given, whether it is a meaningful sequence of instructions or not.

Data has no inherent meaning. There is nothing to distinguish between a number that represents a dot of color in an image and a number that represents a character in a text document. Meaning comes from how these numbers are treated under the execution of a program.

Data and instructions share the same memory. This means that sequences of instructions in a program may be treated as data by another program. A compiler creates a program binary by generating a sequence of numbers (instructions) in memory. To the compiler, the compiled program is just data, and it is treated as such. It is a program only when the processor begins execution. Similarly, an operating system loading an application program from disk does so by treating the sequence of instructions of that program as data. The program is loaded to memory just as an image or text file would be, and this is possible due to the shared memory space.

Memory is a linear (one-dimensional) array of storage locations. The processor's memory space may contain the operating system, various programs, and their associated data, all within the same linear space.

Each location in the memory space has a unique, sequential address. The address of a memory location is used to specify (and select) that location. The memory space is also known as the *address space*, and how that address space is partitioned between different memory and I/O devices is known as the *memory map*. The address space is the array of all addressable memory locations. In an 8-bit processor (such as the 68HC11) with a 16-bit address bus, this works out to be $2^{16} = 65,536 = 64K$ of memory. Hence, the processor is said to have a 64K address space. Processors with 32-bit address buses can access $2^{32} = 4,294,967,296 = 4G$ of memory.

Some processors, notably the Intel x86 family, have a separate address space for I/O devices with separate instructions for accessing this space. This is known as *ported I/O*. However, most processors make no distinction between memory devices and I/O devices within the address space. I/O devices exist within the same linear space as memory devices, and the same instructions are used to access each. This is known as *memory-mapped I/O* (Figure 1-4). Memory-mapped I/O is certainly the most common form. Ported I/O address spaces are becoming rare, and the use of the term even rarer.

Most microprocessors available are standard Von Neumann machines. The main deviation from this is the *Harvard architecture*, in which instructions and data have different memory spaces (Figure 1-5) with separate address, data, and control buses for each memory space. This has a number of advantages in that instruction and data fetches can occur concurrently, and the size of an instruction is not set by the size of the standard data unit (word).

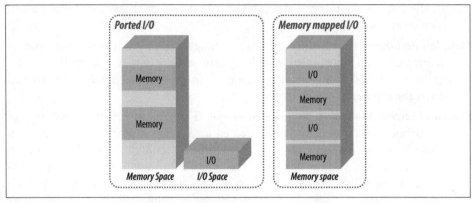

Figure 1-4. Ported versus memory-mapped I/O spaces

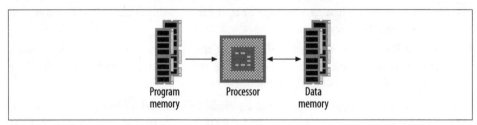

Program memory — Processor — Data memory

Figure 1-5. Harvard architecture

Buses

A bus is a physical group of signal lines that have a related function. Buses allow for the transfer of electrical signals between different parts of the computer system and thereby transfer information from one device to another. For example, the data bus is the group of signal lines that carry data between the processor and the various subsystems that comprise the computer. The "width" of a bus is the number of signal lines dedicated to transferring information. For example, an 8-bit-wide bus transfers 8 bits of data in parallel.

The majority of microprocessors available today (with some exceptions) use the three-bus system architecture (Figure 1-6). The three buses are the *address bus*, the *data bus*, and the *control bus*.

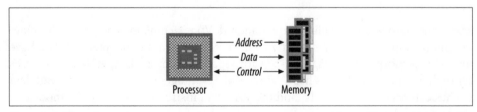

Figure 1-6. Three-bus system

The data bus is bidirectional, the direction of transfer being determined by the processor. The address bus carries the address, which points to the location in memory that the processor is attempting to access. It is the job of external circuitry to determine in which external device a given memory location exists and to activate that device. This is known as *address decoding*. The control bus carries information from the processor about the state of the current access, such as whether it is a write or a read operation. The control bus can also carry information back to the processor regarding the current access, such as an address error. Different processors have different control lines, but there are some control lines that are common among many processors. The control bus may consist of output signals such as read, write, valid address, etc. A processor usually has several input control lines too, such as reset, one or more interrupt lines, and a clock input.

A few years ago, I had the opportunity to wander through, in, and around CSIRAC (pronounced "sigh-rack"). This was one of the world's first digital computers, designed and built in Sydney, Australia, in the late 1940s. It was a massive machine, filling a very big room with the type of solid hardware that you can really kick. It was quite an experience looking over the old machine. I remember at one stage walking *through* the disk controller (it was the size of small room) and looking up at a mass of wires strung overhead. I asked what they were for. "That's the data bus!" came the reply.

CSIRAC is now housed in the museum of the University of Melbourne. You can take an online tour of the machine, and even download a simulator, at *http://www.cs.mu.oz.au/csirac*.

Processor operation

There are six basic types of access that a processor can perform with external chips. The processor can write data to memory or write data to an I/O device, read data from memory or read data from an I/O device, read instructions from memory, and perform internal manipulation of data within the processor.

In many systems, writing data to memory is functionally identical to writing data to an I/O device. Similarly, reading data from memory constitutes the same external operation as reading data from an I/O device, or reading an instruction from memory. In other words, the processor makes no distinction between memory and I/O.

The internal data storage of the processor is known as its *registers*. The processor has a limited number of registers, and these are used to hold the current data/operands that the processor is manipulating.

ALU

The Arithmetic Logic Unit (ALU) performs the internal arithmetic manipulation of data in the processor. The instructions that are read and executed by the processor control the data flow between the registers and the ALU. The instructions also control the arithmetic operations performed by the ALU via the ALU's control inputs. A symbolic representation of an ALU is shown in Figure 1-7.

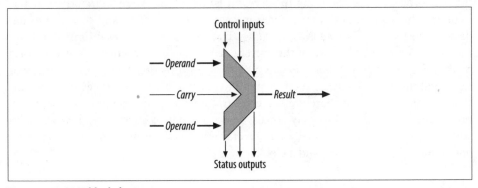

Figure 1-7. ALU block diagram

Whenever instructed by the processor, the ALU performs an operation (typically one of addition, subtraction, NOT, AND, OR, XOR, shift left/right, or rotate left/right) on one or more values. These values, called *operands*, are typically obtained from two registers, or from one register and a memory location. The result of the operation is then placed back into a given destination register or memory location. The status outputs indicate any special attributes about the operation, such as whether the result was zero, negative, or if an overflow or carry occurred. Some processors have separate units for multiplication and division, and for bit shifting, providing faster operation and increased throughput.

Each architecture has its own unique ALU features, and this can vary greatly from one processor to another. However, all are just variations on a theme, and all share the common characteristics just described.

Interrupts

Interrupts (also known as *traps* or *exceptions* in some processors) are a technique of diverting the processor from the execution of the current program so that it may deal with some event that has occurred. Such an event may be an error from a peripheral, or simply that an I/O device has finished the last task it was given and is now ready for another. An interrupt is generated in your computer every time you type a key or move the mouse. You can think of it as a hardware-generated function call.

Interrupts free the processor from having to continuously check the I/O devices to determine whether they require service. Instead, the processor may continue with other tasks. The I/O devices will notify it when they require attention by asserting one of the processor's interrupt inputs. Interrupts can be of varying priorities in some processors, thereby assigning differing importance to the events that can interrupt the processor. If the processor is servicing a low-priority interrupt, it will pause it in order to service a higher-priority interrupt. However, if the processor is servicing an interrupt and a second, lower-priority interrupt occurs, the processor will ignore that interrupt until it has finished the higher-priority service.

When an interrupt occurs, the usual procedure is for the processor to save its state by pushing its registers and program counter onto the stack. The processor then loads an *interrupt vector* into the program counter. The interrupt vector is the address at which an *interrupt service routine* (*ISR*) lies. Thus, loading the vector into the program counter causes the processor to begin execution of the ISR, performing whatever service the interrupting device required. The last instruction of an ISR is always a *Return from Interrupt* instruction. This causes the processor to reload its saved state (registers and program counter) from the stack and resume its original program. Interrupts are largely transparent to the original program. This means that the original program is completely "unaware" that the processor was interrupted, save for a lost interval of time.

Processors with *shadow registers* use these to save their current state, rather than pushing their register bank onto the stack. This saves considerable memory accesses (and therefore time) when processing an interrupt. However, since only one set of shadow registers exists, a processor servicing multiple interrupts must "manually" preserve the state of the registers before servicing the higher interrupt. If it does not, important state information will be lost. Upon returning from an ISR, the contents of the shadow registers are swapped back into the main register array.

Hardware interrupts

There are two ways of telling when an I/O device (such as a serial controller or a disk controller) is ready for the next sequence of data to be transferred. The first is *busy waiting* or *polling*, where the processor continuously checks the device's status register until the device is ready. This wastes the processor's time but is the simplest to implement. For some time-critical applications, polling can reduce the time it takes for the processor to respond to a change of state in a peripheral.

A better way is for the device to generate an interrupt to the processor when it is ready for a transfer to take place. Small, simple processors may only have one (or two) interrupt inputs, so several external devices may have to share the interrupt lines of the processor. When an interrupt occurs, the processor must check each device to determine which one generated the interrupt. (This can also be considered a form of polling.) The advantage of interrupt polling over ordinary polling is that the polling occurs only when there is a need to service a device. Polling interrupts is suitable only in systems that have a small number of devices; otherwise, the processor will spend too long trying to determine the source of the interrupt.

The other technique of servicing an interrupt is by using *vectored interrupts,** by which the interrupting device provides the interrupt vector that the processor is to

---

* Note that this is different from an interrupt vector stored in memory.

take. Vectored interrupts reduce considerably the time it takes the processor to determine the source of the interrupt. If an interrupt request can be generated from more than one source, it is therefore necessary to assign priorities (levels) to the different interrupts. This can be done in either hardware or software, depending on the particular application. In this scheme, the processor has numerous interrupt lines, with each interrupt corresponding to a given interrupt vector. So, for example, when an interrupt of priority 7 occurs (interrupt lines corresponding to "7" are asserted), the processor loads vector 7 into its program counter and starts executing the service routine specific to interrupt 7.

Vectored interrupts can be taken one step further. Some processors and devices support the device by actually placing the appropriate vector onto the data bus when they generate an interrupt. This means the system can be even more versatile, so that instead of being limited to one interrupt per peripheral, each device can supply an interrupt vector specific to the event that is causing the interrupt. However, the processor must support this function, and most do not.

Some processors have a feature known as a *fast hardware interrupt*. With this interrupt, only the program counter is saved. It assumes that the ISR will protect the contents of the registers by manually saving their state as required. Fast interrupts are useful when an I/O device requires a very fast response from a processor and cannot wait for the processor to save all its registers to the stack. A special (and separate) interrupt line is used to generate fast interrupts.

Software interrupts

A software interrupt is generated by an instruction. It is the lowest-priority interrupt and is generally used by programs to request a service to be performed by the system software (operating system or firmware).

So why are software interrupts used? Why isn't the appropriate section of code called directly? For that matter, why use an operating system to perform tasks for us at all? It gets back to compatibility. Jumping to a subroutine (calling a function) is jumping to a specific address in memory. A future version of the system software may not locate the subroutines at the same addresses as earlier versions. By using a software interrupt, our program does not need to know where the routines lie. It relies on the entry in the vector table to direct it to the correct location.

CISC and RISC

There are two major approaches to processor architecture: *Complex Instruction Set Computer* (*CISC*, pronounced "Sisk") processors and *Reduced Instruction Set Computer* (*RISC*) processors. Classic CISC processors are the Intel x86, Motorola 68xxx, and National Semiconductor 32xxx processors, and, to a lesser degree, the

Intel Pentium. Common RISC architectures are the Freescale/IBM PowerPC, the MIPS architecture, Sun's SPARC, the ARM, the Atmel AVR, and the Microchip PIC.

CISC processors have a single processing unit, external memory, and a relatively small register set and many hundreds of different instructions. In many ways, they are just smaller versions of the processing units of mainframe computers from the 1960s.

The tendency in processor design throughout the late 70s and early 80s was toward bigger and more complicated instruction sets. Need to input a string of characters from an I/O port? Well, with CISC (80x86 family), there's a *single instruction* to do it! The diversity of instructions in a CISC processor can run to well over 1,000 opcodes in some processors, such as the Motorola 68000. This had the advantage of making the job of the assembly-language programmer easier, since you had to write fewer lines of code to get the job done. As memory was slow and expensive, it also made sense to make each instruction do more. This reduced the number of instructions needed to perform a given function, and thereby reduced memory space and the number of memory accesses required to fetch instructions. As memory got cheaper and faster, and compilers became more efficient, the relative advantages of the CISC approach began to diminish. One main disadvantage of CISC is that the processors themselves get increasingly complicated as a consequence of supporting such a large and diverse instruction set. The control and instruction decode units are complex and slow, the silicon is large and hard to produce, and they consume a lot of power and therefore generate a lot of heat. As processors became more advanced, the overheads that CISC imposed on the silicon became oppressive.

A given processor feature when considered alone may increase processor performance but may actually decrease the performance of the total system, if it increases the total complexity of the device. It was found that by streamlining the instruction set to the most commonly used instructions, the processors become simpler and faster. Fewer cycles are required to decode and execute each instruction, and the cycles are shorter. The drawback is that more (simpler) instructions are required to perform a task, but this is more than made up for in the performance boost to the processor. For example, if both cycle time and the number of cycles per instruction are each reduced by a factor of four, while the number of instructions required to perform a task grows by 50%, the execution of the processor is sped up by a factor of eight.

The realization of this led to a rethink of processor design. The result was the RISC architecture, which has led to the development of very high-performance processors. The basic philosophy behind RISC is to move the complexity from the silicon to the language compiler. The hardware is kept as simple and fast as possible.

A given complex instruction can be performed by a sequence of much simpler instructions. For example, many processors have an xor (exclusive OR) instruction for bit manipulation, and they also have a clear instruction to set a given register to zero. However, a register can also be set to zero by xor-ing it with itself. Thus, the separate clear instruction is no longer required. It can be replaced with the already present xor. Further, many processors are able to clear a memory location directly by writing a zero to it. That same function can be implemented by clearing a register and then storing that register to the memory location. The instruction to load a register with a literal number can be replaced with the instruction for clearing a register, followed by an add instruction with the literal number as its operand. Thus, six instructions (xor, clear *reg*, clear *memory*, load *literal*, store, and add) can be replaced with just three (xor, store, and add).

So the following CISC assembly pseudocode:

```
clear 0x1000    ; clear memory location 0x1000
load  r1,#5     ; load register 1 with the value 5
```

becomes the following RISC pseudocode:

```
xor   r1,r1     ; clear register 1
store r1,0x1000 ; clear memory location 0x1000
add   r1,#5     ; load register 1 with the value 5
```

The resulting code size is bigger, but the reduced complexity of the instruction decode unit can result in faster overall operation. Dozens of such code optimizations exist to give RISC its simplicity.

RISC processors have a number of distinguishing characteristics. They have large register sets (in some architectures numbering over 1,000), thereby reducing the number of times the processor must access main memory. Often-used variables can be left inside the processor, reducing the number of accesses to (slow) external memory. Compilers of high-level languages (such as C) take advantage of this to optimize processor performance.

By having smaller and simpler instruction decode units, RISC processors have fast instruction execution, and this also reduces the size and power consumption of the processing unit. Generally, RISC instructions will take only one or two cycles to execute (this depends greatly on the particular processor). This is in contrast to instructions for a CISC processor, whose instructions may take many tens of cycles to execute. For example, one instruction (integer multiplication) on an 80486 CISC processor takes 42 cycles to complete. The same instruction on a RISC processor may take just one cycle. Instructions on a RISC processor have a simple format. All instructions are generally the same length (which makes instruction decode units simpler).

RISC processors implement what is known as a "load/store" architecture. This means that the only instructions that actually reference memory are load and store. In contrast, many (most) instructions on a CISC processor may access or manipulate memory. On a RISC processor, all other instructions (aside from load and store) work on the registers only. This facilitates the ability of RISC processors to complete (most of) their instructions in a single cycle. Consequently, RISC processors do not have the range of addressing modes that are found on CISC processors.

RISC processors also often have pipelined instruction execution. This means that while one instruction is being executed, the next instruction in the sequence is being decoded, while the third one is being fetched. At any given moment, several instructions will be in the pipeline and in the process of being executed. Again, this provides improved processor performance. Thus, even though not all instructions may be completed in a single cycle, the processor may issue and retire instructions on each cycle, thereby achieving effective single-cycle execution. Some RISC processors have overlapped instruction execution, in which load operations may allow the execution of subsequent, unrelated instructions to continue before the data requested by the load has been returned from memory. This allows these instructions to overlap the load, thereby improving processor performance.

Due to their low power consumption and computing power, RISC processors are becoming widely used, particularly in embedded computer systems, and many RISC attributes are appearing in what are traditionally CISC architectures (such as with the Intel Pentium). Ironically, many RISC architectures are adding some CISC-like features, and so the distinction between RISC and CISC is blurring.

An excellent discussion of RISC architectures and processor performance topics can be found in Kevin Dowd and Charles Severance's *High Performance Computing* (O'Reilly).

So, which is better for embedded and industrial applications, RISC or CISC? If power consumption needs to be low, then RISC is probably the better architecture to use. However, if the available space for program storage is small, then a CISC processor may be a better alternative, since CISC instructions get more "bang" for the byte.

Digital Signal Processors

A special type of processor architecture is that of the *Digital Signal Processor* (*DSP*). These processors have instruction sets and architectures optimized for numerical processing of array data. They often extend the Harvard architecture concept further by not only having separate data and code spaces, but also by splitting the data spaces into two or more banks. This allows concurrent instruction fetch and data accesses for multiple operands. As such, DSPs can have very high throughput and can outperform both CISC and RISC processors in certain applications.

DSPs have special hardware well suited to numerical processing of arrays. They often have *hardware looping*, whereby special registers allow for and control the repeated execution of an instruction sequence. This is also often known as *zero-overhead looping*, since no conditions need to be explicitly tested by the software as part of the looping process. DSPs often have dedicated hardware for increasing the speed of arithmetic operations. High-speed multipliers, Multiply-And-Accumulate (MAC) units, and barrel shifters are common features.

DSP processors are commonly used in embedded applications, and many conventional embedded microcontrollers include some DSP functionality.

Memory

Memory is used to hold data and software for the processor. There is a variety of memory types, and often a mix is used within a single system. Some memory will retain its contents while there is no power, yet will be slow to access. Other memory devices will be high-capacity, yet will require additional support circuitry and will be slower to access. Still other memory devices will trade capacity for speed, yielding relatively small devices, yet will be capable of keeping up with the fastest of processors.

Memory chips can be organized in two ways, either in *word-organized* or *bit-organized* schemes. In the word-organized scheme, complete nybbles, bytes, or words are stored within a single component, whereas with bit-organized memory, each bit of a byte or word is allocated to a separate component (Figure 1-8).

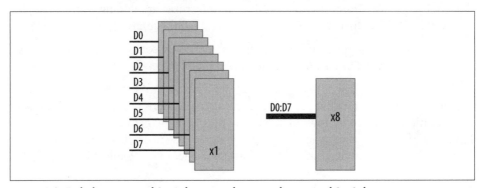

Figure 1-8. Eight bit-organized 8 × 1 devices and one word-organized 8 × 8 device

Memory chips come in different sizes, with the width specified as part of the size description. For instance, a DRAM (dynamic RAM) chip might be described as being 4M × 1 (bit-organized), whereas a SRAM (static RAM) may be 512K × 8 (word-organized). In both cases, each chip has exactly the same storage capacity, but organized in different ways. In the DRAM case, it would take eight chips to complete a memory block for an 8-bit data bus, whereas the SRAM would only require one chip. However, because the DRAMs are organized in parallel, they are accessed simultaneously. The final size of the DRAM block is (4M × 1) × 8 devices, which is 32M. It is common practice for multiple DRAMs to be placed on a *memory module*. This is the common way that DRAMs are installed in standard computers.

The common widths for memory chips are x1, x4, and x8, although x16 devices are available. A 32-bit-wide bus can be implemented with thirty-two x1 devices, eight x4 devices, or four x8 devices.

RAM

RAM stands for *Random Access Memory*. This is a bit of a misnomer, since most (all) computer memory may be considered "random access." RAM is the "working memory" in the computer system. It is where the processor may easily write data for temporary storage. RAM is generally *volatile*, losing its contents when the system loses power. Any information stored in RAM that must be retained must be written to some form of permanent storage before the system powers down. There are special nonvolatile RAMs that integrate a battery-backup system, such that the RAM remains powered even when the rest of the computer system has shut down.

RAMs generally fall into two categories: *static RAM* (also known as *SRAM*) and *dynamic RAM* (also known as *DRAM*).

SRAMs use pairs of logic gates to hold each bit of data. SRAMs are the fastest form of RAM available, require little external support circuitry, and have relatively low power consumption. Their drawbacks are that their capacity is considerably less than DRAM, while being much more expensive. Their relatively low capacity requires more chips to be used to implement the same amount of memory. A modern PC built using nothing but SRAM would be a *considerably* bigger machine and would cost a small fortune to produce. (It would be *very* fast, however.)

DRAM uses arrays of what are essentially capacitors to hold individual bits of data. The capacitor arrays will hold their charge only for a short period before it begins to diminish. Therefore, DRAMs need continuous refreshing, every few milliseconds or so. This perpetual need for refreshing requires additional support and can delay processor access to the memory. If a processor access conflicts with the need to refresh the array, the refresh cycle must take precedence.

DRAMs are the highest-capacity memory devices available and come in a wide and diverse variety of subspecies. Interfacing DRAMs to small microcontrollers is generally not possible, and certainly not practical. Most processors with large address spaces include support for DRAMs. Connecting DRAMs to such processors is simply a case of "connecting the dots" (or pins, as the case may be). For those processors that do not include DRAM support, special DRAM controller chips are available that make interfacing the DRAMs very simple indeed.

Many processors have instruction and/or data *caches*, which store recent memory accesses. These caches are (often, but not always) internal to the processors and are implemented with fast memory cells and high-speed data paths. Instruction execution normally runs out of the instruction cache, providing for fast execution. The processor is capable of rapidly reloading the caches from main memory should a cache miss occur. Some processors have logic that is able to anticipate a cache miss and begin the cache reload prior to the cache miss occurring. Caches are implemented using very fast SRAM and are most often used in large systems to compensate for the slowness of DRAM.

ROM

ROM stands for *Read-Only Memory*. This is also a bit of a misnomer, since many (modern) ROMs can also be written to. ROMs are *nonvolatile memory*, requiring no power to retain their contents. They are generally slower than RAM, and considerably slower than fast static RAM.

The primary purpose of ROM within a system is to hold the code (and sometimes data) that needs to be present at power-up. Such software is generally known as *firmware* and contains software to initialize the computer by placing I/O devices into a known state. It may contain either a bootloader program to load an operating system off disk or network or, in the case of an embedded system, it may contain the application itself.

Many microcontrollers contain on-chip ROM, thereby reducing component count and simplifying system design.

Standard ROM is fabricated (in a simplistic sense) from a large array of diodes. The unwritten bit state for a ROM is all 1s, each byte location reading as 0xFF. The process of loading software into a ROM is known as *burning the ROM*. This term comes from the fact that the programming process is performed by passing a sufficiently large current through the appropriate diodes to "blow them," or *burn* them, thereby creating a zero at that bit location. A device known as a *ROM burner* can accomplish this, or, if the system supports it, the ROM may be programmed in-circuit. This is known as *In-System Programming (ISP)* or, sometimes, *In-Circuit Programming (ICP)*.

One-Time Programmable (OTP) ROMs, as the name implies, can be burned once only. Computer manufacturers typically use them in systems where the firmware is stable and the product is shipping in bulk to customers. *Mask-programmable* ROMs are also one-time programmable, but unlike OTPs, they are burned by the chip manufacturer prior to shipping. Like OTPs, they are used once the software is known to be stable and have the advantage of lowering production costs for large shipments.

EPROM

OTP ROMs are great for shipping in final products, but they are wasteful for debugging, since with each iteration of code change, a new chip must be burned and the old one thrown away. As such, OTPs make for a very expensive development option. No sane person uses OTPs for development work.

A (slightly) better choice for system development and debugging is the *Erasable Programmable Read-Only Memory*, or EPROM. Shining ultraviolet light through a small window on the top of the chip can erase the EPROM, allowing it to be reprogrammed and reused. They are pin- and signal-compatible with comparable OTP and mask devices. Thus, an EPROM can be used during development, while OTPs can be used in production with no change to the rest of the system.

EPROMs and their equivalent OTP cousins range in capacity from a few kilobytes (exceedingly rare these days) to a megabyte or more.

The drawback with EPROM technology is that the chip must be removed from the circuit to be erased, and the erasure can take many minutes to complete. The chip is then inserted into the burner, loaded with software, and then placed back in-circuit. This can lead to very slow debug cycles. Further, it makes the device useless for storing changeable system parameters. EPROMs are relatively rare these days. You can still buy them, but flash-based memory (to be discussed shortly) is far more common and is the medium of choice.

EEROM

EEROM is *Electrically Erasable Read-Only Memory*, also known as *EEPROM* (*Electrically Erasable Programmable Read-Only Memory*). Very rarely, it is also called *Electrically Alterable Read-Only Memory* (*EAROM*). EEROM can be pronounced as either "e-e ROM" or "e-squared ROM," or sometimes just "e-squared" for short.

EEROMs can be erased and reprogrammed in-circuit. Their capacity is significantly smaller than standard ROM (typically only a few kilobytes), and so they are not suited to holding firmware. Instead, they are typically used for holding system parameters and mode information to be retained during power-off.

It is common for many microcontrollers to incorporate a small EEROM on-chip for holding system parameters. This is especially useful in embedded systems and may be used for storing network addresses, configuration settings, serial numbers, servicing records, and so on.

Flash

Flash is the newest ROM technology and is now dominant. Flash memory has the reprogrammability of EEROM and the large capacity of standard ROMs. Flash chips are sometimes referred to as "flash ROMs" or "flash RAMs." Since they are not like standard ROMs or standard RAMs, I prefer just to call them "flash" and save on the confusion.

Flash is normally organized as sectors and has the advantage that individual sectors may be erased and rewritten without affecting the contents of the rest of the device. Typically, before a sector can be written, it must be erased. It can't just be written over as with a RAM.

There are several different flash technologies, and the erasing and programming requirements of flash devices vary from manufacturer to manufacturer.

Input/Output

The address space of the processor can contain devices other than memory. These are input/output devices (I/O devices, also known as *peripherals*) and are used by the processor to communicate with the external world. Some examples are serial controllers that communicate with keyboards, mice, modems, etc.; parallel I/O devices that control some external subsystem; or disk-drive controllers, video and audio controllers, or network interfaces.

There are three main ways in which data may be exchanged with the external world:

Programmed I/O
> The processor accepts or delivers data at times convenient to it (the processor).

Interrupt-driven I/O
> External events control the processor by requesting the current program be suspended and the external event be serviced. An external device will interrupt the processor (assert an interrupt control line into the processor), at which time the processor will suspend the current task (program) and begin executing an interrupt service routine. The service of an interrupt may involve transferring data from input to memory, or from memory to output.

Direct Memory Access (DMA)
> DMA allows data to be transferred from I/O devices to memory directly without the continuous involvement of the processor. DMA is used in high-speed systems, where the rate of data transfer is important. Not all processors support DMA.

DMA

DMA is a way of streamlining transfers of large blocks of data between two sections of memory, or between memory and an I/O device. Let's say you want to read in 100M from disk and store it in memory. You have two options.

One option is for the processor to read one byte at a time from the disk controller into a register and then store the contents of the register to the appropriate memory location. For each byte transferred, the processor must read an instruction, decode the instruction, read the data, read the next instruction, decode the instruction, and then store the data. Then the process starts over again for the next byte.

The second option in moving large amounts of data around the system is DMA. A special device, called a *DMA Controller (DMAC)*, performs high-speed transfers between memory and I/O devices. Using DMA bypasses the processor by setting up a *channel* between the I/O device and the memory. Thus, data is read from the I/O device and written into memory without the need to execute code to perform the transfer on a byte-by-byte (or word-by-word) basis.

In order for a DMA transfer to occur, the DMAC must have use of the address and data buses. There are several ways in which this could be implemented by the system designer. The most common approach (and probably the simplest) is to suspend the operation of the processor and for the processor to "release" its buses (the buses are tristate). This allows the DMAC to "take over" the buses for the short period required to perform the transfer. Processors that support DMA usually have a special control input that enables a DMAC (or some other processor) to request the buses.

There are four basic types of DMA:

Standard block transfer

Accomplished by the DMA controller performing a sequence of memory transfers. The transfers involve a load operation from a source address followed by a store operation to a destination address. Standard block transfers are initiated under software control and are used for moving data structures from one region of memory to another.

Demand-mode transfers

Similar to standard mode except that the transfer is controlled by an external device. Demand-mode transfers are used to move data between memory and I/O or vice versa. The I/O device requests and synchronizes the movement of data.

Fly-by transfer

Provides high-speed data movement in the system. Instead of using multiple bus accesses as with conventional DMA transfers, fly-by transfers move data from source to destination in a single access. The data is not read into the DMAC before going to its destination. During a fly-by transfer, memory and I/O are given different bus control signals. For example, an I/O device is given a read request at the same time that memory is given a write request. Data moves from the I/O device straight into the memory device.

Data-chaining transfers

Allow DMA transfers to be performed as specified by a linked-list in memory. Data chaining is started by specifying a pointer to a *descriptor* in memory. The descriptor is a table specifying byte count, source address, destination address, and a pointer to the next descriptor. The DMAC loads the relevant information about the transfer from this table and begins moving data. The transfer continues until the number of bytes transferred is equal to the entry in the byte-count field. On completion, the pointer to the next descriptor is loaded. This continues until a null pointer is found.

To illustrate the use of DMA, let's consider the example of a fly-by transfer of data from a hard-disk controller to memory. A DMA transfer begins by the processor configuring the DMAC for the transfer. This setup involves specifying the source, destination, and size of the data, as well as other parameters. The disk controller generates a request for service to the DMAC (not the processor). The DMAC then generates a HOLD or BR (bus request) to the processor. The processor completes the current instruction; places the address, control, and data buses in a high-impedance state (*floats*, tristates, or releases them); and responds to the DMAC with a HOLD-acknowledge or BG (bus granted) and enters a dormant state. Upon receiving a HOLD-acknowledge, the DMAC places the address of the memory location where the transfer to memory will begin onto the address bus and generates a WRITE to the memory while the disk controller places the data on the data bus. Hence, a direct memory access is accomplished from the disk controller to the memory.

In a similar fashion, transfers from memory to I/O devices are also possible. DMACs are capable of handling block transfers of data. The DMAC automatically increments the address on the address bus to point to each successive memory location as the I/O device generates (or receives) data. Once the transfer is complete, the buses are returned to the processor and it resumes normal operation.

Not all DMA controllers support all forms of DMA. Some DMA controllers simply read data from a source, hold it internally, and then store it to a destination. They perform the transfer in exactly the same way that a processor would. The advantage in using a DMA controller instead of a processor is that if the transfer were to be performed by the processor, each transfer would still have program fetches associated with it. Thus, even though the transfer takes place by sequential reads and writes, the DMA controller does not also have to fetch and execute code, thereby providing a faster transfer than a processor.

Support for DMA is normally not found in small microcontrollers. Some mid-range processors (16-bit, low-end 32-bit) may have DMA support. All high-end processors (32-bit and above) will have DMA support, and many include a DMA controller on-chip. Similarly, peripherals intended for small-scale computers will not provide DMA support, whereas peripherals intended for high-speed and powerful computers definitely *will* have DMA support.

Parallel and Distributed Computers

Some embedded applications require greater performance than is achievable from a single processor. For cost reasons, it may not be practical to implement a design with the latest superscalar RISC processor, or perhaps the application lends itself to distributed processing where the tasks are run across several communicating machines. It may make more sense to use a fleet of lower-cost processors, distributed throughout the installation. It is becoming increasingly common to see embedded systems implemented using parallel processors.

Introduction to parallel architectures

The traditional architecture for computers follows the conventional, Von Neumann serial architecture. Computers based on this form usually have a single, sequential processor. The main limitation of this form of computing architecture is that the conventional processor is able to execute only one instruction at a time. Algorithms that run on these machines must therefore be expressed as a sequential problem. A given task must be broken down into a series of sequential steps, each to be executed in order, one at a time.

Many problems that are computationally intensive are also highly parallel. An algorithm that is applied to a large data set characterizes these problems. Often the computation for each element in the data set is the same and is only loosely reliant on the results from computations on neighboring data. Thus, speed advantages may be gained from performing calculations in parallel for each element in the data set, rather than sequentially moving through the data set and computing each result in a serial manner. Machines with multitudes of processors working on a data structure in parallel often far outperform conventional computers in such applications.

The *grain* of the computer is defined as the number of processing elements within the machine. A *coarsely grained* machine has relatively few processors, whereas a *finely grained* machine may have tens of thousands of processing elements. Typically, the processing elements of a finely grained machine are much less powerful than those of a coarsely grained computer. The processing power is achieved through the brute-force approach of having such a large number of processing elements.

There are several different forms of parallel machine. Each architecture has its own advantages and limitations, and each has its share of supporters.

SIMD computers

Single-Instruction Multiple-Data (*SIMD*) computers are highly parallel machines, employing large arrays of simple processing elements. In an SIMD machine, each processing element has a small amount of local memory. The instructions executed by the SIMD computer are broadcast from a central instruction server to every processing element within the machine. In this way, each processor executes the same instruction as all other processing elements within the machine. Since each processor executes the instruction on its local data, all elements within the data structure are worked upon simultaneously.

The SIMD machine is generally used in conjunction with a conventional computer. An example of this was the Connection Machine (CM-1) by Thinking Machines Corporation that used either a VAX minicomputer or a Silicon Graphics or Sun workstation as the "host" computer. The CM-1 was a finely grained SIMD computer with up to 64K of processing elements that appeared as a block of 64K of "intelligent memory" to the host system. An application running on the host downloaded a data set into the processor array of the CM-1, each processor within the CM-1 acting as a single memory unit. The host then issued instructions to each processing element of the CM-1 simultaneously. After the computations were completed, the host then read back the result from the CM-1 as though it were conventional memory.

The primary advantage of the SIMD machine is that simple and cheap processing elements are used to form the computer. Thus, significant computing power is available using inexpensive, off-the-shelf components. In addition, since each processor is executing the same instructions and therefore sharing a common instruction fetch, the architecture of the machine is somewhat simpler. Only one instruction store is required for the entire computer.

The use of multiple processing elements, each executing the same instructions in unison, is also the SIMD's main disadvantage. Many problems do not lend themselves to being broken down into a form suitable for executing on an SIMD computer. In addition, the data sets associated with a given problem may not match well with a given SIMD architecture. For example, an SIMD machine with 10k processing elements does not mesh well with a data set of 12k data elements.

MIMD computers

The other major form of parallel machine is the *Multiple-Instruction Multiple-Data* (*MIMD*) computer. These machines are typically coarsely grained collections of semi-autonomous processors, each with their own local memory and local programs. An algorithm being executed on an MIMD computer is typically broken up into a series of smaller sub-problems, each executed on a processor of the MIMD machine. By giving each processing element in the MIMD machine identical programs to execute, the MIMD machine may be treated as an SIMD computer. The grain of an MIMD computer is much less than that of an SIMD machine. MIMD computers tend to use a smaller number of very powerful processors, rather than a large number of less powerful ones.

MIMD computers can be of one of two types: *shared-memory MIMD* and *message-passing MIMD*. Shared-memory MIMD systems have an array of high-speed processors, each with local memory or cache, and each with access to a large, global memory (Figure 1-9). The global memory contains the data and programs to be executed by the machine. Also in this memory is a table of processes (or sub-programs) awaiting execution. Each processor will fetch a process and associated data into its local memory or cache and will run semi-autonomously of the other processors in the system. Process communication also takes place through the global memory.

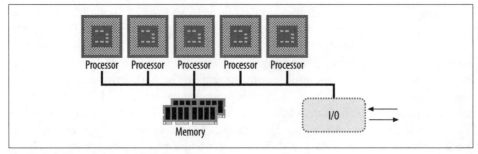

Figure 1-9. Shared-memory MIMD

A speed advantage is gained by sharing the program among several, powerful processors. However, logic within the system must arbitrate between processors for access to the shared memory and associated shared buses of the system. In addition, allowances must be made for a processor attempting to access data in global memory that is out of date. If processor A reads a process and data structure into its local memory and subsequently modifies that data structure, processor B attempting to access the same data structure in main memory must be notified that a more recent version of the data structure exists. Such arbitration is implemented in processors like the (now extinct) Motorola MC88110, which was intended for use in shared-memory MIMD machines.

An alternative MIMD architecture is that of the message-passing MIMD computer (Figure 1-10). In this system, each processor has its own local, main memory. No global memory exists for the machine. Each processing element (processor with local memory) either loads, or has loaded into it, the programs (and associated data) that it is to execute. Each process runs autonomously on its local processor, and interprocess communication is achieved by message-passing through a common medium. The processors may communicate through a single, shared bus (such as Ethernet, CAN, or SCSI) or by using a more elaborate interprocessor connection architecture, such as 2-D arrays, N-dimensional hypercubes, rings, stars, trees, or fully interconnected systems.

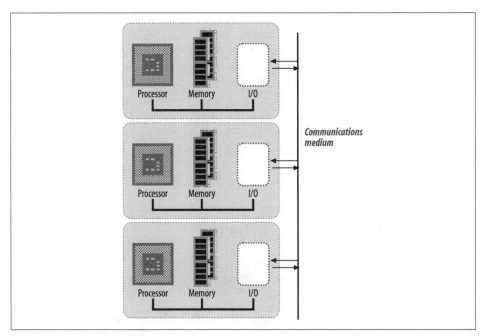

Figure 1-10. Message-passing MIMD

Such machines do not suffer the bus-contention problems of shared-memory machines. However, the most effective and efficient means of interconnecting the processing nodes of a message-passing MIMD machine is still a major area of research. Each different architecture has its own merits, and which is best for a given application depends to a certain degree on what that application is. Problems that require only a limited amount of interprocess communication may work effectively on a machine without high interconnectivity, whereas other applications may weigh down the communications medium with their message passing. If a percentage of a processing node's time is spent in message-routing for its neighbors, a machine with a high degree of interprocess communication but a low degree of interconnectivity may spend most of its time dealing in message passing, with little time spent on actual computation.

The ideal interconnection architecture is that of the fully interconnected system, where every processing node has a direct communications link with every other processing node. However, this is not always practical, due to the costs and logistics of such a high degree of interconnectivity. A solution to this problem is to provide each processing element in the machine with a limited number of connections, based on the assumption that a processing element will not need or be able to communicate with every other processing element in the machine simultaneously. These limited connections from each processing node may then be interconnected using a *crossbar switch*, thereby providing full interconnectivity for the machine through only a limited number of links per node.

A *distributed* machine is composed of individual computers networked together as a loosely coupled MIMD parallel machine. Projects such as *Beowulf* and even *SETI@Home* can be considered MIMD machines. Distributed machines are common in the embedded world. A collection of small processing nodes may be distributed across a factory, providing local monitoring and control, and together forming a parallel machine executing the global control algorithm. The avionics of commercial and military aircraft are also distributed parallel computers.

Now let's take a look at computer applications and how they relate to the architecture of the machine.

Embedded Computer Architecture

What a computer is used for, what tasks it must perform, and how it interacts with humans and other systems determine the functionality of the machine and, therefore, its architecture, memory, and I/O.

An arbitrary desktop computer (not necessarily a PC) is shown in Figure 1-11. It has a large main memory to hold the operating system, applications, and data, and an interface to mass storage devices (disks and DVD/CD-ROMs). It has a variety of I/O devices for user input (keyboard, mouse, and audio), user output (display interface and audio), and connectivity (networking and peripherals). The fast processor requires a system manager to monitor its core temperature and supply voltages, and to generate a system reset.

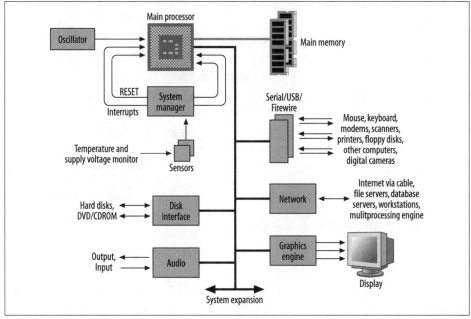

Figure 1-11. Block diagram of a generic computer

Large-scale embedded computers may also take the same form. For example, they may act as a network router or gateway, and so will require one or more network interfaces, large memory, and fast operation. They may also require some form of user interface as part of their embedded application and, in many ways, may simply be a conventional computer dedicated to a specific task. Thus, in terms of hardware, many high-performance embedded systems are not that much different from a conventional desktop machine.

Smaller embedded systems use microcontrollers as their processor, with the advantage that this processor will incorporate much of the computer's functionality on a single chip. An arbitrary embedded system, based on a generic microcontroller, is shown in Figure 1-12.

The microcontroller has, at a minimum, a CPU, a small amount of internal memory (ROM and/or RAM), and some form of I/O, which is implemented within a microcontroller as subsystem blocks. These subsystems provide the additional functionality for the processor and are common across many processors. The subsystems that you will typically find in microcontrollers will be discussed in the coming chapters.

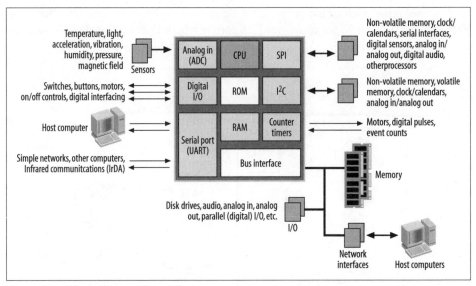

Figure 1-12. Block diagram of an embedded computer

For the moment, though, let's take a quick tour and examine the purposes for which they can be used.

The most common I/O is *digital I/O*, commonly called *general-purpose I/O*, or *GPIO*. These are ports that may be configured by software, on a pin-by-pin basis, as either a digital input or digital output. As digital inputs, they may be used to read the state of switches or push buttons, or to read the digital status of another device. As outputs, they may be used to turn external devices on or off, or to convey status to an external device. For example, a digital output may be used to activate the control circuitry for a motor, turn a light on or off, or perhaps activate some other device such as a water valve for a garden-watering system. Used in combination, the digital inputs and outputs may be used to synthesize an interface and protocol to another chip. Most microcontrollers have other subsystems besides digital I/O but provide the ability to convert the other subsystems to general-purpose digital I/O if the functionality of the other subsystems is not required. This gives you great versatility as a system designer in how you use your microcontroller within your application.

Many microcontrollers also have analog inputs, allowing sensors to be sampled for monitoring or recording purposes. Thus, an embedded computer may measure light levels, temperature, vibration or acceleration, air or water pressure, humidity, or magnetic field, to name just some. Alternatively, the analog inputs may be used to monitor simple voltages, perhaps to ensure the reliable operation of a larger system.

Some microcontrollers have serial ports, which enable the embedded computer to be interfaced to a host computer, a modem, another embedded system, or perhaps a simple network. Specialized forms of serial interface, such as SPI and I²C, provide a simple way of expanding the microcontroller's functionality. They allow peripherals to be interfaced to the microcontroller, providing access to such devices as off-chip memories (for data or parameter storage), clock/calendar chips (for timekeeping), sensors with digital interfaces, external analog input or output, and even audio chips and other processors. Most microcontrollers have timers and counters. These may be used to generate internal interrupts at regular intervals for multitasking, to generate external triggers for off-chip systems, or to provide control pulses for motors. Alternatively, they may be used to count external triggers (pulses) from another system. A few microcontrollers also include network interfaces, such as USB, Ethernet, or CAN. In this book, we'll look at many of these peripheral subsystems in detail and see how to utilize them to increase an embedded computer's functionality.

Some of the larger microcontrollers also provide a bus interface, bringing the internal address, data, and control buses to the outside world. This allows the processor to be interfaced to a huge variety of possible peripherals in very much the same way as a conventional processor. All of the possible devices and interfaces described previously may also be implemented through the bus interface and the appropriately chosen peripheral. A bus interface provides enormous possibility.

The mix of I/O subsystems that microcontrollers may have varies considerably. Some microcontrollers are intended for simple digital control and may have only digital I/O. Others may be intended for industrial applications, and may have digital I/O, analog input, motor control, and networking. The choice of microcontroller (and there are literally thousands of subspecies available from dozens of manufacturers) depends on your processing needs and your interfacing requirements. Choose the one that best suits your purposes.

CHAPTER 2

Assembly Language

For the things we have to learn before we can do them,
we learn by doing them.
—Aristotle
   Nichomachean Ethics

This chapter is about writing assembly-language software. This is a difficult subject to present, as it is a very diverse topic. There are many processors covered in this book. The assembly language of one processor bears no relation to that of another. To delve into the assembly language of each would require an entire book in its own right (or several books). Hence, I'm not even going to attempt to cover each one's instruction set. Instead, I'm going to concentrate on just two processors, the 68HC11 and the PIC, and use these as vehicles to show you some basic assembly-language techniques. I'm not going to dissect the instruction sets in detail. The User's Manual/datasheets for the processors give full descriptions of the instructions and their operation.

Assembly-language programming works down at the machine level, and as such, you really get a feel for what the processor is doing and how your computer actually works. While assembly-language programming can be fun, it can also be a daunting task to code major applications in it. To this end, assembly is usually used in only two instances. The first is for the development of simple test software during the early prototype development of a system. Such software may simply initialize the machine to a known state and perform some simple task such as flashing a LED or outputting the venerable "hello world" to a terminal or host.

With assembly language, you work with data in single bytes or words at a time. Processors store data within memory, and this is usually implemented using external chips in the computer system. To manipulate data, processors use registers within the CPU.

No computer can understand assembly directly. Back in the olden days, when computers were steam-driven and tended by gnomes, software was compiled manually.

Each instruction mnemonic was looked up and converted to the appropriate opcode by the programmer. While it is certainly character-building, converting from assembly to opcodes is very tiresome, particularly where large programs are concerned. To make life easier, special compilers, called *assemblers*, take mnemonics and convert them to opcodes.

Assembly language has been described as the "nuts and bolts language," because you are writing code directly for the processor. For a lot of the software you will write, a high-level language like C will be the language of choice. High-level languages make developing software much easier, and your code is also portable (to a degree) between different target machines. Compilers of high-level languages convert your source code down to machine opcodes. Thus, by using a compiler, the programmer is relieved of having to know the specific details of the processor, and of having to code his program directly in machine code.

So there are good reasons for using a high-level language, yet programmers often write directly in assembly language. Why? Assembly and machine code, because they are "hand-written," can be finely tuned to get optimum performance out of the processor and computer hardware. This can be particularly important when dealing with time-critical operations with I/O devices. Further, coding directly in assembly can sometimes (but not always) result in a smaller code space. So, if you're trying to cram complex software into a small amount of memory and need that software to execute quickly and efficiently, assembly language may be your best (and only) choice. The drawback, of course, is that the software is harder to maintain and has zero portability to other processors. A good software engineer can create more efficient code than the average optimizing C compiler; however, a good optimizing compiler will probably produce tighter code than a mediocre assembly-language software engineer. Typically, you can include *in-line assembly* within your C code, and thereby get the best of both worlds.

At the mere mention of assembly language, many a die-hard programmer begins to quiver in fear, as if just invited into a tiger's cage. However, assembly-language programming is not that hard and can often be a lot of fun. Think of it as being "as one" with the processor.

That said, this is a book predominantly about hardware, not software. In this chapter, we'll take a quick tour of assembly-language programming, just to give you an overview. In the next chapter, we'll take a look at the Forth programming language, widely used in many embedded systems. For more information on embedded software development, I highly recommend two O'Reilly books: *Programming Embedded Systems* by Michael Barr and Anthony Massa, and *Programming with GNU Software* by Mike Loukides and Andy Oram. If you want to build a Linux-based embedded computer, I recommend *Building Embedded Linux Systems* by Karim Yaghmour, also published by O'Reilly.

Let's start by looking at the internal storage of the processor.

Registers

Registers are the internal (working) storage for the processor. The number of registers varies significantly among processor architectures. Typically, the processor will have one or more *accumulators*. These are registers that may have arithmetic operations performed on them. In some architectures, all the registers function as accumulators, whereas in others, some registers are dedicated for storage only and have limited functionality.

Some processors have *index registers* that can function as pointers into the memory space. In some architectures, all general-purpose registers can act as index registers; in others, dedicated index registers exist.

All processors have a *program counter* (also known as an *instruction pointer*) that tracks the location in memory of the next instruction to be fetched and executed. All processors have a *status register* (also known as a *condition-code register*, or *CCR*) that consists of various status bits (flags) that reflect the current operational state. Such flags might indicate whether the result of the last operation was zero or negative, whether a carry occurred, if an interrupt is being serviced, etc.

Some processors also have one or more control registers consisting of configuration bits that affect processor operation and the operating modes of various internal subsystems. Many peripherals also have registers that control their operation and registers that contain the results of operations. These peripheral registers are normally mapped into the address space of the processor.

Some processors have banks of *shadow registers*, which save the state of the main registers when the processor begins servicing an interrupt. By using shadow registers, there is no need to save processor state to the stack. This can save significant time in servicing an interrupt. (We'll look at stack operations in more detail shortly.)

Processors are commonly 8-bit, 16-bit, 32-bit, or 64-bit, referring to the width of their registers. An 8-bit processor is invariably low-cost and is suitable for relatively simple control and monitoring applications. If more processing power is required, the larger processors are preferable, although cost and system complexity increase accordingly.

Machine Code

Everything that a processor deals with is expressed as numbers in memory. That applies to data, and to software as well. Your compiled C program is converted to a sequence of numbers that is meaningful to the processor as a sequence of instructions. A program that a processor (in this case, a 68HC11) can execute might look something like:

```
86 41 B7 01 00 BD 02 00
```

This is known as *machine code*, and each numeric instruction is called an *opcode*. Humans find such programs very hard to write and even harder to understand. To make this easier to cope with, we use a notation called *assembly language*. Assembly-language instructions equate directly to their machine code counterparts. Since machine code is difficult to read and write (for a human), a *mnemonic* is used to represent the opcode. For example, the 68HC11 instruction 86 41 is more easily understood by its mnemonic LDAA #$41. (The dollar sign [$] represents a hex value in some assembly languages.) This is still a bit cryptic, so we usually add comments on the righthand side to help us follow what is going on. The previous machine code sequence written as 68HC11 assembly would be:

```
Machine code   Assembly      Comment
86 41          LDAA #$41     ; anything after a semi-colon
B7 01 00       STAA $0100    ; is a comment
BD 02 00       JSR $0200     ;
```

LDAA #$41 means "load accumulator A with the immediate value (signified by the #) of 0x41." *Immediate* means that the operand is to be treated as a number, rather than as a pointer to an address. With some processors, this is known as a *literal*. LDAA corresponds to the machine opcode 86.

STAA $0100 tells the processor to store the contents of accumulator A to the *memory location* (no # this time) 0x0100.

JSR $0200 means "jump to the subroutine at address 0x0200." A subroutine is essentially a procedure or function call. In some processors, the instruction to do this is call, rather than jump.

The instructions of a Freescale Semiconductor 68HC11 series processor (Chapter 16) can be from one to three bytes in length. The first byte is always an opcode and may be followed by one or two bytes of data. For example, consider the following assembly-language program:

```
Machine code   Assembly      Comment
CE 10 02       LDX #$1002    ; load index register X with 0x1002
5F             CLRB          ; clear accumulator B
86 41          LDAA #$41     ; load accumulator A with 0x41.
```

Note the length of each instruction. The first instruction takes three bytes, the second takes only one, and the third is two bytes in length. The number of bytes an instruction takes depends on what it does. This is true for CISC processors, but not RISC. In order to achieve simpler instruction decode units, RISC processors have instructions of a fixed size, with operands buried inside the instruction. For example, all instructions of a PIC16 processor are 14 bits wide, regardless of what operation they perform.

Different processors use different assemblies. No two are alike. The previous examples are written in 68HC11 assembly. This assembly is applicable only to the 6800 family of processors, of which the 68HC11 is a member. Other assembly languages, because they are based on very different processor hardware, have very different syntax. Some examples of different versions of the same operation are given in Table 2-1. In each case, a register is loaded with a byte value of 0x41. (Note also the different ways of expressing hex notation.)

Table 2-1. Comparison of some different assembly languages

Processor	Instruction	
Motorola 6800/68HC11	LDAA	#$41
Intel x86	mov	al,41h
Motorola 680x0	move.b	#$41,D0
PIC16xx	movlw	0x41
Motorola 56000	move	#$0041,A
Intel 80960	lda	0x41,r4

Signed Numbers

Before getting into the nuts and bolts of assembly, let's take a quick look at how signed numbers are represented within the machine. Negative and positive numbers can be represented in binary (or hex) number systems by the state of the most significant bit. If the most significant bit is set, this indicates that the number is negative.

> It is up to the programmer whether to treat the content of a register or memory location as signed or unsigned. In C, we are used to explicitly declaring a variable or pointer as either signed or unsigned. In assembly, it's up to you.

An 8-bit accumulator can have (in decimal) 0 to 255 (unsigned) or -128 to +127 (signed). Given a positive number, we use *two's complement* to convert this to its negative equivalent. Taking the two's complement of a number is done by inverting the bits (a *one's compliment*) and adding one to the result. So 0xFF is 1111 1111 (in binary) and is therefore negative. 0xFF is used to represent -1, 0xFE is -2, etc., all the way to 0x80, which is -128 (decimal).

For example, -3 as an 8-bit hex value is calculated in this way:

```
              0 0 0 0   0 0 1 1  (0x03)
Invert bits: 1 1 1 1   1 1 0 0  (0xFC)
Add 1 gives: 1 1 1 1   1 1 0 1  (0xFD)
```

So -3 is 0xFD in hex.

Note that we are not limited to using signed (positive and negative) numbers. We are free to ignore the sign bit and treat the byte as an unsigned number, giving us a range of 0x00 to 0xFF (255 decimal). It all depends on what we want the byte to represent.

16-bit, 32-bit, and 64-bit signed numbers work in the same way. The most significant bit represents the sign, and the remaining bits constitute the number.

Addressing Modes

The different ways in which an instruction can reference a register or memory location are known as the *addressing modes* of the processor. The types of addressing modes available within different architectures vary. To illustrate some of the more common modes, let's take a look at those available in the 68HC11 architecture:

Inherent

The instruction deals purely with registers. CLRB clears the B accumulator, for example.

Immediate/Literal

The instruction has a literal number as an operand.

Direct

The instruction accesses a memory location, specified by a short address. In other words, direct addressing provides access to a subset of the total address space. On a given processor with a 16-bit address bus, a direct access may, for example, specify an address within the first 256 bytes. On a 32-bit processor, a direct access may specify an address within the first 64K of memory, for example. Direct addressing is used (when possible) to reduce the length of instruction-referencing memory. This can reduce code size, and therefore instruction fetch time, in time-critical applications. Many processors, especially RISC, do not use direct addressing.

Extended

The instruction accesses a memory location, specified by the full address. So LDAA $B098 means load accumulator A with the contents of address 0xB098 in memory.

Indexed

The instruction uses the contents of a register as a pointer into memory. If, for example, the X register is equal to 0x5034, then LDAA 0,X means "load accumulator A with the contents of the location pointed to by X." In this example, this means "load accumulator A with the contents of address 0x5034." Whereas LDAA 2,X means "load accumulator A with the contents of the memory location pointed to by X, but with an offset of 2." So if X = 0x5034, then 2,X is 0x5036. So LDAA 2,X loads from address 0x5036. Indexed addressing is useful when your program needs to reference data in a table or list. The index is an easy way of moving through the data structure.

Relative

An offset is specified as part of the addressing. A branch instruction uses relative addressing to add (or subtract) a value from the program counter. For example, bra 02 (branch) adds 2 to the program counter, whereas bra $FF adds –1 to the program counter. Note that the instruction counter always points to the next instruction, not the one currently being executed.

Big-Endian and Little-Endian Addressing

Microprocessors are either *big endian* or *little endian* in their architecture. This refers to the way in which the processor stores data (16 bits or greater) to memory. A big-endian processor stores the most significant byte at the least significant address, as illustrated in Figure 2-1. In each case, the data has been stored to address 0x0100.

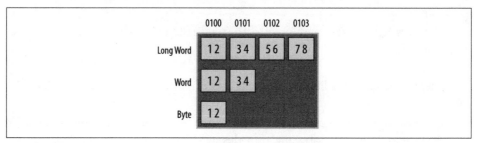

Figure 2-1. Big endian

A little-endian processor stores the most significant byte at the most significant address, as shown in Figure 2-2.

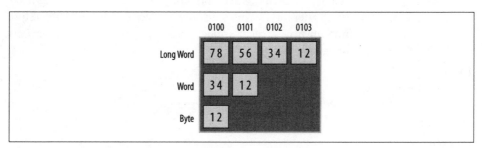

Figure 2-2. Little endian

With the little-endian scheme, the least significant data travels over the least significant part of the data bus and is stored at the least significant memory location. For a programmer, it is conceptually easier to understand in terms of data path. The inconvenience of little endian is that data appears "backwards" in the computer's memory if you display a block of locations. Storing the value 0x12345678 to memory results in 0x78563412 in the memory space. Note that a little-endian processor will read this data back correctly; it's just that it makes it harder to understand the numbers if a human is looking at the memory directly. Alternatively, a big-endian processor storing 0x12345678 to memory results in 0x12345678 sitting inside the memory chip. This appears (to a human) to make more sense. Neither scheme has much advantage over the other in terms of operation; they are just two different ways of doing the same thing. When you're doing high-level programming on a system, the "endian-ness" makes little difference. The only time you are really exposed to it is when you are dealing with multibyte data and accessing it on a byte-by-byte basis. However, when you are developing and debugging hardware and low-level firmware, you come across it all the time, and so an understanding of big endian and little endian is important.

Coding in Assembly

Assembly-language programming is not difficult, particularly with the smaller microcontroller and microprocessor architectures. The main difficulty many people seem to have is knowing how to tackle a given programming problem. As with any other language, there are always many ways in which a program may be written. There is rarely a single "right way" (although there may be a "most efficient way"). It is simply a matter of breaking down the problem into a series of tiny steps.

For example, let's say we want a 68HC11 processor to add three numbers together (0x10, 0x1F, and 0x0C) and store the result at address 0x0027. This problem is easily broken down into four steps. We take the first number (step one), add the second number (step two), add the third number (step three), and store the result (step four). We want to do some arithmetic, so we choose an accumulator to hold our numbers, since accumulators are registers designed for this type of operation. We start by loading an accumulator with the first number:

```
LDAA    #$10    ; load first number into the A accumulator
```

The A accumulator now contains the number 0x10 (16 in decimal). Remember that the "#" in the instruction means that the addressing mode is immediate. In other words, the processor is to load the actual number 0x10, not use the operand as a pointer. We then want to add the number 0x1F. So our next instruction is:

```
ADDA    #$1F    ; add the second number to the A accumulator
```

This causes 0x1F to be added to accumulator A. Again note the "#." Similarly, to add the third number, we have:

```
ADDA    #$0C    ; add the third number to the A accumulator
```

Finally, we store the result at address 0x0027:

```
STAA    $0027   ; store the contents of the A accumulator to address 0x0027
```

This time, note that there is no "#." This is an extended instruction. It means "Store the contents of accumulator A to the memory location 0x0027." It does not treat 0x0027 as a number, but rather as the address of a location in memory.

So our complete program is:

```
LDAA    #$10    ; load first number in the A accumulator
ADDA    #$1F    ; add the second number to the A accumulator
ADDA    #$0C    ; add the third number to the A accumulator
STAA    $0027   ; store the contents of the A accumulator to address 0x0027
```

To make this program into a subroutine (a callable function or procedure), we simply add a label at the start and a return-from-subroutine (RTS) instruction at the end. (We'll look at subroutines in more detail shortly.) A *label* is used by the assembler during compilation to identify a given address location. It has no direct meaning in the machine code:

```
add_numbers
    LDAA   #$10    ; load first number in the A accumulator
    ADDA   #$1F    ; add the second number to A
    ADDA   #$0C    ; add the third number to A
    STAA   $0027   ; store the contents of A to address 0x0027
    RTS            ; return to main program
```

To call our subroutine from our main program, we simply use a jump-to-subroutine instruction (JSR) with the label as an operand:

```
JSR    add_numbers
```

For comparison, this is what the same subroutine looks like in PIC16 assembly:

```
add_numbers
    movlw  0x10    ; load first number in the w accumulator
    addlw  0x1F    ; add the second number to the w accumulator
    addlw  0x0C    ; add the third number to the w accumulator
    movwf  0x27    ; store the content of w to address 0x27
    return         ; return to main program
```

movlw is "move literal to w," and, similarly, addlw is "add literal to w." movwf is "move w to register file (f)." (Microchip calls the processor's on-chip RAM "registers.") The PIC's return instruction is exactly the same as the 68HC11's RTS. Both perform exactly the same function; just the mnemonic is different.

To call our PIC subroutine, we use the PIC's call instruction with the label as an operand:

```
call   add_numbers
```

The program can be converted to machine code by looking up each instruction in the datasheet or by using an assembler running on a host computer. Let's manually assemble the 68HC11 subroutine so that you can see the process. (Opcodes are always assumed to be hex and carry no prefix.)

LDAA (immediate) is 86 and takes two bytes, the other byte being the data operand, 0x10. Similarly, ADDA (immediate) is 8B and also takes two bytes. Looking up the remaining opcodes in the datasheet or programmer's reference gives us:

```
0100  86 10     LDAA #$10  ; load first number in the A accumulator
0102  8B 1F     ADDA #$1F  ; add the second number to the A accumulator
0104  8B 0C     ADDA #$0C  ; add the third number to the A accumulator
0106  B7 00 27  STAA $0027 ; store the contents of A to address 0x0027
0109  39        RTS        ; return to main program
```

Here I have (arbitrarily) assumed that the program will start at address 0x0100 and have added the address of each instruction at the far left. Note how the addresses change in relation to the size of the instructions.

If I want to explicitly tell an assembler to start the code at address 0x0100, I could use the org *assembler directive*:

```
org  $0100
```

The org directive always precedes the first instruction at that address. org is useful for locating code at specific locations, such as on-chip ROM.

Let's now see how this program is executed by the processor by manually stepping through the code. Assuming that the program counter points to address 0x0100, the first step taken by the processor is loading the byte located at address 0x0100 and decoding it as an instruction. The processor does this by placing 0x0100 on the address bus and performing a read cycle. The memory device responds by placing the content of address 0x0100 (86) onto the data bus. This is then read by the processor into its instruction decode unit. 86 is a LDAA (immediate) instruction, so this causes the processor to load the next byte of the instruction (at address 0x0101) and place this in the A accumulator. As part of the instruction decode in the processor, the program counter is incremented by the size of the current instruction so that it points to the next instruction. Hence, the program counter is now 0x0102, as the first instruction occupied two bytes.

The processor loads the instruction at 0x0102 by placing this address on the address bus and performing a read cycle. The processor decodes it to be an ADDA (immediate). The processor then fetches the next byte and adds this to accumulator A. Similarly, it executes the next ADDA instruction and adds the byte at 0x0105 to the A accumulator.

The program counter now points to address 0x0106. The processor fetches this instruction by placing 0x0106 on the address bus and performing a read cycle. The memory device responds by placing B7 on the data bus. The processor decodes B7 to be an extended store operation. It then loads the next *two* bytes by placing 0x0107 on the address bus and performing a read, then placing 0x0108 on the address bus and performing another read. The processor takes the two bytes that were read and constructs the address 0x0027. The processor then places 0x0027 on the address bus, places the contents of accumulator A on the data bus, and performs a write cycle. The memory chip or peripheral mapped by the address decoder to address 0x0027 latches and stores the written data.

Normally, the program counter is incremented as each instruction is executed, so that it points to the next instruction. Some instructions, such as jump (JMP) or branch (BRA) directly modify the program counter, thus giving you control over the flow of the program. These instructions effectively reload the program counter with a new value (as with jump) or add to the program counter (branch), so that it points to a different location in memory. This means that the next instruction to be executed will come from a new address, not the address immediately following the current instruction.

Disassembly

Disassembly is the conversion from a sequence of machine code back to the mnemonics that represent that code. This is done when we have a machine code program (perhaps written by someone else) and we want to know what it does and how it works.

For example, suppose we have the following sequence of bytes that constitute a 68HC11 machine code program:

```
8E 56 78 86 56 84 06 36 4C 36
```

We start by assuming that the first byte is an opcode. By looking up the opcode 0x8E in the Motorola 6800 (or 68HC11) datasheet, you will find that it is the LDS instruction (load stack pointer) and that it takes three bytes (one for opcode, two for data). Therefore, if the first byte is the instruction, the next two bytes are its associated data. So that gives us the first instruction:

```
8E 56 78   LDS #$5678 ; load stack pointer with the number 0x5678
```

If the first instruction was three bytes long, then the fourth byte in the sequence must be the second instruction. Therefore, the next opcode is 0x86, which, according to the datasheet, is LDAA # (load accumulator A with an immediate value) and takes two bytes.

So we now have:

```
8E 56 78   LDS  #$5678 ; load stack pointer with the number 0x5678
86 56      LDAA #$56   ; load Acc A with 0x56
```

The next opcode is 0x84, which is an ANDA # instruction taking two bytes. Then we have a 0x36 (PSHA), a 0x4C (INCA), and finally another 0x36 (PSHA).

So, from:

```
8E 56 78 86 56 84 06 36 4C 36
```

our disassembled program is:

```
8E 56 78   LDS  #$5678 ; load stack pointer with the number 0x5678
86 56      LDAA #$56   ; load Acc A with 0x56
84 06      ANDA #$06   ; AND Acc A with 0x06
36         PSHA        ; push Acc A onto the stack
4C         INCA        ; increment Acc A
36         PSHA        ; push Acc A onto the stack
```

Position-Independent Code

When we jump to an address or subroutine within our program, we could use an absolute address. For example, JSR $0200 jumps to a subroutine at the absolute address 0x0200. This means that for our program to work, that subroutine must always be at address 0x0200. A program (and hence its subroutines) could be located (or relocated) by the computer's operating system to anywhere in memory. If this were to happen, JSR $0200 would no longer jump to the location of our subroutine because that subroutine would no longer be at address 0x0200. Therefore the program would crash. For this reason, it is good practice to employ *position-independent code*. This method of programming avoids the use of absolute addresses (except where appropriate). It means that rather than jumping to the absolute address of our subroutine, we branch to the subroutine relative to the program counter's contents. It sounds complicated, but all it really means is that we should use BRA (or BSR) rather than JMP (or JSR). By using a branch rather than a jump, we are adding a number to the program counter rather than replacing its contents. This means that we are not jumping to an absolute position in memory, but branching relative to our current location.

Absolute addressing is used when we branch or jump to some code that we know will always be at a given address. For example, a subroutine that is located in ROM (permanent memory) is not going to move somewhere else.

Loops

It is often useful to repeat an instruction or series of instructions. Using branch instructions allows us to redirect the program counter and hence control the flow of the program. Here is a simple example of a loop that executes 15 times:

```
        LDAA #$0F   ; load the count into the A accumulator
again               ;
        DECA        ; count down (decrement the A accumulator)
        BNE again   ; repeat until we have counted down to zero
```

DECA decrements the A accumulator and sets the status flags as appropriate. If the result of the decrement was a zero in the A accumulator, the zero flag in the CCR (Condition Code Register) is set; otherwise, the flag is cleared. The BNE instruction is "branch not equal (to zero)." This checks the state of the zero flag. If it is clear (not equal to zero), then the branch is taken; otherwise, execution continues on with the next instruction after BNE. Hence, the above code fragment will start with the A accumulator equal to 15 and will decrement this value until is has reached zero. At this point, the loop will terminate. Now, to get the loop to actually perform work for you, place your code between the again label and the DECA instruction.

In machine code, this is:

```
Address  Opcodes        Assembly
0100     86 OF          LDAA #$0F
0102     4A       again DECA
0103     26 FD          BNE  again
0105     ...            ; address of instruction after BNE
```

Note the instruction BNE. Where did the 0xFD come from? We want the processor to branch back to address 0x0102. As with all instructions, when executing the BNE the program counter points to the next instruction, so as BNE is being executed, the program counter contains 0x0105. We want the program counter to be 0x0102, so we need to subtract 3 from it. We do this by adding –3, which in 8-bit hex is 0xFD. (0xFF is -1, 0xFE is -2, 0xFD is -3, and so on.) To branch forward, we add a positive number. To branch backward, we add a negative number. In both cases, we must remember to take into account that the program counter will be pointing to the address *after* the branch when determining the value to add.

Masking

It is often useful to examine the state of certain bits (such as the status of a peripheral chip or a flag). We are interested in the state of a given bit, but the state of the other bits is unknown (and unimportant to us).

For example, assume we want to check the state of bit 0 in a byte that has been read from a status register. To do this, we need to compare the byte with a constant. But what constant should we choose? In both the following examples of a byte read from a status register, bit 0 is set. Comparing the byte with the constant 0x65 will work in the first instance but not the second:

```
0 1 1 0 0 1 0 1 (0x65)
1 1 0 0 1 1 0 1 (0xCD)
```

There is no single number with which we can compare the byte that will work in all instances. We need to set all the other bits to a known state before we can do a comparison. To do this, it is necessary to *mask* out any bits in which we are not interested. This may be accomplished by using an AND instruction.

In the previous example, we need to AND the byte from the status register with 0x01 to clear the other bits. This will preserve bit 0 (regardless of its state) and clear all other bits. The result of this operation is 0x01 if bit 0 was set or 0x00 if bit 0 was clear:

```
0 1 1 0 0 1 0 1   (0x65)
0 0 0 0 0 0 0 1   (0x01)  AND
```

This gives:

```
0 0 0 0 0 0 0 1   (0x01)
```

The following operation:

```
1 1 0 0 1 1 0 1    (0xCD)
0 0 0 0 0 0 0 1    (0x01)  AND
```

gives:

```
0 0 0 0 0 0 0 1    (0x01)
```

Finally, this operation:

```
1 0 0 0 1 1 0 0    (0x8C)
0 0 0 0 0 0 0 1    (0x01)  AND
```

gives:

```
0 0 0 0 0 0 0 0    (0x00)
```

In each of these examples, the state of bit 0 in the original byte is preserved. All other bits are cleared. Therefore, to determine the state of bit 0, we need now only compare the byte with 0x01. If it is equal, the bit is set; otherwise, the bit is clear.

So let's convert this into assembly. Here I am assuming that we want to check the status of an I/O device located at address 0x0700:

```
check   LDAB $0700 ; load status register located at 0x0700 into B
        ANDB #$01  ; mask out unwanted bits
        CMPB #$01  ; check to see if bit 0 is set
        BNE  check ; if it is not, go back and check once more
```

This code fragment loops until bit 0 is found to be set.

Indexed Addressing

It is often useful to use a pointer to reference a section of memory. The 68HC11 has two index registers, X and Y. These are the equivalent of pointers in C.

For example, let's say we want to fill the address range 0x0200 to 0x2FF with the number 0x0F. One way would be to load an accumulator with 0x60 and store that to address 0x0200. Then we could store the value to address 0x0201, and so on:

```
LDAA #$60    ;
STAA $0200   ;
STAA $0201   ;
STAA $0202   ;
STAA $0203   ;
STAA $0204   ;
STAA $0205   ;
STAA $0206   ; ... and so it goes
```

While this would do what we want, it makes for a long (and tedious) program. A simpler way is to use indexed addressing, with an index register pointing to each memory location in turn. The following program uses indexed addressing to achieve our goal:

```
        LDX   #$0200   ; load the X register with the number 0x0200
        LDAA  #$60     ; load the A accumulator with the value to be stored
        LDAB  #$FF     ; load the B accumulator with the count
   loop STAA  0,X      ; store acc A to address pointed to by X with no offset
        INX            ; increment X to point to next address
        DECB           ; count down
        BNE   loop     ; repeat until we have counted down to zero
```

The LDX instruction loads an immediate value into the 16-bit X register. This is now our pointer into memory. The A accumulator is then loaded with the value to be stored in memory, and the B accumulator is loaded with the number of locations in memory we will be accessing. This will act as the counter for our loop.

The loop begins by storing the content of the A accumulator to the memory location pointed to by the X register. The 0,X means there is no offset. (If we wanted to store the value not to the address pointed to by X, but the one three locations further on, we would use 3,X.) The X register is then incremented to point to the next address in memory, and the B accumulator is decremented since we have completed an iteration of the loop. In the process of decrementing the accumulator, the zero flag will be set or cleared, and this will be checked by the subsequent branch instruction. If the result of the decrement is not zero, then the loop isn't finished. Execution branches back to the STAA 0,X instruction, and the content of A is stored to the next location in memory. The process repeats.

Stacks

Many processors implement one or more *stacks*, which serve as temporary storage in external memory. The processor can *push* a value from a register on the stack to preserve it for later use. The processor retrieves this value by *popping* from the stack back into a register. In some processor architectures, popping is also known as *pulling*.

Most processors have a special register known as a *stack pointer*, which references the next free location on the stack. Some processors implement more than one stack and so have more than one stack pointer. Most stacks grow down through memory. (Some processors have stacks that grow up as the stack is filled.) When the processor pushes or pops a value to or from the stack, the stack pointer automatically decrements or increments to point to the next free location.

Figure 2-3 shows the steps that occur when the content of a register (in this case, 72) is pushed onto the stack. These steps are normally performed by a single instruction (for example, PSHA). First, the value is copied from the register and stored to the location pointed to by the stack pointer. The stack pointer is then decremented. Again, these operations take place automatically by executing a single push instruction.

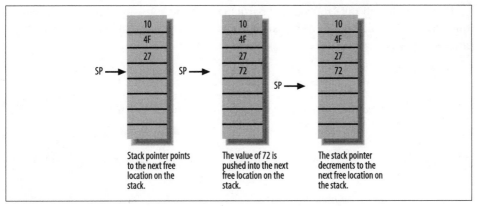

Figure 2-3. *Pushing a register onto the stack*

Most processors automatically save registers to the stack when events such as interrupts occur. However, the stack is also available to you as a programmer to temporarily store values. Some processors have two stacks, with one reserved for system use and the other available to the application programmer.

Stacks are particularly useful for the temporary storage of data. For example, let's say we wish to call a subroutine, but we know that the subroutine changes the contents of the B accumulator as part of its operation. If there was nothing of importance in the B accumulator before we called the subroutine, this would be of little consequence. But if we wished to preserve the B accumulator, we would push the accumulator onto the stack before we called the subroutine and then pull it back after the subroutine ends:

```
PSHB       ; save B accumulator onto the stack
BSR   fred ; branch to subroutine fred
PULB       ; restore B accumulator from the stack
```

In this way, we have used the stack as a temporary storage location for data that we required later in the program. Alternatively, a good programmer would write the subroutine to preserve any affected registers:

```
fred
      PSHB  ; save B accumulator onto the stack
            ;
            ; (subroutine code here)
            ;
      PULB  ; restore B accumulator from the stack
      RTS   ;
```

Timing of Instructions

On some processors, particularly CISC chips, different instructions take varying lengths of time to complete. Sometimes it is important to know how long a given section of code will take to execute, particularly if the software is interacting with a time-critical external system. The execution time can be calculated by looking up the number of cycles each instruction takes and adding them together.

 A "cycle" relates to the internal clock that is driving the processor. This is not necessarily the same speed as the crystal. The datasheet will tell you how the crystal frequency relates to the internal clock for a given processor.

The following example shows some 68HC11 assembly language and the number of cycles associated with each instruction:

```
      LDAA #$0F ; 2 cycles
again DECA      ; 2 cycles
      BNE again ; 3 cycles
exit  JMP $1000 ; 3 cycles
```

From examining the code, we can see that the loop is executed 15 (0x0F) times. This loop comprises five cycles in total. Therefore, the above program will take:

```
2 + (15 * 5) + 3 cycles = 80 cycles
```

For a 2 MHz 68HC11, a cycle is 500 ns. Hence, this code fragment will take 40,000 ns (or 40 μsecs) to complete.

Knowing the timing of instructions is often very useful. For example, suppose we need to have a program that will provide a delay of approximately 9 msec. To do this, we need to load a value into a register and count it down to zero. This will provide the delay.

So a program that would do this is simply:

```
       LDX #some_number ; load X with a number
repeat DECX             ; count down        3 cycles
       BNE repeat       ; not zero, repeat  3 cycles
```

For a 2 MHz 68HC11, a cycle is 500 ns. So for 9 msec, we require 18,000 cycles. The loop takes six cycles per iteration. Therefore, we need to run through the loop 3,000 times. In hex, 3,000 is 0x0BB8. So our program becomes:

```
       LDX #$0BB8   ; load X with 3000 decimal
repeat DECX         ; count down       3 cycles
       BNE repeat   ; not zero, repeat 3 cycles
```

Now, let me make some important points here. If an interrupt occurs during the loop, the processor will service the interrupt, and this will add an unknown (and unknowable) delay to the execution. If this code was controlling something critical, such an event would be disastrous. Most processors have instructions to disable and re-enable interrupts, and you would be well advised to turn off all interrupts prior to this code executing. Of course, you have to remember to re-enable them afterward as well. The other important point is that this code will provide a delay only of 9 msec, provided it is running on a 68HC11 at 2 MHz. If the code were run on a computer with a processor kicking along at 2.1 MHz, we would not get our 9 msec delay. In other words, techniques like this are not very portable and are generally considered bad practice. Use it only if you really have to. Programmers using code such as this often get caught when they move their code to a newer version of the hardware. Code that used to work is suddenly broken.

A better way to provide a fixed delay is to use a hardware timer, either as an internal peripheral to the microcontroller (and most have them) or as an external device. The timer generates an interrupt to the processor, and this gives a much more precise, reliable, and portable way of implementing a timing delay.

CHAPTER 3

Forth/Open Firmware

Verbum sat sapienti

At the beginning of this book, I said I would talk about hardware, not software. There are many good books already written on C programming, embedded firmware development in C, porting Linux, coding in Python, writing Java software, and so on. However, there is one software topic that is rare, and chances are you may not happen upon it or become exposed to it. And that is a pity, because for the hardware developer, this topic can be very important. It is the programming language, Forth. So, I will break with the general "stuff you can kick" theme of this book to give you an overview of this important language.

Introducing Forth

Forth was originally written by Charles (Chuck) Moore (*http://www.colorforth.com/ bio.html*) in 1970 to control the 30 ft telescope at the Kitt Peak Observatory. When he created Forth, Charles Moore envisioned that the "fourth" generation of computers would be distributed controllers, in essence embedded systems, although that term had not yet been invented. Hence, he called his programming language "Fourth." However, since the machine that was used for development allowed only five-character filenames, the programming language became simply Forth. The name has stuck ever since.

Forth is unlike any other conventional programming language (although there are some vague similarities to Adobe's PostScript). Forth is an extensible, highly interactive, stack-based language. It is extremely efficient and extremely versatile. In addition, Forth is relatively easy to "bring up" on a virgin machine, and the structure and functionality of the language make it ideal for debugging both system hardware and software. In fact, it is fantastic for debugging new hardware. Forth is commonly used in systems under development and is often retained by manufacturers in their computers. You can often find Forth sitting deep inside a machine's ROM. NASA's Voyager spacecraft run Forth, providing for both efficient firmware and the ability to interactively debug across the vastness of space, and Forth is also used by NASA in the Space Shuttle's Star Tracker subsystem. (More information may be found at *http://forth.gsfc.nasa.gov*.) The Open Firmware standard (IEEE 1275) is based on Forth and is used by both Apple Computer and Sun Microsystems, as well as many others. Hardware engineers love Forth. Traditional computer scientists hate it.

 If you have an Apple Macintosh and like living life on the edge, hold down command-option-O-F immediately after pushing the power button. You'll boot into the Open Firmware Forth instead of Mac OS X.

Forth is predominantly written in Forth and is interpreted by itself at runtime. The virtual machine running Forth is typically coded directly in the assembler both for speed of operation and to take advantage of the characteristics of the target computer directly. Moore explains that his concept for Forth is that each implementation of the language should be optimized to take advantage of the machine it is running on, even if this optimization compromises the portability of the language. This philosophy is a major departure from conventional programming ideology. With Forth, speed and robustness are the goals, not the ability to port applications between platforms.

Forth is at once a compiler, an interpreter, and, in a fashion, an operating system too. The majority of computer languages share many characteristics, many of them coming from common origins. Languages in this category include C and C++, Pascal, Modula-2, ADA, Fortran, and BASIC, to name just a few. With the exception of BASIC, which is (typically) an interpreted language, all these languages are compiled. Forth is also a compiled language, but it is a compiled language with a difference. It is *interactive*. Commands (known as *words* in Forth) get an immediate response. This, coupled with Forth's ability to talk directly to hardware, makes it an excellent environment for hardware development.

Forth allows the execution of any subroutine (word) of a program in isolation. The programmer is also able to create new programs (words) based on previously defined words. So rather than writing a single, large program, small segments of code are written and tested independently. These words are then combined to create new words, eventually ending up with a single word that is the whole program. This new word is also available to the programmer, and in this way the language both grows and becomes richer as the programmer works with it. In addition, the words used to create the new word are still available and can be run as programs in their own right or used to create other new words. This modular form of program construction makes Forth a "bottom-up" language, rather than the conventional "top-down" programming methodology. This interactive, yet low-level, nature makes Forth a very powerful tool for debugging microprocessor hardware. Words written to interact with specific aspects of hardware (at the initial debugging stage) may be later incorporated in higher-level diagnostics or in the final application itself.

The most notable aspect of Forth is that data (arguments) are passed to the words (subroutines, if you like) via a stack. (Note that this stack is not necessarily the processor's stack. Often it is a virtual stack created by the Forth kernel.) While it is true that many languages use stacks for parameter passing, the programmer is usually unaware of this aspect. Forth, however, is quite different. In Forth, arguments required by a word are pushed onto the stack explicitly, and then the word is called. The values can be pushed or pulled from the stack by other words or by the user.

In Forth, the words that a programmer writes directly manipulate the stack, taking parameters off and putting new values (return parameters) back. In addition, the programmer can directly manipulate the stack at the prompt, manually pushing or popping stack values prior to running a given word. This feature encompasses the power and beauty of Forth. As a consequence of the stack, Forth uses a form of syntax known as *Reverse Polish Notation* (*RPN*). Anyone who has used an old-style Hewlett-Packard calculator is familiar with RPN. In this notation, the operator follows the arguments. So the conventional expression $a + b$ becomes $a \, b \, +$ in RPN. In this example, first the number represented by a is pushed onto the stack, then b. In Forth, the + word takes these values off the stack, performs the addition, and places the result back on the stack.

So:

```
4  5  +
```

gives a result of 9 on the top of the stack. To display this result, we use *dot* (.), which pulls the topmost value from the stack and prints it to the console as a signed number. As an example, to add three numbers together and print the result, we would type the following at the prompt:

```
5  25  98  +  +  .
```

The first + adds 98 and 25, leaving the result on the stack. The second + adds this result to 5. This could also be done as:

```
5  25  +  98  +  .
```

Most versions of Forth use signed 16-bit numbers, although there are some Forths that are explicitly 32-bit. 16-bit Forths do provide access to 32-bit arithmetic using doubles.

By default, Forth works in base 10 (decimal). hex changes the base to base 16, and decimal returns it to base 10. As an example, let's add (hex) 0x4F to (decimal) 255 and print out the result in decimal:

```
hex 4f decimal 255 + .
```

This gives a result of 334 on the console.

To output the top stack value as an unsigned number, use u. rather than the . operator. To output a right-justified number, use the .r word, which uses the top parameter to specify the spacing for the second parameter. For example:

```
123456  6  .r
1234  6  .r
12  6  .r
```

results in the following output:

```
123456
  1234
    12
```

Standard arithmetic is available using +, -, *, and /. These arithmetic operators are Forth words, and so must be surrounded by spaces. To multiply 2 and 3:

```
2  3  *
```

The / operator performs integer division. In some Forths, this rounds toward zero. In other Forths, it rounds toward minus infinity. To divide 9 by 3:

```
9  3  /
```

We can increment the top of the stack using the word 1+ and decrement it using 1-. As a nonsensical example, to convert 2 to 3:

```
2  1+
```

Let's take a look at some words common to all/most implementations of Forth. I won't provide an exhaustive list, as a complete discussion of the language would take a book in its own right. Remember, all words in Forth must be separated by one or more spaces.

String Words

We'll start with that perennial favorite of programmers, "hello world," to illustrate how to print out a string of characters. The word to output a string is ." (pronounced *dot quote*) and is used thus:

```
." hello world"
```

Note the space between ." and the string, and the *absence* of a space before the final quote. That's because ." is a Forth word, and all words must be separated by a space. The final quote character is not a Forth word, merely a string terminator.

A carriage-return/line-feed pair is output using the Forth word cr, and a space is output using space. For more than one space, use the spaces word that takes a parameter from the stack to specify the number of spaces to be printed. For example, the following code prints 20 spaces to the console:

```
20 spaces
```

To output a number as an ASCII character, we use the word emit. This is equivalent to the C function putchar. For example, to output an asterisk, we would use:

```
42 emit
```

The Forth word key waits for a character to be input from the console, and the word key? (*key query*) checks to see if a key has been pressed. Note that I have seen some implementations of Forth that use different words for character input. As the saying goes, your mileage may vary.

The word expect is used to input a string of characters from the console.

 Some Forths don't use the word expect, but use the word accept instead. accept works in exactly the same way as expect.

expect uses two parameters from the stack. The *topmost parameter* (the last parameter to go on the stack) is the number of characters to be read from the console. expect will wait for this number of characters to be entered or for a carriage return to be typed, whichever comes first. The other parameter used by expect is a pointer (address) to a scratchpad in memory where the string is to be placed. How do you know where to put a string? Easy, Forth has a scratchpad already for you. Use the word pad to place the address of the scratchpad onto the stack.

 Note that the scratchpad is not fixed in memory. It is merely a temporary storage place for strings. As words are defined and memory is used, the address supplied by pad will change.

To show you how this works, here is some code that will input 20 characters from the console:

```
pad 20 expect
```

Stack Manipulation

Since all words operate using parameters on the stack, Forth provides tools for the programmer to change the contents of the stack, or to alter the order of values on the stack.

The Forth word .s shows the current stack without removing any entries. This is a useful tool for the programmer, enabling you to nondestructively monitor the stack.

Other useful stack words are dup (duplicate the entry on top of the stack), drop (discard the entry on top of the stack), swap (exchange the two top entries on the stack), and over (copy the second-to-the-top entry to the top of the stack).

For example, entering 5 dup results in 5 5 on the stack. 3 4 swap results in 4 3 on the stack. 1 2 over results in 1 2 1 on the stack. dup is most often used to preserve stack entries when they are used with words that remove values from the stack. For example, here is Forth code that prints out the ASCII character A with its corresponding numeric code:

```
65 dup emit space . cr
```

Since both emit and . take a parameter from the stack, a dup is required to produce two copies of the required operand.

?dup will duplicate the top of the stack *only* if it isn't zero. 2dup will duplicate the top *two* stack entries. For example:

    10 23 2dup

gives:

    10 23 10 23

Similarly 2swap, 2over, and 2drop also operate on the top two stack entries.

The Forth word rot rotates the third stack parameter to the top. For example:

    1 2 3 rot

results in:

    2 3 1

The word -rot rotates the other way and is, in effect, the exact opposite of rot:

    1 2 3 -rot

This gives:

    3 1 2

The word pick allows you to arbitrarily grab an item from the stack, with the top-most stack entry specifying from where the item comes. For example, *n* pick will pick the nth item from the stack.

 pick will work in different ways depending on which variety of Forth you are using. Consult the documentation specific to your Forth.

Forth-79 and FIG Forth have pick numbering that starts from 1. So if our stack looks like:

    54 46 32 29 10 5

then:

    3 pick .

will output 29 to the console.

However, Forth-83, ANSI Forth, and gnu Forth have pick numbering that starts from 0. If you are using one of these Forths (with the same stack values), then:

    3 pick .

will output 32 to the console.

The word nip removes the second item from the stack, while the word tuck copies the top item to the third position:

    78 12 nip

This gives:

    12

and:

    78 12 tuck

gives:

    12 78 12

Creating New Words

A new word is created by using a *colon definition*. An example of this is shown in Figure 3-1. This simple program prints "A" to the console.

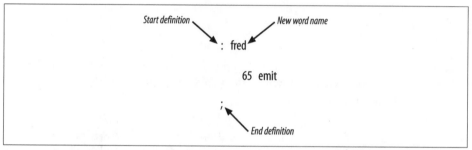

Figure 3-1. Colon definition

The colon (:) tells the compiler that a definition is starting, and that what comes next is the name of the word, in this case "fred." The definition is finished with a semicolon (;), the equivalent of a return in C or assembler. Everything in between : and ; constitutes the new program. In this example, the decimal value of 65 (the ASCII code for "A") is loaded onto the stack, and then the word emit is called. To run our new word, we simply type fred at the prompt. To run fred three times, we simply type fred fred fred at the prompt.

Forth uses *threaded code*, which is a list of subroutine identifiers (*words*). Each word within a program is called in turn, thus producing the sequence of running code. The interpreter is responsible for calling words as appropriate and is capable of only three operations. The first of these is the *call*, which, as the name implies, begins execution of a given word. The second operation is known as the *next* operation and passes control from one word to the next word in the list. The *return* operation passes control back to the calling list of words. The call is often known as *nesting*, and the return is known as *unnesting*. As a consequence of this structure, Forth is capable of recursion; the degree of recursion (or nesting) is limited only by the available memory.

Forth uses two stacks for its operation. The first stack is the *parameter stack* used to pass data between words. The second stack is the *return stack* and holds the return addresses for currently running words. Typically, the return stack is the system stack of the processor. Often, both stacks are implemented within a virtual machine (in the same way that Java runs under a virtual machine). The virtual machine also has an *Interpretive Pointer* (IP), the equivalent to the instruction pointer (or program counter) of a conventional processor. A *Word Pointer* (WP) is used to track words within a definition.

Words are stored in a linked list known as a *dictionary*, shown in Figure 3-2.

	Name	Address of code	Next word
1000	test	2000	1010
1010	fred	2010	1020
1020	check	2036	1030
1030	status	20F5	1040
1040	calc	2107	1050

Figure 3-2. Dictionary structure

In this data structure, words are stored in their order of definition. So when the user types fred on the console or uses fred in a word definition, Forth looks through the dictionary for a match and then simply calls the appropriate subroutine.

Writing your own Forth for your target machine is easy. It is simply a set of stack-manipulation primitives, a string parser, and a simple compiler. The compiler is trivial as it just builds a list of subroutine addresses, adds a return instruction, and then adds an entry in the linked list.

Words may be redefined by the programmer, the new word appearing in the dictionary list before the previous definition. When the input is parsed by the Forth interpreter, the dictionary is searched for a match. Thus, a redefined word will be matched before the parser reaches an earlier definition. Early words that used the prior definition reference that word by its address rather than its dictionary entry, and therefore still point to the original definition. Thus, redefining a word will not compromise the operation of other words based on the earlier definition. However, if a word is redefined as a bug fix, other words relying on it must subsequently be recompiled to use the newer definition.

It is possible to redefine a word based on a variation of its previous definition. For example, a word fred may be redefined to run its previous definition twice:

```
: fred
    fred fred
;
```

In this example, the new dictionary entry fred points to code that executes the previous definition of fred twice, referenced by the address of the original fred. When the compiler creates a new entry for fred, it searches the dictionary for the old reference, adding a subroutine call to the appropriate address. The original code for fred still exists in memory and is accessed by the call to its address. When you type fred at the prompt to run the new word, Forth searches the dictionary until it finds a match. Forth finds the newer definition first, and that is the code that is executed. Words that were written to use the previous definition of fred still work, as they reference that word by its address in memory.

Now, since Forth is written in Forth with much of the compiler and language sitting in the dictionary as Forth words, it is possible (and completely legal) to redefine the compiler (or aspects of the compiler) while it is running! Try doing that in C!

Comments

Comments in Forth are enclosed in parentheses:

```
( Here is a comment )
```

Note the spaces before and after the parentheses. The parentheses are Forth words, and therefore the spaces are required. Leaving the spaces out will not work:

```
(This ISN'T a comment)
```

Forth will try to interpret (This, ISN'T, a, and comment) as individual words, and if it does not find them in the dictionary (word list), it will complain bitterly.

Comments are also used to specify *stack diagrams*. A stack diagram indicates the stack usage of a word, as well as what it does. The general format of a stack diagram specifies the parameters taken off the stack (N1), the parameters placed back on the stack (N2), and a comment indicating the purpose of the word:

```
wordname ( N1 -- N2 , what this word does )
```

Here are stack diagrams for some common Forth words:

```
1+ ( N -- N+1, increments the top of the stack )
dup ( N -- N N, duplicates the top of the stack )
swap ( A B -- B A, swap top two values on stack )
```

Typically, stack diagrams are used within a word definition as a simple way of documenting the stack use and purpose of a word. Here are some examples:

```
: helloworld ( -- , says hi )
    ." hello world"
;

: square ( A -- A*A , squares top of stack )
    dup *
;
```

Because stack diagrams are comments, exactly how you specify the parameters is up to you, just so long as it makes sense to you and to anyone else likely to read your code.

if ... else

Forth has if ... else ... like other languages, but the structure is quite different from that which you are used to. if treats the topmost stack entry as a boolean. Any nonzero value is considered as true. Here is some sample code that shows you how to use if:

```
: is_it_true
    if
      ." That is true"
      cr
    else
      ." Not true"
      cr
    then
;
```

Note that the if statement is terminated by then. This is somewhat counterintuitive if you're used to other programming languages. To show how this new word works, if we typed:

```
5 is_it_true
```

we'd get:

```
That is true
```

but, if we typed:

```
0 is_it_true
```

we'd then get:

```
Not true
```

For a simple if statement with no need of else, the format is simply:

```
: is_it_true
    if
      ." That is true"
      cr
    then
;
```

Now, rather than using then to end the if structure, you can also use endif:

```
: is_it_true
    if
      ." That is true"
      cr
    endif
;
```

then and endif work in exactly the same way. Using endif rather than then makes code a little easier to read. Which code structure you use is up to you.

Loops

Loops may be created using the Forth words do and loop. The following simple example prints out five new lines:

```
5  0  do
   cr
loop
```

This is equivalent to the following for loop in C:

```
for (i = 0; i < 5; i++)
{
   printf("\n");
}
```

 Note that in some Forths, the loop constructs described in this section may be used only inside word definitions. Gnu's *gforth* is an example of such a Forth. In other Forths, you can quite happily use them from the command line. It all depends on which implementation you are using.

Now in C, you're not limited to incrementing the loop counter by 1. Forth doesn't have this limitation either. Instead of using loop, the word +loop takes a value from the stack and uses it to increment the loop count. Here is an example where the loop is incremented by 2 each iteration:

```
10 0 do
   cr
2 +loop
```

This is very versatile. In the previous example, the value by which the loop was incremented was specified just prior to +loop. However, since +loop takes a value from the stack, that value could just as easily be unspecified until runtime, and it could also be varied for each iteration of the loop simply by modifying that stack entry.

do (destructively) takes two operands off the stack and uses these for the loop count. In the previous examples, the loop executes the word cr five times. The operands can just as easily be supplied by other Forth words. In this example, the loop executes twice:

```
100 98 - 0 do cr loop
```

Alternatively, a word definition using do ... loop may take one or both of the loop operands from the stack. In the following example, the number of times to execute the loop is left to the user at runtime:

```
: stars ( N -- , prints N asterisks to the console )
   0 do
   42 emit
   loop
;
```

To output 10 asterisks:

```
10 stars
```

The loop count is accessible inside the loop using the Forth word i. In this example, we print out the loop count as the loop executes:

```
10 0 do i . cr loop
```

Loops can also be nested. In this example, 50 spaces are printed to the console:

```
10 0 do 5 0 do space loop loop
```

A counter for the outer loop can be accessed by the Forth word j:

```
10 0 do 5 0 do i . space j . loop cr loop
```

This is not limited to two nested loops:

```
10 0 do            ( loop 1 )
   5 0 do          ( loop 2 )
      i j          ( counts of loops 2 and 1 )
      20 0 do      ( loop 3 )
         i         ( count of loop 3 )
         4 0 do    ( loop 4 )
            10 0 do  ( loop 5 )
               i j   ( counts of loops 5 and 4 )
            loop
         loop
      loop
   loop
loop
```

As you can see, at any stage, i can be used to access the count of the current loop, and j can be used to access the count of the loop containing the current loop. For three nested loops, access to the outermost counter is provided by k.

The mechanics of do ... loop are interesting. do places the top two stack parameters onto the return stack and sets up a target address to which loop branches back. This target address is that of the word immediately following do. When loop executes, it increments a counter and compares this with the loop limit on the return stack. If they are equal, the loop terminates; otherwise, execution branches back to the target address set up by do.

A loop can be prematurely terminated by using the leave word. For example, this loop will execute 10 times, provided a key is not typed:

```
10 0 do
   key? if leave endif
loop
```

key? checks whether a character has been input from the console and places a boolean onto the stack to indicate this. if removes the boolean and conditionally executes the leave word.

Conditional loops are created using the Forth words begin and until. until checks for a boolean on top of the stack. If one is found, the loop terminates; otherwise, execution branches back to the word following begin. The following example word reads characters from the console until an "A" is typed:

```
: wait_for_A
    begin
        key
        65 =
    until
;
```

The equal operator (=) takes the top two values from the stack (in this case, the ASCII code obtained using key and the value 65) and compares them. If they are equal, it places a true (-1) on the stack; otherwise a false (0) is placed on the stack. The Forth operator = is equivalent to = = in C.

An alternative conditional loop construct is begin *condition* while *code* repeat. Everything between begin and repeat is executed with each iteration, but only provided that the condition is met. The code between begin and while is used to evaluate the condition, thus determining whether execution will continue or whether the loop will terminate. For example, the following word definition will run only while the user types an "A" on the console:

```
: while_A
    begin
        key 65 =
    while
        ." That was an A"
        cr
    repeat
;
```

Infinite loops may be implemented using begin ... again. Here is a word that, once run, will never terminate:

```
: semper
    begin
        ." Once more through the loop, dear friends."
        cr
    again
;
```

Such loops are particularly useful in embedded systems, where the code must repeat forever.

The Forth-83 standard doesn't implement begin ... again. Instead, use begin 1 while ... repeat or begin ... 0 until as a replacement.

Forth-79, ANSI-Forth, and gnu Forth *do* implement begin ... again, so if you're using one of those Forths, you have nothing to worry about.

Data Structures

The fact that Forth uses a stack for parameter passing between words makes it very powerful. It is because of the stack that the language is re-entrant and supports recursion. However, the dynamic nature of the stack makes it unsuitable for global data. Fortunately, Forth is not limited to using the stack, as the language provides for both named constants and variables.

A constant is declared by placing the value for the constant onto the stack, then the word constant followed by the constant name. For example, the following code declares a constant called kilobyte (representing the number of bytes in a K) to have a value of 1024:

```
1024 constant kilobyte
```

Using the constant in your code is trivial. Simply use the constant name to place the value onto the stack:

```
kilobyte
```

For example, here is a word definition that takes a value from the stack for a number of kilobytes, converts this into bytes, and prints out the result:

```
: kilobytes  ( N --  , convert N to bytes )
    kilobyte  *  .
    ." bytes"  cr
;
```

So, typing:

```
32 kilobytes
```

gives a result on the console of:

```
32768 bytes
```

There is an alternative way to declare a constant. Simply define a word that places that value onto the stack:

```
: myconstant
    908612
;
```

This is not as efficient as using the constant word, but it works just the same.

Variables are declared in a similar way to constants, but the way they are used is quite different. Rather than placing a value onto the stack, the variable name will place a pointer to the variable onto the stack. A variable is declared by placing an initial value for the variable onto the stack, then the word `variable` followed by the variable name:

```
0 variable my_var
```

The pointer is used in conjunction with the words @ (pronounced *fetch*) and ! (pronounced *store*). Let's say we want to make `my_var` equal to 32. We do it by placing the value (32) onto the stack, using the variable name to place the pointer onto the stack, and then using store to assign the value to the variable:

```
32 my_var !
```

To recall the variable's value, we use the variable name to place the pointer onto the stack and then use fetch to retrieve the value and place it on the stack:

```
my_var @
```

For example, let's say we want to add 5 to the current value of `my_var`:

```
my_var @    ( get the current value )
5 +         ( add 5 )
my_var !     ( put the result back into my_var )
```

This might seem a bit strange, but it is very close to what goes on behind the scenes when you say `my_var = my_var + 5;` in C. In C, the mechanics of the process are hidden from you. In Forth, the nuts and bolts are there for all to see (and to play with).

Interacting with Hardware and Memory

Forth is great for debugging embedded hardware. You can use Forth to examine the contents of memory or peripheral registers:

```
2000 @
```

This places the content of address 2000 onto the stack. You can also use Forth to set memory or peripheral registers:

```
41 2000 !
```

This sets the content of address 2000 to 41. Remember that you can do this from within a word or interactively from the command prompt. This means that from the prompt, you can interactively probe and change peripheral registers—a very powerful debugging tool.

 If you're using a version of Forth that is running on a desktop computer (such as a Mac or PC), don't try using store (!) or any other word that directly modifies memory, as it may have unforeseen (and possibly disastrous) results.

Fetch (@) and store (!) work with 16-bit-wide locations. To access 8-bit-wide locations, use the words c@ ("c-fetch") and c! ("c-store"), respectively. To access 32-bit-wide locations, use 2@ and 2!.

 On some versions of Forth, such as gnu's gforth running on a PowerPC processor, @ and ! operate on 32-bit values rather than 16-bit values. Similarly, on the same platform, 2@ and 2! are 64-bit operations.

As an example, let's create a Forth program called status that will read the content of an 8-bit register located at address 2100 and place the result onto the stack.

```
: status 2100 c@ ;
```

This can be manually run from the prompt to examine the register during debugging:

```
status .
```

Perhaps you would like to continually monitor the status register while you tweak some hardware. Here is a Forth program that will do just that, until you press a key on the console:

```
: showstatus
   begin
      status .
      cr
      key?
   until
;
```

Once debugging is complete, the word status can be used as part of the main application:

```
: main
   begin
      status 5 =
   until
   41 TxRegister c!
;
```

The word dump is useful for examining a region of memory. dump takes two operands from the stack in the form *address size* dump. For example, to output 256 values starting at the current scratchpad location:

```
pad 256 dump
   BB1D4: 0C 30 C3 0C  C3 0C 30 C3 - 0C 30 C3 0C  33 33 33 30  .0....0..0..3330
   BB1E4: C3 0C 30 C3  0C 30 C3 0C - 30 C3 0C 30  C3 0C 30 30  ..0..0..0..0..00
   BB1F4: C0 C0 C0 C3  0C 2C 2F 89 - 09 24 24 90  92 49 09 02  .....,./..$$..I..
   BB204: 42 00 00 00  20 B0 B0 B0 - 90 90 B0 00  3C 00 00 00  B... .......<...
   BB214: 00 00 00 00  00 00 00 00 - 00 00 00 00  00 00 00 00  ................
   BB224: 00 00 00 00  00 00 00 00 - 00 00 22 42  42 42 49 32  ........."BBBI2
   BB234: 4C 92 4C 24  09 02 42 42 - 40 92 49 09  09 24 24 90  L.L$..BB@.I..$$.
   BB244: 24 09 02 42  4B C0 BF CB - C9 30 AD C3  0B 30 2F F0  $..BK....0...0/.
```

```
BB254:  OB B8 BF 82  FE 2B 8B E2 - FC BF 2F E2  FF FE 2F FC   .....+..../.../.
BB264:  2F 8B FF BF  2F FE FC 2B - 7F BB DD FF  7F F8 2F 7D   /.../..+....../}
BB274:  F8 AF FF BF  E2 F0 B7 FC - AC 2A D8 AB  FF F7 F0 AD   .........*......
BB284:  E2 FE DF 0A  F0 B7 DE FB - C2 DF E0 AF  2F FE 2F CB   ............././.
BB294:  E2 AE 2A E0  90 90 BF 0B - F0 BE 2F 8B  2C B2 CB F8   ..*......../.,...
BB2A4:  BE 24 92 49  24 92 4B FF - 2F 8B F0 80  00 02 DB F7   .$.I$.K./.......
BB2B4:  FE 08 00 00  2D BF 7F E2 - FF 2B FF BF  2F FE 2F FE   ....-....+../././.
BB2C4:  2F FF F8 BF  DF FF 8B DE - 2B EF B7 CB  FE 2F FF FF   /.......+..../..
```

For each line, dump prints out an address followed by 16 bytes of data and the ASCII interpretation of those bytes. Any hex byte that doesn't have an ASCII representation appears as a dot.

Memory can be cleared (each location made equal to 0) using the erase word. For example, to write 32 zeros starting from address 2100:

```
2100 32 erase
```

Similar to erase, fill can be used to fill a region of memory with a particular value. In this example, we store the value 255 to 32 locations starting from 2100:

```
2100 32 255 fill
```

Forth Programming Guidelines

As with any other programming language, it's possible to write good Forth, and just as easy to write bad Forth. Here are some Forth tips:

- Limit your stack usage to three or four words. Any more than this, and you will find it very hard to keep mental track of where you're up to.

- Use several short word definitions rather than one long word definition. Don't ever create a Forth word that is hundreds of lines of code long. The beauty of Forth is its ability to build upon itself, allowing you to test as you go. To this end, keep your Forth words to three or four lines of code where possible. That might sound strange if you're used to other languages, but once you get into the swing of Forth, you'll understand that this is a logical approach to coding.

- Keep it simple and focus on what you're trying to achieve. A simple Forth word that solves a specific, simple problem is better than a complicated do-all word that is difficult to write and hard to debug.

- Check for data that is out of range or erroneous and generate useful error messages or diagnostics.

There's a lot more to this powerful language than I've shown here. For more information on Forth, visit the Forth Interest Group (FIG) at *http://www.forth.org* or go to Forth, Inc. at *http://www.forth.com*. Charles Moore, the creator of Forth, has a web site at *http://www.colorforth.com*. If you'd like to play with Forth, there are dozens of free Forths available for download over the Internet. For gnu's Forth, go to *http://www.gnu.org/software/gforth*. Alternatively, just use your favorite search engine to search for a Forth for your platform.

CHAPTER 4

Electronics 101

...in reality, nothing but atoms and void
—Democritus

In writing this book, my hope is to bring to you an understanding of the design process involved in producing an embedded computer system. To this end, I have kept the electronics, the chips, and the systems I have used as simple as possible. I want you to understand the big picture without getting lost in detail. But, however simple I keep the computer designs, you won't get very far without at least a very rudimentary understanding of electronics. So what I want to do in this chapter is give some basic background theory to guide you on your way. Electronics is a truly vast and complicated multidisciplinary field, and it is not possible to cover even a thousandth of it here. I won't even attempt to. What I will do is give you an understanding of the basic principles necessary for embedded computer engineering in a simplified, and hopefully easy to understand, way. The rest of the vast mountain, I will leave unvisited. If you want to learn more, pick up a copy of Paul Horowitz and Winfield Hill's *The Art of Electronics* (Cambridge University Press). It's a great introductory text.

Voltage and Current

It's all about electrons. It is from their very name that we derive the term *electronics*. Electrons are subatomic particles with a negative charge. They are bound to positively charged atomic nuclei through Coulombic attraction. The classical physics view was to think of electrons "orbiting" the nucleus, analogous to planets orbiting in a solar system. While not at all correct,[*] it makes it easier to visualize what goes on. The strength by which electrons are bound to the nucleus varies from atomic element to atomic element, and from molecule to molecule. Substances are either

---

[*] The truth, as always, is far stranger. The quantum view is both beautiful and bizarre. For a simple and elegant introduction, read Richard Feynman's brilliant *QED* (Quantum Electro Dynamics) (Princeton University Press).

conductors, *insulators*, or *semiconductors*. In a conductor, such as a metal, the energy required to shift an electron from one nucleus to another is negligible, and the electrons may easily exchange with nearby atomic nuclei. In effect, the metal is a collection of nuclei surround by a "sea" of semi-free electrons. In an insulator, the opposite is true. The energy required to shift an electron from a nucleus is excessive, and so electrons tend to stay put. In a semiconductor, the substance may act either as a conductor or as an insulator, depending on external influences. By controlling the external influences, you change the conductivity of the substance and therefore change the way electrons move within that substance. In effect, a semiconductor is a switch that may be controlled by other semiconductors. It is this basic principle that is the basis of all modern electronics. It is the cornerstone upon which everything digital is founded.

The flow of electrons through a conductor or a semiconductor is known as *current*. Current is measured in *Amperes*, more commonly called just plain *Amps* (with the unit symbol "A," equation symbol "I"). For an electron to move through a conductor,[*] there must be a "vacancy" at the next nucleus into which it can shift. (If the next nucleus has a full complement of electrons, the Coulombic repulsion of those electrons will prevent any others from slotting in.) Semiconductor physicists term these vacancies *holes*. An electron shifting into a neighboring hole leaves a new hole behind it. This new hole is then filled by another electron further down the line, which, in turn, creates another new hole. So current flow is, in effect, a movement of electrons in one direction and a "movement of holes" in another. The electrons are negatively charged, and the holes may be thought of as positive charges. (A missing electron at a nucleus means that the positive charge of the nucleus isn't fully canceled, and so a net positive charge exists at that location.) So while electrons move from negative to positive, the holes move from positive to negative, and it is the movement of holes (rather than electrons) that we refer to when we talk about current. Current flow, which we work with in electronics, is deemed to be from *positive* to *negative*. For continued current flow, there must be a continuous circular flow of electrons in one direction and holes in the other direction. It is from this circular flow that we derive the term *circuit*.

For current flow to occur between two points, there must exist an imbalance between electrons at one end and holes at the other. The size of this imbalance is known as the *potential difference*, or *voltage difference,* between two points. (It is also sometimes termed "the *voltage drop* across an electronic component.") The unit of voltage difference is the *Volt* (unit symbol "V"). The greater the voltage difference, the greater the opportunity for current flow. It is very important to note that voltage refers to the *difference* between two points. A voltage cannot exist in isolation. Although you will sometimes see a statement like "the voltage at this point is...," it is

---

[*] I'm treating a conducting semiconductor as though it were an ordinary conductor.

taken as given that it is relative to some common reference point, usually *ground* (the zero-volt reference point).

 A common beginner's mistake in testing electronic circuits is to wire up only one lead of a piece of test equipment. Without both leads, there is no common reference point, and, therefore, any measurement taken is meaningless.

Analog Signals

An analog signal can have an amplitude of any voltage within a range, unlike a digital signal, which can be in one of two defined voltage states (either *high* or *low*). Figure 4-1 shows a typical analog signal (in this case, a sine wave).

Figure 4-1. An analog waveform

The voltage of a signal may vary over time, or it may be constant. If the voltage varies, it may repeat at regular intervals, in which case the signal is said to be *periodic*. The *period* is the interval of time it takes the signal pattern to repeat (for example, from one wave crest to another). The *frequency* of the signal is the number of times per second that the pattern repeats.

Frequency is measured in Hertz (Hz) and relates to the period in the following way:

```
Frequency = 1 / Period
```

Thus, a signal with a period of 1 ms has a frequency of 1 kHz.

A *unipolar signal* (Figure 4-2) has component voltages that are either all positive or all negative. A *bipolar signal* (Figure 4-3) has both positive and negative voltages.

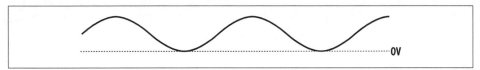

Figure 4-2. Unipolar signal

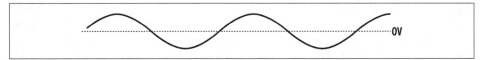

Figure 4-3. Bipolar signal

A typical analog signal will have both an *AC component* and a *DC component* (Figure 4-4). The DC component is the fixed voltage of the signal. The AC component is a varying voltage imposed on the DC component. The AC component is sometimes referred to as the *peak-to-peak* amplitude of a signal and is denoted with the suffix "pp." For example, an AC component of 5 V would be written as 5 Vpp.

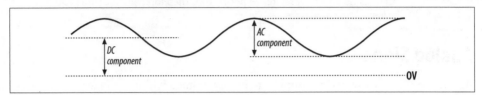

Figure 4-4. DC and AC components of an analog signal

Power

A voltage difference is generated by a difference in potential energy between two points. Therefore, to generate a voltage, you use a device that can create such an energy difference. Such devices may be mechanical (generators), converting motion into a potential difference by electromagnetics; photovoltaic (solar cells); or chemical (batteries). Conversely, a voltage difference (and therefore current flow) can be used to produce mechanical movement (motors), light emission (light bulbs, LEDs), and heat (toasters, Pentium 4 processors).

Power is the amount of work per time (Joules per second) and is measured in *Watts* (unit symbol "W"). The equation for calculating power is simply:

```
P = V * I
```

No electronic device is 100% efficient (far from it!), and so it will consume power as it performs its task. The power consumed by a device may be calculated using the above equation, from the voltage difference across the device and the current flowing through the device. A typical embedded computer may consume a few hundred mW (milliWatts) of power, but it can vary quite considerably. A large and powerful embedded machine may use several tens (or even hundreds) of Watts, while a tiny embedded controller may use just microWatts.

Reading Schematics

You won't get very far in electronics unless you know how to draw and read schematics. They crop up everywhere, and understanding them is a must. The schematics are like an architect's blueprint. They show what components will be used in a circuit and how they are connected together. The schematics may also include other information such as construction directives. A schematic may have a list of revisions indicating what changes have been made to the original design. These are commonly called *Engineering Change Orders* (*ECOs*). As a design grows and changes over time, it's a good idea to keep track of what changes were made and, more importantly, *why* they were made. Just as commenting source code is important, so is keeping track of the ECOs.

You will come across two types of schematics. There are the schematics you see in datasheets, books (like this one), and other technical documents. These schematics will just show the circuit (or partial circuit) and maybe a note or two, and that's all. The other sort of schematic is the actual drawing(s) used to generate a *Printed Circuit Board* (*PCB*). These schematics represent a full system design and will often have a title block located in the lower right of the sheet, indicating what the sheet represents, who drew it, and when. Figure 4-5 shows a sample title block.

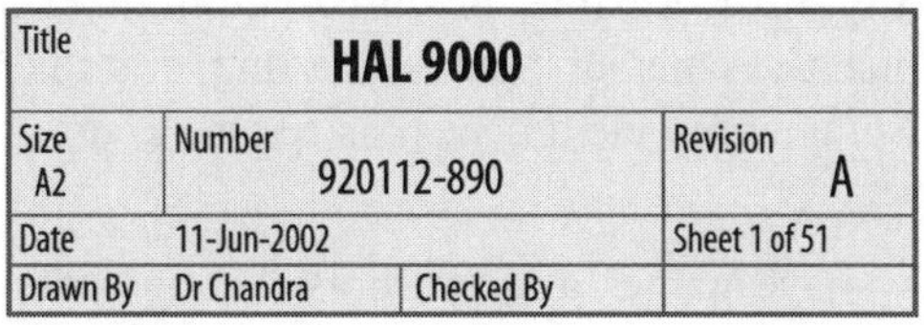

Title	**HAL 9000**		
Size A2	Number 920112-890		Revision A
Date	11-Jun-2002		Sheet 1 of 51
Drawn By	Dr Chandra	Checked By	

Figure 4-5. Title block

Essentially, there are two types of objects on a schematic: component symbols and nets. *Nets* are the wires that show what is connected to what, and *component symbols* represent physical devices. A component symbol will have a component name and a component type. For example, a memory chip may have the name U3 and have a component type AT45DB161. The component name is simply a reference label, much like a variable name in source code. It's important to keep component labels unique. Having two devices labeled U3 on a schematic may cause a great deal of confusion for the design automation software. The component type is the actual part number used by the component manufacturer.

It is common practice with component names to use common prefixes for components of the same type. For example, resistors have the prefix R. You will see resistors on a schematic labeled R1, R2, R3, etc. Similarly, capacitors carry the prefix C, inductors L, diodes D, transistors Q, crystals X, and connectors and jumpers J. Semiconductors often carry the prefix U, but not always. Logic gates and other small, nondescript semiconductors may have the prefix U, but larger semiconductors may have a more informative name. For example, a processor may be labeled PROC, while four memory chips may carry the names RAM0, RAM1, RAM2, and RAM3. Giving larger devices more meaningful names often makes schematics easier to understand. However, that being said, a lot of people still give every semiconductor the U prefix.

Figure 4-6 shows an example component with a net.

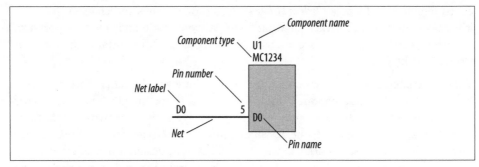

Figure 4-6. Signal net and component

As well as the name and part number, the component will also have an array of pins. The pins may have a number, a name, or both. The number indicates the physical pin on the chip to which the schematic pin is referring, and the name gives an indication of its function. Some components, such as resistors, do not have pin names or numbers shown.

Component pins may have names and symbols that indicate their characteristics. Figure 4-7 shows an example component with a variety of pin types.

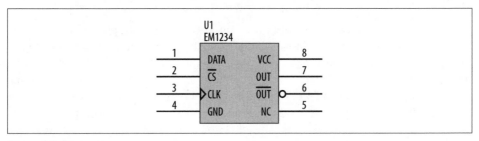

Figure 4-7. Pin types

Pin 1 is a generic pin. Pin 2 has a bar over the pin name that indicates that it is *active low*. This means that a logic 0 on this pin will activate its function, while a logic 1 will deactivate it. Pin 2's name is $\overline{\text{CS}}$, which typically means *chip select*. In other words, this pin is used to activate the chip. Most peripherals and memory chips have a chip-select input. Chip selects are important since there are many memory and peripheral chips within a computer system. It is through the chip select that the processor will enable the chip so that it can write data to it or read data from it. Some devices have an input called $\overline{\text{CE}}$, which means *chip enable*. It's exactly the same as a chip select. They are just two different names for the same function.

The little triangle on pin 3 indicates that it is an edge-triggered input. This simply means that the input responds to a *change* in signal.

Pins 4 and 8 are ground (**GND**) and power (**VCC**), respectively. "VCC" and "VDD" are used to label voltage sources for powering the circuits. The terminology originates from transistors and solid-state electronics, where "collectors" (VCC) and "drains" (VDD) are common parlance. You don't need to worry about what the names mean, just know that when you see "VCC" or "VDD," we're talking about supply voltages.

Pin 7 is an output that is active high, and pin 6 is an output that is active low. Note the circle on pin 6. This indicates that it is an inverted output. The fact that it has the same name as pin 7 indicates that pin 6 is the inversion of the output of pin 7. Finally, pin 5 is labeled "NC." This is commonly used to represent "No Connect," which means that this pin has no function. No net should be connected to it. (Very rarely, you'll also see a pin name "Do Not Wire." It means the same thing.) However, just because you see a pin name "NC" doesn't mean that you should *assume* that it is a no-connect. It may just be that the chip manufacturer labeled the pin NC for some other reason. As always, check the datasheet carefully for each device.

A net may be drawn between two components or may simply have a *net label* giving the net a name and indicating that it is connected to every other net with the same name. With complicated schematics, it may not be practical to show every wire that must be connected. There would simply be wires going everywhere, and the resulting schematic would be impossible to understand. Therefore, it is common practice to simply use the net labels to locally name a net, and this alone is enough to indicate what is connected to what (Figure 4-8).

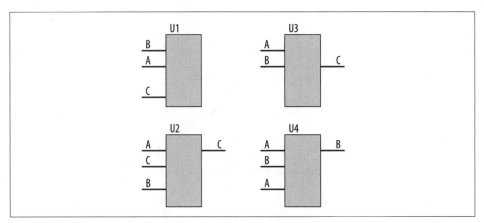

Figure 4-8. Net labels show which pins are connected without the need for drawing every wire

Signals that are functionally related, such as buses, are drawn using a bus net (Figure 4-9).

It is common practice to use more than one schematic sheet for a design. Just as a program is broken up into functions, with commonly used code placed in libraries, designs are also broken into functional units, allowing subsystem reuse in multiple designs. For example, the same power-supply circuit may be used in several different embedded computer designs. By placing the power-supply circuit on its own sheet,

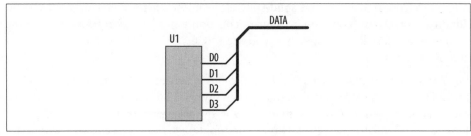

Figure 4-9. Related signals are routed using a bus

that same subsystem design may be reused in many designs. *Ports* are used to indicate when a schematic's nets are connected to another schematic sheet. Figure 4-10 shows a component with connections to off-sheet objects. In this case, the "D0:D3" port is a bidirectional bus, the "A0:A3" port is an output bus from this sheet (and therefore an input to another sheet), and the "MODE" port is an input net to this sheet.

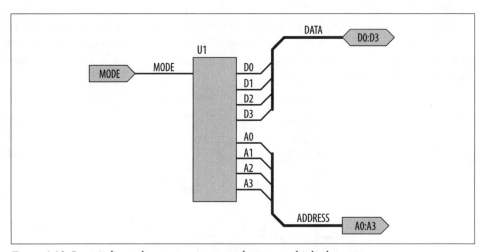

Figure 4-10. Ports indicate that nets are connected across multiple sheets

Figure 4-11 shows nets crossing each other. The vertical net on the left *is not* connected to the horizontal net. It simply crosses over on its way to another part of the circuit. The vertical net on the right *is* connected to the horizontal net, and this is indicated by a *junction* dot.

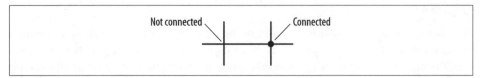

Figure 4-11. Nets crossing

In some hobbyist electronics magazines and old textbooks, you'll sometimes see nets with "little bridges" as they cross other nets (Figure 4-12). This is definitely *not* the way to draw it—very unprofessional, very uncool.

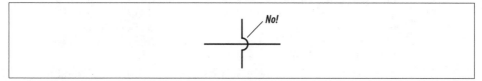

Figure 4-12. How not to draw one net crossing the other

Figure 4-13 shows common *power ports*. These indicate connections to voltage sources (power supplies) and grounds. The ground symbols all mean a potential of zero volts. The different symbols are used to differentiate between different ground networks. In microprocessor schematics, you'll commonly see the two leftmost ground symbols (usually only one or the other) and rarely see the other two.

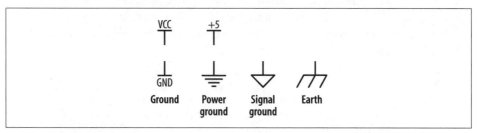

Figure 4-13. Power ports

By the way, always place your power ports vertically, *never* horizontally. Horizontal power ports are like source code that isn't indented—frowned upon as the work of the Unenlightened. Also, voltage ports (like VCC) should point up, while ground ports should point down. A ground port should never be pointing skyward, nor should a voltage port be pointing down. For a professional engineer, they're a vexation to the spirit.

Resistors

Even a conductor (such as a metal wire) is not 100% efficient at conducting current flow. As current flows through the wire, energy will be lost as heat (and sometimes light). For very small currents, this energy loss is negligible, but for large currents, the loss can cause the conductor to become quite hot (an effect utilized in toasters) or glow brightly (light bulbs). This loss of energy results in a voltage difference across the wire (or component). The component is said to resist the current flow. This *resistance* (also known as *impedance*, although impedance is somewhat more complex than simple resistance) is measured in *Ohms* (unit symbol "Ω," equation symbol

"R"). In schematics, it is common to leave off the Ω symbol, so 100 kΩ is usually written as just 100 k.

On a schematic, a 4.7 kΩ value is often not written as 4.7 k, but rather as 4k7. The reason is that it is too easy for a decimal point to be missed, or lost when the document is photocopied. The solution is to place the multiplier ("k") in the position of the decimal point. Resistors such as 24.9 Ω are written as 24R9.

This convention is used by design engineers in most of the world. However, in North America it is only sometimes followed.

The relationship between voltage, current, and resistance is known as *Ohm's Law*, and is given by:

```
V = I * R
```

For a fixed resistance, a varying voltage will produce a varying current, while a constant voltage will produce a constant current. Hence, a varying voltage source is known as an *Alternating Current* source (or *AC*), while a constant voltage source is known as a *Direct Current* source (*DC*). An AC voltage is normally specified as *VAC*, while a DC voltage is either *VDC* or more often just *V*.

The stuff that comes out of your wall socket is AC, and is nominally 110–120 VAC (at 60 Hz) if you live in North America; 100 VAC if you're in Japan (50 Hz in the eastern half [Tokyo] and 60 Hz in the western half [Osaka, Kyoto, and Nagoya]); and 220–240 VAC (at 50 Hz) if you're in Australia, New Zealand, the UK, or Europe. All digital electronics, and that includes computers, use DC internally and operate at typical voltages of either 5 V or 3.3 V. (Some digital electronics will operate at voltages as low as 1.8 V or lower.) The *power supply* of the computer (or TV or stereo or...) converts the high-voltage AC supply into the lower DC required by the electronics. The AC adaptor or plug pack (charger) for your cell phone is also an example of a power supply.

For a given voltage difference, the smaller the resistance, the larger the current flow. Conversely, the bigger the resistance, the smaller the current flow. In this way, resistance can be used to limit the current flow through a particular part of a circuit. Special components, known as *resistors*, are produced for precisely this purpose. Resistors are part of a family of devices known as *passive components*.

Figure 4-14 shows "through-hole" resistors. From top to bottom, they are 0.5 W, 0.25 W, and 0.125 W, respectively.

Figure 4-15 shows surface-mount resistors. Surface-mount technology is now far more common than the older "through-hole" style of component. The components shown in Figure 4-15 are a "1206" footprint (left) and a "0603" footprint (right).

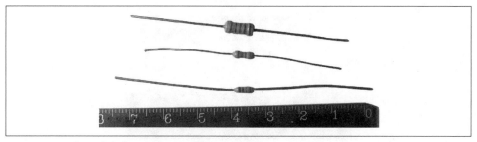

Figure 4-14. Through-hole resistors (scale in centimeters)

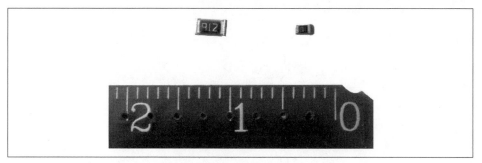

Figure 4-15. Surface-mount resistors (scale in centimeters)

There are smaller footprints than these available, but if you're hand-soldering, you are more likely to suffer a nervous breakdown before you successfully solder the component to the circuit board!

The schematic component symbols for a resistor are shown in Figure 4-16. Both symbols mean the same thing. The more commonly seen symbol is on the left.

Figure 4-16. Resistor symbols

A resistor may be used to *pull up* (or *pull down*) a signal line to a given voltage level. If you have many pull-up resistors in your circuit, all of the same value, it may be convenient to use a resistor network, or "resnet," shown in Figure 4-17. Resnets combine several resistors (typically eight, but available in other sizes as well) in a single package. All the resistors are tied to one pin, which is connected to the power supply such that all resistors act as pull-ups.

Figure 4-18 shows a pull-up resistor and a push button. When the button is open (not pressed), there is no current flow through the resistor, and, therefore, the voltage at V_{OUT} is (in this case) +5 V. (Since there is no current flow through the resistor, there is no voltage drop across it.) When the button is pushed, V_{OUT} is connected to ground, and, consequently, current will flow through the resistor. This simple circuit can be used to switch an input between two logic level thresholds.

Figure 4-17. Resnet

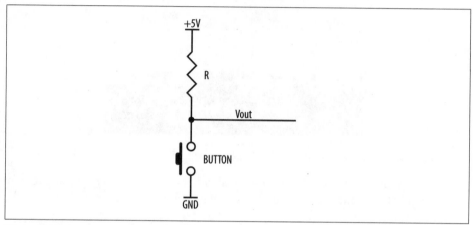

Figure 4-18. A pull-up resistor and a push button

Resistors may be daisy-chained together to increase resistance. This is known as a *series* connection (Figure 4-19).

Figure 4-19. Resistors in series

The combined total resistance is given by the relation:

$$R_{TOTAL} = R1 + R2$$

The current flow through *any* of the components in series connection will be the same for each component. In other words, the current flowing through the first resistor will be the same as that flowing through the second resistor. This derives from *Kirchhoff's Current Law*.

Kirchhoff's Current Law:

The current flowing through a given circuit point is equal to the sum of the currents flowing into that circuit point, and is also equal to the sum of currents flowing out of that circuit point.

In other words, what flows in must flow out.

Series resistors may be used to create a *voltage divider* (Figure 4-20) to provide an intermediate voltage.

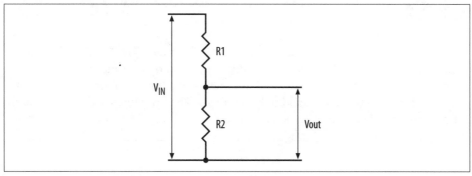

Figure 4-20. Voltage divider

The output voltage is given by:

$$V_{OUT} = V_{IN} * R2 / (R1 + R2)$$

For example, if the input voltage is 5 V, and the two resistors are both 1 kΩ, then the output voltage is:

```
VOUT = 5V * 1k / (1k + 1k)
     = 5V * 1k / 2k
     = 5V * 0.5
     = 2.5V
```

As you would expect, a voltage divider using equal resistors halves the input voltage.

Resistors combined in *parallel* (Figure 4-21) will decrease the total resistance.

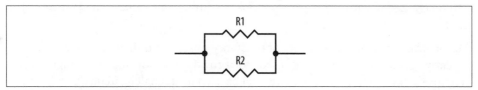

Figure 4-21. Resistors in parallel

The combined total resistance is given by the relation:

$$R_{TOTAL} = 1 / (1/R1 + 1/R2)$$

The voltage drop across R1 must be the same as the voltage drop across R2. However, unless R1 is equal to R2 (and there is no requirement for them to be so), the current flow through each will be different. This is derived from *Kirchhoff's Voltage Law*.

Kirchhoff's Voltage Law:

The sum of the voltage differences around a closed circuit is zero.

A *potentiometer* (also known simply as a "pot," "trimmer," or "trim pot") is just a variable resistor. The schematic symbol for a pot is shown in Figure 4-22. Pots are normally mechanical components and are manually adjusted. Your stereo probably uses pots for its volume, bass, and treble controls. The brightness and contrast knobs for monitors and LCDs are also potentiometers.

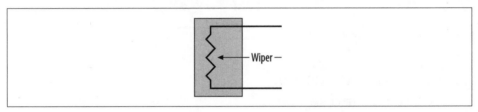

Figure 4-22. A potentiometer

A standard potentiometer consists of two terminals (the upper and lower pins in the diagram) that connect to either end of a resistor. A third terminal, known as the *wiper*, moves up or down the resistor, effectively tapping into the voltage present at a given point. Move the wiper one way, and the amount of resistance the wiper sees is increased. Move it the other way, and the resistance decreases.

There are many different types of pots available. Figure 4-23 shows several pots, including a slider pot and two types of rotary pot. Usually, the pot is fitted inside the equipment casing with the wiper shaft poking through an appropriate hole or slot. A knob is then screwed to the shaft.

Mechanical pots come in a variety of resistance ranges, and their accuracy is not particularly good. They may be used to provide an adjustable voltage output (Figure 4-24) or simply to vary the resistance used in an analog circuit.

As a simple example, you could use a pot to vary the intensity of a LED by varying the current flow through it. A circuit to do this is shown in Figure 4-25. Here, the fixed resistance between the LED's anode and the pot's wiper is 330 Ω. By adjusting the wiper, we add to this resistance, thus decreasing the current flow through the LED and reducing its brightness.

Figure 4-23. Some of the different potentiometers that are available

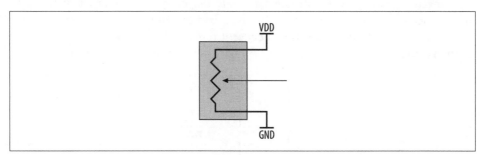

Figure 4-24. Using a potentiometer to provide a variable voltage between VDD and ground

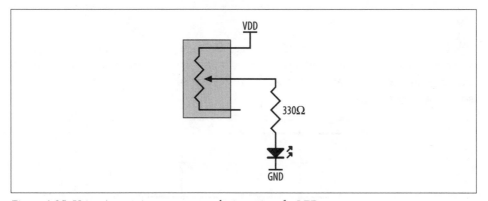

Figure 4-25. Using a potentiometer to vary the intensity of a LED

Note how one terminal of the pot is unconnected. This is fine, since in this case we are not using the pot to provide an intermediate voltage between two values. Rather, we are simply using the pot as a variable resistor, increasing the impedance between the wiper and **VDD**.

Capacitors

While a resistor is a component that resists the flow of charge through it, a capacitor stores charge. Capacitance is measured in Farads (or more formally, "Faradays") with an equation symbol "C" and a unit symbol "F." Typical capacitors you will use range in value from uF (micro-Farads) down to pF (pico-Farads).

The relationship between current, capacitance, and voltage is given by:

```
I = C * dV/dt
```

where dV/dt is the rate of voltage change over time.

The schematic symbols for capacitors are shown in Figure 4-26. The component on the far left is *bipolar*, while the other two are *unipolar*. A unipolar capacitor has a positive lead and a negative lead, and it must be inserted into a circuit with the correct orientation. Failing to do so will cause it to explode. (Unipolar capacitors have markings to indicate their orientation.) A bipolar capacitor has no polarity.

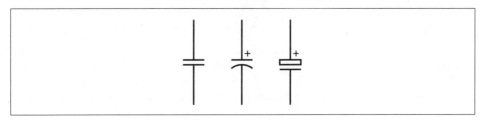

Figure 4-26. Capacitor symbols

Applying a voltage across a capacitor causes the capacitor to become charged. If the voltage source is removed, and a path for current flow exists elsewhere in the circuit, the capacitor will discharge and thereby provide a (temporary) voltage and current source (Figure 4-27).

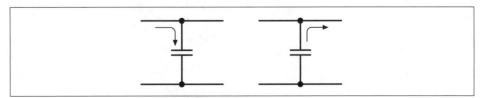

Figure 4-27. Capacitor charging and discharging

This is an extremely useful characteristic. A given voltage source may have a *DC component* (a fixed voltage) and an *AC component* (a ripple voltage superimposed). (Here, "component" does not mean a physical device, but rather a fractional part of a voltage.) The capacitor becomes charged by the DC component of the voltage source to a given level and is then alternately charged and discharged with the AC component. In effect, the capacitor averages out the peaks and troughs of the AC component and, as a result, removes the AC ripple from the voltage source. This is known as the capacitor *decoupling* the AC and DC components of the voltage source. This is a common technique used to remove electrical noise from power supplies, for example.

The flip side of this is that a capacitor can also be used to block the DC component of a voltage, allowing only the AC component to pass through (Figure 4-28).

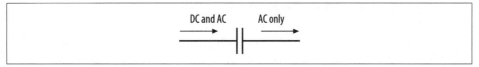

Figure 4-28. Blocking capacitor

Capacitors may also be used in series or parallel (Figure 4-29).

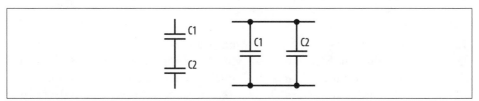

Figure 4-29. Capacitors in series and in parallel

The relationship is the opposite of what it is for resistors. In the series case, the total capacitance is calculated by:

$$C_{TOTAL} = C1 * C2 / (C1 + C2)$$

In the parallel case, the total capacitance is given by:

$$C_{TOTAL} = C1 + C2$$

Types of Capacitors

There are over a dozen different types of capacitor, each based on a different technology. The ones you are most likely to come across are *ceramic*, *electrolytic*, and *tantalum*.

Ceramic capacitors are small in size and small in value. They range from a few picofarads (pF) up to around 1 uF. They are commonly used as decoupling capacitors for power-supply pins of integrated circuits and as bypass capacitors in crystal circuits (among other uses).

Electrolytics look like small cylinders and are used primarily for decoupling power supplies. They range in value from 100 nF to several F (and we're talking *big* capacitors here). Their accuracy is terrible. Their actual value can vary quite a bit from what it is supposed to be. Therefore, they are not used where critical tolerances are required. Use them only where "ballpark" values are sufficient.

The other problem with electrolytics is that they age, and the older they get, the worse they become. Expect a circuit using electrolytics to eventually fail. Having said that, most consumer electronics still use them heavily, and for one reason—they are very cheap. By the time they've failed, the product will be well out of the warranty period. However, electrolytics will outlast the useful lifetime of your average computer product. You'll have upgraded your PC to a newer model long before its electrolytics have passed on.

 The most common cause of failure in old radios and hi-fi gear is that the electrolytics have failed. You can often pick up a very cheap bargain at a garage sale. Ten minutes with the soldering iron and you've replaced the electrolytics, and what "doesn't work anymore" suddenly comes back to life as good as new. Well, most of the time anyway.

Tantalum capacitors are somewhat larger than ceramics but not as physically large as electrolytics. In through-hole devices, they have the appearance of small, shiny plastic bulbs. Surface-mount tantalums look much like all other surface-mount capacitors: small ubiquitous rectangles. They range in value from around 100 nF up to several hundred uF. They are commonly used to decouple power supplies. They are more accurate than electrolytics, meaning their actual value is closer to their stated value. I always use tantalums in preference to electrolytics in my designs where possible. I like my machines to *last*.

Some common capacitors are shown in Figure 4-30.

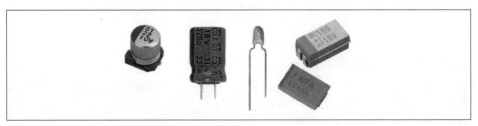

Figure 4-30. Capacitors (not to scale)

RC Circuits

Combining resistors and capacitors can yield some interesting and useful effects. A resistor-capacitor combination is known as an *RC circuit*, and it can take one of three forms. The first form is where the resistor and capacitor are in parallel (Figure 4-31).

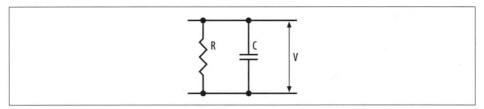

Figure 4-31. Resistor and capacitor in parallel

Now, what does this do? A voltage (V) applied across the pair will charge the capacitor (as well as some current flowing down through the resistor). When the applied voltage is removed, the capacitor will discharge through the resistor. The resistor will limit the rate of discharge, since it limits current flow. From Ohm's Law, we have:

    I = - V / R

(The negative voltage is because we're discharging the capacitor.) Now, the current flow out of a capacitor is given by:

    I = C * dV/dt

So, we have:

    dV/dt = - V / RC

Integrating this with respect to time, with zero initial conditions, gives us:

    $V = e^{-t/RC}$

This gives us the discharge waveform shown in Figure 4-32, which represents the voltage across the capacitor.

A parallel RC circuit will provide an exponential decay in the output voltage. The value for t when the output voltage is at 37% of the maximum is known as the *time constant* for the circuit and is simply the product of R and C:

    t = R * C

For example, a parallel RC circuit where the resistor is 100 kΩ and the capacitor is 10 uF gives a time constant of 1 second.

The second form of RC circuit is the series RC circuit, shown in Figure 4-33.

When a voltage is applied at the input to the RC circuit (on the left), current will flow through the resistor and the capacitor will begin to charge. However, the resistor limits current flow and therefore will limit the rate at which the capacitor charges.

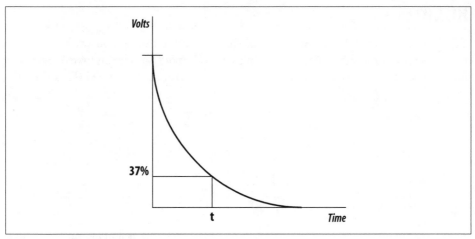

Figure 4-32. Discharge of a parallel RC circuit

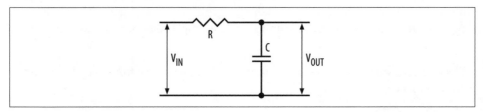

Figure 4-33. Series RC circuit

Now, the current flowing into the capacitor is again given by the relation:

    I = C * dV/dt

This current is the same as that which is flowing through the resistor, and by Ohm's Law, we have that this current is given by:

    I = (V_{IN} - V_{OUT}) / R

where V_{IN} - V_{OUT} is the voltage drop across the resistor. Combining these two equations gives us the differential equation:

    dV / dt = (V_{IN} - V_{OUT}) / RC

Integrating this gives us the voltage at the capacitor as:

    V_{OUT} = V_{IN} (1 - e^{-t/RC})

Again, this is an exponential equation; however, this time it represents an exponential charging of the capacitor. The waveform for the voltage at the capacitor is shown in Figure 4-34.

In this case, the time constant is the time for the voltage at the capacitor to reach 63% (total − 37%) of the input voltage. As before, this time constant is simply the product of R and C.

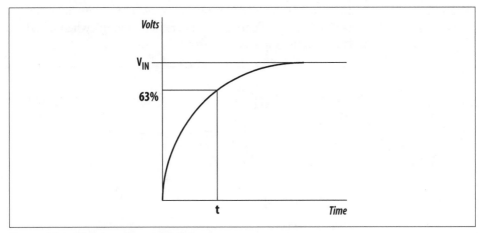

Figure 4-34. Charging of a series RC circuit

This form of RC circuit is a simple type of *low-pass filter*. This is a circuit that provides a path to ground for high-frequency components of a signal, thereby attenuating them from the main signal, while the low-frequency components suffer far less attenuation. This type of circuit is very useful for removing high-frequency noise that may be superimposed on a signal.

A given processor or peripheral chip will have a small amount of *input capacitance* on each input pin. This, combined with the small inherent impedance of a circuit connection and the input impedance of the pin, means that an applied digital voltage to the pin will actually appear as an exponential rise, rather than as a sharp (digital) edge (Figure 4-35). These effects are minimal but can be significant in high-speed circuits or where several devices are connected to the same signal line and the overall input capacitance is not insignificant.

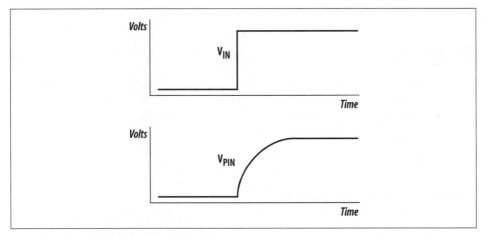

Figure 4-35. RC charging at a chip's input pin

The effect of lead inductance can contribute second-order characteristics, such as those shown in Figure 4-36. These inductive effects create "ringing" when a sudden voltage change is applied. Inductors will be discussed shortly.

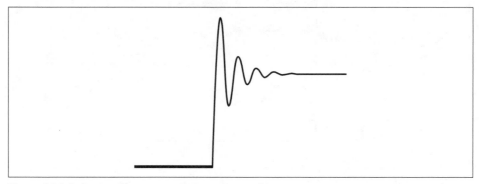

Figure 4-36. Inductive effects cause ringing on a signal input

The third form of an RC circuit is shown in Figure 4-37.

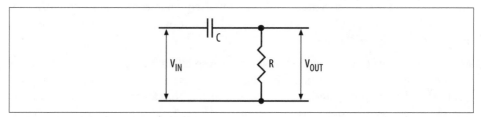

Figure 4-37. RC filter

This type of circuit is a simple form of a *high-pass filter*, since it passes only the high frequencies through to the output. The capacitor in such a circuit is known as a *blocking capacitor*.

Inductors

Inductors are passive components that are essentially coils of conductive wire. The schematic symbol for an inductor is shown in Figure 4-38. Inductance is measured in Henries, with an equation symbol "L" and a unit symbol "H."

Figure 4-38. Schematic symbol for an inductor

The voltage across an inductor changes the current flow through it, measured with the following relation:

```
V = L * dI / dt
```

Whereas applying a current to a capacitor caused the voltage to build across it, the opposite is true for an inductor. Applying a voltage across it builds current flow through it, and the resulting energy is stored in the inductor as a magnetic field. When the applied voltage is removed, the field collapses and returns the stored energy as a voltage spike.

Figure 4-39 shows a series R-L circuit.

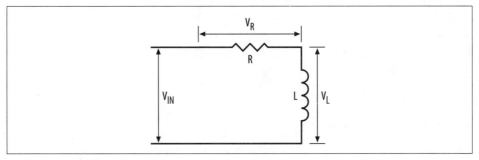

Figure 4-39. Series R-L circuit

The voltage across the resistor (V_R) and the voltage across the inductor (V_L) are shown in Figure 4-40. When a voltage is applied at V_{IN}, the voltage across the resistor is initially small, whereas the voltage across the inductor is large. As the current flow through the inductor builds, the voltage across the resistor increases, while the voltage across the inductor diminishes accordingly.

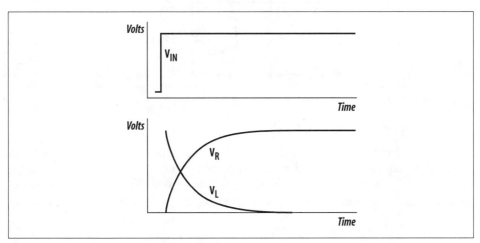

Figure 4-40. Series R-L response to a step input

Figure 4-41 shows a series R-L-C circuit.

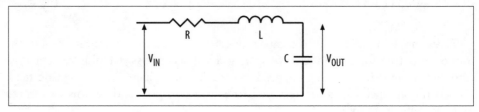

Figure 4-41. R-L-C circuit

The response (V$_{OUT}$ versus time) of an R-L-C circuit to a step input is shown in Figure 4-42.

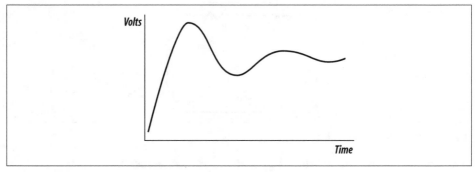

Figure 4-42. R-L-C circuit response

Figure 4-43 shows an R-L-C circuit where all the components are in parallel.

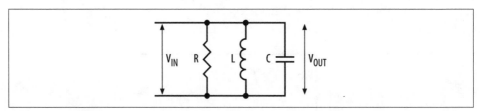

Figure 4-43. Parallel R-L-C circuit

The step response of this circuit is shown in Figure 4-44.

Inductors are commonly used in switching voltage regulators (Chapter 5) and are also employed (in combination with a resistor and capacitor) as filters to remove unwanted frequency components from a signal. Inductive effects exist in many components, and inductive voltage spikes are the bane of the embedded-system designer.

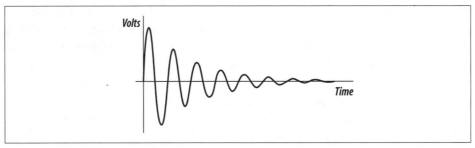

Figure 4-44. Parallel R-L-C circuit response

Transformers

Transformers are related to inductors. A transformer consists of two coils of wire, known as the *primary* and the *secondary*, that are closely coupled magnetically. The schematic symbol for a transformer is shown in Figure 4-45.

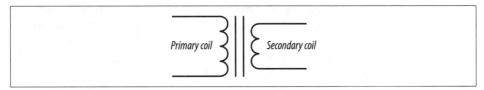

Figure 4-45. Schematic symbol for a transformer

An AC current flowing through the primary will generate an associated electro-magnetic field. The strength of the field is proportional to the number of turns in the coil of the primary. Because the secondary is within this field, the field will generate a current flow through (and therefore a voltage difference across) the secondary. Since the secondary has a different number of windings in the coil than the primary, the field generated by the primary will create a different voltage and current in the secondary (provided, of course, that the secondary is part of a circuit so that current can flow). Therefore, a transformer can be thought of as a voltage multiplier (or divider). The ratio of the number of turns in the primary and secondary will determine the voltage multiplication.

Since transformers are usually exceptionally efficient, most of the power in the primary is transferred across to the secondary. If the secondary increases the voltage of the primary, then the secondary's current will correspondingly be smaller than in the primary. Conversely, if the voltage across the secondary is less than the primary, the current through the secondary will therefore be larger than in the primary.

Transformers are commonly used inside power supplies to convert the high line voltage (110 VAC or 240 VAC, depending on where you live) to a much lower voltage for use by electronic systems and other appliances. They also provide isolation between the powered system, and the high-voltage supply.

A transformer with a ratio of n turns has an increase in impedance of n^2. Therefore, another use of transformers is to provide a way of changing the impedance of a transmission line. For example, an Ethernet port will have a transformer between the interface chip and the cable.

Diodes

Diodes are semiconductor devices that are extremely useful. They have the interesting characteristic that they will pass a current in one direction but block it from the other. They can be used to allow currents to flow from one part of a circuit to another but prevent other currents from "backwashing" where you don't want them.

The schematic symbol for a diode is shown in Figure 4-46. The arrow indicates the direction of conduction. The arrow represents the *anode*, or positive side, of the diode, while the bar represents the *cathode*, or negative side, of the diode. A higher voltage on the left of the component will allow current to be passed through to the right. However, a higher voltage on the right will be prevented from causing current flow to the left.

Figure 4-46. Schematic symbol for a diode

Diodes have a *forward voltage drop* when conducting. This means there will be a voltage difference between the anode and the cathode. For example, a diode may have a forward voltage drop of 0.7 V. If this diode is part of a larger circuit and the voltage at the anode is 5 V, then the voltage at the cathode will be 4.3 V.

Diodes come in a variety of shapes and sizes. Figure 4-47 shows a small power diode. The white stripe indicates the cathode (negative) end of the diode.

Figure 4-47. Power diode (1N4004)

Diodes are useful for removing negative voltages from a signal, a process known as *rectification*. Four diodes may be combined to form a bridge rectifier, as shown in Figure 4-48. The bridge "flips" the negative components of the wave, so that only a positive voltage is present at the output. A capacitor on the output can be used to smooth the rectified wave.

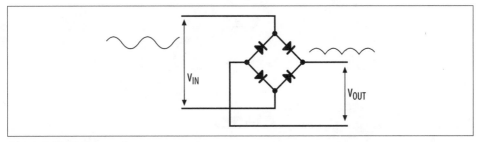

Figure 4-48. Bridge rectifier

Such configurations are commonly used on the power inputs of embedded comput-ers and other digital systems. A voltage can be applied across the inputs on the left, with no regard as to which should be positive or negative. The bridge rectifier ensures that a positive voltage will always be conducted to the upper right, and at the same time current flow is returned from the lower right through the bridge rectifier to whichever lefthand connection is negative.

If you'll forgive the pun, the most commonly seen diode is the LED (Light Emitting Diode). The schematic symbol is shown in Figure 4-49, and a through-hole LED is shown in Figure 4-50. All diodes produce a small amount of light as a consequence of their operation (although you don't normally see it because of the diode casing); it's just that LEDs are especially good at it.

Figure 4-49. Schematic symbol for a LED

Figure 4-50. LED (5 mm through-hole)

There is a limit to the amount of current that can pass through a LED. Exceeding this current will potentially damage or destroy the LED. For this reason, LEDs are used in conjunction with a current-limiting resistor. Figure 4-51 shows such a circuit. Some LEDs will incorporate a current-limiting resistor internally. However, most do not, so it is important to check the manufacturer's datasheet. Generally, you'll need to include the resistor, and calculating the required value (R) is easy.

Let's say that the LED has a forward voltage drop of 1.6 V and a current limit of 36 mA. We need to select a resistor that will limit the current flowing through the LED

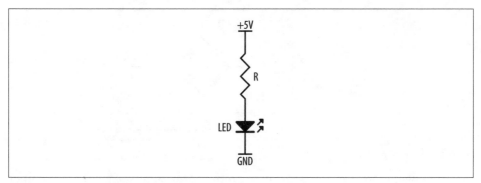

Figure 4-51. Using a resistor to limit the current flow through a LED

to this value. In our circuit, the LED and resistor are in series, and the total voltage across them is 5 V. So, if the LED has a voltage drop of 1.6 V, then we can easily calculate the voltage drop across the resistor:

```
VR = 5 - 1.6
   = 3.4 V
```

So, if the voltage drop across the resistor is 3.4 V, and we need to limit the current to 36 mA, then using Ohm's Law we can calculate a value for R:

```
R = V / I
  = 3.4 / 0.036
  = 94.44 Ω
```

A 100 Ω resistor will therefore do fine and will result in a brightly glowing LED. If you want lower-intensity light, you just need to limit the current further, and you would therefore use a larger resistor. Note that since 36 mA is the maximum current the LED can handle, we will always need a resistor that keeps the current flow below this. Therefore, we always opt for a larger R.

The power that the resistor must dissipate is given by the relation:

```
P = V * I
  = 3.4 * 0.036
  = 0.1224 W
```

Resistors are available with different power-dissipation ratings. It is important to choose a resistor with the correct rating. In this instance, we would use a 0.125 W resistor.

The ubiquitous power-on LED you see in your home appliances works in this exact same way. This simple LED circuit (or variations of it) drives the LEDs on your PC's front panel, on your VCR and DVD player, your cell phone, and a host of other appliances. Many traffic lights and railroad signals are replacing conventional bulbs with arrays of LEDs, as the LEDs last longer and produce more light (per area).

LEDs are available in red, green, yellow, blue, and white. The last two colors are very hard to produce and therefore relatively expensive.

There are two more types of diodes about which it is useful to know: *Zener diodes* and *Schottky diodes* (Figure 4-52).

Figure 4-52. *Zener and Schottky diodes*

Zener diodes exhibit a characteristic known as *dynamic resistance*, or *small-signal resistance*. The voltage drop across a Zener diode will not change as the current through it changes. In effect, it acts as a variable resistor whose resistance is current-dependent. Zener diodes are commonly used to provide a reference voltage (Figure 4-53).

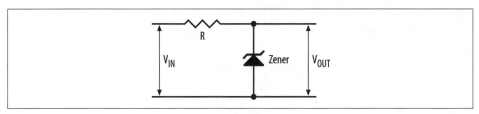

Figure 4-53. *Using a Zener diode to provide a reference voltage*

From Ohm's Law, we have:

$(V_{IN} - V_{OUT}) = I * R$

Now, if V_{IN} changes, it logically follows that the current will also change. So we can modify our equation thus:

$(\Delta V_{IN} - \Delta V_{OUT}) = \Delta I * R$

The Zener acts as a source of *dynamic resistance*, which we'll designate R_d. Now what we have is effectively a voltage divider. So, our equation for V_{OUT} is:

$\Delta V_{OUT} = \Delta V_{IN} * R_d / (R + R_d)$

Schottky diodes are also known as *hot-carrier diodes* and behave like conventional diodes, save for a very small forward voltage drop. They are commonly used in power-supply circuits and signal rectification for this reason.

Crystals

Finally in our component tour, we come to crystals. Just as their name suggests, they are small blocks of quartz (silicon dioxide). Quartz crystal is a type of material known as a *piezo-electric*. This is a substance that generates a voltage when it is stressed (compressed, stretched, twisted). This effect is utilized in microphones. The sound vibrates the piezo-electric material, and it produces a small AC voltage that is directly proportional to the original sound that created it. This voltage is then amplified for broadcast, recording, or processing.

The opposite effect is also true for piezo-electric materials. Apply a voltage and the piezo-electric material will contort or vibrate. Some speakers use piezo-electric materials to produce sound. (However, most use other techniques, such as electromagnetics.) Most loud buzzers are based on piezo-electrics.

Now, the neat thing about quartz is that for a block of a given size, it will vibrate at a given (and fixed) frequency. As such, it can be used as an oscillator to generate a sine wave, which in turn can be used to generate timing signals for microprocessors and other digital circuits. Just about every computer system will have a crystal (or two) somewhere on its circuit board, generating the timing that ultimately drives the whole machine. That crystal is simply a small block of quartz, plated at either end with wires attached and encased in a metal can.

The schematic symbol for a crystal is shown in Figure 4-54, and a real crystal is shown in Figure 4-55.

Figure 4-54. Schematic symbol for a crystal

Figure 4-55. A crystal

Crystals require a drive circuit to make them go. These tend to be a bit temperamental and don't always oscillate at the frequency you expect, due to a range of effects that are hard to track down. Fortunately, there are two easy ways around this problem. The first is that most processors (and other chips requiring timing) have internal oscillator circuits. All you need to do is add the external crystal (and maybe a capacitor or two), and it will work beautifully. For those chips that don't make life quite so easy, you can get complete oscillator modules, which include the crystal and drive circuit. All you need to do is give them power and ground, and they too will work beautifully.

Clocks and Oscillators

All microprocessors (and quite a few other digital devices too) require a clock. A *clock* is an output from an oscillator that runs the processor and all system events related to the clock. (And just in case you're wondering, this "clock" has nothing to do with the time of day. Think of it as a stream of digital pulses.) The clock frequency is normally expressed in kiloHertz (kHz), MegaHertz (MHz, 1,000 kHz), or GigaHertz (GHz, 1,000 MHz). The clock frequency of a processor is also known as its *clock speed*. (Note the capital "H" in Hz. It is never "hz," always "Hz.")

A given processor will have a maximum and a minimum clock frequency. This specifies the range in which the oscillator driving the processor can operate. A processor with a minimum clock speed of zero is said to have *static operation*, or *DC operation*. This means that the processor can have its clock stopped and still be able to resume operation at a later time with no ill effect. If the minimum operating frequency of a processor is specified to be greater than zero, then that processor is said to have *dynamic operation*. If the oscillator frequency falls below the minimum of a dynamic processor, then that processor may suffer corruption of its registers.

The clock speed of a processor relates to how quickly a processor can execute software. A processor running at a faster clock speed will execute software faster than a processor *of the same type* running at a slower clock speed. But clock speed is not the whole story in terms of processor speed. One processor architecture may take 32 clock cycles to execute an instruction, whereas another processor may complete one instruction every clock cycle. So, even though these two processors are running at the same clock speed, the latter will be significantly faster than the former.

There are several ways of generating a clock. Which is appropriate depends largely on the processor you are using. Some processors expect a digital (square-wave) clock input. For a processor running at common frequencies, and this includes most processors, the best choice is to use a device called an *oscillator module* (Figure 4-56). These four-pin components provide a square-wave clock output at a given frequency, requiring only power and ground connections. These simplify the system design, as they are "plug and go" devices.

Many processors (including all the microcontrollers I can think of) contain oscillator circuitry and generally require only the addition of an external crystal and bypass capacitors (Figure 4-57). The capacitors remove higher-order harmonics from the oscillation.

Power versus speed

Often it is necessary to design a system with minimal power consumption. This may be done to reduce the heat produced by a system or to make the system portable.

Figure 4-56. Microprocessor oscillator modules

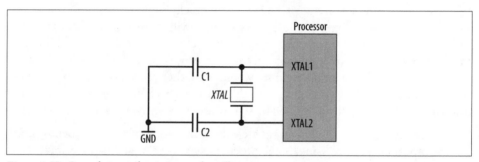

Figure 4-57. Crystal circuit for an internal oscillator

The more current that devices within a system use, the hotter they become. Too much heat will cause them to stop working. While it is possible to provide cooling subsystems and temperature monitors, the better approach is simply to reduce the power consumption and therefore the heat. When a system is powered by batteries, the lower its current draw, the longer the batteries will last. For these reasons, low-powered design is advantageous.

Most of the current usage of a digital system occurs during transitions of state—in other words, during the clock edges. The more frequent the clock edges, the more the average current usage goes up. Therefore, the faster a processor runs, the more power it consumes. Conversely, the lower the processor's operating voltage, the less its power consumption is. Many embedded processors are available in lower-voltage versions. Power consumption can also vary between architectures. An ARM processor running at the same clock speed and operating voltage as a Pentium will have *considerably* less power consumption. It is for this reason that ARMs are common in PDA devices.

Using chips with *static operation* allows the clock of the system to be slowed (or stopped), and since power consumption relates directly to speed, this can reduce the overall power usage of the machine. The clock may be slowed in several ways. First, the clock can be kept permanently slow. For an application that does not require a lot of computing power (a traffic-light controller, for example), a processor clock of 32 kHz (rather than, say, 20 MHz) may be used.

Alternatively, in systems that occasionally require heavy computation, the system clock may be slowed only when the processor is idle. Many laptop computers use this technique to reduce their power consumption. The processor runs at full speed when in use. If the system sits idle for 30 seconds, the clock is slowed down into the kHz range. If the system remains idle for several minutes, the clock is slowed down into the Hz range. Since the user is not actively working with the machine (that's why it is idle), the user doesn't notice any difference. The moment the processor is required to perform a task (such as when a key is pressed), the clock is switched back to full speed and normal operation is resumed.

 Palm computers use this technique very effectively. The machines are event-driven, meaning they do something when the user taps the screen, or when an I/O device requires servicing. Therefore, in between events, the processor slows down considerably. When an event occurs, the system switches back to full speed, processes the event, and then returns to idle mode. The processor spends far more time in idle mode than in operating mode, and, therefore, the battery use is minimal. It is by using this technique that Palms get such long operating life from their batteries. It is also why you never see (or shouldn't see) computationally intensive applications on Palm computers. The batteries would be flat in no time.

Some computer systems may even halt the clock completely until the processor is required, at which point an external device reactivates the system clock.

Many processors have SLEEP and HALT modes, reducing the processor's power consumption. Some processors extend this to SLEEP, NAP, DOZE, SNOOZE, etc., each with a different level of power usage and each requiring a different period of time for the processor to "awaken." (The deeper the sleep, the longer it takes for the processor to resume operation.)

This concludes the discussion of electronic components. One major type of component that I haven't covered is transistors. They have been left out simply because they are not commonly seen in embedded systems, and a proper coverage of transistors would occupy a large volume in its own right. If you are interested in learning about transistors, there are plenty of excellent books available. Just visit your local technical bookstore or cruise the Internet.

Digital Signals

Being an electronic circuit, the operation of a computer is about voltages and current flow. Understanding the basic principles of voltages and current flow within the computer is mandatory if you're going to produce a working system. Common operating voltages inside a computer are normally either 5 V or 3.3 V. For some low-power or exceptionally fast computers, voltages may be as small as 1.8 V or lower.

An output pin of a digital device can be in one of three states. It can be *high* (logic 1), *low* (logic 0), or *tristate* (*high-impedance*, also known as floating). A logic high is defined as the output voltage at the pin being higher than a given threshold. When a device's pin is outputting a high, it is said to be *sourcing current* to that connection. Similarly, a logic low is where the output voltage is below a given threshold, and the device's pin is said to be *sinking current*. Typically, components can sink more current than they can source.

A tristate pin is outputting neither a high nor a low. Instead, it becomes high-impedance (high-resistance) such that current flow in or out of the pin is negligible. It is, in effect, invisible to other components to which it is connected. For example, within a computer system there may be several memory devices connected to the data bus. When a particular device is being read, its data outputs will be either high or low (corresponding to the bit pattern being read back). All other memory devices in the system, because they are not being accessed, will have tristate data buses. They take no part in the read transaction between the processor and the accessed memory device.

The threshold for logic high and the threshold for logic low can vary from device type to device type. For an input device to recognize a given signal as high or low, the output device must provide that signal within the appropriate limits. The thresholds can vary but are always consistent across devices of the same *logic families*. Back in the good old days, there were a limited number of logic families, and each device within a family conformed to the thresholds of that family. Life, and designing digital systems, was easier. Now, with the quest for ever lower-powered devices and the desire for devices to be as versatile as possible, the thresholds for logic high and logic low are considerably diverse. So the input low threshold for a given chip may not match the output low threshold for the chip to which it is to be connected. Therefore, it is vitally important to check the datasheets of all the components you are using and ensure they will work together.

When a device outputs a logic high, and its output voltage is greater than the high threshold for the input device, current will flow from the output pin to the input pin. The output device is sourcing current, while the input device is sinking current.

Conversely, for certain types of digital logic, when a device outputs a logic low, and its output voltage is lower than the low threshold of the input device, current will flow from the *input* pin to the *output* pin, even though the output device is the one controlling the voltage. The output device is sinking current, while the input device is sourcing current (Figure 4-58).

Voltage Thresholds

The voltages for the TTL logic family (Transistor-Transistor Logic) define a logic low as a maximum input voltage of 0.8 V and a maximum output voltage of 0.4 V, and a logic high as a minimum input voltage of 2.0 V and a minimum output voltage of 2.4 V. Many processors accept TTL inputs, though relatively few of them are actually TTL-compatible devices. This is important. You can never assume that a given output or a given input will be within voltage specifications. For instance, a *minimum* high voltage for an old 80386 processor on its clock input is 4.2 V at 20 MHz and 3.7 V at 25 MHz. These are significantly higher than standard TTL levels. A standard TTL device driving this input may not be able to achieve a voltage sufficiently large enough to be recognized as a high by this processor. The moral of the story is *check the datasheet*! The electrical (and timing) specifications listed in datasheets are there for very good reasons.

There are many different logic families, each with their own threshold voltages and other characteristics. Beyond that, there are many components that don't fit into any particular logic family. The component datasheets are your best guide as to what will work with what.

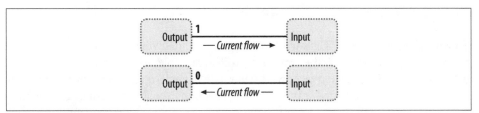

Figure 4-58. Current flow between digital devices

The magnitude of the current flow is important. A given device will have limitations on how much current it can sink or source. Exceeding this current limit can permanently damage an integrated circuit. It is therefore important to calculate the current flows within your system and ensure that all the requirements are met.

Electrical Characteristics

Pick up any chip datasheet and you will find three sections, labeled *Absolute Maximum Ratings*, *DC Electrical Characteristics*, and *AC Electrical Characteristics*. These are vitally important, but often poorly understood. So let's see what it all means, and how you work with that information to produce a reliable and effective embedded system. Let's look at the Absolute Maximum Ratings first.

Absolute Maximum Ratings

The very first thing you'll see in the electrical characteristics section is something labeled Absolute Maximum Ratings. A chip will be designed to operate under certain nominal conditions, and exceeding those conditions during normal operation is not advised. But what happens if you do go beyond those parameters? At just what point will you really kill the chip? The Absolute Maximum Ratings tell you just that. They show you how far you can stress the chip, and (sometimes) for how long, before the device will fail.

An example of the Absolute Maximum Ratings for a chip, in this case a Dallas Semiconductor DS87C550 microcontroller, is shown in Table 4-1.

Table 4-1. Absolute Maximum Ratings for a DS87C550 microcontroller

Parameter	Rating
Voltage on any pin relative to ground	−0.3 V to (**VCC** + 0.5V)
Voltage on VCC relative to ground	−0.3 V to 6.0 V
Operating temperature	−40°C to +85°C
Storage temperature	−55°C to +125°C
Soldering temperature	160°C for 10 seconds

So what does it all mean? Let's work through it. The first row of the table refers to the voltage range any pin of this microcontroller can tolerate. Normally, the voltage applied to a pin (be it signal or power) will range from zero volts (ground) to **VCC** (in the case of the DS87C550, this is +5 V). The Absolute Maximum Ratings tell us that if a pin falls to below −0.3 V (in other words, pretty much any negative voltage), the chip may be damaged. Similarly, if a pin has an applied voltage greater than **VCC** + 0. 5 V, then it will also be damaged. Now, a lot of people would interpret **VCC** + 0.5 V to be +5.5 V since the nominal **VCC** is +5 V. This is not necessarily the case. **VCC** + 0.5 V means 0.5 V above the *actual* **VCC** that you're using to power the chip, not the nominal value of +5 V. If you're running a DS87C550 from a supply of +4.5 V (perfectly valid), then the absolute maximum rating for an input is *not* +5.5 V but +5 V. The design engineer (that's you) must ensure that no device connected to this microcontroller will exceed those parameters.

Note that not all chips have an Absolute Maximum Rating for input voltage as tight as the DS87C550. I can think of one memory chip that operates from a +2.7 V supply voltage but can tolerate signals as high a +6 V on its inputs. As always, it's vitally important to check the datasheet for each device you are using to see what is and what is not possible.

Let's look at an example where we have two embedded systems, each using an identical 87C550 microcontroller, cooperating as part of a larger system. In the first embedded system, designed by Company A, the 87C550 is powered from a +4.5 V supply. In the second embedded system, produced by Company B, the 87C550 is running on a +5.5 V supply. Both of these supply voltages are valid, and perfectly allowable within the specifications of these chips. Now, an output high from the second embedded system may be (and probably will be) +5.5 V. (The datasheet only gives a *minimum* value for an output high of +2.4 V, meaning that in reality, a high could be anywhere in the range +2.4 V to **VCC**.) An input high to the first embedded system's microcontroller cannot exceed **VCC** + 0.5 V:

```
Max input = VCC + 0.5V
          = 4.5V + 0.5V
          = 5V
```

So, an output high from the second embedded system could very well exceed the maximum input rating of the first, even though they are based on identical chips. This illustrates the importance of checking everything carefully and *thinking* about what is going on within the system. An engineer assuming that both systems will work together since they use the same microcontroller would be wrong and would very likely kill the first system.

The second row of the table tells us the maximum power supply the chip can tolerate. In the case of this processor, although its nominal operating voltage is +5 V (listed elsewhere in the datasheet), it can actually run off a supply as high as +6 V. However, exceeding +6 V on the power pins will probably damage the chip. Similarly, applying a negative voltage to a power pin will also damage the chip.

The operating temperature (row three in our table) specifies the temperature range at which this chip will operate reliably. If it is colder than −40°C, then the chip may physically fail, or the software it is executing may crash. Similarly, if the microcontroller is run in an environment where the temperature exceeds +85°C, then the chip will also fail. Now, the operating temperature is different from the storage temperature (row four of the table). The device can be stored reliably at any temperature between −55°C and +125°C without stressing the chip and potentially causing it to fail.

 In some datasheets, you'll see operating temperature listed as *junction temperature*, referring to the temperature within the semiconductor. It effectively means the same thing.

The final entry in the table indicates the maximum soldering temperature that the chip can tolerate. In this case, it can withstand +160°C for 10 seconds. Now, 160 degrees is not that hot as far as soldering irons go. In truth, the chip can probably tolerate much higher temperatures than this, but only for significantly shorter periods of time. So, if I was to solder this chip using a standard iron, the final row of the table tells me that I need to be quick when soldering each pin, and that I should let the device cool down between soldering each pin. Holding a hot iron against each pin for several seconds will build up temperature within the chip and will turn a complicated, functioning integrated circuit into a mere ornament in the middle of the circuit board.

DC Characteristics

The DC characteristics specify the voltages and currents pertaining to the chip during normal operations. In datasheets, you'll often see the DC characteristics (and sometimes the Absolute Maximum Ratings) referred to as *commercial grade*, *industrial grade*, or *military grade*. These indicate the robustness of a particular part and its ability to withstand harsh environments. A military-grade part will be able to withstand higher temperatures, have better noise immunity, and have a longer operating life. In some cases, the military-grade part will have *radiation hardness*, meaning that it can survive and continue to operate after exposure to radiation. The downside is that a military-grade part will be more expensive, sometimes harder to get, and may not operate at as high a speed as its commercial-grade cousin. Now, you may think that unless you're designing military hardware, you'll have no need of military-grade parts. However, if you're designing equipment that will be used in space, at high altitude, or in the Arctic or Antarctic, where temperature variations are extreme and radiation levels can be high, military grade may be the better choice.

The DC characteristics data is presented in a table format. An example, showing some typical entries (for an imaginary chip), is given in Table 4-2. Now, I say "typical" in the loosest sense of the word. For each chip manufacturer, there is a different way of presenting the data. But you'll work it out, as it's not that hard once you know what to look for.

Table 4-2. Sample DC characteristics

Parameter	Symbol	Min	Typ	Max	Unit
Supply voltage[a]	VDD	3	-	5.5	V
Input-low voltage	VIL	VSS	-	0.15VDD	V
Input-high voltage	VIH	0.25VDD	-	VDD	V
Output-low voltage[b]	VOL	-	-	0.6	V
Output-high voltage[b]	VOH	VDD - 0.7	-	-	V
Supply current[c]	IDD	-	0.8	1.4	mA
Sleep current[d]	Isleep	-	10	25	nA
Input capacitance				TBD	pF

[a] Referenced to **VSS**
[b] $3 \leq$ **VDD** ≤ 5.5 V
[c] Oscillator $= 4$ MHz
[d] Oscillator $= 32$ kHz

The *supply voltage* tells us the operating voltage needed to supply the chip. The *symbol* is simply a label, used in other parts of the datasheet to refer to this parameter. In this case, the supply voltage is a minimum (Min) of 3 V and a maximum (Max) of 5. 5 V. This means that we can run this chip using a supply voltage anywhere within this range. The typical (Typ) column is left blank, indicating that there is no preferred supply voltage within this range. Sometimes you'll see a chip with a minimum supply voltage of 4.5 V, a maximum of 5.5 V, and a typical supply voltage of 5 V. What this tells us is that this part requires a 5 V supply (indicated by the Typ value) but can tolerate a range of 0.5 V on either side of this. Some manufacturers will use *nominal* (Nom) in place of typical. It means the same thing. The footnote (a) pertaining to this entry indicates that the supply voltage is referenced to **VSS**. This may seem like an obvious thing, but it is important. **VSS** is typically ground (zero volts), but it need not be. In exceptional circumstances, the design may require that **VSS** be some voltage other than ground. Hence the footnote says that the supply voltage must be 3 V to 5.5 V above **VSS**. So, if **VSS** were 2 V, for example, our supply voltage would be 5 V to 7.5 V. (Remember that it is the voltage *difference* that is important.)

The next two rows show us what voltage levels are required on an input pin to register as a low (0) or a high (1). Note that these are not absolute values, but are referenced to **VSS** and **VDD**.

The *output low voltage* is given as a maximum of 0.6 V, with no minimum or typical values. This means that when this chip is outputting a low, it will be no greater than 0.6 V. Although no minimum is given, it can be assumed that the minimum is **VSS**. The chip would not output a low below this value. The footnote for this parameter and the next parameter indicates that the values given are for when the chip is operating from a supply voltage of between 3 V and 5.5 V. Such a range is typically written as "$3\ V \le VDD \le 5.5\ V$." This just means that **VDD** lies between 3 V and 5.5 V.

The *supply current* has a typical value and a maximum value. For some manufacturers, the typical value is what you'll see in reality. For other manufacturers, the typical value could best be described as "wishful thinking." The real value is often closer to the maximum than the typical. The note tells us that the supply current given is for when the chip is running at 4 MHz. Since the current used by a device varies with speed, this parameter is only of limited use. Some manufacturers will give you an equation or a graph that allows you to determine supply current for any oscillator speed.

The *sleep current* shows how much juice this chip will draw when it is in "sleep" or "power down" mode. As you would expect, it is much less than the "awake" supply current given in the row above. But, look at the footnotes. The sleep current is given for an oscillator speed of 32 kHz, while the supply current is for an oscillator speed of 4 MHz. Some manufacturers do this deliberately to make their devices look better than they are, as this can mask the true nature of the part. (Remember that current drops with clock speed anyway.) This makes it hard to determine what the real current draw of the device will be in your application. Sure, the sleep current may be 10nA at 32 kHz, but it might be 0.5 mA at 4 MHz. Another trick manufacturers use is to provide a value for the supply current to the *core* (the CPU) but disregard the current used by all the onboard peripherals. It may look good on paper, but the reality could be quite different. The only way to be really sure is to build the thing into a system and *measure* it.

The final parameter in our example is *input capacitance*. Every input pin has a small capacitance, and this combines with the small inherent resistance of the signal traces (circuit board tracks) to act as an RC circuit. Earlier in this chapter, we saw how an input pulse into an RC circuit results in a rising voltage at the output. This means that although an input may quickly change from a low to a high, the input capacitance of the pin will provide a slight delay before the chip "sees" this change in input. You need to take this into account in your design, especially with respect to rapidly changing signals.

Now, in this particular example, the input capacitance is specified as "TBD." This is the bane of the system designer. "TBD" means "To Be Determined." In other words, this parameter wasn't known at the time the datasheet was written. TBD can pop up in all sorts of places in datasheets and can be a real problem if you're trying to design a machine. I remember one datasheet for a processor many years ago where *every* parameter, from supply voltage and current to voltage levels and timing, was listed as TBD!

Finally, be aware that technical data in some (not all) datasheets is theoretical only. In other words, the design engineers for the chip or part calculated what the values *should* be using their supercomputer (or abacus or Tarot cards). Other manufacturers actually go to great pains to measure their technical parameters, and even provide you with detailed explanations of the test conditions. They take a very thorough approach, and you can use their parts in confidence. Maxim and Texas Instruments are examples of two such companies, although there are many more.

AC Characteristics and Timing

A *timing diagram* is a representation of the input and output signals of a device and how they relate to each other. In essence, it indicates when a signal needs to be asserted and when you can expect a response from the device. For two devices to interact, the timing of signals between the two must be compatible, or you must provide additional circuitry to make them compatible.

Timing diagrams scare and confuse many people and are often ignored completely. Ignoring device timing is a sure way of guaranteeing that your system will not work! However, they are not that hard to understand and use. If you want to design and build reliable systems, remember that *timing is everything*!

Digital signals may be in one of three states: *high*, *low*, or *high-impedance* (*tristate*). On timing diagrams for digital devices, these states are represented as shown in Figure 4-59.

Low   High   Tristate
                   (High impedance)

Figure 4-59. Digital states

Transitions from one state to another are shown in Figure 4-60.

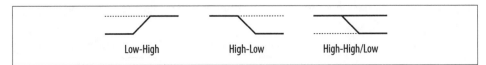

Low-High   High-Low   High-High/Low

Figure 4-60. Transitions

The last waveform (High-High/Low) indicates that a signal is high and, at a given point in time, may either remain high or change to low. Similarly, a signal line that is tristate may go low, high, or either high or low depending on the state of the system. An example of this is a data line, which will be tristate until an information transfer begins. At this point in time, it will either go high (data = 1) or low (data = 0), as shown in Figure 4-61.

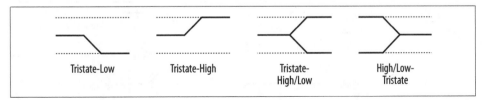

Tristate-Low   Tristate-High   Tristate-   High/Low-
                                     High/Low   Tristate

Figure 4-61. Tristate transitions

The waveforms in Figure 4-62 indicate a change from tristate to high/low and back again. These symbols indicate that the change may happen *anywhere* within a given *range* of time, but *will have happened* by a given *point* in time.

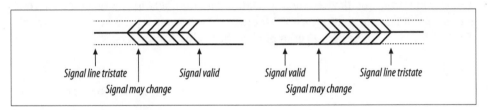

Signal line tristate   *Signal valid*   *Signal valid*   *Signal line tristate*

Signal may change   *Signal may change*

Figure 4-62. Transition timing

The waveform in Figure 4-63 indicates that a signal may/will change at a given point in time. The signal may have been high and will either remain high or go low. Alternatively, the signal may have been low and will either remain low or go high.

Figure 4-63. Change in signal state

The impression given in many texts on digital circuits is that a change in signal state is instantaneous. This is not so. A transition is *never* instant; it can be several nanoseconds in duration, and there is considerable variation between different devices (Figure 4-64). The datasheet for each component will detail the transition times for that particular device.

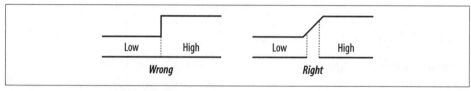

Figure 4-64. Timing of a signal transition

Datasheets from component manufacturers specify timing information for devices. A sample timing diagram for an imaginary chip is shown in Figure 4-65.

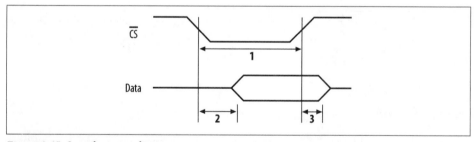

Figure 4-65. Sample timing diagram

The diagram shows the relationship between input signals to the device (such as $\overline{CS}$) and outputs from the device (such as **Data**). The numbers in the diagram are references to timing information within tables. They do *not* represent timing directly. Table 4-3 shows how a datasheet might list the timing parameters.

Table 4-3. Sample timing parameters

Ref	Description	Min	Max	Units
1	CS Hold Time	60		ns
2	CS to Data Valid		30	ns
3	Data Hold Time	5	10	ns

Timing reference "1" (the first row of Table 4-3) shows how long $\overline{CS}$ must be held low. In this instance, it is a *minimum* of 60 ns. This means that the device won't guarantee that $\overline{CS}$ will be recognized unless it is held low for more than this time. There is no maximum specified. This means that it doesn't matter if $\overline{CS}$ is held low for longer than 60 ns. The *only* requirement is that it is low for a *minimum* of 60 ns.

Timing reference "2" shows how long it takes the device to respond to $\overline{CS}$ going low. From when $\overline{CS}$ goes low until this device starts outputting data is a *maximum* of 30 ns. What this means is that 30 ns after $\overline{CS}$ goes low, the device will be driving valid data onto the data bus. It may start driving data earlier than 30 ns. The only guarantee is that it will take *no longer* than 30 ns for this device to respond.

Timing reference "3" specifies when the device will stop driving data once $\overline{CS}$ has been negated. This reference has a minimum of 5 ns and a maximum of 10 ns. This means that data will be held valid for *at least* 5 ns, but *no more than* 10 ns, after $\overline{CS}$ negates.

Some manufacturers use numbers to reference timing; others may use a label (Figure 4-66).

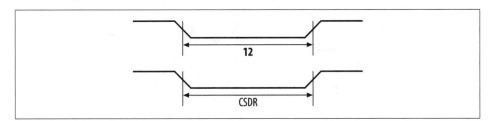

Figure 4-66. Timing reference

Some manufacturers will specify timing from when a signal becomes valid until it is no longer valid. Others specify timing from the middle of a transition to the middle of the next transition (Figure 4-67).

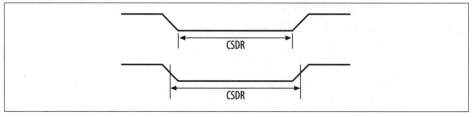

Figure 4-67. Timing length

Logic Gates

In days of old, computers (and other digital electronics) were built using discrete logic gates. Nowadays, these are somewhat rare, with programmable logic being the preferred option. However, it is not unusual to still see the odd logic gate in a schematic. For your reference, Figure 4-68 shows the most common gates and their truth tables. In each case, **A** and **B** are inputs, and **C** is the output.

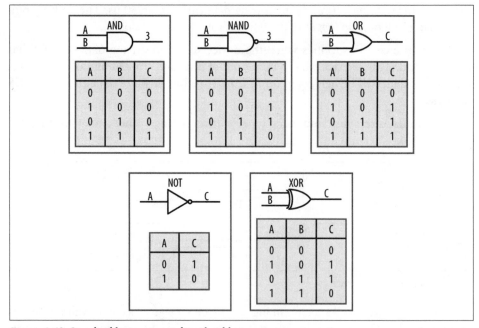

Figure 4-68. Standard logic gates and truth tables

The Importance of Reading the Datasheet

Before starting any design, you need to work out the basic requirements for your system (what it will do, how much it will cost) and select the major components you will need (such as a processor, I/O, and memory). Before you do anything else, obtain the datasheets for these components and read them from beginning to end. These can typically be found on manufacturers' web sites. (Every chip used in this book was specifically chosen because it had full technical data available online.) Just go to the manufacturer's web site and download the relevant documentation.

Once you've read the data thoroughly and feel you understand it, go back and reread it to pick up all the things you missed on the first pass. It's much better to discover something critical that you've missed before you design and build a computer, rather than after.

Always make sure you have the latest datasheets and errata (datasheet bug lists) before you begin a design. Using a datasheet that is even a little bit old is not a good idea. It is not unusual for the electrical and technical specifications to change from time to time, so it's critical that you use the latest (and most accurate) data.

It is very important that you understand how the devices work. When you are debugging your system, you have to know what to look for to know whether different parts of your computer are functioning. Don't assume anything about the functionality of the devices. Read and check everything carefully, including voltage levels, basic timing, and anything else that may be relevant to the system.

 If possible, a very useful thing to include in your design is a serial interface, even if you don't need a serial port for the final application. A serial port is *extremely* useful for printing out diagnostic and status information from the system, and can be an indispensable diagnostic tool (for both hardware and software). The other mandatory debugging tool is the status LED. A flashing LED can tell you volumes about a machine being tested if the LED is used intelligently by the software and programmer. The more status LEDs you have, the better life will be!

Well, that completes the quick tour of this most very basic introduction to electronics. If you're curious to know more, please seek out some more in-depth books on the topic. It really is a fascinating and complex field, worthy of fuller coverage than I am able to give here. Now that we've covered the basics of what the electrons are up to, in the next chapter we'll look at providing power for your embedded system.

CHAPTER 5

Power Sources

The attention span of a computer is only as long as its
electrical cord.
—Turnaucka's Law

There is one important aspect that must be included in all embedded computer designs—power. In this chapter, we look at power sources for your computer and voltage regulation to keep your power smooth and reliable.

Your embedded computer system needs electricity. You have several options when it comes to powering your system: coal, nuclear, hydro, geothermal, or batteries. The first four fall under the general category of "what comes out of the wall."

The Stuff Out of the Wall

If your system doesn't need to be portable, this is the most obvious choice. What comes down the "pipe" is AC and is far too high a voltage to be of immediate use to a digital system. It must be converted to a DC voltage of significantly lower magnitude. There are plenty of solutions for doing this. You can use DC "lab" power supplies, standard PC supplies (probably overkill for your needs), or *AC adaptors*. The last of these is probably the best choice for most applications.

AC adaptors (also known as *plug packs* or sometimes *power bricks*) are the little black boxes that come with your cell phone and a host of other appliances. They are a cheap, easy, and reliable solution and can be purchased from any good electronics vendor. Typically, they will provide an output voltage somewhere in the range of +5 VDC to +12 VDC and can supply a current of up to a few Amps, depending on the particular plug pack. Choose one that will supply an appropriate voltage and current for your system. One caveat with plug packs is the polarity of the connector. Most plug packs have the positive voltage on the center of the connector jack and ground on the outside. Other plug packs have the exact opposite arrangement! Not knowing which you have could lead to disastrous consequences for your embedded system. As always, check the technical data and, if in doubt, use a multimeter to check the output polarity before connecting it to your system.

A better way is to incorporate a bridge rectifier as part of your design (Figure 5-1). That way, the polarity of the power source makes no difference. The input power is DC, but the polarity of the connection makes no difference. The embedded system uses the output of the rectifier as its power source and has internal voltage regulation. (We'll discuss regulators shortly.)

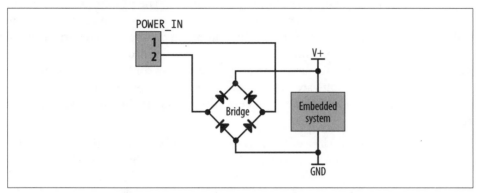

Figure 5-1. A bridge rectifier makes an embedded system "polarity-proof"

Batteries

Batteries are easy to use. The only caveat is to ensure that the battery (or batteries) you have chosen can supply enough current at the right voltage. With the right choice of battery and a carefully designed system, you can achieve extended operation over very long periods. For example, a small PIC- or AVR-based computer can (depending on application and design) operate for up to two years off a single AA battery. A poorly designed system can drain a battery in minutes. A poorly chosen battery unable to supply sufficient current will result in erratic operation, or may result in the system being unable to start at all. When choosing a battery, consider not just its average current capability but also its peak current. An embedded computer may need only an average supply of 20 mA but may require as much as 100 mA at peak loads. This is especially true of systems using flash memory, which may require high currents during write operations. The battery for such a system must be able to supply not just the continuous load, but also the peak load when required.

Low Power Design

There are several ways you can reduce the power consumption in your embedded system. The use of low-power devices is the most obvious place to start. The power consumption of different chips varies considerably, and there are many low-power variants of common devices available. RISC processors often have lower power consumption than comparable CISC processors, so they are often used in preference to CISC in low-power applications. The PIC and AVR microcontrollers can have current draws of less than 5 mA (and as low as 10 nA when in sleep mode). This is considerably less than the 35 mA used by a 68HC11 microcontroller.

Many memory chips and peripherals will automatically enter a low-power mode when they are not in use. Others may be placed in low-power mode by toggling a digital input or by an appropriate software command. The power consumption of some devices can be reduced even further by turning them off when not in use. If the processor is executing code from RAM and outputting data to a serial port, then the power to the ROMs and any other I/O devices may be turned off since they are not in use. Implementing this requires separate power sources for the chips that are to be disabled, switched via software control. Some voltage regulators (discussed in the next section) have shutdown inputs, allowing the subsystem they are powering to be turned off.

Further, some low-power devices (such as sensors) may need very little current, so little that they can be directly powered from the I/O line of a microcontroller. The I/O signal *is* the power supply for the device. The devices can be turned on or off under software control by toggling the I/O line. Some processors, such as the PIC and AVR, can sink relatively large currents (20 mA) through their I/O pins, and these can be used as ground for some devices (such as LEDs).

Regulators

A *voltage regulator* is a semiconductor device that converts an input DC voltage (usually a range of input voltages) to a fixed output DC voltage. They are used to provide a constant supply voltage within a system.

While many components in an embedded system can operate from a wide power-supply range, a fixed operating voltage is necessary for devices such as *Analog-Digital Converters* (*ADCs*), since many use the internal power supply as a reference. In other words, the output voltage of a sensor is sampled as a percentage of the voltage supply of the ADC. If the supply is not a known voltage, then any sampling performed by the ADC is meaningless. (We'll look at ADCs and sampling in Chapter 13.) Therefore, we need a voltage regulator to provide a constant voltage source, and thereby a constant voltage reference. Further, a voltage regulator can assist in removing power-supply noise and can provide a degree of protection and isolation for the embedded system from the external power supply. If your system is operating from a battery, the varying current draw of your computer can combine with the battery's internal resistance to create a varying supply voltage. The addition of a voltage regulator prevents this from becoming a problem since it provides a constant output. Including a voltage regulator in your design is good practice.

National Semiconductor has a good online tutorial on using and designing voltage-regulator circuits based on their chips. It can be found at *http://www.national.com/appinfo/power/webench*.

The types of regulators we will look at are termed *DC-DC converters*. They take an unregulated DC voltage (often over a range of possible voltages) and provide a constant DC voltage output of a fixed value.

There are three types of DC-DC converters: *linear regulators*, which produce lower voltages than the supply voltage; *switching regulators* that can *step up* (*boost*), *step down* (*buck*), or invert the input voltage; and *charge pumps*, which can also step up, step down, or invert the supply voltage, but with limited current-drive capability. (Note that not all charge pumps provide regulated voltage.)

The conversion process of any regulator is not 100% efficient. The regulator itself uses current (known as *quiescent current*), and this is sourced from the input supply. The greater the quiescent current, the more power (and therefore heat) the regulator must dissipate. In choosing a regulator, select one that can supply the appropriate output voltage and the required current needed by your embedded system, yet has the lowest quiescent current.

Linear regulators are small, cheap, low-noise, and very easy to use. The basic circuit for a linear regulator is shown in Figure 5-2. The inputs and outputs are filtered using decoupling capacitors, but beyond that, no other external components are needed.

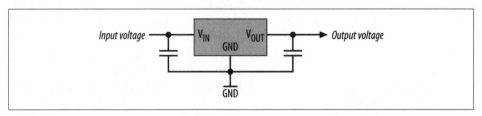

Figure 5-2. Example of a linear regulator circuit

As well as helping to smooth the voltages, the capacitors also help remove momentary glitches in the power source known as *brownouts*. These momentary drops in power are infrequent, but when they occur, they can severely corrupt a computer's operation.

Many microprocessors include brownout detectors that will restart the processor if a brownout gets through to the processor's power inputs.

Switching regulators get their name because they switch a power transistor (MOS-FET) at their output. They tend to be more efficient than linear regulators in converting the input voltage to the output voltage. In other words, they waste less power during the conversion process. However, their drawback is that they require more external components (such as an inductor and diode) and therefore take up more space. They also typically cost more and generate far more noise than linear regulators. Unlike linear regulators, they can step up a voltage as well as stepping one down, and they can also invert. For example, a switching regulator can take a supply voltage of 3.6 V from a battery and provide you with a regulated 5 V supply for your embedded system. Alternatively, a switching regulator may take an unregulated 8 V supply and convert this to a regulated −12 V supply. Switching regulators are far more versatile than linear regulators. However, they do require careful design and board layout, so pay careful attention to the directions of the particular component manufacturer. As always, read the datasheets carefully.

Charge pumps, like switching regulators, can step up, step down, or invert voltages. Unlike switching regulators, they require no external inductor. However, due to their limited capacity to supply current, they are not commonly used. The MAX3222 (and similar devices), discussed in Chapter 9, use internal charge pumps to generate the +12 V and −12 V required for RS-232C level shifting.

LM78xx Regulators

There are literally thousands of voltage regulators available. Probably the most commonly used are the LM78xx linear regulator series made by several manufacturers such as Fairchild (*http://www.fairchildsemi.com*), Semelab (*http://www.semelab.co.uk*), and ST Microelectronics (*http://www.st.com*). They typically come in a TO-220 package (Figure 5-3) and have a metallic attachment point for a heatsink, such as the one shown in Figure 5-4. The regulator is normally mounted flat against the circuit board, and the pins are bent 90 degrees downward.

The part number designates the output voltage. For example, an LM7805 provides a 5 V regulated output, while an LM7812 gives a regulated 12 V output. They can provide an output current of up to 1 Amp (and as much as 2.2 Amps peak), with a quiescent current of between 5 mA and 8 mA. They also feature overload and short-circuit protection. Table 5-1 lists the regulators, their input voltage ranges and their output voltages.

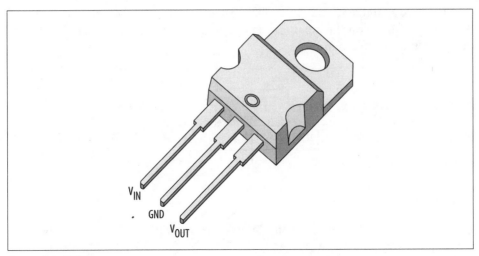

Figure 5-3. LM78xx

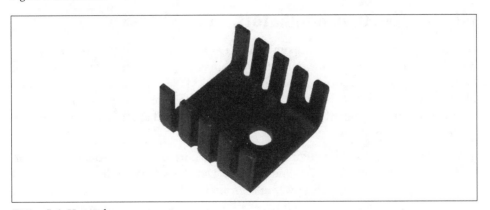

Figure 5-4. Heatsink

Table 5-1. LM78xx voltage regulators

Part	Output (V)	Input range (V)
LM7805	5	7–25
LM7806	6	8–25
LM7808	8	10.5–25
LM7809	9	11.5–25
LM7810	10	12.5–25
LM7812	12	14.5–30
LM7815	15	17.5–30
LM7818	18	21–33
LM7824	24	27–38

The LM78xx is simple to use. Decoupling capacitors (nominally between 10 uF and 47 uF) are required on the input (pin 1) and output (pin 3), as shown in Figure 5-5. Pin 2 is connected to ground.

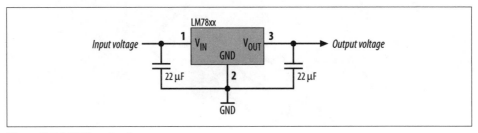

Figure 5-5. LM78xx circuit

For negative output voltages, use an LM79xx regulator. It's used in exactly the same way as an LM78xx.

MAX603/MAX604 Regulators

A good small regulator is the Maxim MAX603 (5 V output) or MAX604 (3.3 V output). I tend to use these as the default "workhorse" regulators for many of my small designs. They use far less quiescent current than LM78xx regulators and as such are ideal for low-power or battery-operated systems. They are available in tiny surface-mount SO-8 or in standard DIP packages (discussed in Chapter 6) and require only two external components.

The MAX603/604 can provide up to 500 mA of current and can operate from an input voltage of between +2.7 V and +11.5 V DC. They have built-in protection in case you inadvertently switch power and ground and consume as little as 15 µA of current for their own use. As such, they are ideal for use in low-power, embedded computers. The schematic for using a voltage regulator such as a MAX603 or a MAX604 is shown in Figure 5-6. In this case, the input supply is a battery, but it could just as easily be a DC plug pack or some other sort of supply.

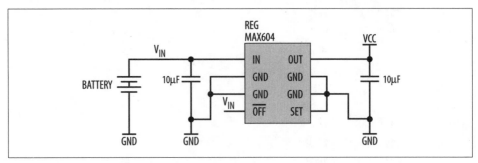

Figure 5-6. MAX603/MAX604 circuit

A capacitor is required at the output (pin 8 of the regulator) to filter the voltage. This capacitor forms part of the regulation circuit and is required. The device will not work without it. The second support component required is a capacitor on the input (pin 1). This stabilizes the input voltage and can provide an additional current source during peak loads. These capacitors are known as *decoupling capacitors* and are discussed in detail later in this chapter.

 Every component should have a decoupling capacitor for every power-supply pin. This is important. Leaving them off is a good way to ensure that your computer will be unreliable.

The ground pins (2, 3, 5, 6, and 7) should all be connected to ground, as they act as a small heatsink for the device. When laying out the PCB, place a ground fill under the regulator and connect these five pins directly to it. Pin 4 ($\overline{\text{OFF}}$) places the regulator in shutdown mode. For constant operation, this pin is connected directly to the power source, such that the device is always on. If you're using this regulator to power a subsystem within your embedded computer, you can use $\overline{\text{OFF}}$ to act as a software-controlled power switch by connecting it to an I/O line of the processor.

A MAX604 gives a regulated 3.3 V output. For a 5 V output, replace the MAX604 with a MAX603. The circuit is otherwise the same.

MAX1615 Regulator

The MAX1615 is a linear regulator that can operate from a supply range between 4 V and 28 V. It is tiny and is capable of supplying 30 mA of output current at either 3.3 V or 5 V. 30 mA is not much current, but for very small (battery-powered) applications, it may be sufficient. The MAX1615 has a shutdown input, allowing an external system to power it down. One use for this regulator could be as a power source to subsystems within an embedded computer, allowing the host processor to turn them off when not in use. Before turning off a subsystem, ensure that its "absence" won't adversely affect the functionality of the rest of the system.

The basic schematic for a MAX1615 circuit is shown in Figure 5-7.

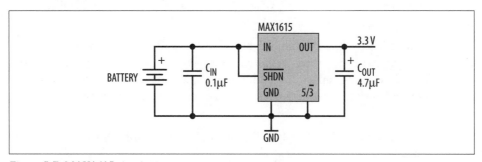

Figure 5-7. MAX1615 circuit

The **5/3** pin determines the output voltage. By tying it to ground, the output is set to 3.3 V. Connect the pin to the input, and the output voltage is set to 5 V. For continuous operation, tie the shutdown pin (**SHDN**) to the input voltage. To allow the regulator to be powered down, connect **SHDN** to a processor I/O line or a simple power switch. (It goes without saying that if you're driving **SHDN** with an I/O line of the processor, then that processor must have a power source other than this regulator! Otherwise, it could lead to some interesting situations.)

MAX724 Regulator

For higher-current situations, the MAX724 can supply up to 5 A from an input supply voltage between 8 V and 40 V. Its output is adjustable from 2.5 V to 35 V, and its quiescent current is 8.5 mA. It comes in a 5-pin TO-220 package, with an attachment point for an external heatsink. The basic circuit for a MAX724 is shown in Figure 5-8. Note that it is a step-down regulator only.

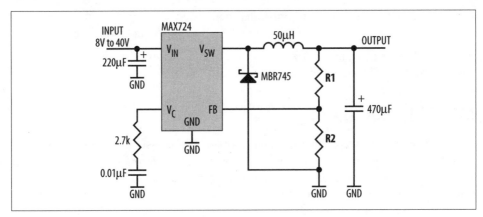

Figure 5-8. MAX724 circuit

The inductor is nominally 50 uH, but can be any value in the range of 5 uH to 200 uH. When the output pin V_{SW} turns off, the diode provides a path to ground for the inductor current. The inductor chosen should have a high saturation current. If it doesn't, the effects will be disastrous. The Maxim datasheet provides detailed information on selecting an appropriate inductor.

It is recommended by Maxim that a Schottky diode, such as an MBR745, be used due to the fast switching times required. Both the regulator's input and output require large decoupling capacitors to filter out ripple. The capacitors must have low *ESR* (*Equivalent Series Resistance*) over the expected temperature range and operating lifetime.

The output voltage is set by resistors R1 and R2. The equation for calculating the output voltage is:

```
VOUT = 2.21 * (R1 + R2) / R2
```

R2 should be less than 4 kΩ. Maxim recommends choosing 2.21 kΩ for R2, as it simplifies the above equation:

```
VOUT = (R1 + 2.21k) / 1000
```

So, the equation to calculate R1 becomes:

```
R1 = 1000 * VOUT - 2.21k
```

The regulators I've covered so far should be useful in most situations. If you're designing a machine with special requirements, there is bound to be a regulator that will suit your needs. Just spend some time browsing component manufacturers' web sites and see what is offered.

Electrical Noise and Interference

Digital systems are inherently analog in operation. Digital signals suffer degradation and noise due to analog effects present in the system. Spurious noise or reflections from nearby electrical machinery or radio transmissions can induce signals within your circuit that can cause false events to occur, or even prevent a digital system from functioning at all. The one way to ensure that your system is immune to electromagnetic interference is to avoid the use of electricity! Unfortunately, the steam-powered microprocessor is not a reality, so if your system is to operate reliably in the real world, you must take electromagnetic effects into account. What follows is not a comprehensive overview of noise and associated problems and solutions, which is far too complex a field to cover properly here. What I will do is provide an introduction. It is worth seeking out information that is more detailed to understand these concepts more thoroughly.

The United States, Australia, the European Union, and many other countries have very strict guidelines and requirements for electromagnetic emission and immunity. The recommendations presented here are good practice only and are not necessarily sufficient to warrant compliance in your country. Therefore, it is important that you check your local regulations and ensure that you meet the appropriate requirements. Compliance cannot be guaranteed just by design. A system must be tested to ensure that it is compliant.

Noise can be a significant problem in digital systems. Noise can disturb signal transmission, leading to corrupted data, or may even cause a program to crash. Problems with an embedded system may or may not be noise-related. Similar problems can also be caused by inadequate power-supply levels, insufficient decoupling capacitors, marginal timing tolerances, and software bugs. However, even a well-conceived system can be disrupted by noise. There may be noise problems inherent in the design. Switching noise from integrated circuits, ringing, and crosstalk (discussed shortly) are all due to aspects of the designed system. Other forms of noise may be due to environmental effects (such as nearby motors or radio emissions). The bad news is that electromagnetic problems are getting worse for digital systems. The environment is bathed in ever-increasing emissions from radio, TV, and cell-phone towers. At the same time, integrated circuits are becoming increasingly sensitive, as designs move towards higher-speed and lower-power operation.

These sources of noise may not be present during the design and test phase of the system but will only manifest themselves once the system is out "in the field" and in service. A crashed embedded system may be due to a hardware problem, a software problem, or the fact that the factory a block away turned on a compressor, which caused a spike on the power supply. Field problems created by noise may only occur very occasionally and can often be very difficult to track down. It is not unusual for some problems to occur only once every few days. Any problem is not satisfactory and must be fixed, but identifying the cause is not always easy. It is better to design the system from the beginning to be as immune to these problems as possible. You have to consider not just what emissions your system may produce, but also how it may be susceptible to external effects. This will not guarantee your system will be problem-free, but every bit of immunity helps.

Electromagnetic interference (EMI) is noise generated by sources external to the embedded system. Some examples of EMI are motors, switches in power consumption, fluorescent lighting, RF emissions, and electrostatic discharges. All can be significant sources of noise. For example, turning on or off a machine with an electric motor can cause a 1000 V spike on the AC power-supply line. An *electrostatic discharge (ESD)* can send a spike of 35 kV from a finger into an integrated circuit with a current rise time of 4 Amps per second! This can be enough to permanently damage a sensitive chip. Cars are particularly noisy environments. The 12 V supply line to the automotive electronics may be reversed, driven at voltages ranging from 6 V to as much as 24 V, and have ± 400 V transient spikes. All of these can have very adverse effects on the operation of an embedded system.

In any circuit, there is a wire carrying current in and a wire carrying current out. Current flowing through a wire generates a magnetic field around that wire. Such a magnetic field can be a source of EMI. The intensity of the magnetic field felt is inversely proportional to the distance from the source of the field, and the orientation of the field relates directly to the direction of current flow in the wire.

Minimize the Current Loop Area

Current flows through a system via the power and signal connections and back to the power supply (thereby completing the *circuit*) through ground. Ground thus forms the *return path* for current flowing within the system. If the signal wire and return wire are located close together, the magnetic fields generated by the currents in the wires cancel out within a short distance of the wires. The objective is to keep all signal and return paths as close together and as short as possible. This is known as *minimizing the current-loop area*. Where there are many current loops present in a system (as is common in many large, high-speed, digital systems), a *ground plane* is used to minimize loop area. A ground plane is a large conducting surface that can serve as the current return path for all loops in the circuit. A ground plane is often implemented as a complete, internal PCB layer.

Capacitive coupling is the coupling of electric fields. A signal on one wire, through its associated electric field, can capacitively induce a phantom "signal" in an adjacent signal line. This is known as *crosstalk* in digital systems. If not designed correctly, the magnitude of the crosstalk in a system can be significant and can easily cause a crash.

Capacitive coupling may be reduced by shielding the signal lines with an *electrostatic* or *Faraday shield*. This shield is a metal conductor placed between the capacitively coupled elements. The shield is simply part of the PCB (discussed in Chapter 6), formed in the same way as the circuit tracks, and is usually grounded (though not always). The shield may be a simple ground plane under an integrated circuit to protect it from signal lines on the underside of the circuit board. Signal lines may be shielded from each other (if necessary) by placing a ground line between them.

Keep the Power Smooth

The principle of keeping current loops small applies as much to power lines within a system as it does to signal lines. However, keeping the loop area small for power is difficult. Power must be distributed throughout the circuit, and to effectively route this throughout a PCB, and keep the loop area small, is very difficult. The power lines can therefore be susceptible to noise, and this can cause major problems to the circuit.

The solution is to provide a path to ground for any noise present in the power supply. This should be done locally for each component in the circuit. It is achieved by adding a *decoupling capacitor* between power and ground for each integrated circuit. The capacitor decouples the noise from the power source and provides a path to ground for it. In this way, noise is removed from the power supply, and the chips have a constant and clean voltage source. The decoupling capacitors should be placed as close as possible to the power pins of the devices. Surface-mount capacitors have very low inductance connections, and so are preferable. Ceramic capacitors are normally used for decoupling capacitors due to their low resistance.

The capacitor has the added advantage of acting as a current source for the device when the device must switch its outputs or internal state. As such, it represents a current source with a much smaller loop area. Generally, the circuit board will be decoupled by a large (22–100 uF, say) electrolytic or tantalum capacitor placed near the power input, and each integrated circuit will be separately decoupled by 10 nF ceramic capacitors. Multiple decoupling capacitors, one for each power pin, improve the situation. You need to ensure that all frequencies that may affect the circuit have a low impedance path to ground. To this end, several capacitors (100 nF, 10 nF, and 100 pF) can be used to decouple a wide range of frequencies and thereby remove noise from the power-supply circuits. You can never have enough decoupling capacitors (within reason). Additionally, an onboard voltage regulator can provide a degree of isolation between your circuit and the external power supply.

The Importance of Decoupling Capacitors

Many years ago, when I used to teach embedded-system design at a university, I had a final-year student undertaking a project in which she had to design and build a 64-bit embedded computer engine using the now long-vanished Motorola 88110 MIMD processor. The machine mysteriously failed to go, even though she'd verified the design and its construction. The fault was that she had neglected decoupling capacitors in the design. When the fault was pointed out and corrected, the machine roared to life. Those simple capacitors were the difference between a working 64-bit computer and a system that never managed to climb out of reset.

Noise can also be present in ground lines. Ground is not always at the same potential in all locations. There can be a voltage difference between the local grounds in different parts of a circuit that are both connected to "ground." In some instances, this voltage difference can drive currents of several Amps through the ground line. This is referred to as a *ground loop*, and can result in serious problems. Shielding, decoupling, and minimizing the current-loop area can help protect against ground noise.

Ground bounce is ringing (oscillation) on signal lines caused when one or more outputs on the same device are being switched from high to low. This ringing can be of significant amplitude and can adversely affect the system. Some devices are designed so that ground-bounce effects are minimized. Using devices in packages with shorter leads (such as PLCC and surface-mount) can reduce ringing effects. Devices with ground and power pins toward the center of the package have shorter lead lengths, and this also helps to reduce ringing effects. Termination techniques can also help to reduce ground bounce.

Another effect you are likely to encounter is caused by the simultaneous switching of several outputs at once. Like ground bounce, it is due to parasitic effects relating to packaging and internal wiring of the chips. When several outputs switch at once, these effects can cause a delay of several nanoseconds in the changing output signals. Component datasheets usually specify timing parameters for a single changing output. You need to consider the effect that several changing outputs may have on your circuit.

How to Destroy a Computer Without Really Trying

Walk across a carpet on a dry day, or rub a cat against some plastic, and a static charge will build up. If you or the cat then touches something metallic, the jolt you both feel is an *electrostatic discharge (ESD)*. An ESD can destroy an integrated circuit permanently. The ESD may be too small to be felt, but it can still send a semiconductor to that great beach in the sky.

Many integrated circuits have internal protection against ESD. Semiconductor manufacturers, such as Maxim, are now building protection into their devices that can withstand ESDs of 15 kV or more. This protection is sufficient to safeguard the device against the charge build-up that can occur during normal handling. It is not, however, sufficient to protect the device against the huge electrostatic sparks that can sometimes occur. Once a device is in-circuit, it should not be considered safe. It is possible for a processor to be destroyed by a spark received when a typist puts fingers on a keyboard. The spark, like a lightning strike, will attempt to find a path to ground, even if that means traveling down a data line and through the processor to get there.

One solution is to include a buffer chip to isolate the important components in the system from those that may come in contact with an ESD. This is not an ideal solution. It simply means that the buffer will be destroyed instead of the processor. You still have a system that has failed.

Transient suppressors are available that can provide protection. Such suppressors act as an open circuit at normal voltage levels, but conduct power to ground at higher voltages. At no time should a signal ground be used to earth an ESD. Most integrated circuits don't respond very well to having their ground pins raised to several hundred volts above their power supply by an ESD!

When handling chips, it's a good idea to use a *grounding mat*. This is a conductive sheet that you connect to the ground of a handy power supply. You then wear a *grounding strap* around your arm, connecting you to the grounding mat. Thus, any electrostatic charge is dissipated and never gets the chance to build up.

 If you're using a grounding mat, don't forget to take your embedded system off it before powering up. The grounding mat is conductive, and powering up a system while it is in contact with the mat can be disastrous!

In the next chapter, we'll investigate the process of designing and building a physical computer. We'll look at how you need to consider the electrical environment in which your system will be operating, and then we'll go on to see how you lay out a printed-circuit board.

CHAPTER 6

Building Hardware

Hardware: the part of a computer that you can kick.
—Anon.

Before we get into the designs later in this book, let's spend some time looking at how you would produce the physical machine. Building a computer that doesn't work is really easy. You may have a perfect design and flawless code, but ignore the physical environment in which the machine will exist, and you'll have built yourself a very intricate paperweight. In this chapter, I'll also show you how to lay out a circuit board (and what to be careful of) and how you debug your hardware. We will look at how you physically produce a computer by laying out the design for the ATtiny15 computer, presented in Chapter 15. I'll assume that you're hand-building in small quantities and target the discussion accordingly. What I present here is not the state of the art in circuit board design or assembly, but guidelines for "cottage-industry" computer production. If you need to make production runs of hundreds of thousands, either you already know what you're doing (and can skip this section) or you need to talk to a professional.

Tools

To design and build an embedded computer, you have to start with the right tools. The first thing you will need to design a computer is another computer. It's a chicken-and-egg problem. You will need software tools to create the design (schematic and circuit board layout), and you will need software tools not only to write your code, but also to download it into your embedded target machine.

Development Kits

When you're developing your embedded system, it's best to start with a *development kit* from the processor's manufacturer (Figure 6-1).

Figure 6-1. Microprocessor development system

A good development kit will not only provide you with a working example of the machine you're trying to build (and upon which you can test your code), it should also include a nice *Integrated Development Environment (IDE)*. The IDE will have a windowing editor, a debugger, a simulator too if you're lucky, an assembler, and hopefully a C compiler as well. The kit should also come with cables and tools for downloading code to the processor and circuit schematics so you can see what a working machine should look like. However, treat the schematics with a small degree of caution. Some (but not all) semiconductor manufacturers farm out the design of their development systems to small, external companies. Some of these companies do a fantastic job, while others seem to employ stray chimpanzees as design engineers. In the latter case, the development system will work, but only through a miracle and by the grace of the digital gods. So, treat the schematics as a rough guide only. They are not always the best example of how a system should be designed.

To use the IDE, you will need a desktop computer, and here lies the bad news. Almost without exception, the IDEs will run on only one platform and under only one operating system. No prizes for guessing which one. So, if your preferred environment is a Unix workstation, generally you're out of luck. While the gnu tools are great, they don't support a lot of the smaller processors, and sometimes you just have to resort to the chip maker's IDE to download code into your target computer.

Development kit prices range from free (if you're at the right place at the right time) to many tens of thousands of dollars for some of the really high-end and exotic processors. For most embedded-type processors, you can expect to pay somewhere between $50 and $300, depending on the chip, the manufacturer, and their current whim. For the time they will save you, it's probably worth investing in one.

Measurement Tools

For the systems described in this book, the minimum debugging tools you will need are a *multimeter* (Figure 6-2) and an *oscilloscope*.

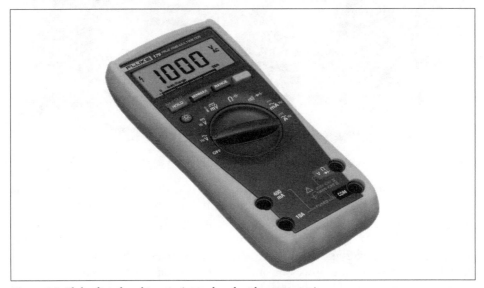

Figure 6-2. Fluke digital multimeter (reproduced with permission)

A multimeter allows you to measure current and voltage, but, more importantly, it also allows you to do a continuity test between two points (and verify that there is a physical, and therefore electrical, connection). However, do *not* do continuity tests if there are sensitive components in your system. The continuity test may cause them damage.

 Don't assume that just because a signal is present at one end of a trace that it is present at all points along the trace. *Check everywhere* with an oscilloscope probe, and use your multimeter to confirm that signal paths are connected properly.

An oscilloscope (Figure 6-3) allows you to view waveforms within your system, and, as such, it is your principle debugging tool. Oscilloscopes range from the crude and ancient to the expensive and sophisticated. While you don't need to spend $100k on an oscilloscope, you will need one that can accurately view waveforms. That rules out the $20 antique you picked up from Mr. Gorsky's garage sale down the road.

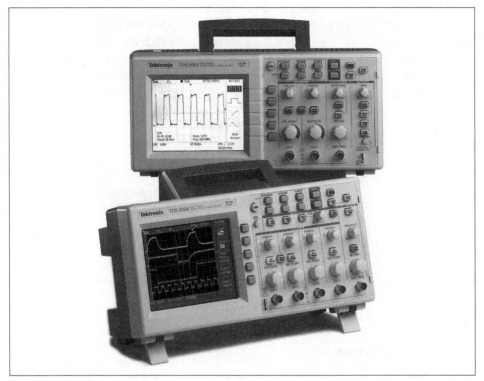

Figure 6-3. Tektronix oscilloscopes

You will need an oscilloscope of sufficient bandwidth to view the signals within your computer. There's no point using a 20 MHz oscilloscope to look at a 100 MHz system clock. The oscilloscope simply won't see it, and therefore neither will you. The higher the bandwidth, the more you will see. While you may think that the signals of a 4 MHz embedded processor might not require a 100 MHz oscilloscope, that oscilloscope will allow you to see the rising edges of the waveforms as rising edges (and not just vertical transitions) and view miniscule timing differences that may be having an adverse effect. It will also allow you to see fine spikes of noise or ringing on your signal lines, which may be adversely affecting your machine.

I really like the (relatively) low-cost Tektronix oscilloscopes for debugging embedded systems. HP and others also make nice units. If you're serious about developing embedded hardware, it's worth investing in one. Keep an eye out for startup companies going under—you may be able to pick up some great test gear going cheap!

When using an oscilloscope, it is critical that you connect the ground clip of the probe to a ground connection close to (or better, *on*) your embedded system. Without this, your measurement of the signal will be affected by ground loop problems, and you will not get an accurate reading. You'll spend ages chasing phantoms, all the while missing the real problem.

Logic analyzers (Figure 6-4) are very expensive tools that allow you to monitor and diagnose a multitude of digital signals simultaneously. They are essential for developing high-speed and complex systems (especially those with buses), but you should be able to get by without them for the simpler designs in this book. Certainly, for a completely self-contained microcontroller, a logic analyzer is of no use at all.

Figure 6-4. Tektronix logic analyzers

In-Circuit Emulators

Another development tool is the *In-Circuit Emulator* (ICE). This is a small module with the same footprint as the processor, which is placed into the target system under development. Under the control of software executing on a PC and emulating the embedded processor, the ICE behaves just as the processor would in-circuit. This allows you to interactively debug your hardware and software. This can be especially useful in systems based on self-contained microcontrollers, where it would be otherwise difficult (impossible) to get to the system internals.

Some ICEs are better than others, and, as with everything, you get what you pay for. For really sophisticated tools that closely match the timing and electrical characteristics of the processor, expect to pay big bucks. Cheaper systems will emulate the processor's operation but will do so with completely different signal timings. Also, for each processor type around which you develop systems, you'll need a different ICE.

Some engineers use ICEs heavily during their embedded system's development process. Call me a heretic, but I get by quite well without them. The catch with an ICE is that no matter how good a particular tool is, it is never going to be *exactly* like the real thing. There will always be some slight difference in the electrical characteristics or in the timing. The engineers at Boeing have a saying: "Test what you fly; fly what you test." In other words, there's no substitute for the real thing.

Construction Tools

Finally, you'll need a good soldering iron, some side-cutters, a pair of pliers, and other construction tools. Don't use the same pliers you use to build your fence; get some high-quality pliers with very fine jaws. I have six pairs of pliers, all suited to very fine work, and each is slightly different. I also have a set of jeweler's tools, useful for very fine and delicate assembly work. If you can afford it, a quality binocular microscope is very useful not only for construction, but also for verification of the final assembled circuit. Figure 6-5 shows just a sampling of some of the tools I regularly use during construction.

Figure 6-5. Construction tools

Soldering

Soldering is very easy to do well, and very easy to do badly. The basic skills are simple to learn. Becoming a wizard with the soldering iron is not hard to achieve.

Safety First

The most important thing to note about solder is that it contains lead. Therefore, all soldering should be done in a well-ventilated work area, and avoid breathing the fumes! After soldering, wash your hands, especially before eating!

Solder can splatter, so always wear protective eyewear and clothes.

Solder is a metal alloy with a relatively low melting point. It is used to bond components to circuit boards and forms a conductive join. Solder is available as either *strand solder* (like a spool of wire) or *solder paste* (out of a syringe). There are two basic categories of soldering tool: the standard *soldering iron* and the *rework station*. Weller (*http://www.cooperhandtools.com/brands/weller*) and Hakko (*http://www.hakko.com*) both make excellent soldering tools. Weller has kindly supplied photographs of some of its products so you may see examples of each type of tool.

A soldering iron (Figure 6-6) is used with strand solder to mount through-hole components. Note the sponge used for cleaning the iron's tip. The sponge should be kept *very* wet at all times, and the iron's tip should be wiped regularly. (Don't squeeze out the sponge as you would a dishcloth. It needs to be really wet, although not drenched.)

Figure 6-6. Weller WES51 soldering iron (reproduced with permission)

There are many different tips available, depending on the type of work you are doing and the temperature at which you want to solder. When the iron is cold, it is a simple matter to unscrew the tip and replace it with another. Tips eventually wear out and need replacing. Spare parts are readily available from most electronics suppliers.

 Never remove the iron's tip when the iron is on. The tip contains a sensor that controls the heating element. Removing the tip will cause the iron to overheat and may damage the unit.

Also never leave a soldering iron turned on for extended periods when it is not in use. Doing so will reduce the life of the tool.

Always ensure that the iron's tip has a fine coating of solder, as this prevents oxidization and prolongs the life of the tip. As you work with the tip, it will become discolored. Simply feed some strand solder onto it when it is hot and wipe this excess off on the sponge. This will ensure that your iron's tip is kept in good condition. A well-cared-for tip will allow you to solder successfully. A poorly maintained tip will make the job of soldering very difficult indeed.

Rework stations (Figure 6-7) blow heated air through a small nozzle and are primarily used with surface-mount components and solder paste. However, it is relatively straightforward to solder some surface-mount components using a standard soldering iron. You don't necessarily need the more expensive rework stations, although they do make a lot of surface-mount work easier. Regardless of whether you invest in a rework station, you will always need a conventional soldering iron. There are many components (such as through-hole connectors) that require a standard iron.

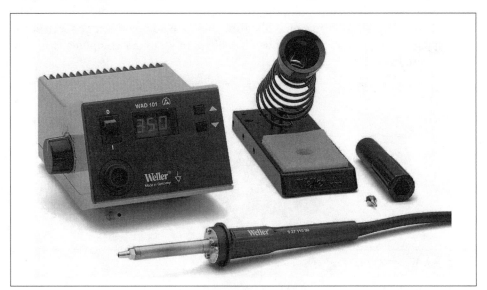

Figure 6-7. Simple Weller WAD101 rework station (reproduced with permission)

Integrated stations that combine both standard soldering tools and hot-air guns are also available. Figure 6-8 shows a Weller WRS3000ST unit.

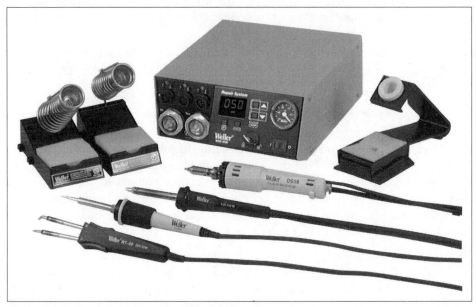

Figure 6-8. Weller WRS3000ST (reproduced with permission)

For working on ball-grid array (BGA) packaged chips, you'll need access to a rework station like the Weller WQB 3000 (Figure 6-9). These allow you to accurately place components and successfully bond the many hundreds of solder balls (pads) under a BGA. If you can't afford a machine like this, there are companies that specialize in assembling electronic systems. They will be able to mount your components to your circuit board for a price.

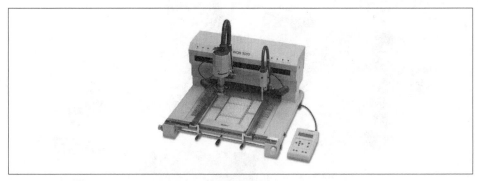

Figure 6-9. Weller WQB 3000 (reproduced with permission)

Solder fumes are toxic, and prolonged exposure to them is bad for your health. When soldering, ensure that your work area is well ventilated. It may also be worth investing in a fume extractor, such as that shown in Figure 6-10.

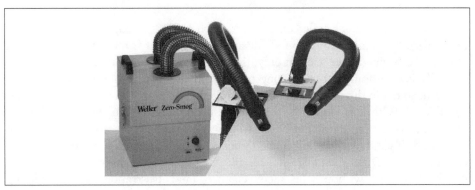

Figure 6-10. Weller fume extractor (reproduced with permission)

How to Solder

The key to soldering well is to control the heat and the amount of solder that flows onto component pins. Too much heat can damage a component (especially sensitive integrated circuits) and can overheat the solder as well. Read the datasheets to determine the maximum temperature (and duration) that the components can take and ensure that your soldering does not exceed this. Variable-temperature irons allow you to set the temperature, thereby avoiding overheating. The tip of your soldering iron should be thin, allowing you to do fine work. An old-style iron with a large, bulky tip (intended for electrical work) is not appropriate for soldering electronics.

 Whenever you solder your PCB, make sure it is not powered! The tip of a soldering iron is grounded, and touching this to a pad with volts on it is *not* a good idea!

Similarly, when inserting or removing socketed components, ensure that the system is powered down. Most semiconductors do not appreciate being plugged into a live system.

There should be enough solder to make a good contact, but not so much that it bulges up or, worse, shorts a neighboring pin (Figure 6-11).

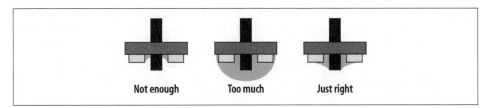

Figure 6-11. Component pins soldered to a PCB

During the Apollo/Saturn missions, NASA found that teaching its technicians the correct way to solder saved several hundred pounds in takeoff weight.

When soldering through-hole components (such as DIP-packaged chips or connectors), place the component into its hole and ensure that it is mounted correctly and sits flat. To begin, solder one pin only, then check that the component is still seated correctly before doing the remaining pins. With the iron in one hand and a thin strand of solder in the other, bring the two together such that they meet at the pin to be soldered. Within a second, the solder will flow around the pin and you will have a good join. As soon as the solder begins to flow, remove both the iron tip and the solder strand. If you are using DIP chips, rather than soldering the chip directly into the circuit, solder a DIP socket instead. This allows you to easily remove/replace the chip if you have to, without the inconvenience (and frustration) of desoldering. Figure 6-12 shows a machined socket (left) and a "dual-wipe" socket (right). Machined sockets, while they cost more, are more reliable and will last longer.

Figure 6-12. Chip sockets

Common mistakes when soldering are to heat the component pin for several seconds before applying solder (causing the component to become too hot) or to apply the solder directly to the iron and then dab the molten solder onto the pin.

Soldering surface-mount components requires a different procedure. If you're using a rework station, you will need to use solder paste. This is sold in a large syringe. Solder paste dries out easily inside the syringe, so ensure that you seal the end when it is not in use. Before soldering a surface-mount chip, place a thin squirt of solder paste along each row of pads on the PCB. If there is too much paste, it can flow under the chip and create a short, so keep the application light. You can always add a small quantity later. Place the chip onto its PCB pads and ensure that it is lined up correctly; then use the rework station to apply heated air (Figure 6-13). Too much airflow will either shift the chip off its correct orientation or, worse, blow solder paste underneath. Since solder paste is electrically conductive, this is not a good thing. Too little heat will result in poorly soldered joints, whereas too much heat can easily overheat and damage the chip. It is something of an art to get it just right, so it's best to do considerable practice before tackling the real thing.

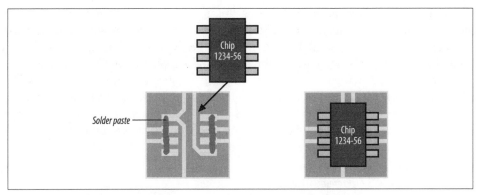

Figure 6-13. Soldering surface-mount components using a rework station

Surface-mount chips can also be soldered using a standard iron, although it's not recommended for really finely spaced chip pins. Unlike the technique with the rework station, solder paste is applied after the chip is in place. To begin, before putting the chip on the PCB, use the iron and either strand solder or solder paste to place a small dab of solder directly onto one of the pads where the chip is to be mounted. Place the chip in position, aligning it carefully, and then use the iron to heat the pin resting on the solder dab. The dab will melt and fix the chip in place. Check the alignment again to ensure that the chip did not shift. If it did, reheat the pin again, and carefully shift the chip as appropriate. Once you are happy with the alignment, place a thin squirt of solder paste down each row of pins, as far from the edge of the chip as possible. Too much paste will flow between the pins, creating shorts, so keep it light. Gently and quickly run the tip of the soldering iron down each row of pins. The solder paste will melt and flow as you go, bonding the chip to the PCB (Figure 6-14).

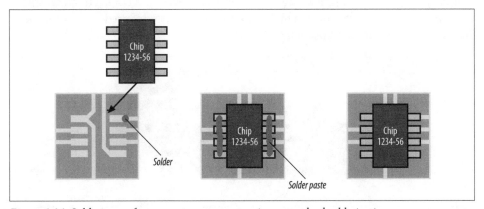

Figure 6-14. Soldering surface-mount components using a standard soldering iron

Solder is a metal alloy and incorporates a flux to assist flow. When heating the solder, it is common for the flux to separate and flow out onto the surrounding PCB, leaving a thin brown residue. Excess flux can be removed using special solvents, available from most electronics hobby stores and suppliers. Flux removers can be nasty stuff, so keep them away from skin and plastics and use them in a well-ventilated work area. Flux residue is removed for cosmetic reasons only, making your circuit boards look more professional for your customers. However, as it is for appearances only, and since flux solvents are not good for either you or the environment, if you can avoid using them, please do so.

A Note on Pronunciation:

If you are a resident of North America, solder is pronounced "sodder." If you live anywhere else in the English-speaking world, you will pronounce it as "sol-der." So Americans, be advised that if you say the word as "sodder" to non-Americans, they may not know what you're talking about. Instead, they may think you're confessing to strange and unspeakable acts, rather than talking about bonding metals together.

So, with all that in mind, what are your options for construction? There are several ways of fabricating a computer (or any other circuit). Let's take a look at them.

Quick Construction

It is possible to build very simple circuits by just soldering the components together in free space. For example, the leads of a watch crystal can be soldered directly onto the pins of the processor, with the crystal lying across the top of the processor. Wires are soldered onto the pins bringing in ground and power, and connecting the processor's I/O to the outside world. This technique is variously referred to as a *rat's nest*, *bird's nest*, or *"what the hell is that?"* (Figure 6-15).

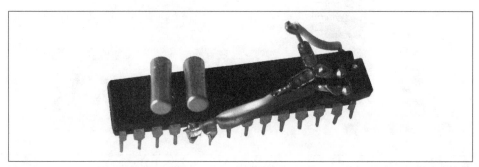

Figure 6-15. Rat's nest construction of a small microcontroller system

This is a quick-and-dirty method, useful for rapid prototyping of extremely simple circuits. It's not really recommended, but you can get away with it in a pinch. Don't try it with anything that is even slightly complicated or running at any reasonable speed. If you do, you'll spend more time debugging the construction than debugging the actual design or code!

Breadboarding

Breadboards are plastic blocks with arrays of electrically connected holes (Figure 6-16). They are designed to hold *DIP* (Dual Inline Package) integrated circuits and discrete components. The term "breadboard" dates back to the olden days when valve radios were constructed on a base of solid wood (a cutting board for bread). The term has stuck, and the modern breadboard can still be found in electronics hobbyist stores, and even the occasional university teaching lab.

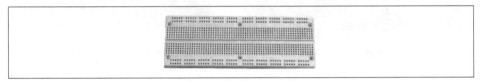

Figure 6-16. Breadboard

As a general rule, breadboards are *bad news*, and their use should be avoided at all costs. (Think of them as the hardware equivalent of COBOL.) They suffer from excessive capacitance, crosstalk, and noise susceptibility and, as such, are completely inappropriate for microprocessor system construction. It's hard enough trying to debug microprocessor hardware and software (together) without the additional complications that breadboards can add. Breadboards can also suffer from mechanical failure after extended use, leading to short circuits. Circuit interconnections on a breadboard are done with small sections of wire. These make great little antennas and will pick up every scrap of stray electromagnetic radiation, channeling it straight into your circuit! Microprocessors don't, as a rule, like "Classic Rock FM" modulated onto their data bus.

Using a breadboard is not the way to construct a robust and reliable system. If you really must, you could probably build the ATtiny15 or PIC12C805 computers (discussed in later chapters) on a breadboard, using their internal RC oscillators. But I'd advise against using breadboards for anything that uses a crystal or that has any fast-switching digital signals. While it is possible to build very low-speed microprocessor systems and general digital circuits on breadboards, *try not to*. There be dragons!

Wirewrapping

Once common as a construction technique, wirewrapping is now relatively rare. It is intended for use with DIP-packaged integrated circuits, mounted into sockets with long pins (0.6"). Figure 6-17 shows an embedded computer built as a student project using wirewrapping.

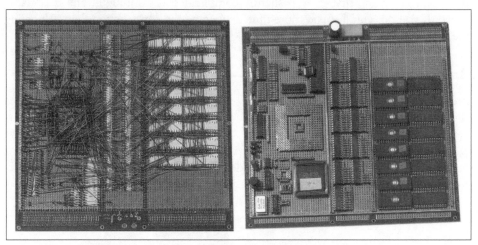

Figure 6-17. Bottom and top views of a wirewrapped embedded computer

Special tools, known as *wrapping tools*, allow you to quickly and efficiently wind thin wire around the pins. Figure 6-18 shows a low-cost, hand (manual) wrapping tool on the left and a wire stripper on the right. Automatic tools are also available.

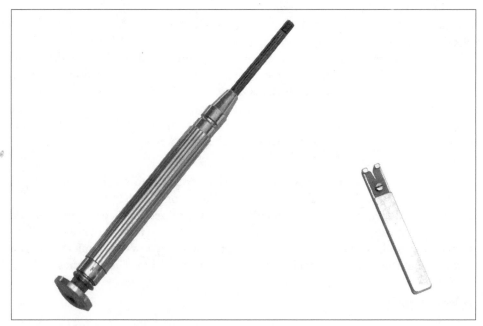

Figure 6-18. Wirewrapping tool and wire stripper

The wire stripper is used to remove the insulation from fine-gauge wire (Figure 6-19).

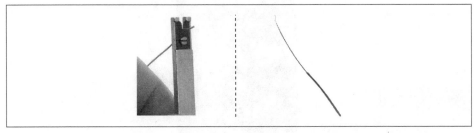

Figure 6-19. Stripping wire

The stripped wire is then inserted into the notch of the wrapping tool (Figure 6-20), and the tool is then placed over a socket's pin. The tool is rotated so that the wire is wound onto the pin.

Figure 6-20. Wirewrapping tool with wire inserted

The pins are square in cross-section, and wrapping a wire around a pin forms a *cold weld*—a tight electrical connection between wire and pin with no soldering (Figure 6-21). In this way, a circuit is constructed by individually wiring point-to-point each connection within the system.

Figure 6-21. Close-up of wirewrapped pins (image courtesy of Peter Paine)

Figure 6-22 is a photo of the underside of a wirewrapped computer (in this case, a LISP engine designed and built by Peter Paine). Note the square cross section of the pins and the tightly wound wires.

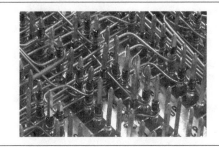

Figure 6-22. Close-up of a wirewrapped circuit (image courtesy of Peter Paine)

Wirewrapping is a very fast prototyping technique and is very robust and reliable. In the early days, NASA used wirewrapping for the construction of spacecraft avionics, and many mainframe computers were also built using the technique. Wirewrapping is good for prototyping (especially if you're unclear as to the final form of the design and expect to make lots of changes to the hardware) or for building one-off designs. If you intend to make more than one computer based on your design (and you probably will), then skip wirewrapping and do it on a printed-circuit board.

Printed-Circuit Boards

Printed-circuit boards (PCBs) are epoxy-bonded fiberglass sheets plated with copper. The copper plating is etched away, leaving tracks (traces) that form the interconnections of the circuit (Figure 6-23). PCBs are very reliable and are the only realistic option if you intend to produce more than one system. It is possible to etch your own PCBs, but commercial PCB production isn't that expensive, and it is worth the cost to get professionally produced boards.

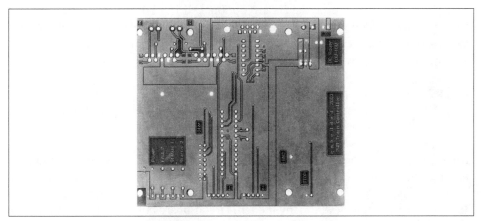

Figure 6-23. PCB for a PIC-based model train controller (Chapter 14)

EDA (*Electronic Design Automation*) software is used to create the schematic and PCB design. The most popular EDA software comes from Mentor Graphics (*http:// www.mentor.com*) and Protel (*http://www.protel.com*). There is also a gnu (*http:// www.gnu.org*) PCB editor, called *PCB*, which is freely available. Such programs normally come with several tools, allowing schematic entry, netlist generation (a list of what needs to be connected to what), PCB layout, manual routing (making the connections), and autorouting. There's a great temptation to use autorouters, as they simplify the process of generating the PCB by getting your workstation to do the hard work of routing. However, I prefer to lay out the circuit board myself. (I've seen some autorouters make a real mess of a design.) Routing the board manually can take a long while, but it is often worth the extra effort. It can also be very absorbing, much like spending hours in deep meditation. (It's very Zen.)

PCBs can be either single-sided (one layer), double-sided (two layers), or 4-layered, 6-layered, 8-layered, 12-layered, or more. The more layers you have, the easier it is to route your interconnections, but the costs of fabrication go up considerably with extra layers. Further, it's much easier to debug a 2-layered board than a 12-layered board. An advantage of using additional layers dedicated to power and ground planes is that your system will have greater noise immunity. While not so critical for slow 8-bit systems, they are mandatory for high-speed computers.

Multilayered boards will be *plated through*, meaning there will be metallic connections through the holes in the board, connecting traces of different layers together, as appropriate. A *solder mask* is the (normally) green coating on circuit boards, and it prevents solder from flowing between pads and tracks during construction. It is possible to order commercial PCBs without plating through and without solder mask, but the small amount you will save is not worth the hassle.

The *overlay layers* (also known as *silkscreen layers*) are painted on and contain labels (such as "R30" or "RAM4") used during construction and repair to show component placement. The overlay layers are optional. If the boards are to be manually populated with components by someone else, the overlay layers are helpful during construction. If you're building them yourself, then you can easily do without the overlays and save a few bucks.

 A useful trick if you're skipping the overlays is to place component information as text on the copper layers. Just be sure to avoid making contact with the circuit tracks!

The external copper layers are called *top* and *bottom* (no surprises there). Traditionally, the top layer was called the *component layer*, and the bottom layer was called the *solder layer*, since components used to be mounted on top and their pins soldered underneath. However, many modern circuit boards place surface-mount components on both sides and are soldered on both sides. Thus, the terms "component layer" and "solder layer" are seeing less use.

There are also internal copper layers for multilayer boards, *mechanical layers* (indicating any special physical features), the *keepout layer* (showing the actual PCB shape), and others. In four-layer boards, it is common practice to use the outer layers for signals and the internal layers for power and ground. This not only provides shielding, but also minimizes the current-loop area, thereby giving your design greater stability.

The five types of objects that can be placed on a copper layer are tracks, individual pads, components (arrays of pads grouped together), vias, and fills.

Tracks are used to interconnect components. Track width is expressed in thousandths of an inch ("mils") or in millimeters (mm). Tracks can be of varying thickness, and often a PCB will have different widths for different tracks. The fatter the track, the more current it can carry. The thinner the track, the easier it is to fit more tracks in a given space, and, therefore, the easier it is to route the PCB. As a general guide, Table 6-1 gives a list of the current-carrying capacity of different track widths for a temperature rise of +10°C.

Table 6-1. Track width versus current flow

Mils	mm	Amps
8	0.2	0.5
12	0.3	0.75
20	0.5	1.25

Table 6-1. Track width versus current flow (continued)

Mils	mm	Amps
50	1.25	2.5
100	2.5	4
200	5	7
325	8.12	10

Check with the company doing your PCB fabrication as to what tolerances it can manufacture. There's no point in doing a PCB with 4 mils tracks if your local PCB fab company can only etch as small as 8 mils.

Pads are used to mount component pins, and they can be round, rectangular, or oval. They consist of a hole and a copper surround. A pad for a component in a DIP, for example, will be a multilayered pad, meaning that the pad appears on all copper layers, and the hole is drilled through the entire PCB. A surface-mount component will have pads that appear on one layer only (Figure 6-24). An array of pads grouped together to form a component package is known as a *footprint*. Surface-mount components have holes of zero diameter (in other words, they aren't drilled). These components are small, with "gull-wing" pins that mount flat on the PCB. They are less susceptible to noise interference than the older DIP-style of packaging. However, DIP (through-hole) components may be easily mounted in sockets and are therefore easily removed during debugging. DIPs are sometimes preferable (although not always feasible) during early development, while surface-mount is the only option for production. Surface-mount components radiate less noise and are less susceptible to external interference. Conversely, DIPs have terrible noise-related characteristics.

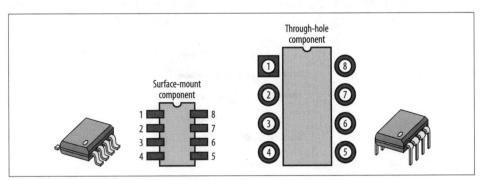

Figure 6-24. Footprints of surface-mount and through-hole (multilayer) components

Tracks entering a pad should "aim" directly for the pad center, as shown in Figure 6-25, and *not* as in Figure 6-26.

When specifying the pads for a component, ensure that the pad size is large enough to accommodate the pins and to allow enough space on which to solder. Also ensure that the holes (for through-hole components) are large enough to take the pins. A

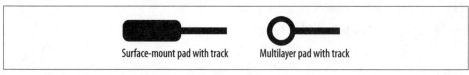

Surface-mount pad with track   Multilayer pad with track

Figure 6-25. Surface-mount and through-hole pads

Figure 6-26. The incorrect way for a track to enter a surface-mount pad

standard DIP pin will happily go into a 0.7 mm hole, while a DB connector requires 0.9 mm holes for the signal pins and 3 mm holes for the mounting pins.

Don't assume that the libraries of predefined components that came with your PCB CAD software have the pads, spacings, or holes right. It is not uncommon for CAD libraries to get it very wrong. (No kidding.) There's nothing worse than getting a beautiful new PCB back and finding that you can't mount the components! So, check and recheck.

When routing tracks around pads, ensure that there is sufficient clearance, as shown in Figure 6-27. Tracks should always change direction by 45-degree turns. Some PCB editing programs allow you to do a *design rule check* (also known as an *electrical rule check*) to ensure that correct clearances are maintained and that there are no potential shorts. (It's no guarantee that there won't be a problem, but it's a start!)

Figure 6-27. Routing tracks around a component pad

Avoid close passes and right-angle turns, as shown in Figure 6-28.

Closely spaced pads on surface-mount components can present a problem. Often the tracks leaving a surface-mount device are too close together to easily route tracks. The solution is to *fan out* the tracks, thereby giving greater spacing. This is shown in a simplified form in Figure 6-29.

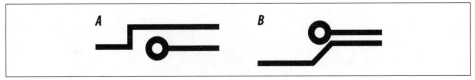

Figure 6-28. How not to route tracks around pads

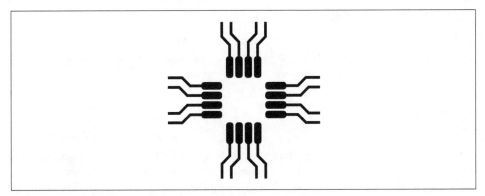

Figure 6-29. Fan out from a surface-mount device

Vias are used to connect tracks on different layers together (Figure 6-30). They are, in effect, little pads. Vias can either be through-hole vias appearing on all layers (Figure 6-31), or *blind* or *buried vias*, appearing only on the layers they are interconnecting and on intermediate layers. Making the vias as small as possible aids in routing the PCB, but check with your PCB manufacturer as to how small you can go. Remember to ensure that the outside diameter of the via is sufficiently bigger than the hole, such that the entire via is not drilled out during fabrication. If space permits, a useful trick is to make the vias with 0.4 mm holes. That way, if there is a bug in the PCB layout or a manufacturing fault, you can use the vias to solder in wire-wrap wire and manually make (or remake) a connection.

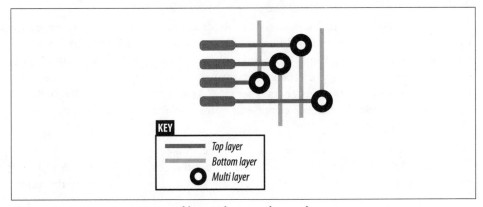

Figure 6-30. Vias connecting top and bottom layer tracks together

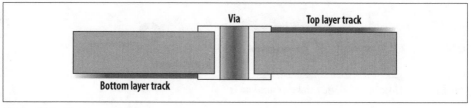

Figure 6-31. Via in cross section

Fills are used to provide shielding to certain sections of the PCB, and also for circuit paths that carry a lot of current. It is common to place ground fills in and around analog sections of the circuit to isolate them from digital crosstalk.

Laying Out a PCB

The first thing to note when laying out a PCB is that someone (or some robot) is going to have to assemble it. As tempting as it might be to cram everything into the smallest space possible, remember the limitations of whoever (or whatever) will be building it. That's not to say you should make the PCB as big as possible—just be realistic. Also, don't bring components and tracks right to the edge of the PCB. Leave a spacing of 5 mm (200 mils) around the outside. If your PCB is to go inside a case, or be mounted in some way, make sure you have the dimensions correct and don't forget to add mounting holes.

There are two schools of thought in placing components (especially integrated circuits) on a PCB. The first is that all components should be placed with the same orientation. For instance, the "pin 1" of each chip should point to the upper lefthand corner of the PCB. This simplifies populating (or *stuffing*) the board with components, especially if this is to be done by a contract manufacturer in an automated process. Having varying orientations may add to the expense of production if you're not hand-assembling the boards yourself. Some people also think that this makes a board look neater.

The second school of thought is that you orientate the chips so as to optimize the routing process. The pinouts of different chips are not necessarily conducive to uniform orientation, and spinning one chip 90 or 180 degrees to its neighbor may greatly simplify the routing of tracks between the two. This can lead to a smaller board size, fewer vias, and shorter track lengths. This then results in lower PCB cost, less noise, less crosstalk, and better noise immunity, which is especially important in higher-speed systems.

Whatever you decide about orientation, group related components together. Put the voltage regulator and its support components near the power connector. Any analog circuitry (such as sensors or amplifier circuits) should be as far from the power connector and its support components as possible. By placing chips into functional groups, routing is made easier. This may seem like obvious stuff, but it's amazing how often it's ignored.

The clocks and high-speed signals should be routed first, to ensure that they take the most direct path possible from source to destination. Where appropriate, place shielding (fills) to isolate these signals from other parts of the PCB. This should be done prior to routing other connections; otherwise, there may not be sufficient space later on. In particular, tracks should never be routed under or around crystals, oscillators, or any clock-generation circuit, and these components should be isolated by fills (connected to ground) from the rest of the circuit. Crystals should lie flat against the PCB (rather than being mounted vertically), and a ground plane should be placed under them to shield from emissions.

For high-speed signals, make sure there is a ground return path close to the track so that the current-loop area is minimized. Allow as much space as possible between high-speed tracks. Having two rapidly changing signals in close proximity will result in crosstalk, and this will cause unreliable operation. Every track has an inherent impedance (resistance); although small, it can affect the transmission of fast signals. In particular, a via or sharp corner represents a change of impedance along the track, and this can cause signal reflections. Therefore, it's important to keep the number of vias to an absolute minimum and avoid right-angle turns in tracks. If you need to make a track turn 90 degrees, use two 45-degree turns in succession.

In high-speed systems, you need power and ground planes that are continuous. In other words, you need planes that cover the entire PCB with no breaks. Any break in the power or ground plane makes the current-loop area larger, and this can increase inductance and radiation. This means that for high-speed systems, you really need to use four or more layers on the PCB. For low-speed microcontrollers, you can get by without separate planes or by providing fills in and around components on the signal layers.

When routing buses (such as data and address), keep the tracks running parallel if possible (Figure 6-32). This is bad practice for clock signals, since it can induce crosstalk in neighboring tracks, but is appropriate for buses. The reason is that bus signals will change state together and will then hold that state until the next transaction. The device receiving the bus signals will sample their state only when they are stable (unchanging). Since crosstalk is generated when a signal state changes, running parallel buses is not a problem. By keeping the bus tracks parallel, the signals travel approximately the same distance for each track. A track that takes a different path completely will have a trace-length mismatch, and this can increase signal *skew*, in which the time it takes for a signal to propagate is shifted. This can adversely affect signal quality in high-speed systems.

Figure 6-32. Keep buses parallel to minimize skew

Stubs are short tracks that leave a main track to connect to a component (Figure 6-33). A stub represents an impedance mismatch for a signal and can result in reflections. A better way is to place the component such that the pad lies on the primary signal track (Figure 6-34).

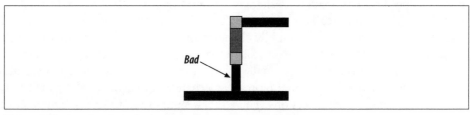

Figure 6-33. Avoid stub tracks

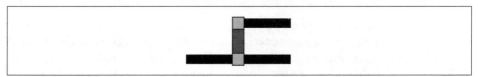

Figure 6-34. Place surface-mount components directly onto tracks, where possible

All power and ground traces should be as fat as possible, and, if feasible, separate power and ground planes (layers) should be used. The *power ground* (ground coming in with the power supply) should be separate from the *signal ground* or *digital ground* (the ground running to all your chips), and both should be separate from the *analog ground* (the ground for your analog components), if one is present. They should all be connected together, but only at one point. This helps isolate the digital and analog sections from each other's noise, as well as from the power-supply noise. Decoupling capacitors should be as close as possible to each power pin of each integrated circuit. Figure 6-35 shows two components on a two-layer PCB, with power and ground tracks routed horizontally through the middle and decoupling capacitors placed close to the power pins.

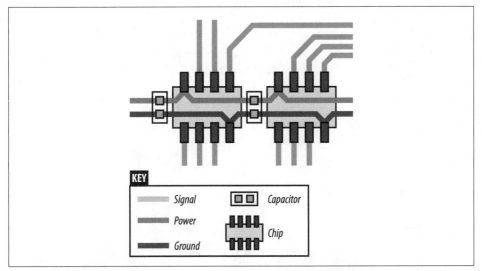

Figure 6-35. Decoupling capacitors should be placed as close as possible to the chips' power and ground pins

 A very useful and simple idea is to place a single pad in the middle of a ground plane (or fill) off to the side of the board. Solder in a post (or even a wirewrap pin), and use this to connect the ground lead of your oscilloscope probe. This can make the debugging process a lot less awkward. You must always use the ground lead of your oscilloscope probe. Without it, you can't get an accurate picture of the timing and voltages of your signals. (Voltage is the potential difference between two points, so you must have a reference.) It's very important.

So, with all that in mind, let's create a simple circuit board for an AVR computer. This design is covered in detail in Chapter 15, but for the moment, we'll just use it as an example so that we can see the process of producing a printed-circuit board.

We start with the schematic (Figure 6-36). This design brings together the voltage regulator circuit (top), the AVR processor (left) with a status LED (far left), and the in-circuit programming interface (right).

Note that no connection is made for pin 2 of the connector. This is the +5 V supply provided by the in-circuit programmer. Since our embedded system has its own supply of +5 V (**VCC**), the external source is not required. (If we were building a 3 V version of this computer, then we would need to use the programmer's +5 V supply, and we'd have to disable the output from the voltage regulator during programming.)

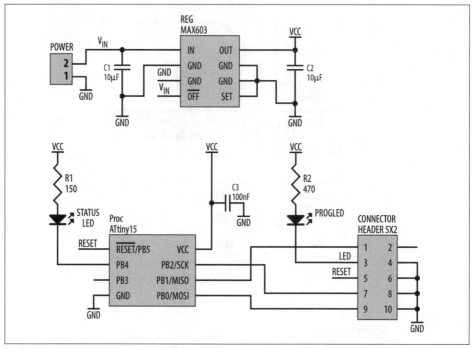

Figure 6-36. The full schematic, including connector for I/O and programming

From this design, we use our schematic editor to generate a *netlist* file, which tells the PCB editing software what interconnections need to be made.

Importing the netlist file into the PCB editor automatically loads the component *footprints*. These are manually rearranged to provide optimum placement, ensuring the shortest track runs between components (Figure 6-37). Note how related components are placed together, such as the voltage regulator, C1, C2, and the power connector. The silkscreen (overlay) layer shows the outline of the components, as well as the component labels. In this example, surface-mount components have been used for the resistors, capacitors, and LEDs, while the two integrated circuits are DIPs. Note the three-pad triangular LEDs ("STATUS" and "PROGRAM"). Only two of the pads are connected to the internal LED; the third is unused. This tiny circuit board measures just 2" by 0.6".

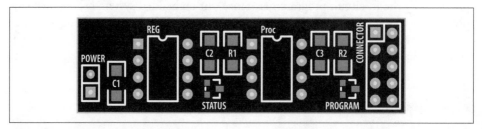

Figure 6-37. Components placed onto PCB

Once you're satisfied with the component placement (and this may need tweaking as you go), the connections are routed. Figure 6-38 shows the PCB with manually routed connections. In this case, the overlay layer has been "turned off" for clarity. Note the use of fills for power and ground connections. For such a simple circuit, operating at low speed with no external system buses, the PCB layout is relatively trivial.

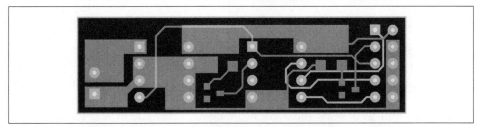

Figure 6-38. Manually routed board, using fills for power and ground

Just for comparison, Figure 6-39 shows the same board, but this time using the EDA software's autorouter to make the connections. Note the bizarre track loop near pin 8 of the processor, the strange meandering track paths, and the unnecessary via in the middle of the PCB.

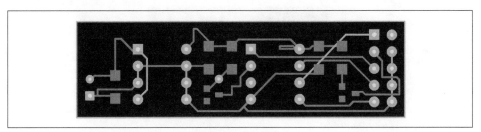

Figure 6-39. The psychedelic results of using an autorouter

This is a simple board, so even an autorouter can make most of the connections. On complex boards, the average autorouter gives up about halfway through, after first making a complete mess. There are autorouters that do a *much* better job than this, but they are very expensive.

For greater noise immunity, a polygon plane is placed on the bottom layer of the manually routed PCB to act as a Faraday shield (Figure 6-40). Note how the polygon has "flowed" around the component pins, yet has connected to the ground pins. In this way, the polygon is a ground plane, providing a (small) degree of noise immunity for the system. The "void" region in the middle right is where it could not reach due to the prerouted tracks. If you are designing a four-layer board, the polygon fill would be placed on a separate layer and should have no discontinuities at all, except where it flows around the pads of through-hole components.

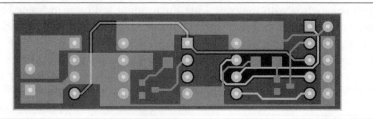

Figure 6-40. Manually routed PCB, with Faraday shield

Using all surface-mount parts (where possible) makes the design even smaller. Figure 6-41 shows the same design (manually routed), but this time using surface-mount versions of the processor and regulator, and even smaller-sized resistors and capacitors. The new board size is just 1" by 0.5". (The pads for the regulator are covered by fills and so are not apparent in the figure. Once the PCB is fabricated, the pads stand out easily.) The only "through-hole" components are the power connector (lower left) and the I/O connector (upper right). Note the four vias needed to route the tracks. For the previous design, the pads of the DIP components effectively acted as vias. On the all-surface-mount version, since just about everything is on the same layer, vias are required to take tracks to the bottom layer of the PCB.

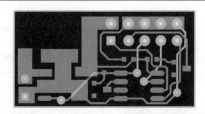

Figure 6-41. Surface-mount PCB

You could make this board even smaller (perhaps 0.5" by 0.5") by placing surface-mount components on both sides of the PCB. This adds to the cost of construction if you're having it professionally done.

Figure 6-42 shows the surface-mount PCB, now with a Faraday shield.

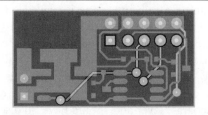

Figure 6-42. Surface-mount PCB, with Faraday shield

Before sending off your circuit board design to be fabricated, print it out and carefully look at it. Check clearances to ensure that there are no potential shorts. Just because there's a whisker gap between a track and a via on the screen doesn't mean there won't be a short between the two when the PCB is made. Give enough clearance to make this an impossibility. Good practice is to set your clearances to be equal to or greater than the minimum track width to which the PCB manufacturer can etch. Anything finer, and you're asking for trouble.

When your design is printed out, place the physical components on the paper and check for clearances. Just because the component outlines in the CAD package didn't collide does not mean the physical chips won't. It is much easier to solve these problems before the PCB is fabricated than after.

Building It

Once the PCB has been fabricated and checked carefully to ensure that all pads and tracks are intact and properly etched, do the construction one step at a time and check everything as you go. Using a multimeter, do a continuity test between the ground pads and the ground pin on the power connector.

Powering Up for the First Time

Start construction by soldering in the power connector, voltage regulator, and its support components, including the "power" LED if you've included one in your design.

Once you've soldered in the components needed for the power supply, power up the board and check that it is operational. Also check that you have power on every pad on the board where you expect power to be, and check the ground pads to make sure there is no power where you expect no power to be.

Next, solder in the power-decoupling capacitors for the ICs. Add the processor's oscillator and decoupling capacitors. If the oscillator is a module, check its operation with an oscilloscope. Does it have the right waveform on its output pin?

If IC sockets are used, solder these next and then insert the components. If you're using a processor that needs to be externally reprogrammed, then a socket is a good idea.

Add in the Processor

Make sure once again that the system is powered down. Using a multimeter's continuity test function, check that the processor footprint has the appropriate power and ground connections to the right pins. Solder the processor to the board (or plug it into a socket if you've used one), remembering to ensure that the system is powered down before you do so. If your processor needs to be externally programmed with your code, make sure you do so before putting it into your circuit. Power it up and check the clock to the processor with an oscilloscope to confirm that it is oscillating. You should see a nice sine wave of the appropriate amplitude. Check the voltage levels you measure against those stated in the datasheet. If the oscillation doesn't have the right amplitude (perhaps due to a poor connection or a partial short), it may not be able to drive the processor.

If the system you are building uses a microcontroller with no external ROM (such as the example presented in this section), the first test software you will write will simply waggle an I/O line. Observing this with an oscilloscope will allow you to see if your system is executing code correctly. If you included a status LED in your design, turn it on! Seeing a status LED blink on for the first time in a machine you've designed and built yourself is sure to bring a smile to your face.

Once you've confirmed that the processor is operating under software control, you can begin to add in the other hardware and software components of your application.

 Don't try to be too adventurous at any stage of the building process. If everything suddenly stops working, it's much easier to find the cause if you've only made one change or addition. Take things one step at a time.

Some Thoughts on Debugging

Debugging is as much an art as it is a science. You can load a workbench to its breaking point with all sorts of expensive test equipment, yet without a logical approach and a clear mind, elusive bugs will never be found. Conversely, by "right thinking," the strangest of bugs can be isolated with a minimum of tools. While it is true that the more complex the system being tested, the harder it is to nail down a fault through detection, it is also true that the most advanced and useful debugging tool you have at your disposal is your own brain. Therefore, learning to debug is learning to think carefully and clearly.

Debugging hardware can be a lot trickier than debugging software. With code, you can always put in some diagnostics to inspect the execution. That's not to say that debugging software is trivial—far from it. But with hardware, it is often either a case of everything working or nothing working. Software has the advantage of being able to be brought into operation gracefully. For hardware, you need to have an awful lot working right from the start.

The essence of debugging is establishing what works and what doesn't work. The design presented in this chapter is intentionally simple and should require little or no hardware debugging. But as the designs grow in complexity, finding hardware and design faults can become quite an involved problem.

For example, your embedded system may not be outputting characters through its serial port. Why? Perhaps it's a bug in the code. Maybe there's a cable fault. Maybe the RS-232C interface chip is dead. Maybe the serial chip itself is dead. It might be that there is a timing problem with the serial chip's oscillator, or a voltage-level problem. Perhaps the processor itself is not coming out of reset and therefore not executing code at all. If so, maybe it's the power-on reset circuit failing to kick in, or the brownout detector kicking in when it shouldn't. Maybe a data line between the processor and the serial chip is not connected, perhaps due to a manufacturing fault with the PCB. Or maybe it wasn't soldered correctly. Perhaps your voltage regulator isn't operating properly, or maybe you have a faulty power supply. And those are just the obvious causes that spring to mind. There are a thousand others lurking, with big teeth and a nasty disposition.

For any one problem, there is a multitude of possible causes. Debugging is therefore about isolating a fault, and this is best done by a "20 questions" approach. Divide and conquer to solve the problem.

Let's take the example of the faulty serial-port problem above. You discover the problem when you first try to test the serial port. Your simple test code fails to output a character. Is the problem in software or hardware? If hardware, is the problem with the cable, the serial chip(s), or is it a more fundamental problem with the core system? Check the cable and the terminal (or host PC) first. Disconnect the cable from the embedded computer, and with a piece of metal (a screwdriver blade will do), short out pins two and three (**Rx** and **Tx**) on the cable connector. Now type something on the terminal (or the terminal software on the PC). What comes out of the terminal should echo back through the short and appear on the screen. That will tell you whether there is a cable fault and whether the terminal is set up correctly.

If that works, then the problems lie in your embedded system. Replace your serial test code with code that does something else that is simpler (like waggle a digital I/O line, or flash a LED). That simple action will tell you volumes. (Archimedes once said, "Give me a lever long enough and I will move the world." Well, give me a status LED and enough time, and I'll debug the world too!) It will tell you whether your processor is executing code correctly, which in turn shows that the processor and ROM (if a separate chip) have power and are communicating correctly. It shows that the reset circuit, brownout detector, oscillator, voltage regulator, address decoder, and other support logic are OK. If any of these are failing, then the processor will not be executing code, and therefore that I/O line will not waggle or that LED will not flash. With that simple test, you have ruled out a plethora of possible faults.

Otherwise, you know to look elsewhere for the problem, such as checking the oscillator, reset, or voltage regulator for correct operation. Divide and conquer. If the test passed, then the fault lies with the serial chip. Most serial chips include some digital

I/O that can be manually set (such as **RTS**). Write some test code that does this. This simple test will show whether or not you can talk to the chip. If the test passes, you know to look at either your character-output software or the RS-232 driver. If the test fails, then the problem lies in talking to the chip. Use an oscilloscope to check the chip select and other control signals going to the serial chip. Are they active? Are they reasonable? Write some software that continually "jams" a byte at a register in the serial chip. While meaningless to the serial chip, a continuous write of the same number allows you to observe the bus activity. So, your (pseudo) code to do this is:

```
        load    r1,#0x55        ; load %01010101
loop    store   serial_control  ; write it
        jump    loop            ; continuously
```

You will expect to see the above bit pattern on the data bus (and, importantly, on the appropriate pins of the serial chip) at the same time the chip select and write enable are asserted.

This will enable to you to locate a problem with the processor writing to the serial chip. Alternatively, if you can demonstrate that you can write to the chip correctly, then the problem lies either in the software or between the serial chip and the serial connector. By using the divide-and-conquer approach, you can isolate where a problem lies. Devise tests to prove each aspect of system operation.

Often you will be faced with a bug that makes no sense. Something should be working, and it is not. Everything you check seems right, but the total system just isn't working. It can be very perplexing. You have made a common error—you have made an assumption. Somewhere, even though you may not be consciously aware of it, you have assumed that some little detail is correct, when in fact it is not. This is the hardest obstacle to overcome. When you say to yourself, "It should be working, but it isn't! It doesn't make sense!" then say to yourself, "There is still something I haven't checked." Go looking for it. If you can't find it, then you haven't looked hard enough.

When designing your system and laying out the PCB, remember that you will have to debug it. So, design it with debugging in mind. Include one or more status LEDs. These are invaluable for debugging embedded hardware. Sure, you can do a lot with a remote debugger (such as gnu's gdb), but you have to get the hardware working to a certain level before the debugger can be made to run. Status LEDs will help you get there.

You are also going to need to look at signals with an oscilloscope, so include a ground pin on your circuit board onto which you can clip it. Also, make sure that you will be able to get an oscilloscope probe to every circuit trace on the board to examine what's going on. If you can't get to a track, you can't ensure that there's no problem with that particular signal.

So even at the design stage, think carefully about how you can test the subsystems and isolate problems and put the necessary support into your design.

Read the Electrical Specifications!

I once designed a system that operated on a 5 V supply. It worked wonderfully. I then went to produce the same system operating on a 3.3 V supply by using 3.3 V versions of the same parts. It should have worked. It didn't. All the timing was correct; all the voltages were correct. Everything I checked was right, and yet nothing. No activity, not even a trace of a signal from anything. I couldn't understand it. There was nothing left to test.

I knew the design and code were correct because they worked beautifully in the 5 V version. It had to be something specific to the hardware in the 3.3 V system. But what? The processor had power, the regulator was working, the oscillator was going, and the reset circuit was operational. It should have been executing code. Yet, even the simplest of test software failed to go.

Somewhere, there was an incorrect assumption I was making. It took me over a week to find it, and it was as subtle as they come. In going from the 5 V system to the 3.3 V system, I had chosen the 3.3 V version of the processor. What I had *assumed* (logically, but incorrectly) was that the brownout detector (inbuilt in the processor) was designed to work at the correct levels. You'd expect that, but it was wrong. The manufacturer of the processor, when producing the 3.3 V chip, had changed the operating voltage of the device but had left the brownout detector *unchanged*. So, in the 3.3 V processor, the brownout detector kicked in if the supply was less than 4.5 V! Hence, the processor never came out of reset and therefore never executed code.

I had assumed, *incorrectly*, that everything about the 3.3 V processor was designed to work at 3.3 V. For correct operation, the 3.3 V processor needed to have the (optional) brownout detector disabled. This was not explicitly stated in the datasheet, merely implied through careful reading of the electrical specifications.

The moral of the story: don't assume *anything*, and check *everything*. If it still doesn't work, you haven't done the checking carefully enough.

JTAG

A *JTAG* (Joint Test Action Group) port provides access to the internals of the processor and, through it, the rest of the computer system. JTAG is defined under IEEE standard *1149.1a-1993 Standard Test Access Port and Boundary Scan Architecture*. It is sometimes also known as a *Test Access Port*, or *TAP*. Commercially available test suites use JTAG to provide in-circuit debug capability. The adventurous among you can also drive JTAG "manually," using the information in the aforementioned document.

The JTAG port allows for real-time debugging of hardware and software. It allows you to single-step or multi-step through code running directly on the target system. You can individually (and manually) toggle signal lines of the processor to test external subsystems in the computer (also known as *boundary scan*). You can set breakpoints both at locations in code or for when a particular address (or device) is accessed. The JTAG port allows you to examine and modify registers and memory locations. To utilize the JTAG interface, you need to have support tools that are JTAG compliant. For more information, refer to IEEE standard 1149.1a.

Boundary scan allows you to probe the microprocessor and the circuit connections between peripherals and memories. It does this by asserting outputs (independently of the CPU) and reading the response from external devices on input pins. It is useful for testing not only interconnections on the PCB, but also for design verification and even correct timing. JTAG can operate independently of the CPU, "manually" driving outputs, and can interrogate the processor as to its manufacturer, processor type, and revision number. JTAG can also be used to disable output pins while a board is undergoing a test. Freescale Semiconductor (formerly Motorola) has added functionality to the JTAG interface through an *On-Chip Emulation module* (*OnCE*) found on many of its processors. The OnCE can let the processor run and watch system activity in response to the executing software. It can retrieve or set parameters in registers or memory, as well as provide a host of debugging features (such as setting breakpoints, single-stepping, and instruction tracing).

A JTAG port provides access to a state machine that implements the boundary-scan functionality. The state machine has four registers. These are the *Instruction Register*, the *Boundary Scan Register*, the *Device Identification Register*, and the *Bypass Register*.

A JTAG port consists of four dedicated signals (Table 6-2). If you think those signals sound suspiciously like a synchronous serial interface, you'd be right, because that is exactly what JTAG is.

Table 6-2. JTAG signals

Signal name	Function
TDI	Test Data Input
TDO	Test Data Output
TMS	Test Mode Select
TCK	Test Clock

JTAG is becoming increasingly common due to the many advantages it brings to the system designer. Most new processor releases are including JTAG in their design. For information regarding the use of JTAG for a specific processor, check the manufacturer's technical data.

CHAPTER 7

Adding Peripherals Using SPI

Thirty spokes meet at a nave;
Because of the hole we may use the wheel.
Clay is molded into a vessel;
Because of the hollow we may use the cup.
Walls are built around a hearth;
Because of the doors we may use the house.
Thus tools come from what exists,
But use from what does not.

—Lao Tse
   Tao Te Ching

In this chapter and the next, we'll look at two low-cost interfaces used to connect peripheral chips to microcontrollers, within a single embedded system. These interfaces allow you to connect devices such as real-time clocks, nonvolatile memories for parameter storage, sensor interfaces, and much more. The interfaces are easy to use and cheap to implement, making them ideal for small, embedded applications. Some microcontrollers incorporate both types of interface, whereas others may only have one or the other. The one to use really depends on what your processor has to offer and the requirements of the particular peripheral you're using.

Serial Peripheral Interface

The *Serial Peripheral Interface* (known as *SPI*) was developed by Motorola to provide a low-cost and simple interface between microcontrollers and peripheral chips. (SPI is sometimes also known as a *four-wire* interface.) It can be used to interface to memory (for data storage), analog-digital converters, digital-analog converters, real-time clock calendars, LCD drivers, sensors, audio chips, and even other processors. The range of components that support SPI is large and growing all the time.

Unlike a standard serial port, SPI is a synchronous protocol in which all transmissions are referenced to a common clock, generated by the *master* (processor). The receiving peripheral (*slave*) uses the clock to synchronize its acquisition of the serial bit stream. Many chips may be connected to the same SPI interface of a master. A master selects a slave to receive by asserting the slave's chip select input. A peripheral that is not selected will not take part in a SPI transfer.

SPI uses four main signals: *Master Out Slave In* (**MOSI**), *Master In Slave Out* (**MISO**), *Serial CLocK* (**SCLK** or **SCK**) and *Chip Select* (**CS**) for the peripheral. Some processors have a dedicated chip select for SPI interfacing called *Slave Select* (**SS**).

MOSI is generated by the master and is received by the slave. On some chips, **MOSI** is labeled simply as *Serial In* (**SI**) or *Serial Data In* (**SDI**). **MISO** is produced by the slave, but its generation is controlled by the master. **MISO** is sometimes known as *Serial Out* (**SO**) or *Serial Data Out* (**SDO**) on some chips. The chip select to the peripheral is normally generated by simply using a spare I/O pin of the master. Figure 7-1 shows a microprocessor interfaced to a peripheral using SPI.

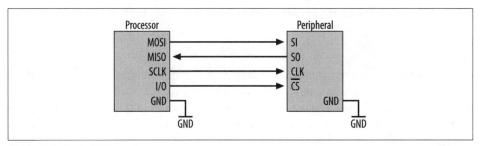

Figure 7-1. Basic SPI interface

Both masters and slaves contain a serial shift register. The master starts a transfer of a byte by writing it to its SPI shift register. As the register transmits the byte to the slave on the **MOSI** signal line, the slave transfers the contents of *its* shift register back to the master on the **MISO** signal line (Figure 7-2). In this way, the contents of the two shift registers are exchanged. Both a write and a read operation are performed with the slave simultaneously. SPI can therefore be a very efficient protocol.

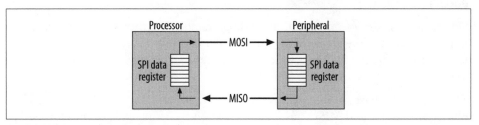

Figure 7-2. SPI transmission

If only a write operation is desired, the master just ignores the byte it receives. Conversely, if the master just wishes to read a byte from the slave, it must transfer a dummy byte in order to initiate a slave transmission.

Some peripherals can handle multiple byte transfers, where a continuous stream of data is shifted from the master. Many memory chips with SPI interfaces work this way. With this type of transfer, the chip select for the SPI slave must remain low for the entire duration of the transmission. For example, a memory chip might expect a "write" command to be followed by four address bytes (starting address), then the data bytes to be stored. A single transfer may involve the shifting of a kilobyte or more of information.

Other slaves need only a single byte (for example, a command byte for an analog-digital converter), and some even support being *daisy-chained* together (Figure 7-3).

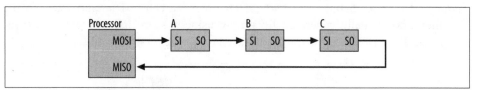

Figure 7-3. Daisy-chaining three SPI devices

In this example, the master processor transmits three bytes out of its SPI interface. The first byte is shifted into slave A. As the second byte is transferred to slave A, the first byte is shifted out of slave A and into slave B. Similarly, as the third byte is shifted into slave A, the second byte is shifted into slave B, and the first byte is shifted into slave C. If the master wishes to read a result from slave A, it must again transfer a three-byte (dummy) sequence. This will move the byte from slave A into slave B, then into slave C, and finally into the master. In the process, the master also receives bytes from slave C and slave B in turn.

Note that daisy chaining won't necessarily work with all SPI devices, especially ones that require multibyte transfers (such as memory chips). Again, it's a case of checking the slave chips' datasheets carefully to determine what you can and can't do. If the datasheet doesn't explicitly mention daisy chaining, then it's a fair bet the device doesn't support it.

SPI has four modes of operation, depending on clock polarity and clock phase. For low clock polarity, the clock (**SCK**) is low when idle and toggles high during a transfer. When configured for high clock polarity, the clock is high when idle and toggles low during a transfer.

The two clock phases are known as *clock phase zero* and *clock phase one*. For clock phase zero, **MOSI** and **MISO** outputs are valid on the rising edge of the clock (**SCK**) if the clock polarity is low (Figure 7-4). If the clock polarity is high, these outputs are valid on the falling edge of **SCK**, for clock phase zero (Figure 7-5). The "X" bit output on **MISO** is an undefined extra bit and is a consequence of the SPI interface. You don't need to worry about it, as the SPI interfaces ignore it.

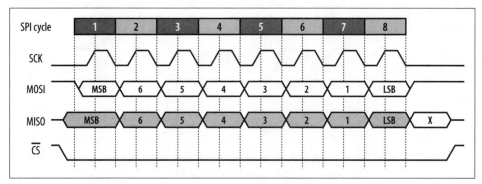

Figure 7-4. SPI timing with clock polarity low and clock phase zero

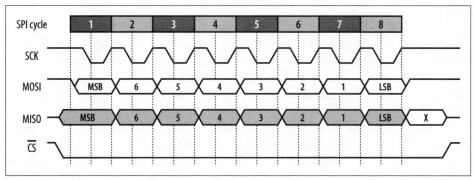

Figure 7-5. SPI timing with clock polarity high and clock phase zero

Conversely, for clock phase one, the opposite is true. **MOSI** and **MISO** are valid on the falling edge of the clock if clock polarity is low (Figure 7-6). They are valid on the rising edge of the clock if the clock polarity is high (Figure 7-7).

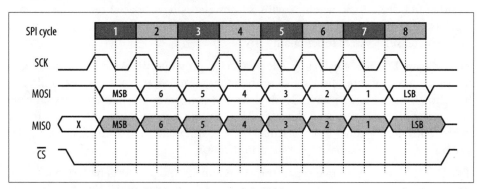

Figure 7-6. SPI timing with clock polarity low and clock phase one

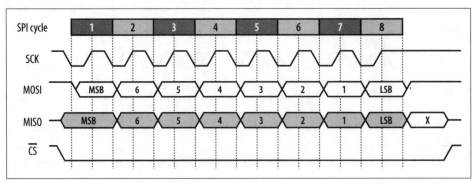

Figure 7-7. SPI timing with clock polarity high and clock phase one

SPI-Based Clock/Calendar

There is a wide variety of SPI devices available, and we'll be looking at several in the coming chapters. In the meantime, to see how a SPI interface is used to add a peripheral to a microcontroller, let's look at interfacing a processor to a clock/calendar chip. Such chips contain an oscillator module driven by a crystal, just like a processor. The oscillator module ticks over internal counters that track milliseconds, seconds, minutes, hours, days, months, and years. They are specifically designed to provide accurate timekeeping, and many have additional functions such as an "alarm" (whereby the processor is interrupted at a specific time) and a watchdog. Some also include voltage monitoring, such that the clock chip may act as a system monitor, alerting the processor should the power supply be wavering. There are a number of clock chips available (and not all are interfaced using SPI). For this example, we will use the Maxim DS1305.

The way in which we interface the clock chip to a processor is virtually identical for all other SPI devices. Some chips with SPI interfaces have special requirements, but most are very simple and straightforward. This makes SPI a very useful interface that makes increasing system functionality trivial.

The Maxim DS1305 Real-Time Clock (RTC) provides timekeeping services and tracks seconds, minutes, hours, day of the month, month, day of the week, and year. It knows which months have 30 days and which have 31. It even automatically adjusts for leap years, up to the year 2100. It can generate two interrupts to the microcontroller for time-of-day alarms. These alarms can be used to trigger a regular system event, such as a backup or user notification.

The DS1305 can run off two separate power sources and supports battery backup of its internal state. The chip can use a power supply in the range of 2 V to 5.5 V, allowing it to be powered from a variety of sources. It also has 96 bytes of static RAM, used for parameter storage. You could use the RAM for holding variables indicating system mode, secure password storage, or even authorization codes for your embedded software, just as desktop software does.

If you are producing commercial embedded systems and have problems with late-paying customers, you can use this RAM to hold a license number. When you ship the system, you design it to work for perhaps 45 days before shutting down. When your customer pays her bill, and you supply her with the right magic number, the system comes back to life again. The system stores the license number in the RAM of the RTC and from then on works as normal.

The RAM, like the timekeeping function, is battery-backed, and so its contents will be retained for the life of the battery. This can be up to 10 years, depending on the battery chosen. Thus, the contents of the internal parameter RAM will probably last for the expected operational lifespan of an embedded system.

The DS1305 is versatile in the way it can be powered. It has three power-supply inputs—**VCC1**, **VCC2**, and **VBAT**—from which it can choose to draw power. **VCC1** is the primary supply input and is connected directly to the system's power supply. When the computer is up and running, the DS1305 draws its current from this source. **VCC2** is the secondary power source, and this can be a rechargeable battery. **VBAT** is the third power source and is for nonrechargeable batteries.

There are three, and only three, possible configurations for powering the DS1305, and it is important for correct operation that the power inputs are appropriately driven. Figure 7-8 shows the DS1305 powered by a primary DC supply connected to **VCC1** and a secondary, nonrechargeable battery connected to **VBAT**. (To keep the diagram simple, only the power pins are shown. We'll look at the data interface in a moment.) For this configuration, **VCC2** is unused and must be connected to **GND**. When **VCC1** falls below a given threshold voltage (the primary power source has failed), the internal memory and registers of the DS1305 become write-protected to prevent them from being corrupted by a failing microprocessor.

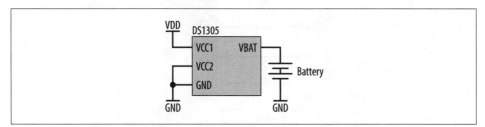

Figure 7-8. Using the DS1305 with a nonrechargeable battery

If the secondary power source is a rechargeable battery, then the DS1305 may be wired as shown in Figure 7-9. When using a rechargeable battery on **VCC2**, **VBAT** must be connected to **GND**. When the device is used in this mode, there is no automatic write protection for the DS1305 if **VCC1** fails.

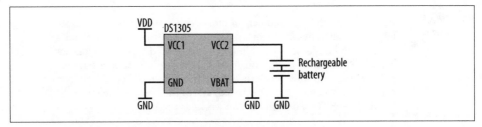

Figure 7-9. Using the DS1305 with a rechargeable battery

Finally, the DS1305 may be used with only a battery as its primary power source and no backup power supply. This is shown in Figure 7-10. For this configuration, both **VCC1** and **VBAT** are connected to ground, while the battery is connected to **VCC2**.

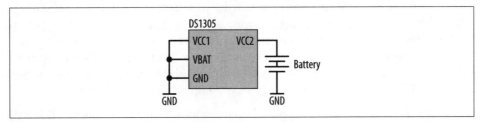

Figure 7-10. Using the DS1305 with a battery as its only power source

Using the DS1305 is very simple. The schematic showing a DS1305 interfaced to a microcontroller is shown in Figure 7-11.

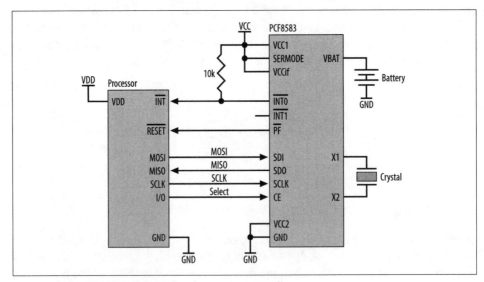

Figure 7-11. A DS1305 RTC interfaced to a microcontroller

The serial interface of the DS1305 can operate as either a SPI port or a three-wire* port. The input **SERMODE** (SERial MODE) selects which serial mode to use. Connecting **SERMODE** to the power supply selects SPI operation. Connecting **SERMODE** to **GND** selects three-wire operation. (For three-wire operation, **SDO** and **SDI** are tied together.) The connection to a microcontroller's SPI port is straightforward, with **MOSI, MISO, SCLK**, and a chip select, as we've seen previously. There is one important difference, though, for the DS1305. It has an active-high **CE** (Chip Enable), rather than the more common active-low chip selects of other SPI devices. Therefore, the processor's I/O line driving **CE** must be low when the device is not selected and high when the device is selected.

The DS1305 has a special Power Fail ($\overline{PF}$) output that is asserted low when the primary power source **VCC1** falls below the secondary power source (**VCC2** or **VBAT**). This can be used to alert the processor of the power fail (by using it as an interrupt) or to stop the processor (by connecting it to the processor's $\overline{RESET}$). This is used to prevent a failing processor from corrupting devices as the power dies. If you don't require a power-fail notification, $\overline{PF}$ may be left unconnected.

The input **VCCif** (**VCC** for the interface logic) selects the output voltage levels of **SDO** and $\overline{PF}$. Since the DS1305 can be used in both 5 V and 3.3 V systems, this input allows the output levels of these pins to be set to the appropriate high voltage. **VCCif** is just connected to the system's power supply. Thus, for a 5 V system, **VCCif** is 5 V, and the outputs of the DS1305 are also 5 V. Similarly, for a 3.3 V system, **VCCif** is 3.3 V and so are the outputs.

Finally, the DS1305 has two interrupt outputs, $\overline{INT0}$ and $\overline{INT1}$. These may be used to interrupt the processor when a DS1305 alarm function triggers. As the interrupt outputs are open-drain, they each require a 10k resistor to pull them high when they are inactive. If one or both of the interrupts are not required, just leave them unconnected. Only $\overline{INT0}$ is used in our example, and so $\overline{INT1}$ is safely ignored.

Finally, the DS1305 has two crystal inputs, **X1** and **X2**. A 32.768 kHz watch crystal is connected across these pins, providing the timing source for the internal clock.

So that is the DS1305, a versatile little chip that can provide timekeeping for your embedded system. It's easy to use, and the programming information for it is contained in the device's datasheet.

SPI-Based Digital Potentiometer

Let's look at another simple SPI example. This time, we will interface a digital potentiometer to a microprocessor. We looked at analog potentiometers in Chapter 4.

---

* Developed by National Semiconductor, three-wire, also known as *MicroWire*, is very similar to SPI and is found is some microcontrollers and DSP processors. Unlike SPI, which has separate data lines for reading and writing, three-wire uses a common bidirectional data line.

Now, a standard pot is manually adjusted. It will either have a knob attached (as in a volume control or brightness adjustment), or it will have a small notch for screwdriver adjustment. Wouldn't it be great if your microprocessor could adjust the pots in your analog circuits, under software control? That way, your application software could adjust the brightness of the display or change the volume of the sound system. Well, by using a *digital potentiometer*, you can do just that. Televisions, computer monitors, and stereos with internal embedded controllers use digital pots to adjust settings such as volume. When you hit a volume button on a remote control, the TV or stereo adjusts the settings of digital pots, which are part of the amplifiers driving the speakers.

Figure 7-12 shows an Analog Devices AD5203 digital potentiometer with a SPI interface. This chip has four potentiometers, all of which may be adjusted under software control. Each pot has 64 possible positions, and versions of the chip are available with either 10 kΩ or 100 kΩ impedances. For higher resolution, the pin-compatible AD8403 has a possible 256 settings, also configurable through a SPI interface.

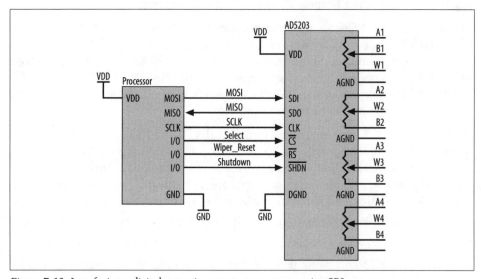

Figure 7-12. Interfacing a digital potentiometer to a processor using SPI

The AD5203 has a Serial Data Input (**SDI**), which is connected to the processor's **MOSI** output. Similarly, the device's Serial Data Output (**SDO**) is connected to **MISO**. The AD5203's clock input (**CLK**) is positive-edge triggered midway through each SPI cycle, which means that any processor communicating with it must use high clock polarity and clock phase one on **SCLK**. The Chip Select ($\overline{\text{CS}}$) of the AD5203 may be driven by a processor digital I/O line. The AD5203 has two other inputs, Shutdown ($\overline{\text{SHDN}}$) and Reset ($\overline{\text{RS}}$). $\overline{\text{SHDN}}$ places the device in low-power mode, and $\overline{\text{RS}}$ resets the potentiometer wipers to their midpoint. Both of these inputs may also be driven by a processor I/O line, or, if their functionality is not needed, they may be simply tied high using 10 kΩ pull-up resistors.

The potentiometers within the AD5203 are used as any other pots would be. The **A** and **B** terminals connect to either end of the internal resistors, and the position of the wiper (**W**) is adjusted under software control.

The AD5203 has several ground connections. **DGND** is the digital ground for the SPI interface and control logic of the chip. The **AGND**s are the analog grounds of the internal potentiometers, and they should all be connected to **DGND** at a single point.

The datasheet for the AD5203 provides the control codes needed to configure the chip, and its use is simple and straightforward.

Adding Nonvolatile Data Memory with SPI

The internal memory of microcontrollers is very small, and their data storage capabilities are severely limited. We're now going to look at how you can increase the storage capacity of your embedded system by adding an Atmel AT45DB161 2M serial DataFlash using SPI. These chips are commonly used in low-cost digital cameras and answering machines. You could also use this flash chip as a virtual disk drive in your embedded system.

Most other flash chips have a bus interface, but the AT45DB161 has a serial interface, making it well suited for use with small microcontrollers. The AT45DB161 is a 2M chip, but you can get similar chips in capacities ranging from 512K to 32M. They all use the same (or similar) SPI interface, so the same design works for all. (Note, however, that their pinouts and physical packages vary, so one chip will not mount onto a circuit board design for another.)

The chip consists of an array of flash memory, organized as individual pages of 528 bytes each, and two RAM buffers, also 528 bytes each (Figure 7-13). To write data into the main flash array, the processor must first write data into one of the buffers and then issue a command to write that buffer into the array. A processor can read the contents of either of the buffers, transfer a flash page to the buffers, or read from the flash array directly. The operation of the buffers is independent, and one buffer may be accessed by the processor (via SPI) while the contents of the other buffer are being written into the flash array.

The flash supports numerous commands for writing to and reading from the buffers, writing the buffers to the main array, and transferring an array page back to a buffer. The Atmel datasheet has full details of the software protocols and command set.

There are a few things to note about the internal architecture and the flash array. The first is that one 528-byte page of the flash array is not contiguous with the next. In

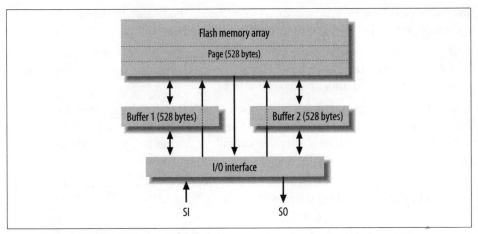

Figure 7-13. AT45DB161 internal architecture

other words, if you are using a pointer in your software to track the current location in the memory, you can't just increment it from the end of one page and expect it to be pointing to the next. Every 528 bytes (and it's a strange number), you have to leap forward to the next page. Think of it as pages of 528 bytes with big gaps in between.

The second catch with this memory is that it has a lifetime of only 1,000 write cycles per page. Most flash technologies (and there are several different types) support 100,000 write cycles or better, and you can normally exceed this limit and the device will keep working reliably for you. This isn't the case with the AT45DB161. Once the 1,000-write limit is exceeded, memory locations will start failing on you. The chip will read existing data back correctly, but new pages will not write successfully. Depending on the application, this limit may not be a problem. I've used this particular chip in my design for long-duration data loggers. These machines are deployed for yearlong deployments, collecting (and compressing) data and storing it away in the flash chip. The logger gradually builds a page image in one of the buffers before storing it to the array in a single write. Since during a deployment, a page will be written only once (and then the logger will move on to the next page), the 1,000-write limitation isn't a problem. It would take 1,000 deployments before the chip would fail. However, if you're using the chip for variable storage and are modifying the flash pages on a byte-by-byte basis, you're in trouble. Individually changing 528 bytes within a page counts as 528 writes. So do that twice to a page, and suddenly you're over the limit. Therefore, this flash is well suited to some applications and not others.

The basic design for using an AT45DB161 is shown in Figure 7-14.

On the left of the chip are the SPI interface connections, **MOSI**, **MISO**, **SCK**, and a chip select (**FLASH**). The chip will support SPI transfers at up to 20 MHz, so the SPI interface can be run very fast indeed. On the right of the chip is the power supply, **VDD**, which is decoupled to ground using a 100 nF capacitor. The AT45DB161

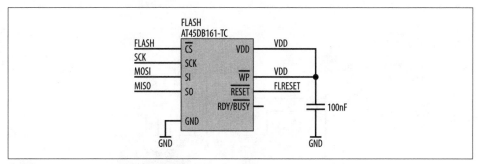

Figure 7-14. 2M Serial DataFlash

requires a power supply in the range 2.5 V to 3.6 V. However, its logic inputs are *5 V tolerant*, meaning this chip can be used in systems with mixed power supplies. In other words, while this chip requires a 3 V power supply, it can be directly interfaced to a processor with a 5 V supply (and 5 V logic levels). The AT45DB161 has a write-protect pin (**WP**), which, when driven low, prevents the contents of the flash from being modified. If you don't require write protection, simply tie this input high, as shown in the schematic. The flash also has a **RESET** input so that the chip can be manually reset under software control. The flash incorporates an inbuilt power-on reset that will put the device into a known state, and therefore a "manual" reset at power up should be unnecessary. However, I've found that the internal power-on reset generator is somewhat finicky and doesn't always kick in as it should. Under such circumstances, the flash fails to enter a known state and is unusable in the system. Therefore, I have found it good practice to give the processor control of the flash's reset. As part of the processor's initialization routines executed in its reset firmware, I get the processor to reset the flash, nudging it into reality. It's a simple thing, but it makes all the difference for a reliable system. Pin 1 is a status output (**RDY/BUSY**) indicating whether the device is ready or if it is still completing an internal operation.

The connections for interfacing this memory chip to an Atmel 90S4434 AVR processor are shown in Figure 7-15. The AVR portion of the schematic is no different from the examples we have seen previously. That's the nice thing about simple interfaces such as SPI. They form little subsystem modules that "bolt together" like building blocks. Start with the basic core design and just add peripherals as you need them. The schematic also shows decoupling capacitors for the power supplies, the crystal oscillator for the processor, and a pull-up resistor for **RESET**. Pin 41 (**PB1**) is used as a "manual" (processor-controlled) reset input to the flash.

Adding a Parameter Memory Using SPI

We saw in the previous section how to add a large-capacity serial flash for data storage. It is often useful to use nonvolatile memory to hold system parameters, a way of preserving important variables during periods of no power. But the AT45DB161

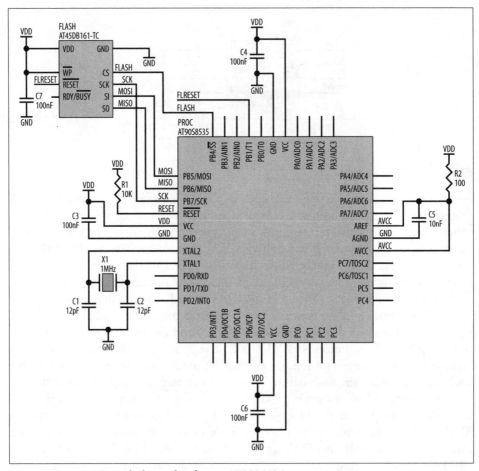

Figure 7-15. A 2M DataFlash interfaced to an AT90S4434

DataFlash is just not the device for that task. It is better suited to data recording, and its large capacity is overkill for parameter storage. So, now we're going to look at how you can use SPI to add a small parameter memory (in the form on an EEPROM) to your embedded system. The EEPROM I've chosen is the Atmel AT25640. This device will hold data for at least 100 years without power, and will endure more than one million write cycles (significantly more than an AT45DB161!). As such, your software can happily alter parameter variables without fear of limiting the lifespan of the chip. The AT25640 has only 8K of memory, which might not sound like much. But don't forget, that's 8192 char variables, which is more than enough storage space for most parameters. If 8K is too much, there are also versions of the chip with 1K (AT25080), 2K (AT25160), and 4K (AT25320) bytes of memory.

The architecture and use of the AT25640 is much simpler than that of the AT45DB161. Full details of the required software protocol are in the Atmel datasheet for this chip.

The schematic for an AT25640 circuit is shown in Figure 7-16.

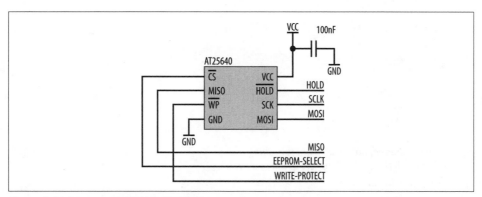

Figure 7-16. Using an AT25640 EEPROM

The interface is standard SPI, and the chip also has a write-protect input and a hold input. Asserting **HOLD** allows the processor to temporarily stall a serial transfer (while it performs other tasks) without terminating the access to the AT25640. And as you might expect, write-protect, when asserted, turns the chip into a read-only device. These control inputs may be driven by programmable I/O lines of the processor. The only other requirement is power (which is decoupled to ground using a 100 nF capacitor) and ground. The chip is available in two types. One will operate from a supply voltage of between 2.7 V and 5.5 V, while the other needs a supply voltage of between 1.8 V and 3.6 V.

CHAPTER 8

Adding Peripherals Using I²C

*Perfection is achieved, not when there is nothing more
to add, but when there is nothing left to take away.*
—Antoine de Saint-Exupéry

In the last chapter, we looked at the low-cost SPI interface used to connect peripheral chips to microcontrollers. In this chapter, we'll examine the alternate serial interface for connecting peripherals, I²C.

Overview of I²C

I²C (Inter-Integrated Circuit) bus is a very cheap yet effective network used to interconnect peripheral devices within small-scale embedded systems. It is sometimes also known as *IIC* and has been in existence for more than 20 years. It is the equivalent of SPI, but its operation is somewhat different.

I²C uses two wires to connect multiple devices in a multi-drop bus. The bus is bidirectional, low-speed, and synchronous to a common clock. Devices may be attached or detached from the I²C bus without affecting other devices. Several manufacturers, such as Microchip, Philips, Intel, and others produce small microcontrollers with I²C built in. The data rate of I²C is somewhat slower than SPI, at 100 kbps in standard mode, and 400 kbps in fast mode.

The two wires used to interconnect with I²C are **SDA** (serial data) and **SCL** (serial clock). Both lines are open-drain.[*] They are connected to a positive supply via a pull-up resistor and therefore remain high when not in use. A device using the I²C bus to

---

[*] An *open-drain* or *open-collector* pin has output drivers that can only pull the signal line to ground. They cannot drive it high. This has the advantage that more than one device connected to a signal line may pull it low. If this were not the case, one device attempting to pull the line low while another tried to pull it high would result in a short circuit, with disastrous results. Interrupt lines are typically open-collector. All open-collector signals need a pull-up resistor and are active low. The idle state (when no device is asserting) is to be pulled high by the resistor.

communicate drives the lines low or leaves them pulled high as appropriate. Each device connected to the I2C bus has a unique address and can operate as either a transmitter (a bus master), a receiver (a bus slave), or both (Figure 8-1). I2C is a *multi-master bus*, meaning that more than one device may assume the role of bus master.

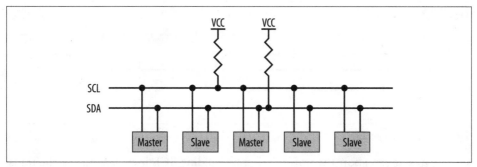

Figure 8-1. I2C network

Both **SDA** and **SCL** are bidirectional. Unlike SPI, which has separate data lines for each direction of communication, I2C shares the same signal line for master transmission and slave response. Also unlike SPI, I2C does not have several modes of operation. The timing relationship between the clock, **SCL**, and the data line, **SDA**, is simple and straightforward. When idle, both **SDA** and **SCL** are high. An I2C transaction begins with **SDA** going low, followed by **SCL** (Figure 8-2). This indicates to all receivers on the bus that a packet transmission is commencing. While **SCL** is low, **SDA** transitions (high or low) for the first valid data bit. This is known as a "START condition."

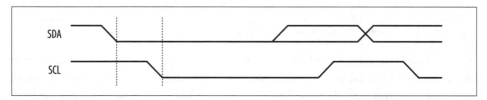

Figure 8-2. Start of packet

For each bit that is transmitted, the bit must become valid on **SDA** while **SCL** is low. The bit is sampled on the rising edge of **SCL** and must remain valid until **SCL** goes low once more. Then **SDA** transitions to the next bit before **SCL** goes high once more (Figure 8-3).

Finally, the transaction completes by **SCL** returning high (inactive) followed by **SDA** (Figure 8-4). This is known as a "STOP condition."

Any number of bytes may be transmitted in an I2C packet. As with SPI, the most significant bit of the packet is transmitted first. If the receiver is unable to accept any

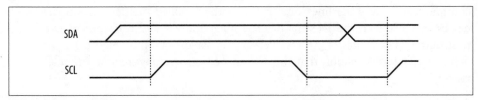

Figure 8-3. Timing relationship between SDA and SCL

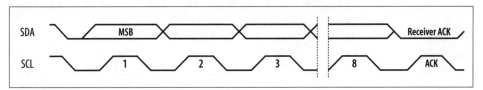

Figure 8-4. End of packet

more bytes, it can abort the transmission by holding **SCL** low. This forces the transmitter to wait until **SCL** is released again.

Each byte transmitted must be acknowledged by the receiver. Upon the transmission of the eighth data bit, the master releases the data line **SDA**. The master then generates an additional clock pulse on **SCL**. This triggers the receiver to acknowledge the byte by pulling **SDA** low (Figure 8-5). If the receiver fails to pull **SDA** low, the master aborts the transfer and takes appropriate error-handling measures.

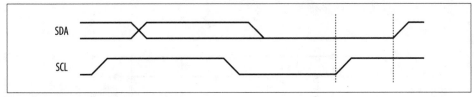

Figure 8-5. I²C packet with receiver acknowledge

Now, I²C is a multi-master bus. So, more than one master may attempt to start transmission at the same time. Since the bus's default state is high, a master transmitting a 0 bit will pull **SDA** low but will leave the bus in its default state if the bit is to be a 1. Thus, if two masters begin simultaneous transmission, a master leaving the bus in its default state for a 1 bit, but detecting the bus pulled low by another master (for a 0 bit), will register an error condition and abort the transmission.

SPI uses a separate chip select to enable a receiving slave. Each SPI slave has a separate chip select that is generated by the master. I²C does not have such a selection mechanism. Instead, each device on the bus has a unique address, and the packet transmission begins with address bits, followed by the data. An address byte consists of seven address bits, followed by a direction bit. If the direction bit is a 0, the transmission is a write cycle and the selected slave will accept the data as input. If the direction bit is a 1, then the request is for the slave to transfer data back to the master. A sample packet, transferring one byte of data, is shown in Figure 8-6.

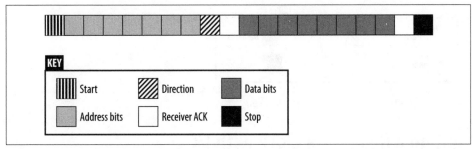

Figure 8-6. An I²C packet

There is a special address, known as the *general call address*, which broadcasts to all I²C devices. This address is %0000000 with a direction bit of 0. The general call is the mechanism by which the master determines what slaves are available, and there are several types of general call. The second byte of a general call indicates the purpose of the general call to the slaves. Upon receiving the second byte, individual slaves will determine whether the command is applicable to them, and, if so, they will acknowledge. If the command is not applicable to a given slave, then the slave simply ignores the general call and does not acknowledge. If the second byte is 0x06 (%00000110), then this indicates that appropriate slaves should reset and respond with their addresses. If the second byte is 0x04 (%00000100), slaves respond with their addresses but do not reset. Any other second byte of a general call, where the least significant bit is a 0, should be ignored.

If the least significant bit of the second byte is a 1, then the general call is by a master device identifying itself to other masters in the system by transmitting its own address. The other bits of the second byte contain the master's address.

There is another special address byte, known as the START byte. This byte is %00000001 (0x01). It is used to indicate to other masters that a long data transfer is beginning. This is particularly important for masters that do not have dedicated I²C hardware and must monitor the bus by software polling. When a master detects a START byte generated by another master, it can reduce its polling rate, allowing it more time for other software tasks.

I²C also supports an extended 10-bit addressing mode, allowing up to 1,024 peripherals. Devices that use 7-bit addressing may be mixed with 10-bit addressing devices in a single system. In 10-bit addressing, two bytes are used to hold the address. If the (first) address byte begins with %11110XX, then a 10-bit address is being generated. The two least significant bits of the first byte, combined with the eight bits of the second byte, form the 10-bit address (Figure 8-7). 7-bit devices will ignore the transaction.

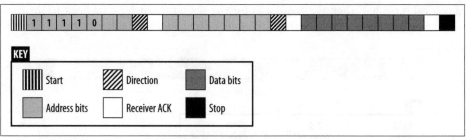

Figure 8-7. An I2C packet with 10-bit addressing

Adding a Real-Time Clock with I2C

We saw in the previous chapter how to interface a Real-Time Clock (RTC) to a microprocessor using a SPI interface. Now let's look at how we'd do the same using the I2C interface. For this example, we'll use the tiny Philips PCF8583. It also has 240 bytes of RAM, which, like the DS1305, may be used for parameter storage. Unlike the DS1305, it does not have an integrated battery-backup system. So, you would need to provide an external battery-backup circuit. There are many other I2C RTCs available, and some do incorporate battery-fail protection. I've chosen to look at this one because it makes for a very simple example of an I2C interface.

The PCF8583 has two pins (**OSCI** and **OSCO**) for connecting a 32.768 kHz watch crystal. This crystal pulses an internal circuit that performs the timekeeping functions. The address pin, **A0**, determines the address of the device on the I2C bus. Most I2C chips provide several address pins, allowing a range of possible addresses to be wired. The PCF8583 has only one, to reduce the pin count of the chip. Six of its address bits are hardwired internally. Only the least significant, **A0**, is available to the system designer. The address configuration of the PCF8583 is shown in Figure 8-8. (Note how the transfer direction [read or write] is incorporated into the address field.)

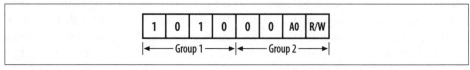

Figure 8-8. PCF8583 addresses

Connecting **A0** directly to ground sets that address bit to 0 and therefore maps the PCF8583 to I2C address 0x50. Alternatively, if **A0** is tied to **VDD**, then the address of the device is 0x51.

The schematic for interfacing the PCF8583 to a microcontroller is shown in Figure 8-9.

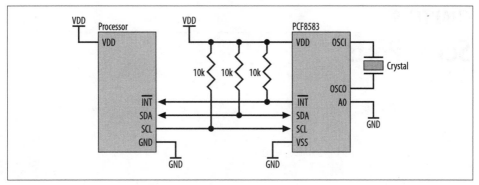

Figure 8-9. Interfacing a PCF8583 to a microcontroller

SDA and **SCL** both require pull-up resistors to **VDD**. The PCF8583 also has an internal alarm function and asserts an output (**INT**) for interrupting the processor. Since this output is open-drain, a pull-up resistor is also required.

Adding a Small Display with I²C

You can use I²C to add simple LCDs (and other equivalent display technologies) to your embedded computer. These LCDs are usually just a few lines of text high, but are useful for simple message display functions. Matrix Orbital (*http://www. matrixorbital.com*) produces a number of display modules that are easy to interface, such as the VFD2041. This display module is 80 characters wide by 4 lines deep. The interface circuit is shown in Figure 8-10, and, as you can see, there's almost nothing to it. The types of LCDs found in laptops are considerably more complicated, and interfacing them to small processors is just not an option. But for simple message displays (such as on the front panel of an appliance), a circuit like this is ideal.

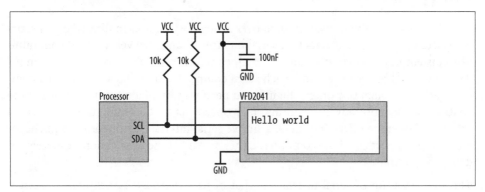

Figure 8-10. Interfacing a VFD2041 display using I²C

Many Matrix Orbital displays also come with RS-232C interfaces, so if your embedded processor doesn't support I²C, it's still easy to add a small display.

CHAPTER 9

Serial Ports

Yet all experience is an arch wherethro'
Gleams that untravell'd world whose margin fades
For ever and for ever when I move.
—Tennyson
  "Ulysses"

In this chapter, we'll look at connecting your embedded systems to the outside world through the ubiquitous serial port. We'll see how you implement the classic serial port, RS-232C, and even take a look at how you can power your embedded system through an RS-232C port. From there, we'll take a look at the more robust RS-422, designed for faster data rates over longer distances. Finally, we'll look at RS-485, an extension of RS-422 designed for low-cost networking of embedded computers.

We'll start our examination of serial interfaces by looking at the engine that drives it all.

UARTs

Serial I/O involves the transfer of data over a single wire for each direction. All serial interfaces convert parallel data to a serial bit stream, and vice versa. Serial communication is employed when it is not practical, either in physical or cost terms, to move data in parallel between systems. Such serial communication may be between a computer and a terminal or printer, the infrared beamings of a Palm computer or remote control, or, in more advanced forms, high-speed network communication such as Ethernet. For embedded computers, a simple serial interface is the easiest and cheapest way to connect to a host computer, either as part of the application or merely for debugging purposes.

The simplest form of serial interface is that of the *Universal Asynchronous Receiver Transmitter (UART)*. UARTs are also sometimes called *Asynchronous Communication Interface Adapters (ACIAs)*. They are termed *asynchronous* because no clock is transmitted with the serial data. The receiver must lock onto the data and detect individual bits without the luxury of a clock for synchronization.

Figure 9-1 shows a functional diagram of a UART. It consists of two sections: a receiver (Rx) that converts a serial bit stream to parallel data for the microprocessor and a transmitter (Tx) that converts parallel data from a microprocessor into serial form for transmission. The UART also provides status information, such as whether the receiver is full (data has arrived) or that the transmitter is empty (a pending transmission has completed). Many microcontrollers incorporate UARTs on-chip, but for larger systems, the UART is often a separate device.

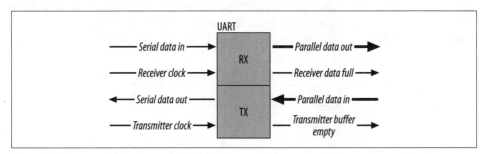

Figure 9-1. Functional diagram of a UART

Serial devices send data one bit at a time, so normal "parallel" data must first be converted to serial form before transfer. Serial transmission consists of breaking down bytes of data into single bits and shifting them out of the device one at a time. A UART's transmitter is essentially just a parallel-to-serial converter with extra features. The essence of the UART transmitter is a shift register that is loaded in parallel, and then each bit is sequentially shifted out of the device on each pulse of the serial clock. Conversely, the receiver accepts a serial bit stream into a shift register, and then this is read out in parallel by the processor.

UARTs actually predate semiconductor-based computers. In the early days of electrical communication, UARTs were mechanical devices with cogs, relays, and electromechanical shift registers. To adjust a UART's settings, you first picked up a wrench!

One of the problems associated with serial transmission is reconstructing the data at the receiving end. Difficulties arise in detecting boundaries between bits. For instance, if the serial line is low for a given length of time, the device receiving the data must be able to identify if the stream represented "00" or "000." It has to know where one bit stops and the next starts. The transmitting and receiving devices can accomplish this by sharing a common clock. Hence, in a synchronous serial system, the serial data stream is synchronized with a clock that is transmitted along with the data stream. This simplifies the recovery of data but requires an extra signal line to carry the serial clock. Asynchronous serial devices, such as UARTs, do not share a common clock; rather, each device has its own, local clock. The devices must operate at exactly the same frequency, and additional logic is required to detect the phase of the transmitted data and *phase lock* the receiver's clock to this.

Asynchronous transmission is used in systems where one character is sent at a time, and the interval of time between each byte transmission may vary. The transmission format uses one start bit at the beginning and one or two stop bits at the end of each character (Figure 9-2). The receiver synchronizes its clock upon receiving the start bit and then samples the data bits (either seven or eight, depending on the system configuration). Upon receiving the stop bit(s) in the correct sequence, the receiver assumes that the transfer was successful and that it has a valid character. If it did not receive an appropriate stop sequence, the receiver assumes that its clock drifted out of phase, and a *framing error* or bit-misalignment error is declared. It's up to the application software to check for such errors and take appropriate action.

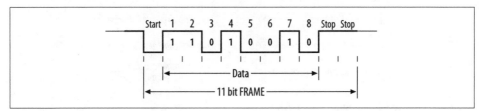

Figure 9-2. Asynchronous serial data

The conversion from parallel to serial format is usually accomplished by dedicated UART hardware, but in systems where only parallel I/O is available, the conversion may be performed by software, which toggles a single bit of a parallel I/O port acting as the serial line.

Error Detection

In any transfer of data over a potentially noisy medium (such as a serial cable), the possibility of errors exists. To detect such errors, many serial systems implement *parity* as a simple check for the validity of the data. The parity bit of a byte to be transmitted is calculated by the sending UART and included with the byte as part of the transmission. The receiving UART also calculates the parity bit for the byte and compares this against the parity bit received. If they match, the receiver assumes that everything is fine. If they do not, the receiver then knows that something went amiss and that an error exists.

There are several types of parity, the main two being *even parity* and *odd parity*. In any byte of data, there is either an even number of "1" bits or an odd number of "1" bits. An extra bit (the parity bit) is added to the byte to make the number of "1" bits even (even parity) or odd (odd parity). For successful transmission, both the receiver and transmitter must be set for the same type of parity generation. There is no protocol for establishing common parity settings between UARTs; it must be done manually at either end.

So for the binary sequence %01000000, the parity bit would be "1" for even parity and "0" for odd parity. Similarly, for %11111111, the parity bit would be "0" if we were using even parity and "1" if we had odd parity. The generation and detection of parity is done automatically by dedicated hardware within the UART. It's not something you explicitly have to calculate. You do have to make sure your UART is set to the correct type of parity generation; otherwise, it will not know how to process the parity information accordingly.

The parity bit is checked at the receiving end against the data to check whether any of the bits were corrupted during transmission. Say we sent %01000000. If our UART was set to even parity, the calculated parity bit from %01000000 would be 1. Now, let's say this transmission was corrupted along the way, such that what was actually received was %01000001. The receiver would calculate the even parity of the byte to be 0. In comparing this to the received parity bit of 1, a parity error would be detected, and the receiver would take appropriate action (such as requesting that the byte be sent again). Note that how parity errors are handled is the responsibility of the programmer. The UART itself takes no action beyond flagging the error. It is up to the software to implement appropriate error handling.

Now, what if the medium was particularly noisy and *two* bits were corrupted? Again, if we sent %01000000 with even parity (computed parity bit = 1), and this was corrupted along the way to be %01001001, the receiver would calculate the even parity of the byte to be 1. The transmission was corrupted, but *no* parity error would be detected! As you can see, the usefulness of this form of error detection is extremely limited, and, for this reason, more complicated error detection (and correction) schemes are often implemented. A good example of this is the *Cyclic Redundancy Check (CRC)* algorithm. If you need to implement CRC, there's plenty of source code available on the Web—just use your favorite search engine.

That covers the basics of how bits are transmitted serially. Now, it's time to look at how you physically implement a serial interface. We'll start with the old standard for serially connecting two computers (or just about anything else digital) together.

Old Faithful: RS-232C

RS-232C is a serial communication interface standard that has been in use, in one form or another, since the 1960s. RS-232C is used for interfacing serial devices over cable lengths of up to 25 meters and at data rates of up to 38.4 kbps. You can use it to connect to other computers, modems, and even old terminals (useful tools for monitoring status messages during debugging). In days of old, printers, plotters, and a host of other devices came with RS-232C interfaces. With the need to transfer large amounts of data rapidly, RS-232C is being supplanted as a connection standard by high-speed networks, such as Ethernet. However, it can still be a useful and (importantly) simple connection tool for your embedded system.

RS-232C is *unbalanced*, meaning that the voltage level of a data bit being transmitted is referenced to local ground. A logic high for RS-232C is a signal voltage in the range of –5 to –15 V (typically –12 V), and a logic low is between +5 and +15 V (typically +12 V). So, just to make that clear, an RS-232C high is a *negative* voltage, and a low is a *positive* voltage, unlike the rest of your computer's logic.

The terminology used in RS-232C also dates back to the 1960s. In those days of mainframes, a high (1) was called a "space," and a low (0) was called a "mark." You'll still find these terms kicking around in RS-232C, where you'll hear phrases like "mark parity" and "space parity." It's also not unheard of to see RS-232C systems still using 7-bit data frames (another leftover from the '60s), rather than the more common 8-bit. In fact, this is one of the reasons why you'll still see email being sent on the Internet limited to a 7-bit character set, just in case the packets happen to be routed via a serial connection that supports only 7-bit transmissions. It's nice how pieces of history still linger around to haunt us! More commonly, RS-232C data transmissions use 8-bit characters, and any serial port you implement should do so, too.

An RS-232C link consists of a driver and a comparator, as shown in Figure 9-3.

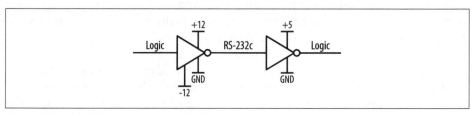

Figure 9-3. RS-232C

RS-232C also defines connectors and pin assignments, although there is a lot a room for variation (and thus a lot of incompatibilities exist). RS-232C was originally intended for connecting *Data Terminal Equipment (DTE)* to *Data Communication Equipment (DCE)* (Figure 9-4). The standard therefore assumes that at one end of an RS-232C link is a DTE device, and at the other end, there is a DCE. Before the advent of computers, a DTE was a terminal or teletype, and a DCE was a modem. The *modem* (MOdulator DEModulator) provided an interface to the phone line, and thereby a connection to a remote modem and terminal.

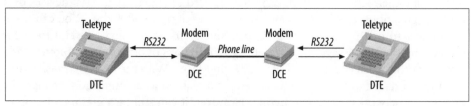

Figure 9-4. Original use of RS232: connecting teletypes to modems

This worked simply and clearly in the days before desktop computers. The "problem" arises when you wish to connect either a terminal or a modem to the serial interface of a computer. Do you treat the computer as a DTE or a DCE? The RS-232C standard implies that if a terminal is at one end of the link, then the other end should be a DCE. So, if you were connecting a terminal to a Unix workstation, the RS-232C standard would like the workstation to be a DCE (Figure 9-5). Conversely, if you were connecting a modem to a computer, the computer should be a DTE (Figure 9-6). It's all a bit schizophrenic.

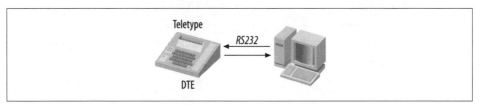

Figure 9-5. DTE device connected to a computer

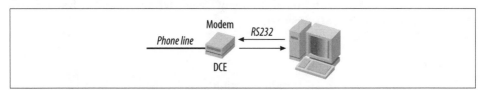

Figure 9-6. DCE device connected to a computer

Manufacturers, when faced with this problem, arbitrarily chose one or the other. The IBM PC has a DTE-type connector, whereas the makers of Unix workstations (such as Sun Microsystems) often choose to make their machines with DCE connectors, since they are more likely to be connected to terminals. To connect a PC to a modem, you need a DTE-DCE cable. To connect a PC to a terminal, you need a DTE-DTE cable. To connect a Sun workstation to a terminal, you need a DCE-DTE cable. To connect a Sun to a modem you need a DCE-DCE cable. To connect a Sun to another Sun, you need a DCE-DCE *null modem* cable (where **Rx** and **Tx** cross over), and to connect a Sun to a PC, you need a DCE-DTE null modem cable. If, however, you need to connect two PCs together, you need a DTE-DTE null modem cable. So, for just two types of device (DTE and DCE), you need six types of cable to cope with the permutations! Variety, as they say, is the spice of life, but it's the bane of RS-232C!

Table 9-1 shows the "standard" connections for RS-232C, for both 25-pin and 9-pin connectors. The signal names are DTE-relative. For example, **Tx** refers to data being *transmitted from* the DTE but *received by* a DCE.

Table 9-1. RS-232C signals

Signal	Function	25-pin	9-pin	Direction
Tx	Transmitted Data	2	3	From DTE to DCE
Rx	Received Data	3	2	To DTE from DCE
RTS	Request To Send	4	7	From DTE to DCE
CTS	Clear To Send	5	8	To DTE from DCE
DTR	Data Terminal Ready	20	4	From DTE to DCE
DSR	Data Set Ready	6	6	To DTE from DCE
DCD	Data Carrier Detect	8	1	To DTE from DCE
RI	Ring Indicator	22	9	To DTE from DCE
FG	Frame Ground (chassis)	1	-	Common
SG	Signal Ground	7	5	Common

Many of these signals are intended for modem control. To form a very simple link between a computer and a terminal, the only signals required are **Tx**, **Rx**, and **SG**. Many systems tie **FG** and **SG** together.

Shake Hands

When two remote systems are communicating serially, there needs to be some way to prevent the transmitter from sending new data before the receiver has had a chance to process the old data. This process is known as *handshaking*, or *flow control*. The way it works is simple. After transmitting a byte (or data packet), the transmitter will not send again until it has been given confirmation that the receiver is ready. There are three forms of handshaking: hardware, software, and none.

The no-handshaking option is obviously the simplest and is used in situations where the transmitting system is much slower in preparing and sending data than the receiver is in processing. For example, if you had a small, embedded computer running at a pokey 1 MHz that was feeding data into a high-speed computer system running at 4 GHz, it would not be unreasonable to assume that the faster machine would be able to keep up. However, if the faster machine is running a certain popular operating system (renowned for poor responsiveness to real-time events), it may very well be the case that it may not be able to keep up. In this case, handshaking would be required, and it's probably good practice to incorporate it anyway. If you're using the serial port to provide a human interface to your computer, then you can safely assume that no human will type faster than your computer can handle. So, for serial ports used solely for user access or debugging purposes, you can skip the handshaking.

Hardware handshaking in RS-232C uses two signals, **RTS** (*Request To Send*) and **CTS** (*Clear To Send*). When the transmitter wishes to send, it asserts **RTS**, indicating to the receiver that there is pending data. The receiver asserts **CTS** when it is ready, indicating to the transmitter that it may send. In this way, the flow of data is limited to the rate at which it may be processed.

Software handshaking, also known as *XON/XOFF*, is used where it is not possible to have hardware handshaking between the transmitter and receiver, such as when the transmission occurs over a phone line. Software handshaking chooses two characters to represent a request to "suspend transmission," and a "clear to resume." These are normally the characters Ctrl-S (0x13) and Ctrl-Q (0x11). The caveat is that you then can't have these characters as part of the transmitted file, because they would be interpreted as flow control by the receiver and not as received data. If you're only sending ASCII text, this is not a problem, but it can be a real headache if you're sending binary data. The common solution is to preprocess the binary data prior to transmission and convert it to ASCII representation. For example, the byte 0x2F becomes the ASCII characters "2" (0x32) and "F" (0x46). Software on the receiving end converts the ASCII characters back into binary data again. Examples of software that will do this are uuencode under Unix and BinHex under Mac OS.

Implementing an RS-232C Interface

Adding an RS-232C interface to a system is easy. Most microcontrollers (except the very tiny) incorporate a UART within the chip, so all that is required is an external *level shifter* to convert the serial transmissions to and from RS-232C levels. Maxim makes a huge range of RS-232C interface chips (level shifters) that greatly simplify your design. No matter what your specific conversion requirements, doubtless there's a Maxim part to meet your need. A good generic choice is the MAX3222 transceiver. Since nearly all RS-232C transceivers are used in the same way, looking at a design with a MAX3222 provides a good example of what to do for any transceiver. Unlike many other level shifters, the Maxim parts can operate from a low supply voltage, in the range of 3.0 V to 5.5 V. Many other manufacturers' devices need supplies of +12 V and −12 V, and therefore require additional voltage regulators. The MAX3222 consumes minimal power (1 mA in normal operation and as low as 1 uA in shutdown mode), making it ideal for portable and battery-powered applications. If the ability to shut down the serial port into low-power operation is not required, the MAX3232 can be substituted. It is functionally the same, except that it lacks shutdown capability.

Using the MAX3222 is trivial, as there is almost no design work involved at all. The only external support components required are capacitors for the chip's internal charge pumps. These pumps generate the +12 V and −12 V voltages required for RS-232C transmission, and they do so without requiring (additional) external voltage regulators. Figure 9-7 shows the schematic.

The capacitor C1 must be a minimum of 0.1 uF. If you are operating the chip at less than 3.6 V, C2, C3, and C4 can also be 0.1 uF. If the supply voltage is to be as high as 5.5 V, then C2, C3, and C4 must be a minimum of 0.47 uF. Since these are

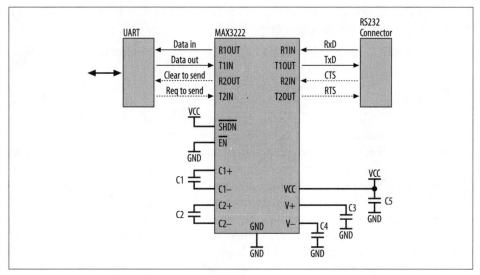

Figure 9-7. RS-232C interface using a MAX3222

minimum values, larger capacitors may be used. However, if C1 is increased, then the remaining capacitors must also be increased accordingly. C5, the decoupling capacitor for **VCC**, is nominally 0.1 uF. All capacitors should be as close to the appropriate pins of the chip as possible.

The only remaining connections are the serial data lines from the UART and the signals to the RS-232C connector. If you are implementing a minimal serial interface, only **Rx**, **Tx**, and ground are required. **RTS** and **CTS** are optional. The RS-232C connector may be either a 25-pin or a 9-pin DB connector (its shape looks like the letter "D"). However, the connector could also be just a row of pins, a parallel header, or even just wires soldered directly onto the PCB.

The MAX3222 has two control inputs, **SHDN** (shutdown) and **EN** (enable). **SHDN** places the RS-232C transmitters in high impedance, thereby disabling them. This reduces the chip's current consumption to less than 1 uA. When in shutdown mode, the receivers are still active. Thus, the UART is still able to receive data even if the MAX3222 is in low-power mode. If **SHDN** is not required, just connect it directly to **VCC**.

Similarly, **EN** is used to control the receiver outputs. Placing **EN** high puts the receiver outputs into high impedance, while the transmitter outputs are unaffected. To enable the receivers, **EN** is asserted (pulled low). If disabling the receivers is not required, then tie **EN** to ground to permanently activate them.

If needed, **SHDN** and **EN** may be controlled by a microcontroller's I/O lines, or by simple digital outputs using a latch.

The MAX3222 is sufficient to implement a minimal RS-232C interface, using just **Rx**, **Tx**, and ground. It also has additional drivers to support **RTS** and **CTS**, allowing for basic flow control. Should you require a full RS-232C interface, the MAX3241 is a good choice. Its operation is similar to the MAX3222, but it has additional transceivers allowing the inclusion of **DTR**, **DSR**, **DCD**, and **RI** for modem control. The MAX3421 may also be used to interface to a serial mouse, since it is able to meet the appropriate voltage and current requirements.

Using a Serial Port as a Power Supply

If an embedded system is to be permanently connected to a host computer via an RS-232C serial interface, it is possible to parasitically power the embedded system *from* the serial interface. Many RS-232C signals go unused and can supply a moderate amount of current, nominally 50 mA. However it can vary (considerably) from device to device, and, as always, you should check the specific system to which you are interfacing. If your embedded system requires less than this for its *total* current draw, you can use an RS-232C control signal for power.

For instance, the **RTS** (Ready To Send) or **DTR** (Data Terminal Ready) signals may not be used in many RS-232C applications. Either can be used as the power input to a voltage regulator, and thereby provide the system with power. The host computer therefore uses **RTS** of its serial port as the power control for the embedded system. Under software, the host sends **RTS** high, and the embedded system is powered up. If the host sends **RTS** low, the embedded system is powered down. The caveat to all this is to ensure that your embedded system's current draw is low enough so that it can be powered by **RTS**. The advantage of this technique is that you require no external power supply for your embedded system. It works, as if by magic, whenever it is plugged into a serial port. The catch is that you can't then use that RS-232C control signal for its original purpose. It must turn on and stay on to provide your embedded computer with power.

A sample schematic of this is shown in Figure 9-8, which also includes an RS-232C interface for a microcontroller, using a MAX3232. Note the diode, D1. Since **RTS** will be a negative voltage (as low as −15 V) when low, some protection is required for the voltage regulator, since it is not designed to have its input taken below zero volts. The diode can be any garden-variety power diode, such as a 1N4004, and will conduct only when **RTS** is positive. The voltage regulator (MAX604) converts the voltage from **RTS** to a supply of 3.3 V for the embedded system. If we required a supply of 5 V, we'd simply use a MAX603 instead. The circuit would otherwise be the same. The output of the regulator is smoothed by the capacitor C5, and a power-on LED is provided to show us when we have power. The MAX3232 sits between the RS-232C port and the processor, level-shifting the serial transmissions from the processor's logic levels to RS-232C, and vice versa.

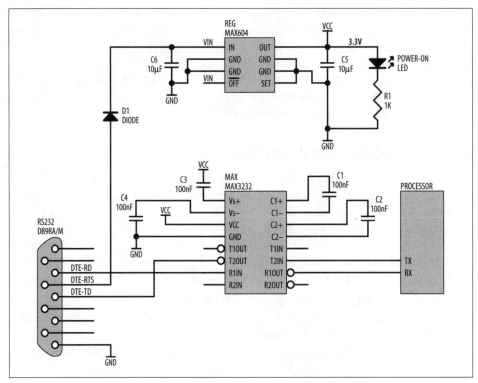

Figure 9-8. Using RTS as a power source in a low-powered embedded system

There we have the basics of RS-232C. It's a very common interface that is easy to use, but it does have its limitations and quirks. It was originally intended for connecting dumb terminals and teletypes to modems, not for interconnecting computers and peripherals. A better choice is RS-422, designed for more robust and versatile serial connections.

RS-422

Unlike RS-232C, which is referenced to local ground, *RS-422* uses the difference between two lines, known as a *twisted pair* or a *differential pair*, to represent the logic level. Thus, RS-422 is a *balanced* transmission, or, in other words, it is not referenced to local ground. Any noise or interference will affect both wires of the twisted pair, but the *difference* between them will be less affected. This is known as *common-mode rejection*. RS-422 can therefore carry data over longer distances and at higher rates with greater noise immunity than RS-232C. RS-422 can support data transmission over cable lengths of up to 1,200 meters (approximately 4,000 feet).

Figure 9-9 shows a basic RS-422 link, where a driver (D) of one embedded system is connected to a receiver (R) of another embedded system via a twisted pair. The resistor, Rt, at receiving end of the twisted pair is a *termination* resistor. It acts to remove signal reflections that may occur during transmission over long distances, and it is required. Rt is nominally 100–120 Ω.

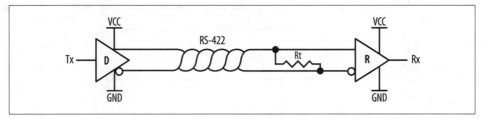

Figure 9-9. RS-422

The voltage difference between an RS-422 twisted pair is between ±4 V and ±12 V between the transmission lines (Figure 9-10). RS-422 is, to a degree, compatible with RS-232C. By connecting the negative side of the twisted pair to ground, RS-422 effectively becomes an unbalanced transmission. It may then be mated with RS-232C. Since the voltage levels of RS-422 fall within the acceptable ranges for RS-232C, the two standards may be interconnected. RS-422 was the serial interface found on early Apple Macintosh computers, quietly dropped with the coming of the iMacs.

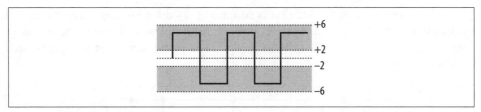

Figure 9-10. RS-422 voltage levels

There is a wide variety of RS-422 interface chips available. Figure 9-11 shows a simple RS-422 bidirectional interface implemented using two Maxim MAX3488s. The **Tx** and **Rx** pairs of each MAX3488 are connected to UARTs within each embedded system, just as we did with RS-232C.

It's important to note that RS-422 specifies only the voltages for the standard, not the physical implementation (pinouts or connectors). That is covered by RS-449. Now, no one seems to bother with RS-449, mainly because it is unnecessarily complex for most uses. People using RS-422 just seem to do their own thing, picking whatever cable and connectors (and pinouts!) they feel are appropriate for their application. Self-expression and RS-422 seem to go hand in hand.

Some RS-422 interface chips have an optional enable input. When enabled, the chip outputs and drives a transmission onto the twisted pair. When disabled, the chip's output is high-impedance, and the chip appears "invisible." Because of the ability of the interface chip to "disappear" from the connection, it is possible to have multiple

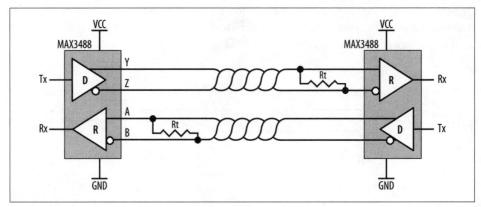

Figure 9-11. Bidirectional RS-422 interface

interface chips (and therefore more than two embedded systems) connected to the twisted pair. In this way, it is possible to extend RS-422 into a low-cost, robust, simple network. When implemented in this fashion, it becomes RS-485.

RS-485

RS-485 is a variation on RS-422 that is commonly used for low-cost networking and in many industrial applications. It is one of the simplest and easiest networks to implement. It allows multiple systems (*nodes*) to exchange data over a single twisted pair (Figure 9-12).

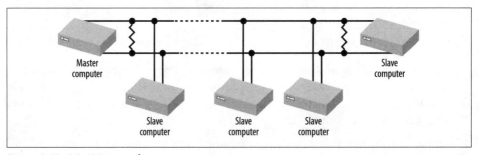

Figure 9-12. RS-485 network

RS-485 is based on a master-slave architecture. All transactions are initiated by the master, and a slave will transmit only when specifically instructed to do so. There are many different protocols that run over RS-485, and often people will do their own thing and create a protocol specific to the application at hand.

The interface to the RS-485 network is provided by a transceiver, such as a Maxim MAX3483 (Figure 9-13).

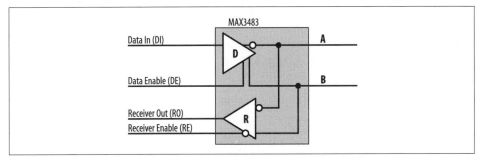

Figure 9-13. RS-485 transceiver

The MAX3483 is just an RS-422 transceiver with enable inputs, and using it in a design is straightforward. On the network side, the MAX3483 has two signal lines, **A** and **B**. This is the twisted pair (network cable) attachment point. The MAX3483 also has Data In (**DI**) and Receiver Out (**RO**). These are connected to the **Tx** and **Rx** signals of the UART (or microcontroller), respectively.

Since it is connected to a common network on which it must both listen and transmit, it has two control inputs, Data Enable (**DE**) and Receiver Enable (**RE**). A high input to **DE** allows the **DI** input to be transmitted on the network. A low input to **DE** disables the output of the transmitter. Similarly, a low input to **RE** enables the receiver, and network traffic is passed through to **RO**. **DE** and **RE** are normally controlled by an I/O line of the processor. Now, you'll notice that **DE** is active high, and **RE** is active low. This is not by chance. A node on the network won't be receiving traffic if it's transmitting and, conversely, won't be transmitting if it is receiving. Therefore, only one of the two—the transmitter or the receiver—should be active at any one time. If the transmitter is on, the receiver should be off, and vice versa. The control for the transmitter is therefore the logical opposite of the control for the receiver. By having **DE** active high and **RE** active low, a single control line may be used for both. Figure 9-14 shows a MAX3483 interfaced to a microcontroller in this way. The microcontroller normally has **DE/RE** low so that it is listening to network traffic. When it wishes to transmit, it sends **DE/RE** high. Upon completion of transmission, it returns **DE/RE** low and resumes listening.

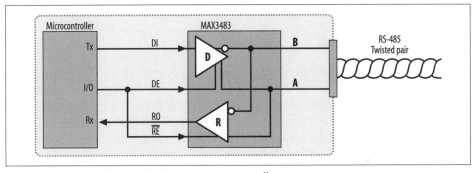

Figure 9-14. Connecting a MAX3483 to a microcontroller

RS-485 may be implemented as *half duplex*, where a single twisted pair is used for both transmission and reception (Figure 9-15), or *full duplex*, where separate twisted pairs are used for each direction (Figure 9-16). Full-duplex RS-485 is sometimes known as *four-wire mode*. Note that for full-duplex operation, the MAX3483s are replaced with MAX3491s that have dual network interfaces.

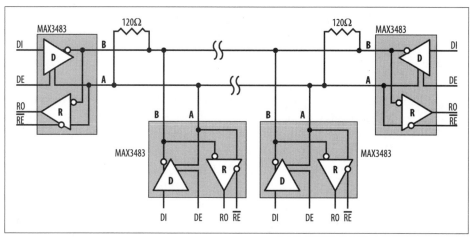

Figure 9-15. Half-duplex RS-485

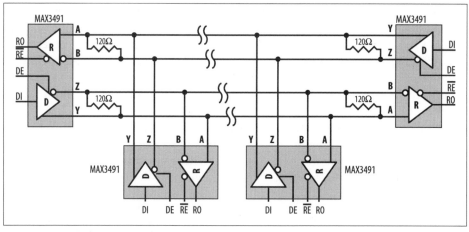

Figure 9-16. Full-duplex RS-485

These examples show four computers (nodes) connected to an RS-485 network. Each RS-485 interface chip (MAX3483 or MAX3491) exists in a separate embedded computer. The UART transmitter output, **Tx**, in each embedded system is connected to the respective **DI** of each of the RS-485 interface chips. Similarly, **RO** connects to the **Rx** input of each UART. The driver of each RS-485 interface chip is enabled by asserting **DE**, and, similarly, reception is enabled by asserting **RE**.

Normally, all systems connected to the RS-485 network have their receivers enabled and listen to the traffic. Only when a system wishes to transmit does it enable its driver. There are a number of formal protocols that use RS-485 as a transmission medium, and twice as many homespun protocols as well. The main problem you need to avoid is the possibility of two nodes of the network transmitting at the same time. The simplest technique is to designate one node as a *master* node and the others as *slaves*. Only the master may initiate a transmission on the network, and a slave may only respond directly to the master, once that master has finished.

The number of nodes possible on the network is limited by the driving capability of the interface chips. Normally, this limit is 32 nodes per network, but some chips can support up to 512 nodes.

CHAPTER 10

IrDA

*It makes all the difference whether one sees darkness
through the light or brightness through the shadows.*
—David Lindsay
  A Voyage to Arcturus

In the last chapter, we looked at serial communication that takes place over copper wire. Now, we'll see a serial interface that uses pulses of infrared light to transmit data across short distances, without the need for interconnecting cables. Infrared (IR) transmission of data is becoming commonplace, and IR transceivers are appearing in laptop computers, PDAs, and cell phones. They are also appearing in peripherals such as printers and network interfaces, allowing no-fuss/no-cable connection for people on the move. IR communication is also used by remote controls to talk to their appliances. Your TV, VCR, and DVD remotes all have an IR LED to beam commands across the room.

We'll start our discussion of IR communication by looking at the most common standard, IrDA. Later, we'll see just how trivial infrared hardware is to implement.

Introduction to IrDA

IrDA is the infrared transmission standard commonly used in computers and peripherals. IrDA, which stands for "Infrared Data Association," is a consortium of over 150 companies that maintain and develop the standard. IrDA owes it origins to the infrared communication links used in Hewlett-Packard calculators, known as HP-SIR (Hewlett-Packard Serial Infra Red). The IrDA standard has expanded on HP-SIR significantly and provides a range of protocols that application software may use in communication.

The basic purpose of IrDA is to provide device-to-device communication over short distances. Mobile devices, such as laptops, present a problem when they must be connected to other machines or networks. Chances are the correct cable is not at hand, or one of the machines is not configured correctly to allow networking to take place. When the users are nontechnical types, this can be a real problem. IrDA was developed as the solution to this problem. With IrDA, no cables are required, and standard protocols ensure that devices can exchange information seamlessly. Full details of the IrDA standard and protocols are available from *http://www.irda.org*.

The expectation is that the IrDA user will be a mobile professional using a laptop or PDA to communicate with other computers, PDAs, or peripherals nearby. This concept has a number of important consequences. The devices communicating will be physically close, so relatively low power transmissions are all that is required. This is important because there are regulations guarding the maximum level of IR radiation that can be emitted. Also, it is reasonable to assume that the two devices that are to communicate will be physically pointed toward each other prior to use. (You don't change your TV channel by aiming the remote at the cat, unless of course your cat is especially reflective.) It can also be assumed that only two devices will be communicating and that their proximity will exclude interference from other IrDA devices. Thus, IrDA does not have to deal with transmission collision and detection issues that standards such as 802.11 (wireless Ethernet) do. Two IrDA devices may be communicating at one end of a desk, while another two devices are communicating at the other, with no problems at all. Further, a transmission will be initiated by the user, which simplifies the software protocols. An overall guiding principle is that IrDA should be cheap to implement, since it must find its way into low-cost consumer devices.

With all that in mind, IrDA is a point-to-point protocol that uses asynchronous serial transmission over short distances. The initial IrDA specification (1.0) supported data rates of between 2,400 bps and 115.2 kbps over distances of one meter, although some IrDA transceivers can achieve greater distances than this. Initial IR communication takes place at 9,600 bps, and devices negotiate the data rate up or down, depending on their capabilities and needs. Unlike RS-232C, the user does not need to set, know about, or even care what bit rate is being used in communication.

An IrDA transmitter will beam out its transmission at an angle of 15 degrees to 30 degrees on either side of the line of sight. The receiver has a "viewing angle" of 15 degrees on either side of its line of sight (Figure 10-1). So, if two IrDA devices are placed a meter or less apart and generally aimed in each other's direction, communication will not be a problem. Since its original specification, the standard has been expanded to support higher data rates of 1.152 Mbps and 4 Mbps.

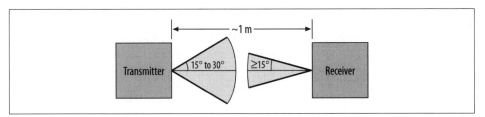

Figure 10-1. IrDA transmission and viewing angles

The IrDA standard specifies a number of protocol layers for communication. The *IrPHY (IR Physical Layer)* specification details the hardware layer, including requirements for modulating the outputs of UARTs prior to transmission. The control protocol is known as *High-level Data Link Control*, or *HDLC. IrLAP (Infrared Link Access Protocol)* uses a HDLC for controlling access to the communication medium. One IrLAP exists per device. An IrLAP connection is essentially a master-slave configuration, or, as they are known in IrDA parlance, *primary* and *secondary* devices. The primary device starts communication, sends commands, and handles data-flow control (handshaking). It is rare for a primary device to be anything other than a computer. Secondaries (such as printers) simply respond to requests from primaries. Two primary devices can communicate by one primary assuming the role of a secondary device. Typically, the device that initiates the transfer remains the primary, while the other device becomes a secondary for the duration of the transaction.

IrLMP (Infrared Link Management Protocol) provides the device's software with a means of sharing the single IrLAP between multiple tasks that wish to communicate using IrDA. IrLMP also provides a query protocol by which one device may interrogate another to determine what services are available on the remote system. This query protocol is known as *LM-IAS*, or *Link Management Information Access Service*. These are the basic IrDA protocols that all devices must support. Beyond these, IrDA also provides a number of optional services. *IrCOMM* provides emulation of standard serial-port and parallel-port devices. For application software, the IR port can then be used as if it were just another serial or parallel port. Using IrCOMM, a laptop or PDA can communicate with an IR-enabled printer just as though that printer were physically plugged into the mobile computer. *IrLAN* allows access to local area networks via the IR interface. *IrOBEX* provides a mechanism for object exchange between devices, in software that supports object-oriented programming. Finally, *Tiny TP* is a lightweight protocol allowing applications to perform flow-control (handshaking) when transferring data from one device to another. Figure 10-2 shows how these protocol layers fit together.

At the lower data rates, all protocol handling, packet forming, and error checking is done in software by the processor within an IrDA-compliant device. At higher data rates, dedicated hardware performs these functions, since low-cost embedded processors may not have the computing horsepower to complete these tasks in the time available.

Since IrDA communicates using light, there must be some way to distinguish between a logic 0 and a logic 1 during transmission. To solve this problem, IrDA uses a bit-encoding scheme known as *Return-to-Zero*, or *RZ*. With RZ, a frame consists of a transmission interval that is divided into subintervals representing individual bits. A logic zero is represented by a pulse that is 3/16 the width of a bit subinterval, while a logic 1 is represented by the absence of a pulse (Figure 10-3).

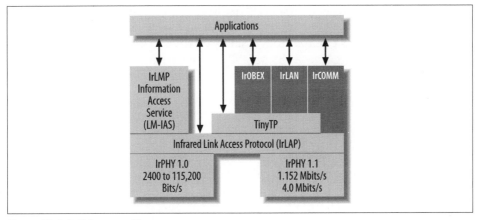

Figure 10-2. IrDA protocol layers

Figure 10-3. RZ encoding

At data rates of 4 Mbps, *PPM*, or *Pulse Position Modulation*, is used to distinguish different bits. With PPM, the position of the pulse is varied. Its location within the subinterval determines the transmitted bit pattern. The PPM used in IrDA is known as *4PPM* and uses one of four positions to provide the transmission of two data bits (Figure 10-4). In PPM terminology, these are known as *cells*.

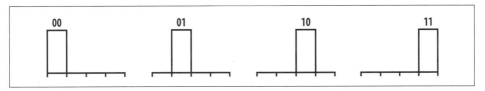

Figure 10-4. 4PPM cell encoding

A sample data packet (for a 4 Mbps transmission) is shown in Figure 10-5. It consists of a 64-cell (128-bit) preamble packet, a start packet, the frame body containing the data to be transmitted, a 32-bit Cyclic Redundancy Check (CRC) code, and a packet stop marker. The data frame can be as little as 2 bytes or as large as 2050 bytes.

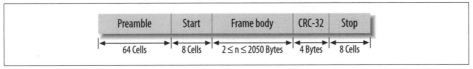

Figure 10-5. A 4 Mbps data packet

Now, most UARTs are not capable of performing transmissions in RZ or PPM encoding. Therefore, a special device, known as an *EnDec* (Encoder Decoder), converts the standard UART output to RZ, and vice versa. A good EnDec to choose is the HSDL-7001 from Agilent or the MCP2120 from Microchip. Some UARTs, such as the MAX3100, incorporate an EnDec on chip and thus may be used to directly interface to an IR transceiver.

An IrDA Interface

For IR transmission and reception, you can use an individual IR LED and an IR photodiode detector. Alternatively, you can use combined IR transceivers that incorporate both the IR LED and photodiode, along with support components, in a convenient package (Figure 10-6). Several manufacturers make such devices, including Agilent (*http://www.agilent.com*) and Vishay (*http://www.vishay.com*). As part of the transceiver packaging, the receiver photodiode is covered by a dark filter to remove visible light and improve IR reception.

Figure 10-6. Agilent IrDA transceivers

The MAX3100 is a general-purpose UART that you can use to add RS-232C or RS-485 interfaces to your embedded computer. It interfaces to a host processor through SPI and can operate on a supply voltage of between 2.7 V and 5.5 V. However, it is also IrDA-compliant and can be configured to output RZ-encoded transmissions and receive RZ-encoded bit streams. All you need to do to make an IrDA interface is add an IR transceiver, some inverter gates, and a few support components. The schematic for the circuit is shown in Figure 10-7.

On the left of the schematic are standard SPI connections to a microcontroller. The MAX3100 also has an interrupt output by which it can notify the host processor of a change in state (such as that it has received data). This interrupt line is pulled high by a 10 kΩ resistor. The MAX3100 also has a shutdown input to place the device in low-power mode. This can be driven by an I/O line of the microcontroller. The MAX3100 also requires a crystal to generate the transmission and reception clocks. This can either be a 1.8432 MHz crystal or a 3.6864 MHz crystal. Either frequency can be used to generate any of the required baud rates through software control of the internal clock dividers. The lower-speed crystal will cause the MAX3100 to use less power.

There are a number of IR transceivers available, and in this schematic I have chosen to use the Agilent HSDL-1001. To interface the MAX3100 to the HSDL-1001, we

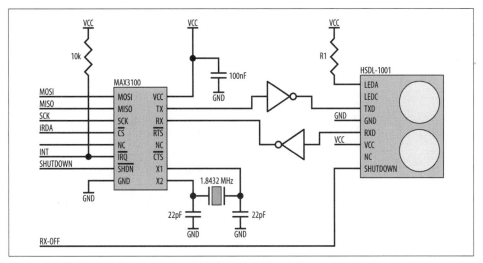

Figure 10-7. IrDA interface for an embedded computer

simply need to invert both the transmit (**TX**) and receive (**RX**) signals. The HSDL-1001 has a shutdown input that is used to put the receiving photodiode in low-power mode. It has no effect on the transmitting LED, however. This shutdown input may also be driven by an I/O line from the processor. For maximum versatility, this shutdown is controlled independently from the MAX3100's shutdown. The transmitter LED of the HSDL-1001 requires a current-limiting resistor, R1. This internal LED circuit is essentially the same as the LED circuit we first saw in Chapter 4. When the LED is turned on, the LED's cathode voltage is a minimum of 2.1 V. The maximum LED current is 240 mA; therefore, from Ohm's Law, the value for the resistor R1 (when operating from a 5 V supply) is approximately 15 Ω.

One final thing to consider is that IrDA is very susceptible to interference and noise; therefore, all power supplies should be properly decoupled using capacitors for *every* power pin. Ground planes should also be used to shield the transceiver and associated signal tracks.

Other Infrared Devices

Your TV, VCR, DVD player, air conditioner, and a host of other devices all have infrared ports for receiving commands from their remote controls. The bad news is that none (or at least very few) are IrDA-compliant. Appliance manufacturers tend to do their own thing, and often at their own weird baud rates too. So the previous circuit, which is IrDA-compliant, may or may not work with a particular appliance. However, something as simple as the circuit in Figure 10-8 may do the trick for you.

The transmitter of the HSDL-1001 may be driven directly by a processor I/O line. Similarly, the receiver may be sampled using an I/O (as an input) too. So, under

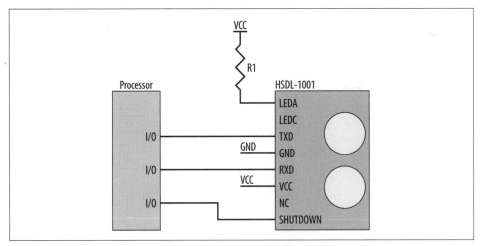

Figure 10-8. A crude infrared interface

software control (and by "manually" toggling the transmitter I/O line as appropriate), the HSDL-1001 may be fed the correct RZ bit stream at the appropriate bit rate. This manual technique is commonly used in standard serial interfaces to implement a serial port on processors that don't have a UART (and that can't be expanded). This *software UART* technique can just as easily be extended to an infrared interface. It's up to you as the programmer to ensure that you get the timing correct.

 You can't see the IR output of a remote control with the naked eye, but if you point a camcorder at it, you can. Point the remote into the camera lens and hit a button or two. If you look in the viewfinder while doing this, you can clearly see the control beaming its bits. The way this works is that the CCD imager inside the camera is sensitive to IR as well as visible light. That's one of the reasons why camcorders are able to shoot so well in low-light levels. To further increase their ability to image at night, some camcorders have IR lights on the front to illuminate the darkness, yet be invisible to people looking on.

Try the trick with the remote. You'll be surprised at just how bright the IR LEDs really are.

For information on appliance (and remote control) IR protocols and programming, go to *http://www.remotecentral.com*.

CHAPTER 11

USB

No thing happens in vain, but everything for a reason
and by necessity.
—Leucippus
On Mind

In Chapter 9, we looked at RS-232C, that old standard of communication that's not so standard after all. RS-232C has lots of problems and lots of limitations. Getting any two RS-232C devices to talk is not as simple as it could or should be. You need the right cable with the right sort of connectors, and then you need to manually coordinate the communication parameters such as data rate, parity, and handshaking. At best it is a nuisance, at worst a headache. For hardware manufacturers, it presents a dilemma. Your goal in developing your product should be to make that product as easy to use as possible. You don't want users stumbling around with incorrect cables, manually configuring settings, and failing to seamlessly integrate your product with the rest of their system. This doesn't make for a happy user.

Universal Serial Bus (*USB*) is the solution. It allows peripherals and computers to interconnect in a standard way with a standard protocol and opens up the possibility of "plug and play" for peripherals. USB is rapidly dominating the desktop computer market, making RS-232C an endangered species. Apple Macintoshes no longer have RS-232C/RS-422 ports, and soon all PCs will go the same way. Therefore, an understanding of USB (and how to build a USB port) is critical if you wish to interface your embedded computer to the desktop machines of the near future. USB supports the connection of printers, modems, mice, keyboards, joysticks, scanners, cameras, and much more.

USB opens a wealth of possibilities, but developing with it is more complex than with RS-232C. USB has the advantage (for the user) that devices interact with the host computer's OS. No manual setup is required. However, it does add an extra layer of complexity to your software, since your embedded code must interact with the host in the appropriate way. USB can even provide power to peripherals through the same cable as data. No external power supply (or power cable) is required. So for the user, a USB peripheral is simplicity itself.

In this chapter, you'll get an overview of USB and then go on to see how you can incorporate a USB interface into your embedded system. The protocols and specifications for USB are long and complex, and well beyond the scope of this book. Fortunately, to design USB-based hardware, the task is much simpler. We'll simply take an overview and then look at a physical USB implementation. For a full look at the standard, a list of vendors, and more documentation than you can shake a cable at, visit *http://www.usb.org*.

Introduction to USB

There are two specifications for USB: USB 1.1 and USB 2.0. USB 2.0 is fully compatible with USB 1.1. USB supports data rates of 12 Mbps and 1.5 Mbps (for slower peripherals) for USB 1.1, and data rates of 480 Mbps for USB 2.0. Data transfers can be either isochronous* or asynchronous.

USB is a high-speed bus that allows up to 127 devices to be connected (Figure 11-1). No longer is having only one or two ports on your computer a limitation. Further, one standard for cables and connectors eliminates the confusion that existed with RS-232C. Devices are able to self-identify to a host computer, and they can be *hot-swapped*, meaning that the systems do not need to be powered down before connection or disconnection.

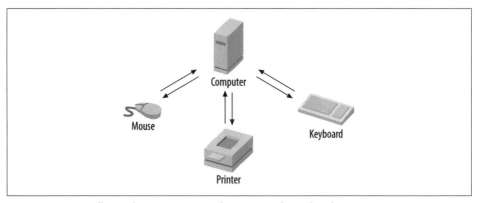

Figure 11-1. USB allows a host to connect with a variety of peripherals

The basic structure of a USB network is a *tiered star*. A USB system consists of one or more *USB devices* (peripherals), one or more *hubs*, and a *host* (controlling computer). The host computer is sometimes known as the *host controller*. Only one host

---

* Occurring at equal intervals of time.

may exist in a USB network. The host controller incorporates a *root hub*, which provides the initial attachment points to the host. The hubs form nodes to which devices or other hubs connect, and they are (largely) invisible to USB communication. In other words, traffic between a device and a host is not affected by the presence of hubs.

Hubs are used to expand a USB network. For example, a given host computer may have five USB ports. By connecting hubs, each with additional ports, to the host, the physical connectivity of the system is increased (Figure 11-2). Many USB devices, such as keyboards, incorporate inbuilt hubs allowing them to provide additional expansion as well as their primary function.

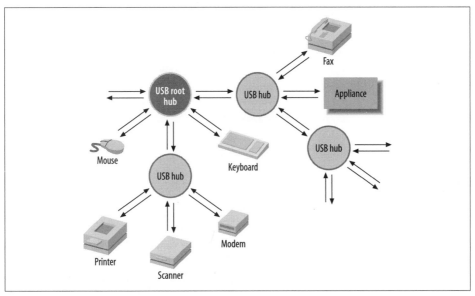

Figure 11-2. USB is expandable using hubs

The host will regularly poll hubs for their status. When a new device is plugged into a hub, the hub advises the host of its change in state. The host issues a command to enable and reset that port. The device attached to that port responds, and the host retrieves information about the device. Based on that information, the host operating system determines what software driver to use for that device. The device is then assigned a unique address, and its internal configuration is requested by the host. When a device is unplugged, the hub advises the host of the change in state when polled, and the host removes the device from its list of available resources. The detection and identification of USB devices by a host is known as *bus enumeration*.

USB "knows" about and supports different *classes* of devices. Each class represents the functionality that the device can provide to the host. Some sample classes (and sample devices) are listed in Table 11-1. A single, physical USB peripheral can encompass several classes.

Table 11-1. USB device classes

Class	Purpose
Audio	Audio and music devices, sound systems
Chip/smart card interface devices (CCID)	Smart card devices
Common class (CCS)	Generic devices
Communications device	Modems, telephones, and network interfaces
HID	*Human Interface Devices* (*HIDs*) such as mice and keyboards
Hub	USB hub
IrDA	Infrared devices
Mass storage	Hard disks, CD-ROMs, DVD-ROMs
Monitor	Computer monitors and display devices
Physical interface devices	Joysticks and other devices (such as motion platforms) that provide physical feedback
POS terminals	Point of Sale (POS) devices such as cash registers and EFTPOS devices
Power	Devices with power control or monitoring (battery backup and recharging, for example)
Printer class	Printers
Imaging class	Scanners and cameras

USB Packets

There are four types of transfers that can take place over USB. A *control transfer* is used to configure the bus and devices on the bus, and to return status information. A *bulk transfer* moves data asynchronously over USB. An *isochronous transfer* is used for moving time-critical data, such as audio data destined for an output device. Unlike a bulk transfer, which can be bidirectional, an isochronous transfer is uni-directional and does not include a cyclic-redundancy-check (CRC) field. An *interrupt transfer* is used to retrieve data at regular intervals, ranging from 1 to 255 milliseconds.

Data is transferred between USB devices using packets, and a transfer can comprise one or more packets. A packet consists of a SYNC (synchronization) byte, a PID (Packet ID), content (data, address, etc.), and a CRC.

The SYNC byte phase locks the receiver's clock. This is equivalent to the start bit of an RS-232C frame. The PID indicates the function of the packet, such as whether it is a data packet or a setup packet. The upper four bits of the packet ID are the inverse of the lower four bits, for additional error checking. For example, the packet ID for a data packet is 0x3C. In binary, this is %0011 1100.

USB packets can be one of four types: token, data, handshaking, or preamble.

Tokens are 24-bit packets that determine the type of transfer that is to take place over the bus. There are four types of token packet (Figure 11-3). A token packet consists of a SYNC byte, a packet ID (indicating packet type), the address of the device being accessed by the host, the end-point address, and a 5-bit CRC field. The end-point address is the *internal* destination of the data within the device.

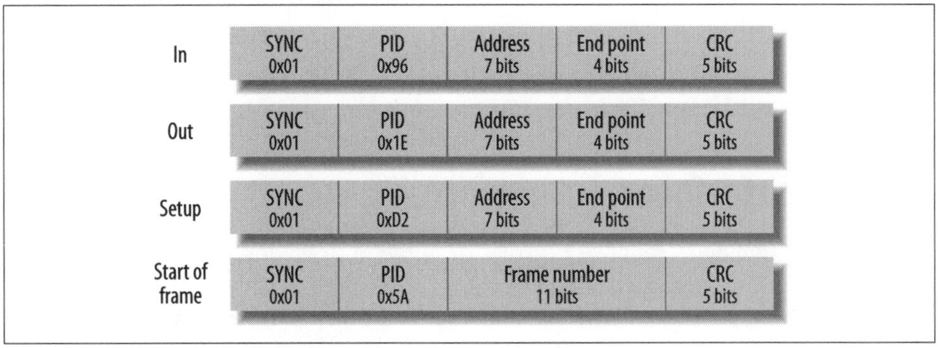

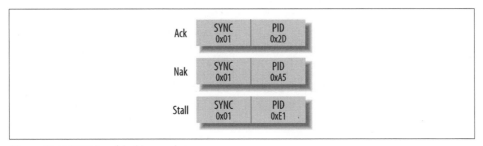

Figure 11-3. USB token packets

There are two types of data packet, known as DATA0 and DATA1 (Figure 11-4). The transmission of data packets alternates between the two types. A single data packet can transfer between 0 and 1,023 bytes, and the data packet's CRC is 16 bits due to the larger packet size.

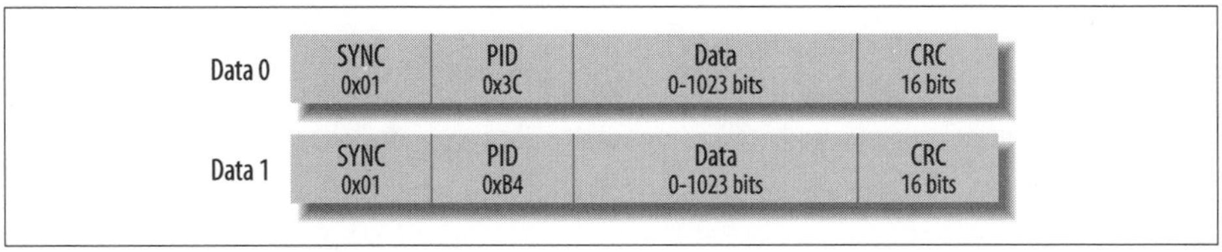

Figure 11-4. USB data packets

There are three types of handshaking packets (Figure 11-5). A successful data reception is acknowledged with an *Ack* packet. The receiver notifies the host of a failed transmission by sending a *Nak* (No Acknowledge) packet. A *Stall* is used to pause a transfer.

Figure 11-5. USB handshaking packets

A *descriptor* is a data packet used to inform the host of the capabilities of the device. It contains an identifier for the device's manufacturer, a product identifier, class type, and the device's internal configuration, such as its power needs and end points. Each manufacturer has a unique ID, and each product in turn will also have a unique ID. Software on the host computer uses information obtained from a descriptor to determine what services a device can perform and how the host can interact with that device.

Full details of the USB protocols may be found in the USB technical documentation available from the USB web site (*http://www.usb.org*).

Physical Interface

USB uses a shielded, four-wire cable to interconnect devices on the network (Table 11-2). Data transmission is accomplished over a differential twisted pair (much like RS-422/485) labeled **D+** and **D-**. The other two wires are V_{BUS}, which carries power to USB devices, and **GND**. Devices that use USB power are known as *bus-powered devices*, while those with their own external power supply are known as *self-powered devices*. To avoid confusion, the wires within a USB cable are color-coded.

Table 11-2. USB wires

Connector pin	Signal	Purpose	Wire color
1	V_{BUS}	USB device power (+5V)	Red
3	D+	Differential data line	Green
2	D-	Differential data line	White
4	GND	Power and signal ground	Black

Some USB chips refer to **D+** and **D-** as **DP** and **DM**, respectively.

The connection from a device back to a host is known as an *upstream connection*. Similarly, connections from the host out to devices are known as *downstream connections*. Different connectors are used for upstream and downstream ports, with the specific intention of preventing loopback. The *only* way to connect a USB network is a tiered star. USB uses two types of plugs (jacks) and two types of receptacles (sockets) for cables and equipment. The first type is Series A, shown in Figure 11-6. Series A connectors are for upstream connections. In other words, a series A receptacle is found on a host or hub, and a series A plug is at the end of the cable that attaches to the host or hub.

Series B connectors are shown in Figure 11-7. A series B receptacle is found on a USB device, and a series B plug is at the end of the cable coming downstream from a host or hub.

Figure 11-6. Series A plug and receptacle

Figure 11-7. Series B plug and receptacle

Figure 11-8 shows how this works in practice. This ensures that USB devices, hosts/hubs, and USB cables are always connected in the right way. It should not be possible to have a cable plugged in the wrong way or to directly connect two USB peripherals.

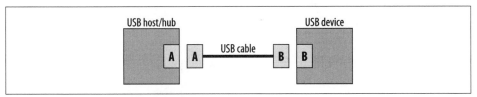

Figure 11-8. USB connectors and cable

Since a hub will be connected to USB devices downstream and to a USB host or hub upstream, it will have both types of receptacle (Figure 11-9).

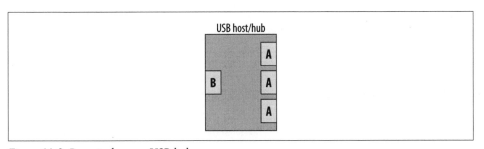

Figure 11-9. Receptacles on a USB hub

Chips that implement a USB interface require very few external components for the USB port. The schematic for an upstream port is shown in Figure 11-10.

In this example, the embedded system is powered from the USB port. If the embedded computer has its own power source, then no connection is made between **VCC** and pin 1 (V_{BUS}) of the USB connector. The pull-up resistor connected to **DP** is

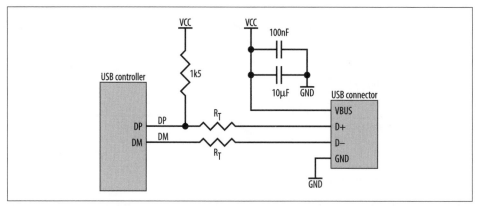

Figure 11-10. Upstream USB port

required only on upstream ports. If you are implementing downstream ports on a hub, the pull-up is not required. However, downstream ports require pull-down resistors on both **DP** and **DM** (Figure 11-11).

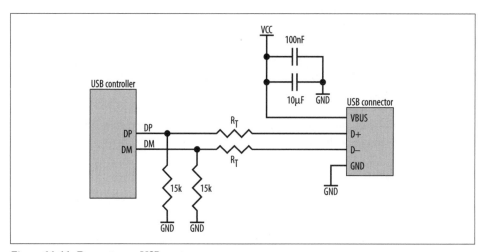

Figure 11-11. Downstream USB port

In both figures, **DP** and **DM** have series resistors (R_T) that terminate the USB connection. The total resistance of the termination should be 45 Ω. However, the pins of the USB controller will have an inherent impedance that will need to be taken into account. If the pin impedance is 21 Ω (say), then the series resistors should be 24 Ω. The catch here is that not all chip manufacturers are thorough enough to specify the pin impedance in their technical data. In such cases, you can either hound the manufacturer for the data, or take a punt. Ballpark values for the series resistors should be between 20 Ω and 30 Ω.

Many microcontrollers, such as the Microchip PIC16C745 and PIC16C765, include USB modules as part of their suite of I/O. Implementing USB with such processors is easy. You simply need to add the physical interface to the **DP** and **DM** pins of the processor. However, if the chip you have chosen to use as the primary embedded processor does not include USB, you have to provide USB functionality with an external device.

Implementing a USB Interface

One possible solution to implementing USB in your embedded system is to use a USB-to-SPI bridge, such as the Atmel AT76C711. This chip is an AVR processor with a USB subsystem, designed to act as a slave USB controller to a host processor. It has 2K of data RAM, 2K of dual-port RAM for packet processing, 16K of program RAM (organized as 8K × 16 words), an inbuilt DMA controller, an upstream USB port (with one control and five data end points), a separate IrDA-compatible UART, and SPI. The processor may be run at up to 24 MHz and operates off a 3.3 V supply. At reset, the AT76C711 automatically loads its software from an external AT45DBxxx data flash (Chapter 7) to the program RAM. Since the AT76C711's program space is small, one of the smaller AT45DBxxx data flashes will be sufficient. Alternatively, a host processor may load the AT76C711's code directly into its program RAM while it is held in reset.

The AT76C711 may act as a standalone processor, performing USB bridging functions to RS-232C, RS-422/RS-485, IrDA, or other protocols. Alternatively, it may be incorporated as a slave processor in a larger embedded system. The host processor may communicate with the AT76C711 either via SPI or by a standard serial interface through one of the AT76C711's UARTs. The AT76C711 also has general-purpose I/O lines and a UART module that supports RZ encoding for IrDA.

If the processor you are using has a bus interface, then you can add USB using a chip such as the USS-820D by Agere Systems (*http://www.agere.com*). It supports transfers of up to 12 Mbps and is specifically designed for use in USB devices, unlike a lot of USB chips that are intended for use in hubs. It can support up to eight endpoints, each with receive and transmit buffers of up 1,120 bytes.

The schematic of an upstream USB interface, using the USS-820D, is shown in Figure 11-12. This chip is available in two footprints; the MQFP is shown in this circuit. For both footprints, the signals are the same. The only difference is the pin numbering.

The USS-820D has several power-supply inputs (V_{DDA}, V_{DDT}, V_{DD0}, V_{DD1}), all of which operate from a 3.3 V supply (**VDD** in the schematic). Each power pin is decoupled to ground using a 100 nF capacitor. The 5 V power (V_{BUS}) available from the USB connector cannot be used to drive the USS-820D directly. However, a

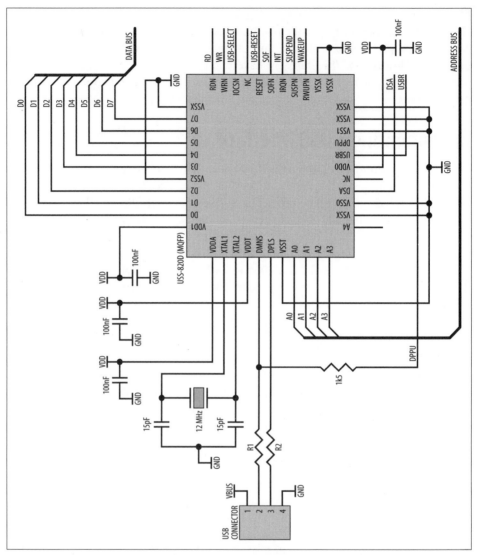

Figure 11-12. USS-820D USB interface

MAX604 voltage regulator circuit (Chapter 5) will convert **V**$_{BUS}$ to the required 3.3 V supply. The USS-820D also has numerous ground pins (**V**$_{SST}$, **V**$_{SSX}$, **V**$_{SS0}$, **V**$_{SS1}$, **V**$_{SS2}$), all of which are connected to ground. Even though this chip uses a 3.3 V supply, its digital (non-USB) inputs are compatible with 5 V logic, and so it may be interfaced directly to a processor operating on a 5 V supply.

XTAL1 and **XTAL2** are the connections for a 12 MHz crystal, providing timing for the USB controller.

The connections to a microprocessor are straightforward. This design, for example, could be included in the AT90S8515-based computer design in Chapter 15 as it is. The USS-820D's data pins, **D0** through **D7**, connect directly to the processor's data bus. Similarly, the low-order address pins, **A0** through **A4**, connect to the corresponding signals from the processor. These address bits are used to select internal registers within the USS-820D. The processor's read (**RD**) and write (**WR**) signals connect directly to USS-820D's read (**RDN**) and write (**WRN**) pins. (Agere places an "N" after pin names that are active low.) The USS-820D is selected when **IOCSN** is asserted low. Therefore, this pin is driven from an address decoder output (which I've labelled **USB-SELECT** in the schematic).

The USS-820D is reset when its **RESET** pin is sent high (not low like most other devices). So, for normal operation this pin should be held low. To allow the USS-820D to be reset under software control, this pin could be driven by a processor digital output line.

The USS-820D has a number of outputs that may be used to notify a host processor of the current USB status. **DSA** (Data Set Available), **USBR** (USB Reset detected), **SUSPN** (Suspend), and **SOFN** (Start Of Frame) may either be read as digital inputs by the host microcontroller, or, for processors that have several interrupt inputs, these signals may be used to generate an interrupt. If the host processor has only a limited interrupt capability, all of these events will trigger the USS-820D interrupt pin (**IRQN**). This pin can therefore serve as the sole interrupt input to the processor. A word of caution, however: this pin can be configured under software control to be either active high or active low. Getting this wrong can put your embedded system in a permanent state of interrupt. The default state for this pin is active low, which suits most processors. For processors that have active-high interrupts, such as Intel processors, the firmware should configure USS-820D for the correct interrupt polarity *before* enabling the processor's interrupt-handling capability.

The **RWUPN** pin is an input that signals a Remote Wake-Up condition. In other words, this embedded system has been asleep (in suspend mode) and has awoken. This pin notifies the USS-820D of the change in state so that it can alert other USB systems. **RWUPN** is simply driven by a processor digital output line.

The USB differential data signals are pins **DPLS** (Data Plus, **D+**) and **DMNS** (Data Minus, **D-**). These are connected to the USB connector through series-termination resistors. Agere Systems suggests a nominal value of 24 Ω. For an upstream connection, **DPLS** (**D+**) requires a pull-up resistor of 1.5 kΩ. Normally, this resistor is connected to +5 V. However, the USS-820D provides a special pin (**DPPU**) specifically for this purpose. Thus, under software control, the USS-820D can simulate a USB-device disconnect. It will appear to an upstream hub that the system containing the USS-820D has been physically disconnected, even though it is still attached. This can be useful during development and testing. It also allows the USB device to decide whether or not a host knows it is connected. **DPPU** may be decoupled to ground using a 10 nF capacitor.

Chips such as the USS-820D make adding USB functionality to your embedded hardware simple and easy. Through USB, you can develop peripherals based on embedded processors for desktop computer systems. Alternatively, you can use USB to connect existing peripherals to your embedded computer to further increase its functionality.

CHAPTER 12

Networks

Never let the future disturb you. You will meet it, if
you have to, with the same weapons of reason that
today arm you against the present.
—Marcus Aurelius Antoninus
Meditations

No town or freeman shall be compelled to build
bridges ... except those with an ancient obligation to
do so.
—The Magna Carta

In this chapter, we'll look at connecting your embedded computer to the real world by adding a *Local Area Network (LAN)* interface. There is a wide variety of networks employed—some very common, some not so common. We'll take a look at CAN and Ethernet, the two most common networks. CAN is a network for industrial applications, where a conventional network just won't do. CAN is suited to electrically noisy and harsh conditions and is the network of choice in electrically severe environments. Ethernet is the intranet network that connects the world's desktop computers, as well as a host of other devices such as routers, gateways, printers, and other peripherals.

Controller Area Network (CAN)

Through the late 70s and 80s, the complexity of automotive electronics grew considerably, with engine-management systems, ABS braking, active suspension, electronic transmissions, automated lighting, air-conditioning, security, and central locking. Each of these systems does not exist in isolation but is part of an integrated whole. A considerable amount of information exchange is required, and, therefore, some means of system interconnection must be provided. The conventional method was point-to-point wiring, which provided discrete interconnection between each subsystem. This methodology was a natural evolution from the simple electrics of earlier cars, but as automotive complexity grew, such a scheme proved vastly inadequate. Each car could have several kilometers worth of wiring and dozens of connectors. Such complex wiring systems added greatly to the cost of producing a car, added unnecessary weight, reduced reliability, and made servicing a nightmare.

The obvious solution was to replace complexity with simplicity and implement inter-system communication using a low-cost digital network. The automotive electrical environment is very noisy. With electric motors, ignition systems, RF emissions, and so on, the 12 V supply to automotive electronics can have ± 400 V transients. The required communication network must therefore be able to cope with this noise and work reliably. The network must provide high-noise immunity and error detection and handling, with retransmission of failed packets. Thus was born the *Controller Area Network*, more commonly known as *CAN*, implementing real-time communication at up to 1 Mbps, over a 2-wire serial network. CAN specifies only the physical and data-link layers of the ISO-OSI model, with higher layers left to the specific implementation.

Bosch developed CAN in Europe in the late 1980s, originally for use in cars. Because of its robustness, CAN has expanded beyond its automotive origins and can now be found in industrial automation, trains, ship navigation and control systems, medical systems, photocopiers, agricultural machinery, household appliances, office automation, and elevators. CAN is now an international standard under *ISO11898* and *ISO11519-2*.

CAN supports multiple masters on the network, with each master responsible for local sensing and control within the distributed system (Figure 12-1).

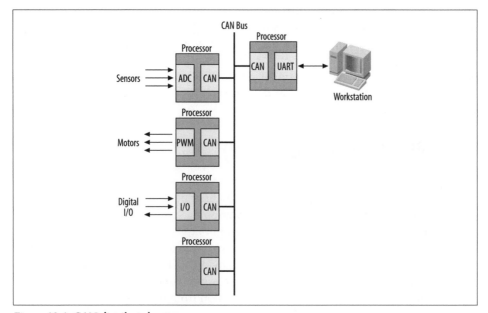

Figure 12-1. CAN distributed system

Each CAN packet contains address information and priority as part of the header, and the nodes may connect to the network, or disconnect from the network, without affecting network traffic between other nodes.

The CAN network uses wired-AND logic, with a maximum bus length of 1,000 meters (3,300 feet), and a bus length of 40 meters (133 feet) at maximum data rate over twisted-pair wiring. Each end of the bus requires termination resistors to prevent transmission reflections (Figure 12-2).

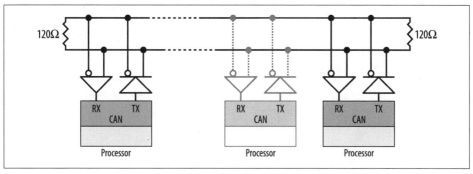

Figure 12-2. CAN bus

Many processors intended for use in harsh or electrically noisy industrial applications include a CAN module. A number of Philips microcontrollers include CAN, as do a few PICs. The DSP56805 processor covered in Chapter 19 also has a CAN interface. For processors that do not include CAN, CAN interface modules are available. The Microchip MCP2510 provides a CAN module and interfaces to a host processor via SPI. Adding CAN to any embedded system is therefore a simple task.

Typically, a microprocessor that supports CAN will include a CAN interface module, which provides most of the functionality. The only additional support required is a CAN interface driver. Philips Semiconductor produces a CAN driver, the PCA82C250T, which makes interfacing to the CAN bus very easy.

Your embedded computer must also have some way of physically attaching to the bus. The simplest method is simply to bring the bus into the computer system on one connector, tap off it, and then route it out through another connector (Figure 12-3).

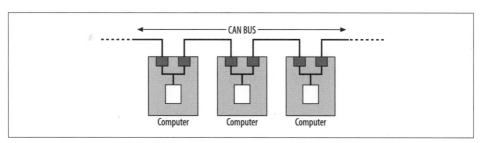

Figure 12-3. Tapping into a CAN bus by using two connectors on a PCB

To see how we can use CAN, let's look at the DSP56805 processor. This processor has a CAN network module as part of its suite of onboard peripherals. The schematic for interfacing a processor's CAN module to a CAN bus is shown in Figure 12-4.

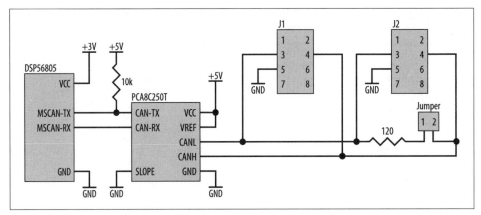

Figure 12-4. CAN interface for a DSP56805 processor

The DSP56805 has two CAN interface signals, **MSCAN-TX** and **MSCAN-RX**, which are the CAN transmitter and receiver, respectively. These are connected to the PCA82C250T, which provides the interface to the CAN bus. Note that the DSP56805 requires a 3.3 V supply, while the PCA82C250T requires a 5 V supply. A pull-up resistor brings the MSCAN-TX output of the processor to the required logic-high level for the PCA82C250T. While CAN requires only two signal lines and ground, the actual connectors have eight pins. Since the CAN bus requires a termination resistor at each end, we provide a 120 Ω resistor should our computer be placed at the bus end. A jumper allows it to be brought in-circuit or disabled as needed. So, if our computer is at the end of the CAN bus, the jumper is closed and the bus is terminated. If our computer is not an endpoint machine, the jumper is left open and the resistor plays no part. Note that having a termination resistor active (jumper closed) when this computer is not at an endpoint is a good way to ensure an unreliable CAN bus! Resistors should be active at bus ends *only*.

Many implementations of CAN just use standard IDC-type headers for the connectors. However, the actual CAN standard specifies that the connector should be a 9-pin Sub-D connector. The pinouts for this connector are listed in Table 12-1.

Table 12-1. CAN pinouts

Pin	Signal/use
1	Reserved
2	CAN_L
3	Ground

Table 12-1. CAN pinouts (continued)

Pin	Signal/use
4	Reserved
5	Reserved
6	Ground
7	CAN_H
8	Reserved
9	V+ (optional power source)

Although this is the same type of connector used in some RS-232C implementations (such as the serial ports on PCs), *do not* connect a CAN bus and RS-232C together. They are not even remotely compatible!

Ethernet

Anyone even remotely involved with computers has heard of Ethernet. Developed at Xerox PARC* in the early 1970s, this local-area networking standard has found its way into every possible application and has evolved over time to encompass a number of standards ranging from wireless networks (802.11) to gigabit Ethernet.

In this section, we'll look at how you add a simple Ethernet interface to your embedded computer. We will develop a 10 Mbps interface only, as higher-speed interfaces require special attention to PCB design and EMC issues. So, for the sake of ease and reliability, we'll keep it simple and low-speed.

The Ethernet standards and protocols are detailed in *Ethernet: The Definitive Guide* (O'Reilly). This excellent book provides definitive coverage of Ethernet, and it is a must for anyone developing Ethernet-based hardware.

By adding Ethernet to your embedded system, you gain access to a network and all the possibilities that it brings. You can send data to a host computer at high speed, as well as access printers, file servers, databases, and even the Internet. You can also monitor and control your embedded system from afar, or even have it send you email when it needs attention. Take an AT90S8515 AVR and add an Ethernet interface and some high-capacity flash memory, and you have yourself a simple web server. Add an ADC and some sensors, and your web server becomes a weather station showing current or past conditions to anyone on the Internet. Use a higher-speed processor, several Ethernet ports, and the appropriate software, and you have yourself a simple gateway or firewall. You could even build an Ethernet-to-Ethernet (or serial, parallel-port, or USB) bridge. The possibilities are limited only by your imagination.

---

* PARC is the Palo Alto Research Center (*http://www.parc.com*). For an interesting history of PARC (and the computer industry in general), read Robert X. Cringely's *Accidental Empires* (HarperBusiness).

There was a time when developing an Ethernet interface was a major exercise. These were complicated circuits, using lots of chips and hundreds of support components. An Ethernet interface could fill a moderate PCB all on its own. Not anymore. In these days of large-scale integration, adding Ethernet to your design is easy, as we will see.

Adding an Ethernet Interface

Crystal Semiconductor, now part of Cirrus Logic (*http://www.cirrus.com*), produces a single-chip Ethernet controller known as the CS8900A. This chip allows you to add a simple (and low-cost) 10 Mbps Ethernet interface to your embedded system. Full documentation on this chip is available from the Cirrus Logic web site. As the CS8900A is a commonly used Ethernet controller, there is plenty of source code available on the Internet. Just use your favorite search engine to hunt it down. When you design a system based on the CS8900A, you can actually email your design to the engineers at Cirrus Logic, and they will check it out for you, offering advice and pointing out mistakes. The email address for this service is *ethernet@crystal.cirrus.com*.

The CS8900A supports *10BASE-2*, *10BASE-T*, and *AUI* (Attachment Unit Interface) Ethernet ports. 10BASE-T and 100BASE-T are by far the most common types of Ethernet interface, supporting data rates of 10 Mbps and 100 Mbps, respectively. Your desktop computer's Ethernet interface is most likely a 10/100BASE-T port with an 8-pin RJ-45 connector. (RJ-45 connectors look like, but are not the same as, standard telephone jacks.) The cabling used is *UTP* (Unshielded Twisted Pair) Category 5 cable, more commonly known simply as *CAT5*. Just like RS-422, RS-485, USB, and CAN, 10/100BASE-T Ethernet transmits using balanced differential signals. Four wires are used: two for the transmitter pair and two for the receiver pair. One wire of the pair carries a signal voltage of 0 to +2.5 V, while the other wire carries a voltage of 0 to –2.5 V, giving a signal difference of 5 Vpp.

Table 12-2 shows the pin connections for an RJ-45 connector. The wires within the CAT5 cable are color-coded for easy identification.

Table 12-2. RJ-45 connector signals

Pin	Signal name	Purpose	Wire color
1	TD+	Transmitted data	White/orange
2	TD–	Transmitted data	Orange
3	RD+	Received data	White/green
4	NC	No connection	Blue
5	NC	No connection	White/blue
6	RD–	Received data	Green
7	NC	No connection	White/brown
8	NC	No connection	Brown

A block diagram of a CS8900A implementation is shown in Figure 12-5.

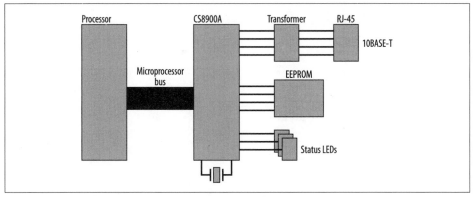

Figure 12-5. Block diagram showing a CS8900A implementation

As the CS8900A has 100 pins and several different modes of operation, we won't cover an entire schematic in one hit. Instead, we'll work through each stage of a CS8900A's design, and learn its functionality and use as we go. This discussion will be targeted at small, embedded application. Some of the more complicated aspects of the CS8900A, which are applicable to desktop PCs, will be left alone.

The CS8900A is connected to its 10BASE-T port through an isolation transformer. This transformer must have a winding ratio of 1:1 for the receiver, and a winding ratio n of 1:1.41 for the transmitter, if the CS8900A is used with a 5 V supply. If used with a 3.3 V supply, the transformer's winding ratio for the transmitter must be 1:2.5. There are a number of manufacturers that make isolation transformers (packaged as chips) with these winding ratios, such as Valor, PCA, YCL, and Bel. The transmitter requires series-termination resistors of 24.9 Ω, ± 1%. The transmitter differential pair must be decoupled with each other using a 68 pF capacitor. A 100 Ω resistor (± 1%) is required in parallel between the receiver's differential pair. The CS8900A can also directly drive LEDs, indicating Ethernet link status and bus and network activity. The CS8900A has an additional pin (RES) that requires a 4.99 kΩ (± 1%) pull-down resistor. Figure 12-6 shows the CS8900A connected to a 10BASE-T port.

An external 20 MHz crystal provides timing for the CS8900A. The crystal is connected across the XTAL1 and XTAL2 pins, and each pin is bypassed to ground using 33 pF capacitors (Figure 12-7).

This Ethernet chip supports the 16-bit ISA bus architecture, the expansion bus found in older-model PCs. However, ISA can easily be adapted to work with a range of non-ISA processors. The CS8900A may therefore be implemented in a variety of computer systems without difficulty. The CS8900A also supports operation in 8-bit mode and thus can also be interfaced to microcontrollers with an 8-bit data bus, such as the AT90S8515 AVR. The CS8900A's input **SBHE** is used to place the chip in 16-bit mode operation after reset. Any activity on **SBHE** will place the CS8900A in 16-bit

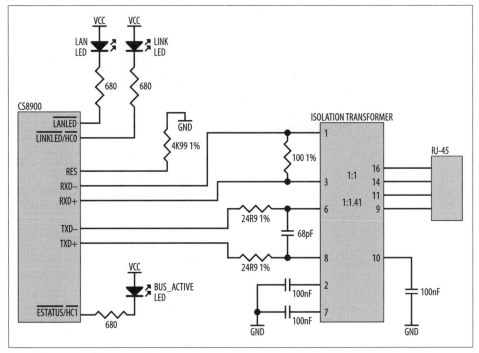

Figure 12-6. 10BASE-T interface

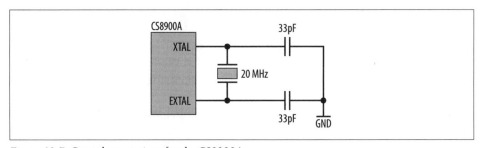

Figure 12-7. Crystal connections for the CS8900A

mode. The easiest way to ensure that there is activity on this input is simply to connect **SBHE** to the processor's address line, **A0**. As soon as the processor begins to use its bus, the activity will place the CS8900A in 16-bit mode. For 8-bit operation, **SBHE** is tied to ground. When used in 8-bit mode, interrupts are disabled and the CS8900A's status must be polled by software.

Before we look at the processor interface of the CS8900A, there are some important characteristics we need to note. On the CS8900A, **RESET** is active high. This can catch an unwary designer used to active-low resets. The reason that **RESET** is active high derives from the fact that this chip was designed principally for use in PCs, as Intel processors also have an active-high reset. The CS8900A's reset may be driven by a digital output of a microcontroller so that it can be reset under software control. Alternatively, in systems where the CS8900A is to have a hardware-generated reset at the same time as the processor, the processor's active-low reset signal must be inverted for the CS8900A. The CS8900A's interrupt outputs (**INTRQ0**, **INTRQ1**, **INTRQ2**, **INTRQ3**) are also active high, and each must be inverted before connecting to an active-low interrupt input of a microprocessor.

Another consequence of its design for use in Intel-based systems is that the CS8900A is little endian in operation. When used in 16-bit mode with big-endian processors such as the MC68000 or the DSP56805, this endian difference is important. There are two possible solutions. The first is to simply byte-swap in software. Your code then changes the 16-bit word to little-endian format before writing to the CS8900A. And when reading from the CS8900A, the processor must byte-swap the retrieved 16-bit word prior to processing.

However, there is an old saying that you should never fix in software what you can correct in hardware. The second solution is simply to byte-swap the data bus between the processor and the CS8900A. **D0:D7** of the processor is connected to **D8:D15** of the CS8900A, and **D8:D15** of the processor similarly go to **D0:D7** of the CS8900A. In this way, the endian-ness is reversed by the actual circuit board, and the software never needs to know the difference (Figure 12-8).

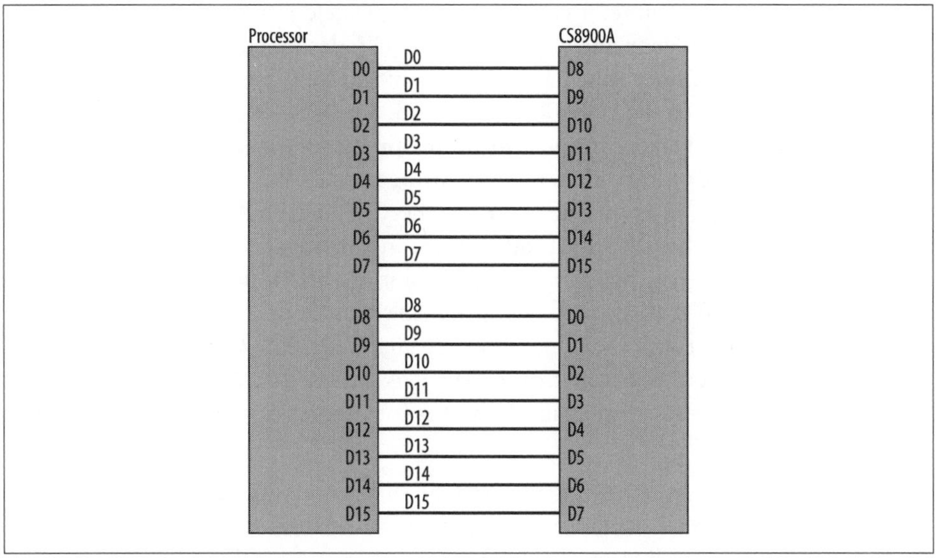

Figure 12-8. Endian swapping in hardware

The CS8900A has 20 address inputs. This may seem like a lot of address inputs for a peripheral, and it is. However, there is a reason. The CS8900A is principally an ISA-bus device, and the ISA bus supports separate memory and I/O memory spaces. Hence, the CS8900 has two separate processor interfaces. In one, it appears as part of the memory space of a processor and is accessed as though it were a memory device. A chip-select input, **CHIPSEL**, enables the CS8900A when it is used as a memory-mapped device. When it is used as a device within an I/O space, there is *no* externally generated chip select. Instead, devices mapped into the I/O space of an ISA bus are expected to do their own address decoding, and *that* is why the CS8900A has 20 address lines. Inside the CS8900A is an address decoder specifically for this chip. When the CS8900A is reset, it defaults to I/O address 0x00300. This address can be remapped under software control by writing to the appropriate register of the CS8900A. When used as an I/O-mapped device, **CHIPSEL** is ignored and the CS8900A will respond to the appropriate address on its address inputs in conjunction with **IOR** (I/O read) and **IOW** (I/O write). You can use the CS8900A in I/O mode within a memory-mapped I/O system. The system address decoder includes the address allocation for the CS8900A but simply does not select it. What the system address decoder must do is ensure that no other device is selected when the address(es) corresponding to the CS8900A is being accessed.

The default setting for the CS8900A is I/O mode operation. To use the CS8900A in memory-mapped mode, and therefore to have it recognize **CHIPSEL** and its memory read (**MEMR**) and memory write (**MEMW**) inputs, the CS8900A must first be accessed as an I/O-mapped device and reconfigured in software. Therefore, to use the memory-mapped option, you still have to support the I/O-mapped addressing scheme to get to it! Therefore, it is much simpler to stick with the I/O-mapped mode and map this within your memory space as just described. If you're using the CS8900A with a processor that has only a 16-bit address bus, simply tie the additional address inputs of the CS8900A to ground. The CS8900A's default address of 0x00300 may be inconvenient for use with some processors that already have internal I/O systems mapped within that region. An access to that address will be intercepted by the internal I/O and never reach the CS8900A. In such cases, it will be impossible to remap the CS8900A's address through software. You will simply never reach the appropriate register. But there is a solution, and it lies within hardware. If you invert some of the address bits from the processor before they reach the CS8900A, you can perform the remapping automatically. The CS8900A still thinks it lies at address 0x00300, but to the processor it is accessed at a completely different address. Figure 12-9 shows an example of this for a processor with a 16-bit address bus.

In this example, address bit **A15** is inverted. So, when the processor accesses address 0x8300 (%1000 0011 0000 0000), this is converted to address 0x0300 (%0000 0011 0000 0000), which is recognized by the CS8900A.

The CS8900A also has support for a serial EEPROM. This can be used to store CS8900A configuration information and the system's unique Ethernet address. Note that this EEPROM is optional, as the host processor can store this data elsewhere in the system. Figure 12-10 shows the CS8900A interfaced to a configuration

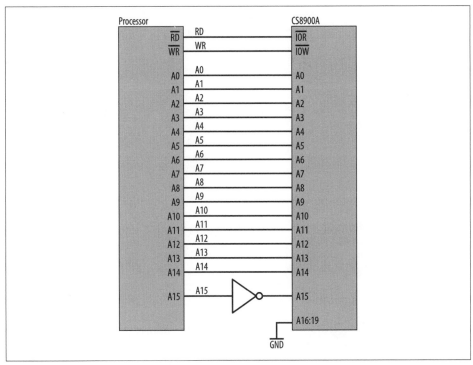

Figure 12-9. Address remapping in hardware

EEPROM. The interface is standard SPI, and the appropriate pins of the CS8900A are directly connected to the corresponding EEPROM pins. The only other component required is a decoupling capacitor for the EEPROM's power-supply pin. The EEPROM interface is disabled in 8-bit mode, so the host processor must supply all configuration information.

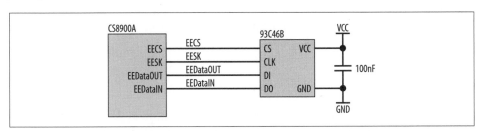

Figure 12-10. CS8900A interfaced to a configuration EEPROM

Finally, any used inputs, such as the DMA signals (**DMACK0**, **DMACK1**, and **DMACK2**), **TEST**, **SLEEP**, **MEMW**, **MEMR**, **AEN**, and **REFRESH** should be tied inactive. These signals are not used in a typical embedded system.

CHAPTER 13

Analog

To experience without abstraction is to sense the world;
To experience with abstraction is to know the world.
These two experiences are indistinguishable;
Their construction differs but their effect is the same.
—Lao Tse
  Tao Te Ching

In this chapter, we'll look at how you sample external voltages and convert these into digital values for processing by your embedded system. Such voltages may be generated by sensors and may represent light levels, temperature, or vibration. Or perhaps the voltages are the output of a microphone or audio system and need to be converted into digital data. Later, we'll take a look at how you turn digital data into an analog output voltage. We'll conclude the chapter with hardware to control electric motors.

First, though, let's take a quick look at amplifiers and sampling theory. Note that this is a very complex field. Since the background theory is well beyond the scope of this book, we'll just take an overview, giving enough background to allow you to interface your embedded system to simple analog circuitry. This discussion is by no means exhaustive, and it is deliberately simplified.

Amplifiers

Amplifiers are used to interface one analog circuit to another. An amplifier is a circuit that increases (or decreases) a given input voltage to produce an output voltage. For example, say you had a sensor that produced a maximum output that was 5 mVpp, and this was to be interfaced to a sampling system that required an input signal of 5 Vpp. You would use an amplifier between the sensor and the sampling system to increase the sensor's output accordingly (Figure 13-1).

The waveform of the amplifier's output signal should be identical to the input signal; only its amplitude will have changed. The amount of increase or decrease in the

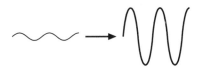

Figure 13-1. Amplifying a waveform

signal is known as the *gain* of the amplifier. Gain is calculated easily by dividing the output voltage by the input voltage:

Gain = V_{OUT} / V_{IN}

Thus, an amplifier that doubles the input signal will have a gain of 2.

The ability of a circuit to respond to a changing signal is typically limited to a given range of frequencies. This is known as the *frequency response* of a circuit. For example, the amplifier in your home stereo may have a frequency response of 20–20 kHz. This means that it will amplify audio signals that have a frequency between 20 Hz (low bass) and 20 kHz (high treble). Try to pump a 100 MHz signal into the audio amp and it simply will not be able to amplify the signal. The signal is said to be outside its frequency range.

Ideally, the frequency response of a circuit, such as the audio amplifier, should be *flat* over its frequency range. This means that its response to an input signal will be the same, no matter the frequency (within the appropriate range). So, in the case of the audio amp, the gain will be constant for any frequency of signal in the appropriate range. Thus, the volume will not vary with frequency (ignoring any differences due to the original music). At either end of the frequency range, the ability of the amplifier to perform ideally degrades. At these extremes of frequency, the amplifier's gain diminishes. This is known as *roll off*. Some small degree of roll off is considered acceptable (and unavoidable). The frequency response is normally defined as the frequency range where the gain is within a certain limit of the ideal.

The limitation of an amplifier to replicate the input signal at its output is the *distortion* of the amplifier. For audio amplifiers, you'll sometimes see the term *Total Harmonic Distortion* (*THD*) listed in the specifications. The smaller this number is, the better the amplifier.

In days of old, amplifiers were constructed using discrete transistors[*] or vacuum tubes (also known as valves). These days, amplifiers are available packaged in integrated circuits. These amplifiers are known as *operational amplifiers*, or *op amps* for short. They make the designer's life much easier. They are cheap, reliable, and so very easy to use. Throughout this chapter, whenever we need to amplify a circuit,

---

[*] In some special applications, amplifiers may still be constructed using discrete transistors (or even valves).

we'll use an appropriate op amp for the job. The schematic symbol for an op amp is shown in Figure 13-2.

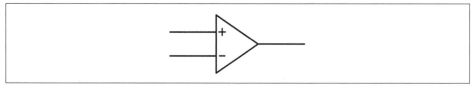

Figure 13-2. Schematic symbol for an op amp

The input marked with "+" is known as the *noninverting input*, and the input marked with "–" is the *inverting input*. If the voltage present at the noninverting input is greater than that present at the inverting input, the output of the op amp is positive. Conversely, if the noninverting input is less than the inverting input, the output is negative. Typically, an op amp's output will not go as low as its negative power supply, nor as high as its positive power supply, due to the limitations of the internal circuitry. An op amp whose output voltage range *does* span the difference between its positive and negative power supplies is said to have *rail-to-rail operation*.

In order to function correctly, an op amp requires *feedback*. Feedback involves coupling the output of an amplifier back to its input. *Negative feedback* uses the output to reduce the gain of the amplifier and, in doing so, improves the amplifier's other characteristics, such as the flatness of the frequency response and immunity to distortion. Negative feedback is achieved simply by connecting a resistor between the output and the inverting input, as we will shortly see. (A circuit with no feedback is said to be *open-loop*.) Op amps are designed in such a way as to make the output change to cancel the difference between the inputs via a feedback resistor. Thus, the output waveform follows the difference between the input waveforms. The magnitude of the output is proportional to the feedback resistor. The larger the resistor, the more the feedback of the output is attenuated. Thus, the op amp makes the output larger to compensate. In this way, the output is an amplified version of the input.

An op amp may either be used as an *inverting amplifier* (Figure 13-3) or a *noninverting amplifier* (Figure 13-4). An inverting amplifier "flips" the signal in addition to amplifying it.

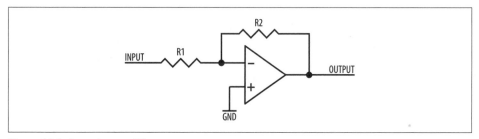

Figure 13-3. Inverting amplifier

The gain of an inverting amplifier is given by:

```
Gain = - R2 / R1
```

Note the minus sign. That's because this amplifier *inverts* the signal.

You are more likely to use a noninverting amplifier (Figure 13-4), which doesn't flip the signal. These are commonly used in audio and sensor applications.

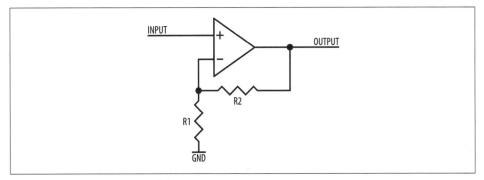

Figure 13-4. Noninverting amplifier

The gain of a noninverting amplifier is given by:

```
Gain = 1 + R2 / R1
```

The gain of the amplifier may be set under software control by using a digital potentiometer (Chapter 7) for R2.

A *differential amplifier* (Figure 13-5) multiplies the *difference* between two input signals and is used to amplify small signals that may be subject to noise. By amplifying the difference between the signal of interest and a reference, any noise present is reduced (since the noise will affect both the signal and the reference equally). When both inputs to a differential amplifier change in the same way, this is known as a *common-mode* change. Ideally, a differential amplifier should be immune to common-mode changes, since its purpose is to amplify the signal difference. Its immunity to common-mode changes is known as its *Common-Mode Rejection Ratio* (*CMRR*). The higher the CMRR, the better. To achieve a high CMRR, it is important to match the values (and tolerances) of the resistors as closely as possible.

The output voltage of this differential amplifier is given by:

```
VOUT = (In2 - In1) * (R2 / R1)
```

Analog to Digital Conversion

A device that converts an analog input voltage to a digital number is known as an *Analog to Digital Converter*, or simply and more commonly as an *ADC*. You may have also heard the term *codec* (COder DECoder) before. A codec is an ADC

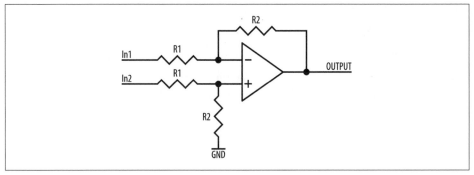

Figure 13-5. Differential amplifier

combined with a *Digital to Analog Converter* (*DAC*), providing both analog input and analog output in one chip. We'll look at DACs in more detail later in this chapter.

ADCs are found in cell phones and digital phones, converting your voice to digital data for transmission. They are also used in your computer to digitize the input from a microphone for speech recognition. Professional recording studios use ADCs to convert audio to digital data in preparation for CD mastering. Similarly, video is sampled using ADCs prior to DVD mastering. Your scanner, web cam, and digital camcorder all have ADCs in them. At the other end of the application spectrum, ADCs are used to sample inputs from sensors. These applications can range from automated weather stations to the system monitoring the processor temperature in your PC.

There are several different types of ADC. *Integrating ADCs* use an internal *voltage-controlled oscillator* to produce a clock signal whose frequency is proportional to the voltage being sampled. The clock signal is used to drive a counter, which provides the digital value for the sample. The higher the sampled voltage, the higher the clock frequency, and therefore the higher the number reached by the counter. The counter is reset prior to each conversion. Because of this conversion technique, integrating ADCs are not known for their speed of conversion.

A *successive approximation ADC* uses a DAC to provide an analog reference voltage that is compared to the input voltage. By incrementing the digital code driving the DAC, the reference voltage is increased until a match is found. Once this happens, the code used to drive the DAC is used as the digital output of the ADC.

Flash ADCs (also known as *parallel ADCs*) use a bank of comparators to compare the input voltage to a range of reference voltages. The conversion of the input analog voltage to a digital value is therefore very fast. The catch is that flash ADCs tend to be more expensive than other types of ADC and, due to their complexity, normally have a lower resolution than other forms of ADC.

The process of converting an analog signal to digital is known as *sampling* or *quantization*. ADCs have two principle characteristics: *sample rate* and *resolution*. Sample rate is expressed as *samples per second* (*SPS*) and refers to how frequently an analog input signal is converted into a digital code. The faster an ADC's sample rate, the more expensive that chip will be. Resolution determines the accuracy of each sample. For example, an "8-bit ADC" will return an 8-bit code representing the sampled input signal. This means that the input has been quantized into one of 256 discrete values. An "11-bit ADC" will quantize the signal into one of 4,096 values, yielding a more accurate result. However, the higher the resolution, the more expensive the ADC. Further, high resolution is not always required. If, for example, you're sampling a temperature sensor that has a range of 0°C to 100°C, with an accuracy of ± 0.5° C, then that sensor has only 200 meaningful voltage levels. For this sensor, an 8-bit ADC is fine. While you could use an 11-bit ADC to sample this sensor, the additional resolution is overkill.

An ADC will convert the analog signal into a number that represents the ratio of the input signal to a given *reference voltage*. For example, if the ADC's reference voltage is 5 V, and the input signal is 3 V, then the ratio of input to reference is 60%. So for an 8-bit ADC, where 255 represents full scale, the sampled input will be returned as 153 (0x99). From your point of view, you receive the value 153 from the ADC, and must work back from this to calculate the original analog voltage:

```
Signal = (sample / max_value) * reference_voltage
       = (153 / 255) * 5
       = 3 Volts
```

Sample Rates

The rate at which a signal is sampled can have a dramatic effect on the quantized result and therefore can also affect the way in which software interprets that result. Figure 13-6 shows a sinusoidal signal that is sampled at a rate equal to its period. In this example, the sample happens to coincide with a peak in the signal. The signal changes in between samples, but our choice of sample rate means that we get the same value each time. We get a completely false picture of what is really happening to that signal. To our sampling software, each value returned is the same, and so the signal appears to us as though it were a flat line!

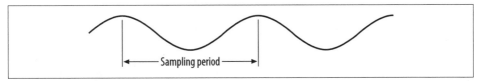

Figure 13-6. Poorly chosen sample rate gives inaccurate signal reading

If we choose a sample rate that is double (or more) than the signal's highest frequency component, we can see the signal in more detail (Figure 13-7). This sampling frequency is known as the *Nyquist frequency* and is the lower limit of what will produce usable results. If the sample rate is slower than the Nyquist frequency, false artifacts (such as our sine wave appearing as a straight line, as we saw previously) may appear in the sampled result. These phantoms are known as *aliasing*.

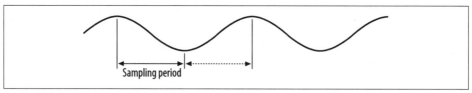

Figure 13-7. Shorter sampling period

 Ever see an old Western movie where the wheels of a wagon appear to be rotating backward, even though the wagon is moving forward? That's an example of aliasing. The frame rate of the camera is effectively sampling the rotation of the wheels. Because the wheel rotation is slightly slower than the frame rate, the wheel doesn't quite make a full revolution per frame. So on each successive frame, the wheel appears a little further behind than it was on the preceding frame. The effect is as though the wheel is rotating backwards—aliasing in action!

The faster the sample rate, the more accurate your sampled results will be. Since your sampling is quantizing the signal both in terms of amplitude (ADC resolution) and time (sample rate), a quantization error will always result (Figure 13-8).

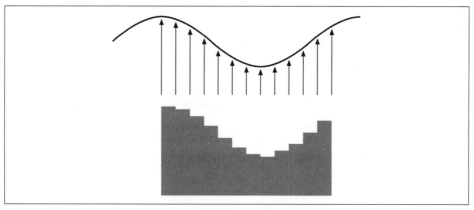

Figure 13-8. Sampling period and corresponding quantization

As you can see, the smooth sine wave of the original signal has become a jagged representation. Now, if you were monitoring temperature, this might be sufficient. You might not care *how* the temperature signal changed. Instead, you might be interested in the temperature only at specific intervals, and with only a limited accuracy. In such a case, this effect is not really a problem.

However, if you were sampling audio, this quantization effect could be a real problem. By increasing the sample rate, a more accurate representation of the original signal is obtained (Figure 13-9).

A voice-mail system may use a sample rate of only 8 kHz and a resolution of 12 bits, and the resultant sound quality is limited. However, CD audio uses a sample rate of

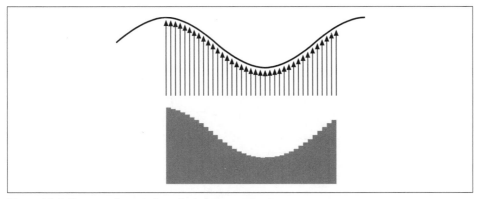

Figure 13-9. Fast sample period results in less quantization

44.1 kHz with 16-bit data and achieves a significant improvement in quality as a result. DVD audio uses a sample rate of 48 kHz with 24-bit data for even greater audio fidelity. To further improve sound quality, both CD and DVD players have special output filters to smooth the transitions between each sample when the data is converted back into analog form.

The take-home message is that you should choose your ADC resolution and sample rate carefully, keeping in mind exactly what you're sampling and what you intend to use it for.

Interfacing an External ADC

There is a very wide range of ADCs available, for every considerable purpose. Choose from very low-cost, low-speed ADCs for simple voltage conversion to very high-speed, precise (and expensive) ADCs for sampling video streams. Many microcontrollers have inbuilt ADC subsystems, making analog interfacing simple. However, if the processor doesn't incorporate an ADC, or its ADC is not suited to your application, it becomes necessary to add an external device.

A good general-purpose ADC for sensor applications is the Maxim MAX1245. It has eight channels of analog input and can sample at 100,000 samples per second, with a resolution of 12 bits. (There are similar devices with resolutions ranging from 8 bits to 16 bits, and with interfaces such as SPI, I²C, and processor bus.) The MAX1245 has an internal track and hold, preventing a changing signal from corrupting the result during a conversion. The MAX1245 is interfaced to a host processor via an interface that is compatible with SPI, Microwire, and the serial interfaces found in Texas Instruments TMS320-series DSP processors (Figure 13-10). As you can see, the MAX1245 is very easy to use. In this schematic, the analog input comes in via an IDC header, the 16-pin connector on the left of the figure. Note that every second pin on the connector is tied to ground. This means that every second wire in the connected cable will be grounded, providing a degree of noise immunity to our analog signals.

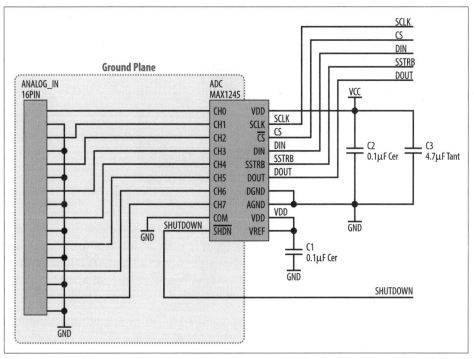

Figure 13-10. MAX1245 interface

The **DOUT**, **DI**, and **SCLK** signals correspond to a processor's SPI **MISO**, **MOSI**, and **SCLK** signals, respectively. $\overline{CS}$ is simply generated using a processor I/O line.

A conversion commences by sending a start command to the ADC via the SPI interface. The start command is simply a byte that specifies the channel and other ADC settings for that particular conversion. (Refer to the MAX1245 datasheet for more information on the software interface.) The MAX1245 may use an internal clock source to drive the conversion process, or it may have an external clock. The SPI **SCLK** also doubles as the conversion clock, when the ADC is used in external-clock mode. When used in internal-clock mode, the output, **SSTRB** (Serial Strobe), goes low at the beginning of a conversion and returns high once the conversion is complete. When an external clock is used, **SSTRB** pulses high in the clock period prior to the most significant bit being processed. **SSTRB** may be used to flag the completion of a conversion to a host processor by acting as an interrupt input. Alternatively, when used in external clock mode, the conversion result is ready once the start command has been sent.

The MAX1245 has the ability to enter low-power mode. This can be done either through hardware or software control. The MAX1245 has an input pin, **SHDN**, which, when asserted low, places the ADC into low-power operation. Now, interestingly, **SHDN** is also used to specify the clock frequency of the ADC's internal sampling. Sending this input high sets the clock to 1.5 MHz, whereas leaving the input to float (no connection) sets the clock to 225 kHz. If $\overline{\text{SHDN}}$ is driven by a microcontroller's I/O pin, changing that pin's configuration from an output to an input will effectively float $\overline{\text{SHDN}}$. In this way, you can still use the "no connection" option even when the pin *is* connected. The MAX1245 can also be placed into low-power mode by software. If the two least significant bits of the start command are both 0, then the MAX1245 is placed into shutdown. The advantage of software power-down is that you can request a conversion *and* place the device into shutdown with a single command. The ADC will complete the conversion before shutting down, and its interface will remain active so that the result may be clocked out to the microcontroller.

Power for the MAX1245 (**VDD**) can be in the range of 2.7 V to 3.3 V. The MAX1245 has three ground pins: **COM**, **DGND**, and **AGND**. **COM** is the ground reference for the analog inputs, **DGND** is the ground connection for the digital section of the ADC, and **AGND** is the ground connection for the analog section of the ADC. These three grounds need to be connected together, but only at a single point, close to **AGND**. This is known as a *star ground point*. The two power inputs (**VDD**) need *two* decoupling capacitors to remove noise from the supply voltage. A 0.1 µF capacitor and a 4.7 µF capacitor should be used to decouple **VDD** and should be placed as close to the star ground point as possible. For particularly noisy power supplies, a 10 Ω resistor should be placed in series between the power source and **VDD**. The analog inputs should be shielded from all nearby digital signals to prevent interference, and a ground shield (a fill) should be placed under the MAX1245 to further isolate the device from noise. (See Chapter 6 for more information on noise and shielding.)

Now that we have seen how to add an ADC to a microcontroller, let's give it something to sample. We'll now take a look at some sensors and see how to interface them to an ADC. There are lots of different sensors available, from many manufacturers. Many are hard to use, awkward to interface, and require much more effort than seems necessary. But not all sensors are created equal. I have sought out and selected a range of sensors that are trivial to use and require little or no design effort. Electronics can be hard, but it doesn't always have to be so, as you will see.

Temperature Sensor

We'll start with something simple: a temperature sensor. This little sensor has a wide range of applications. The most obvious is as an environment monitor or weather station, but you could also use it to sense temperatures inside rooms and to control the appropriate heating or cooling systems. Combine it with a datalogger design, and you have a temperature recorder. Such devices are used in the shipment of fruits, vegetables, frozen foods, and flowers to ensure that they get to market in their best condition. It can also be used in the shipment of blood products and pathology samples, making sure that these critical substances are not exposed to adverse temperatures.

The AD22100 and AD22103 temperature sensors, by Analog Devices, are very easy to use. They are 3-pin devices,* requiring only power (V_S) and ground to give you a voltage output that is proportional to temperature (Figure 13-11). The AD22100 requires a 5 V supply, and the AD22103 requires a 3.3 V supply.

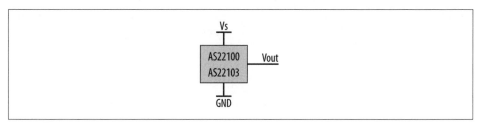

Figure 13-11. AD22100/AD22103

What could be easier than that?

The output voltage corresponds to 22.5 mV/°C over the temperature range –50°C to +150°C for the AD22100 and 28 mV/°C over the temperature range 0°C to 100°C for the AD22103. The transfer functions (how the output relates to the input) for the two devices are given by:

$$V_{OUT} = (V_S / 5) \times [1.375 + (0.0225 \times T_A)] \qquad \text{AD22100}$$
$$V_{OUT} = (V_S / 3.3) \times [0.25 + (0.028 \times T_A)] \qquad \text{AD22103}$$

where V_{OUT} is the output voltage, V_S is the power supply, and T_A is the ambient temperature.

So, turning the equations around, the relationship between temperature and output voltage is:

$$T_A = (((V_{OUT} \times 5) / V_S) - 1.375) / 0.0225 \qquad \text{AD22100}$$
$$T_A = (((V_{OUT} \times 3.3) / V_S) - 0.25) / 0.028 \qquad \text{AD22103}$$

For example, if we were using an AD22100 temperature sensor with a supply voltage of 5 V ($V_S = 5$ V), then our function becomes simply:

$$T_A = (V_{OUT} - 1.375) / 0.0225$$

Thus, if we measured an output voltage of 1.94 V, the corresponding temperature would be 25.1°C.

Interfacing the temperature sensor to an ADC is simple. The output may be directly connected to an input of the ADC. Alternatively, since temperature changes relatively slowly, we can add an *RC filter* between the sensor and the ADC to remove any noise that may be present in the output (Figure 13-12).

---

* These devices are also available in 8-pin surface-mount chips, where five of the pins are unconnected.

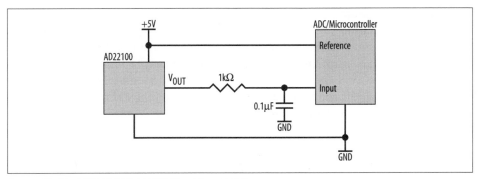

Figure 13-12. ADD22100/AD22103 with an RC filter

Light Sensor

Now we'll take a look at a light sensor. The obvious use of a light sensor is to monitor natural light levels, and perhaps use the results to control artificial-lighting systems. But combine this sensor with a directional light source (such as a bright LED enclosed in a baffle), and you have a security detector. As long as the sensor can "see" the LED, everything's fine. But when the light is interrupted, you know that someone or something has passed between.

I used the particular sensor we're going to look at on a small datalogger. One of my customers is a biologist who studies albatrosses (giant seabirds) of the southern oceans as part of an ongoing conservation program. These birds will fly for years at a time, circumnavigating the world on the ocean winds. The tiny datalogger (smaller than your smallest finger) weighs only a few grams and is attached to the bird's leg. (The attachment is designed and fitted with great care to ensure that the bird is not harmed or adversely affected in any way.) The light sensor is used to record sunlight levels that the bird experiences on its journey.

By comparing the recorded sunrises and sunsets with the reference clock aboard the datalogger, and looking at the duration of twilight, latitude and longitude can be computed. In this way, the simple recording of light levels is used to track an albatross's journey as it circumnavigates the world.

The recorded light profiles also give information about what the albatross does. You can tell whether the bird was flying with feet tucked up in the feathers, flying with feet hanging down, or resting on the water, as each activity has a unique light profile associated with it. You can also see the phases of the moon leaving their trace on the nighttime light levels, as well as which days were cloudy and which were sunny. It even detects when the albatross stumbles across a lonely, and brightly lit, squid boat during the night. One simple sensor can tell you an awful lot. For more information, see *http://www.oreillynet.com/pub/a/oreilly/cprog/news/albatross_1202.html*.

There are lots of commercial light sensors available. We're going to take a look at the TAOS TSL250R sensor. TAOS (*http://www.taosinc.com*) is short for Texas Advanced Optical Solutions, Inc., a spin-off company from the venerable Texas Instruments, Inc. The TSL250R (Figure 13-13) consists of a photodiode (a semiconductor that is responsive to light) and an integrated amplifier. Like the temperature sensor we've just seen, the TSL250R just needs power and ground, and it will give you an analog voltage output that is proportional to incident light.

Figure 13-13. TAOS TSL250R light sensor

The spectral response for the TSL250R, shown in Figure 13-14, ranges from ultraviolet (left) to infrared (right) and peaks in the visible part of the spectrum.

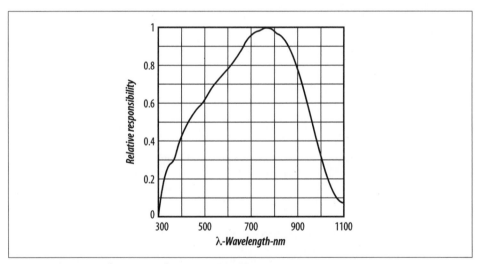

Figure 13-14. Spectral response of a TAOS TSL250R

The TSL250R can operate from a supply voltage of between 2.7 V and 5.5 V and typically consumes only 1.1 mA of current. The basic circuit for the TSL250R is very simple (Figure 13-15).

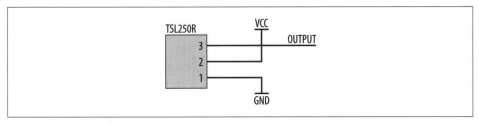

Figure 13-15. Using the TAOS TSL250R

The maximum output voltage (under full irradiance) for this sensor is just under 4 V, when the part is powered from a 5 V supply. So, if we choose, we can interface this sensor directly to a (5 V referenced) ADC without any additional amplification. Now, because the output does not span the full scale of the ADC's range, we lose a small amount of resolution. For an 8-bit ADC, a 4 V input corresponds to 0xCC, and so our range of values for this sensor go from 0x00 to 0xCC. Depending on your application, this may not be a problem. For example, if you are interested only in detecting the difference between light and darkness, or when a given low-light threshold is crossed, this will work fine.

Amplifying the Light Sensor

If you do want to sample the full range of the sensor, you need to amplify the sensor's output. Since the sensor's maximum output is 4 V and the reference of the ADC is 5 V, the gain of the amplifier must be 1.25.

A good general-purpose op amp is the AD623 by Analog Devices. It has rail-to-rail operation, can run from a single supply voltage, requires very little current, and is exceptionally easy to use. Analog Devices has done a lot of the hard work already, and the AD623 requires only a single external resistor to set the gain. The value of the resistor is calculated using the relation:

R_G = 100 kΩ / (Gain - 1)

So, for our required gain of 1.25, we need a resistance of:

R_G = 100 kΩ / (1.25 - 1)
    = 100 kΩ / 0.25
    = 4 kΩ

The resistor should have a *tolerance* (accuracy) of 1% or better. Standard off-the-shelf resistors are normally 5% and just aren't accurate enough.

The circuit with the TSL250R interfaced to the AD623 is shown in Figure 13-16.

The output of the TSL250R sensor (pin 3) is connected to the noninverting input of the AD623 op amp (pin 3), while the inverting input is tied to ground. The gain resistor is connected between pins 1 and 8. The negative power supply, –**VS**, is connected to ground for single-supply operation. The positive power supply, +**VS**, is

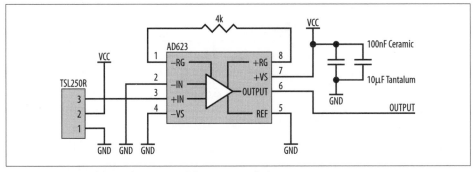

Figure 13-16. Amplifying the output of the TSL250R light sensor

connected to **VCC** and is decoupled to ground using two capacitors. The op amp's reference input (**REF**) is also tied to ground. The output of the op amp at pin 6 is then connected directly to the analog input of an ADC.

Accelerometer

Now we're going to take a look at an interesting sensor. Analog Devices makes some really nice accelerometers, and we'll learn how to interface an ADXL150 to an embedded system. You can use an accelerometer for a number of applications, not just for measuring linear acceleration of vehicles. The ADXL150 is a single-axis (one-dimensional) accelerometer with a resolution of 10 m*g* and a full-scale range of ±50 *g*. For dual-axis (two-dimensional) sensing, choose the ADXL250.

> *g* is the unit of acceleration. One *g* is approximately equal to 9.8 m/sec² (32.2 feet/sec²). As a passenger in a commercial jet aircraft, you'll experience a force of about 2 *g* when the aircraft turns. A fighter aircraft will experience a force of around 8 *g* when turning sharply. Without a special suit, the jet fighter pilot would black out under a force of 8 *g*. So the ADXL150, with a range of ± 50 *g*, can measure a *significant* amount of force!

Such a fine resolution means you can use this sensor to measure gentle vibrations and shifts. You could use it in a seismometer for geophysical applications or to measure vibrations or ground shift in mines, tunnels, or at building sites. You could use it to monitor motion and, by placing three accelerometers orthogonally, get an accurate 3-D motion recorder. The same setup could also be used as a digital carpenter's spirit level by sensing the direction of the Earth's gravitational field. Perhaps you might use it to monitor violent physical shock, such as crash-test measurements. Ever moved to a new house only to discover that Granny's fine crystal glassware was smashed by the movers? Place one of these (along with an appropriate small datalogger) into the packing boxes, and you'll be able to prove just how rough the gorillas from the moving company were. As you can see, this chip has lots of applications.

The axis of sensitivity for the ADXL150 runs along the chip's length from top to bottom (Figure 13-17). It is important when using this device that it be securely mounted to the circuit board. Rather than just relying on solder, also use strong glue under the chip to bind it to the circuit board.

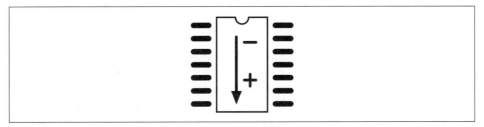

Figure 13-17. Axis of sensitivity

The ADXL150 requires no external components (save for power-supply decoupling) and is a completely self-contained unit, incorporating not only the sensor, but also signal conditioning and amplification. Its output can be interfaced directly to an ADC. The schematic for using the ADXL150 is shown in Figure 13-18.

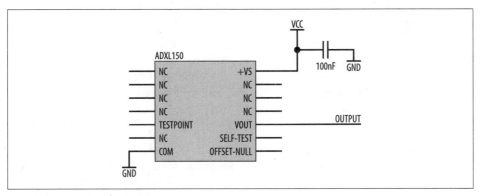

Figure 13-18. Using the ADXL150

Most of the pins are No Connection (NC) and can be ignored, as can the TESTPOINT and SELF-TEST pins. The TESTPOINT pin is used during manufacture only and should be left alone.

The ADXL150 operates off a power supply in the range of 4 V to 6 V. However, for ideal operation, the supply should be exactly 5.0 V. The closer to 5 V the supply is, the more accurate your measurements of acceleration will be. The output voltage is proportional to both acceleration and power supply (V_S) and is given by the relation:

V_{OUT} = V_S/2 - (sensitivity * V_S/5 * acceleration)

The sensitivity value varies from device to device and is in the range 33.0 to 43.0, with a nominal value of 38.0. The standard sensitivity value gives a range of ± 50 *g*; however, the sensitivity may be doubled (giving a range of ± 25 *g*) by connecting the output to the OFFSET-NULL pin.

The SELF-TEST pin is used for verifying the correct operation of both the internal mechanics of the sensor, as well as its signal conditioning and amplification electronics. Applying a logic 1 to this input pin artificially imposes a force on the sensor, and thus the sensor can be shown to be operating correctly.

Pressure Sensors

Now let's take a look at pressure sensors. The most obvious use of these sensors is in measuring air pressure for weather monitoring and prediction. But pressure sensors are also used in cars to measure manifold pressure, in washing machines to measure water levels, and in biomedical applications such as measuring blood pressure. Another application of pressure sensors is to measure altitude, since air pressure changes with height above sea level. Ocean depth can similarly be measured.

When using pressure sensors, the substance you are measuring can adversely affect the device. Remember that these are sensitive electronic components, and fluids or corrosive gases can destroy them. So unless you're measuring clean, dry air, you'll need to provide some degree of environmental protection for your sensor. Just how you do that really depends on what the application is, what environmental conditions you must protect against, and how far your budget stretches.

Pressure sensors work by measuring the deflection of a diaphragm separating two chambers. One chamber is exposed to the pressure that is being measured, while the other chamber holds a reference pressure. The pressure difference between the two chambers causes the diaphragm to deflect, and this deflection is converted into a voltage that is proportional to the pressure difference. Pressure sensors come in three types: *absolute*, *differential*, and *gauge*.

In an absolute pressure sensor, the reference chamber is sealed. Pressure readings are referenced to an absolute pressure, hence the name. Absolute sensors normally have the reference chamber pressure at vacuum, or at 1 atmosphere.

In a differential sensor, the reference chamber is not sealed, and an external pressure reference may be applied. Differential sensors are used to measure the relative pressures between two gases or two liquids. A differential sensor may be treated as an absolute sensor by providing it with a sealed and stable reference pressure.

A gauge sensor is a variation of the differential pressure sensor, where the reference pressure chamber is open to the atmosphere. Thus, the measured pressure is referenced to atmospheric pressure, and variations of atmospheric pressure (such as those caused by weather conditions or altitude) are taken into account. One interesting use of a gauge pressure sensor is to measure airspeed. If the measuring chamber is exposed to the oncoming airflow (caused by the aircraft's motion), and the reference chamber is exposed to the air but sheltered from the effects of the airflow, then the difference in pressure can be used to calculate the airspeed of the aircraft.

So, with all that in mind, let's take a look at some pressure sensors. The first sensor is a Freescale (formerly Motorola) MPXA6115A absolute pressure sensor (Figure 13-19). It operates from a 5 V supply and will give an output voltage of between 0.2 V and 4.8 V, proportional to pressures of 15 kPa to 115 kPa. (*Pa* is short for Pascals, which is a unit of pressure.) Unlike most other pressure sensors, which require external signal conditioning, temperature compensation, and signal amplification, the MPXA6115A integrates it all in one neat little package. It comes in an 8-pin chip package, with or without snorkel!

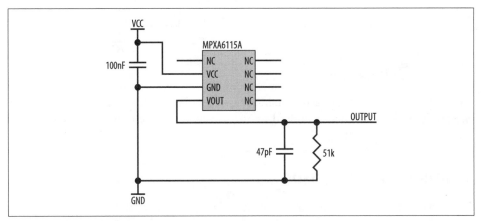

Figure 13-19. Interfacing the Freescale MPXA6115A pressure sensor

The NC pins are no-connection and should be left unwired. The only additional components required are a decoupling capacitor on the power supply and a resistor and capacitor in parallel at the output. The output may be directly connected to an ADC's input.

The second pressure sensor we will look at is also an absolute pressure sensor. But, unusually, rather than producing an analog output, it incorporates an inbuilt ADC. It is interfaced to a microcontroller using SPI and, being digital, it is much less susceptible to noise and interference. The sensor is the KP100, made by Infineon Technologies (*http://www.infineon.com*) in Munich, Germany.

The schematic for a circuit based on the KP100 is shown in Figure 13-20.

The sensor operates off a 5 V supply, and this is decoupled to ground using a 100 nF capacitor to reduce noise. The sensor has a standard SPI-style interface and is connected to a microcontroller, as with any SPI device. The sensor also provides a **READY** output, which may be used to interrupt the host processor, or may simply be connected to a spare I/O and read as a digital status flag. The KP100 also requires a separate clock (**CLK**) input. This clock can be either 4 MHz or 8 MHz. If the processor is running at one of these speeds, then the sensor can share the same clock input as the processor. However, if the processor is operating at a different clock frequency,

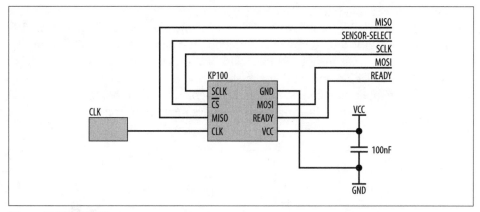

Figure 13-20. KP100 pressure sensor circuit

the KP100's clock may be easily generated using a clock module. These 4-pin devices are available in a variety of standard frequencies and require only power and ground to generate a clock output.

Magnetic-Field Sensor

The final sensor we'll look at is the AD22151 magnetic-field sensor by Analog Devices. Its primary use is for position and proximity sensing. A magnetic source is used as a reference point, and the sensor's distance from that source may be easily determined by the measured field strength. The sensor has inbuilt temperature compensation and amplification.

The circuit for this sensor is shown in Figure 13-21. It's a little bit more complicated than the other sensors we've looked at so far.

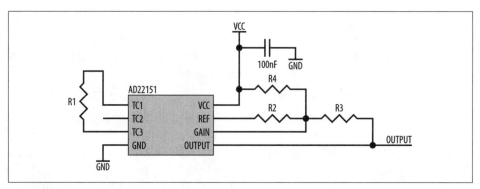

Figure 13-21. AD22151 magnetic-field sensor circuit

The sensor operates off a 5 V supply, decoupled to ground using a 100 nF capacitor. There are four resistors required for correct operation. R1 is the temperature compensation resistor, which should be connected between pins 1 and 3, or pins 2 and 3, depending on the applied magnetic field. For large external fields, R1 connects pins 1 and 3, as shown in Figure 13-21. For smaller fields, connect R1 between pins 2 and 3. The AD22151 datasheet has plots of values for R1 versus required compensation levels. Check with the manufacturer of your magnetic source[*] as to the required compensation value, and use this in conjunction with the datasheet to determine R1.

For magnet data, try *http://www.magtech.com.hk*, *http://www.eastindustries.net*, or *http://www.millennium.com.hk* as places to start.

R2 and R3 set the signal gain of the internal amplifier, and R4 provides a voltage offset. The datasheet for the sensor contains equations and technical data for computing values of these resistors, based on your specific needs.

The output of the sensor circuit may be connected directly to an ADC input for sampling.

Digital to Analog Conversion

So far, we have looked at how you can sense real-world effects and convert these into digital data. Now let's see how to do the reverse: take digital data and convert it into an analog signal by using a chip known as a *Digital-Analog Converter (DAC)*. We'll also look at how you can produce an analog output using nothing more than a single digital I/O line.

All DACs have a digital input (a microprocessor bus, SPI, or I2C) and will provide you with one or more channels of analog output.

The Maxim MAX525 is an 11-bit DAC that interfaces to a host processor using SPI. It has four channels of analog output and incorporates output amplifiers on-chip. The inverting input of each amplifier is accessible so that you can alter their respective gains. A sample circuit for a MAX525 is shown in Figure 13-22.

The four analog output channels are **OUTA**, **OUTB**, **OUTC**, and **OUTD**. These are tied directly to their respective feedback inputs (**FBA**, **FBB**, **FBC**, and **FBD**) for standard unipolar operation. There are two voltage reference inputs, **REFAB** (for channel A and channel B) and **REFCD** (for channels C and D). These two reference inputs *must* be at least 1.4 V or more below **VCC** at all times. The output voltage for each channel is given by the relation:

$V_{OUT} = (V_{REF} * code / 4096) * gain$

---

[*] I'm assuming here that you are using a magnet specifically intended for such applications, and which has data available, rather than a magnet you've found lying around somewhere.

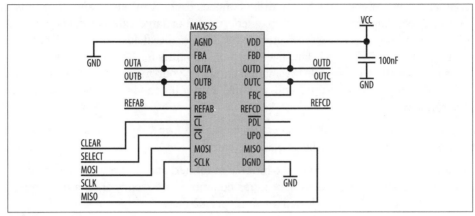

Figure 13-22. MAX525 circuit

where *code* is the digital value written to that channel. In our sample circuit, the gain
is 1. (See "Amplifiers," earlier in this chapter, for an explanation of how to set gains.)
If our reference voltage is set to 3.6 V, the digital value 4095 (0xFFF) generates an output voltage of:

```
VOUT = (VREF * 4095 / 4096) * gain
     = 3.6 * 0.9997 * 1
     = 3.59 V
```

Similarly, the digital value 2048 (0x800) generates an output voltage of:

```
VOUT = (VREF * 2048 / 4096) * gain
     = 3.6 * 0.5 * 1
     = 1.8 V
```

Note the separate analog and digital grounds in the schematic. These should be connected together, but only at a single point close to the DAC.

The MAX525 has a standard SPI connection to a microprocessor. Multiple
MAX525s may be daisy-chained together for efficiency (Figure 13-23).

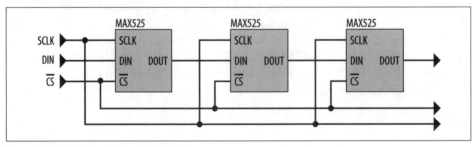

Figure 13-23. Daisy-chained MAX525s

The MAX525 also has a $\overline{\text{CL}}$ input, which, when driven low by an I/O line, sends all outputs to their lowest value. The MAX525 can be put into low-power mode under software control. The input $\overline{\text{PDL}}$ is Power-Down Lockout, and when driven low, it prevents the MAX525 from being shut down. This is important if the outputs are being used to drive a critical circuit or system. You don't want the controlling voltages disappearing by accident. Finally, the good people at Maxim have provided a signal called **UPO** (User Programmable Output). This is a general-purpose output that can be driven high or low under software control. Use it for whatever purpose you require.

Now, if you wanted a gain other than 1 (non-unity gain), external resistors are required for the output amplifier. The schematic for this (for a single output channel) is shown in Figure 13-24.

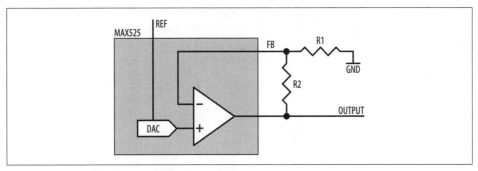

Figure 13-24. Feedback resistors for non-unity gain

From before, we know that the gain of a noninverting amplifier is given by:

```
Gain = 1 + R2 / R1
```

For bipolar output on a given channel, an external amplifier (with bipolar supplies) does the job (Figure 13-25).

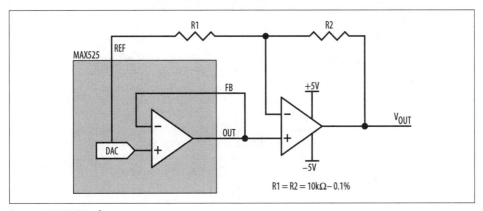

Figure 13-25. Bipolar output

PWM

Using a DAC may seem the obvious way to generate an analog output voltage, but there is another way that uses nothing more than a digital I/O line configured as an output. This technique is known as *Pulse Width Modulation (PWM)*.

Consider the average, garden-variety, square wave shown in Figure 13-26.

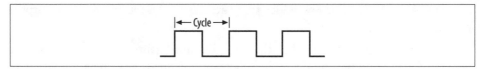

Figure 13-26. A ubiquitous square wave

The width of the high is equal to the width of the low, so this wave is said to have a 50% *duty cycle*. In other words, it is high for exactly half the cycle. Now, if the amplitude of this square wave is 5 V, for example, the *average* voltage over the cycle is 2.5 V. It is as though we had a constant voltage of 2.5 V.

Now consider the square wave in Figure 13-27.

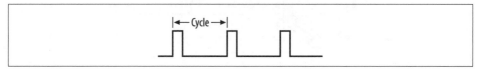

Figure 13-27. 10% duty cycle

This wave has a 10% duty cycle, which means that the average voltage over the cycle is 0.5 V.

A low-pass (averaging) filter on the PWM output will convert the pulses to an analog voltage, proportional to the duty cycle of the PWM signal. By varying the duty cycle, we can vary the analog voltage. Hey, presto! We have digital-to-analog conversion without a DAC. That's the basic idea behind PWM.

 PWM can also be used to drive a LED, and thereby get varying light intensities from a signal that is essentially either on or off. PWM can also be used to generate audio. Early desktop computers, such as the Apple][, used PWM to drive a speaker. Steve Wozniak, the designer of the Apple][, used a spare chip select of the address decoder as his PWM signal. By changing how frequently a particular address was accessed, he was able to change the frequency and duty cycle of his PWM signal and was therefore able to generate simple audio with varying volume and pitch. Sound out of an address decoder!

Motor Control

One of the fun things you can do with an embedded computer is get it to actually *move* something, whether it be an external system or the embedded computer itself. Motion implies motor, and this section will look at how you interface an embedded computer to an electric motor. The possible applications could range from controlling locomotives on your model railroad layout to experiments in robotics, and anything in between. A note of caution, though: if your hardware and software are responsible for moving a physical object, then a bug can easily cause physical damage too. So be careful.

Let's say that we have an electric motor than operates from a 12 V supply. Applying 12 V across the motor will cause it to turn at full speed. Similarly, by applying 6 V, we can get the motor spinning at half speed. By varying the applied voltage, we can vary the speed at which the motor turns.

There are several ways to generate this voltage to drive the electric motor. The most obvious may seem to be to use a DAC to generate an analog output voltage and then use an amplifier to boost the signal to the voltage and current required to turn the motor. The speed of the motor is proportional to the output voltage. However, this technique has a major drawback. For very low-speed operation, the required output voltage may be too low to actually cause the motor to turn.

A better way is to use PWM. Consider the PWM signal in Figure 13-28, with an amplitude of 12 V.

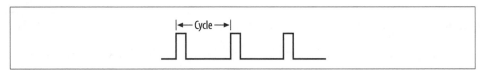

Figure 13-28. PWM signal with a 10% duty cycle

With a 10% duty cycle, the effective analog output voltage of this PWM signal is 1.2 V. Now, by itself, 1.2 V may not be enough to turn a motor. But we're not using 1.2 V; we're actually pulsing the motor with 12 V, its maximum drive voltage. The duration of the pulses gives the *equivalent speed* of a motor voltage of 1.2 V. However, by using a full 12 V amplitude, we're ensuring that the motor will turn. This is the advantage of PWM. To control speed, we vary the width of the pulse and not the amplitude.

Using PWM, you can get very slow motor speeds and very fine control. The pulses can cause a jerkiness to the motor if the overall frequency is low, but by choosing a high frequency, the jerkiness is averaged out.

Many microcontrollers have internal, software-programmable PWM modules that make generating PWM signals easy. Even if a processor does not have a PWM module, you can still generate PWM under software control simply by using a digital output line.

Let's now take a look at how you would interface a processor to an electric motor using PWM. Due to the voltages and currents required by motors, you cannot simply hang a motor off the pins of a processor and expect it to work. You need an interface circuit that will take your logic-level, PWM output and use this to switch much higher voltages and currents.

Figure 13-29 shows a conceptual model (in a crude and simplified form) of such an interface circuit for driving a small electric motor. This type of circuit is known as an *H-bridge*.

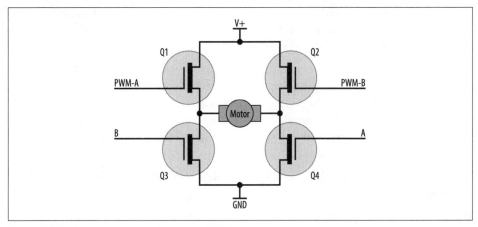

Figure 13-29. Motor drive circuit using an H-bridge

It's not as confusing as it first looks. Don't be too worried about the transistors (Q1–Q4) in the circuit. They simply act as switches. Our motor operates from a supply voltage, **V+**. Apply **V+** with one polarity, and the motor turns in the forward direction. Reverse the polarity, and the motor reverses too. To drive the circuit, we use four outputs from the processor: two PWMs (which I've called **PWM-A** and **PWM-B**) and two general I/O lines (which I've called **A** and **B**). Initially, all outputs are low, everything is turned off, and the motor is stationary.

If we send **A** high, the transistor Q4 turns on and connects the right "side" of the motor to ground. If we then send **PWM-A** high, the transistor Q1 turns on. Thus, the left "side" of the motor is connected to **V+**, and the motor spins. By generating a PWM signal on **PWM-A**, we can control the speed of the motor in that direction.

Conversely, by leaving **A** and **PWM-A** low and setting **B** and **PWM-B** high, transistors Q2 and Q3 turn on, and the motor spins in the reverse direction. By generating a PWM signal on **PWM-B**, we can control the speed in the reverse direction.

Care must be taken in your software. If both Q1 and Q3 are turned on, or both Q2 and Q4 are turned on, then you effectively connect **V+** to ground, with very little resistance in between! The results would be spectacular and short-lived! A proper H-bridge circuit normally contains protection to prevent such a state from occurring.

The actual implementation of an H-bridge is a little more complicated and requires additional components such as protection diodes and so forth. Now, while you could design such an H-bridge circuit using discrete components, there is an easier way. A number of manufacturers—such as Freescale, International Rectifier (*http://www.irf.com*), M. S. Kennedy Corp (*http://www.mskennedy.com*), and others—make H-bridges in easy-to-use integrated circuits.

If you're ever cruising around a component manufacturer's web site looking for devices that will switch high currents at high voltages and you can't find them, scoot over to its "automotive components" section. Such devices are sometimes hidden away in there.

Let's look at a sample H-bridge, the Freescale MC33186. This chip is more sophisticated than the simple H-bridge used to explain the concept. It provides more functionality, yet is easier to control. This chip can operate from a supply voltage (**V+**) of between 5 V and 28 V and can switch continuous currents as high as 5 A, yet it has logic inputs that are compatible with TTL levels. It has inbuilt short-circuit and overcurrent protection. Figure 13-30 shows an MC33186 circuit.

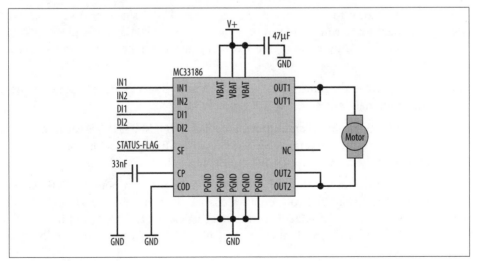

Figure 13-30. MC33186 motor drive circuit

The chip has three power-supply inputs, V_{BAT}, all of which must be connected to the supply voltage, V+. The power-supply input needs to be decoupled using a 47 μF capacitor. The internal charge pump also needs a decoupling capacitor. The pin, **CP**, provides access to the charge pump and is connected to a 33 nF capacitor. The chip also has five ground pins, which, similarly, must all be connected to ground.

OUT1 and **OUT2** are the pins that directly drive the motor. There are two of each, so that the high output currents are not traveling through a single pin.

IN1 and **IN2** control both the motor's speed and direction. **DI1** and **DI2** serve to disable the MC33186. These four control signals may be driven by a microcontroller's I/O lines. For normal operation, **DI1** is low and **DI2** is high. Sending either **DI1** high or **DI2** low will disable the MC33186 and stop the motor. Table 13-1 shows how **IN1**, **IN2**, **DI1**, and **DI2** affect the motor's operation.

Table 13-1. MC33186 states of operation

DI1	DI2	IN1	IN2	OUT1	OUT2	Motor
Low	High	High	Low	V+	Ground	Forward
Low	High	Low	High	Ground	V+	Reverse
Low	High	Low	Low	Ground	Ground	Free-wheeling
Low	High	High	High	V+	V+	Free-wheeling
High	Don't care	Don't care	Don't care	High impedance	High impedance	Disabled
Don't care	Low	Don't care	Don't care	High impedance	High impedance	Disabled

If we want the motor to run forward, we generate a PWM signal on **IN1** and leave **IN2** low. If we want to run the motor backward, we leave **IN1** low and place a PWM signal on **IN2**. The duty cycle of the PWM signal determines the motor's speed. Simple.

If **IN1** and **IN2** are in the same state, then there's no voltage difference applied across the motor's terminals, and so the motor is not driven.

Pin 2 of the MC33186, **SF**, is an output status flag. If the MC33186 is operating correctly, **SF** is high. If there is a fault, **SF** is driven low. **SF** may therefore be used as an interrupt to alert the host processor of a problem.

The input **COD** determines how the chip functions during a fault. If **COD** is left unconnected or is connected to ground, a change on either input **DI1** or **DI2** will reset the fault condition. If **COD** is connected to **VCC** (that's +5 V, not necessarily V+), then **DI1** and **DI2** are disabled. The fault condition can be reset only by a change on **IN1** or **IN2**.

Using an integrated H-bridge circuit, such as the MC33186, greatly simplifies interfacing your embedded system to motors.

Sensing Motor Speed

In a control application, it is very useful to be able to sense a motor's speed. The physical system (load) that the motor is driving will affect the motor's rotation. If the motor must move a heavy load, then its actual speed of rotation may be less than the intended speed. In such situations, it is useful to measure the actual speed so that the embedded control system can compensate.

The easiest way to measure a motor's rotational speed is to use an optical encoder module, such as the Agilent HEDS-9000 or a similar device. The encoder consists of a light source (LED) and an array of photo-detectors, separated from each other by a slotted disc known as a *code wheel* (Figure 13-31). The disc is mounted on the rotating motor shaft. Each time a slot passes between the LED and a detector, the detector receives a flash of light and generates an electrical pulse. The rate at which the pulses are generated corresponds directly to the rotational speed of the motor. The resolution of the code wheel is known as its *counts per revolution (CPR)* value. The HEDS series of encoders are available with CPRs ranging from 96 all the way up to 2,048.

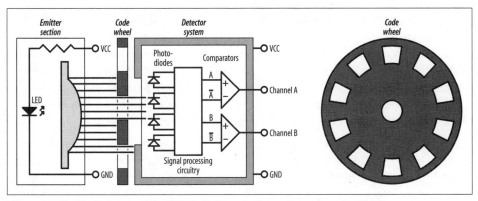

Figure 13-31. Block diagram of a HEDS-9000 optical encoder and a code wheel

The HEDS-9000 optical encoder operates from a 5 V supply and has two outputs, **A** and **B**. These outputs are derived from two adjacent optical sensors. If the code wheel is rotating in one direction, output **A** will trigger before output **B** (Figure 13-32).

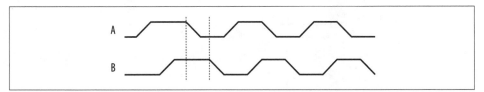

Figure 13-32. Output waveforms for the optical encoder

If the wheel is rotating in the opposite direction, then **B** will trigger before **A** (Figure 13-33).

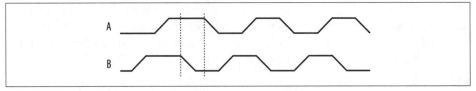

Figure 13-33. Output waveforms for the optical encoder, with rotation in the opposite direction

The rate at which the pulses arrive gives the motor's speed, and the order in which they arrive shows the direction. This is known as *quadrature encoding*.

Most microcontrollers have timer/counter inputs that can measure external trigger events such as these. Under software control, you can use the timers to monitor these quadrature signals. However, Agilent makes a series of devices known as quadrature counters: the 11-bit HCTL-2000, the 16-bit HCTL-2016, and the 16-bit, cascadable HCTL-2020. These chips provide a bus-based interface to a processor and convert quadrature signals into a binary number representing motor position. A 16-bit position counter is capable of measuring 32,767 increments in either direction, which corresponds to approximately 15 turns of a 2,048 CPR encoder. To determine the present motor speed or position, the processor simply reads from the quadrature counter as though it were just another memory location. Quadrature counters also have noise filters on their inputs and so provide a more reliable and accurate way of determining motor position.

The schematics showing an optical encoder and quadrature counter are shown in Figures 13-34 and 13-35, respectively. The optical encoder is placed on a separate, small PCB so that it may be easily mounted next to the motor's shaft. The quadrature counter is located on the embedded computer's PCB. IDC headers (J1 and J2) and a ribbon cable connect the two circuit boards.

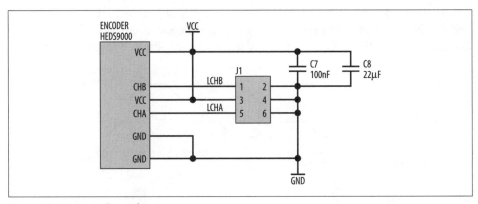

Figure 13-34. Optical encoder circuit

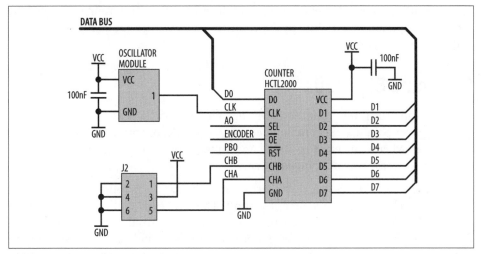

Figure 13-35. Quadrature counter circuit

The quadrature counter requires a 14 MHz clock. This is easily provided by an oscillator module. **CHA** and **CHB** are the quadrature inputs from the encoder. The counter has a reset input, **RST**, which clears the counter. Asserting **RST** zeros the quadrature counter and indicates that the motor is in the "home" position. This input is driven by a digital output of the microcontroller so that the counter can be reset under software control.

D0 to **D7** are the data buses through which the processor reads the current position. Since the counters are either 12 bits or 16 bits, two reads are necessary to retrieve the value through the 8-bit bus. The counter therefore occupies two locations in memory, and the **SEL** input is used to select which byte is being read. If **SEL** is low, then the higher-order bits are read. If **SEL** is high, then the lower-order bits are read. To make these two bytes appear in adjacent memory locations, the processor's address line, **A0**, is used to drive **SEL**. Thus, the least significant address of the two selects the upper eight bits, while the next address selects the lower eight bits.

Now, the counter does not have a chip select as such. Since it is a read-only device, the counter's output enable, **OE**, functions as a combined chip select and output enable. Therefore, this input is driven by the output of the address decoder that corresponds to the region of the address space to which the counter is mapped. When the processor reads from that address range, **OE** is asserted and the counter responds with data. Note that if the processor attempted to write to the counter, the counter would be selected and would respond with data. Therefore, both the processor and the counter would be attempting to drive data onto the data bus. This could potentially damage both chips. Now, with careful coding this would not be a problem. However, a crashing program may inadvertently cause this situation to arise. To prevent this, a better solution is to include the processor's read strobe as part of the address decode for this particular device. In other words, the counter is selected if (and only if) both the address is correct *and* the processor is performing a read. If the processor is performing a write to the counter's address, the counter is not selected and the access is ignored.

Switching Big Loads

We've already seen how to use an H-bridge chip to switch relatively large voltages (and the corresponding big currents) needed to drive electric motors. There are many other cases where you want to turn large voltages on or off, and, in this section, you'll learn an easy way of doing just that.

The Freescale MC33298 is a chip that is controlled by a microprocessor using SPI that can switch eight power sources on or off. This chip can handle voltages between 5 V and 26.5 V, with currents as large as 6 Amps. If you need to turn electrical systems on or off, this chip is for you. Its primary use is for industrial and automotive applications, controlling power to subsystems such as heaters, small air-conditioning units, moderate-voltage light bulbs, small pumps, and so on. Obviously, it won't handle the high AC voltages that come out of your wall socket, so don't use it for switching power to your home appliances!

The basic schematic for the circuit is shown in Figure 13-36.

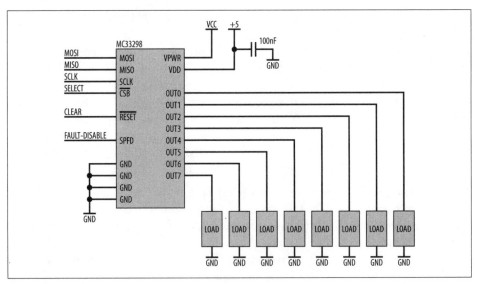

Figure 13-36. MC33298 circuit

The MC33298 has two power-supply pins. **VDD** is a 5 V supply and powers the chip's internal digital logic. It's decoupled to ground using a 100 nF capacitor. V_{PWR} is the supply voltage for the external subsystems (represented in the figure by each "LOAD" rectangle) and can range from 5 V to 26.5 V. There are eight switch outputs, labeled **OUT0** through **OUT7**. When a given switch is activated, the corresponding output is connected to the V_{PWR} supply, thereby turning on that subsystem. The MC33298 has short-circuit detection and shutdown (with automatic retry), over-voltage detection and shutdown, current limiting on the outputs, output clamping during inductive switching, and thermal shutdown if the device is dissipating too much power. Higher currents may be switched by tying two or more outputs together so that the current is shared by more than one pin. By tying all outputs together, currents as high as 48 A may be switched, limited only by the total power dissipation and corresponding thermal shutdown limit.

The chip has a standard SPI port, allowing it to be interfaced to, and therefore controlled by, most microprocessors. The SPI signals **MOSI**, **MISO**, and **SCLK** are connected directly to a processor's SPI pins. The chip's select input, $\overline{\text{CSB}}$, is controlled by a digital output of the processor and is used to select the device during a SPI transfer. The device may be reset and all outputs turned off by asserting its **RESET** input. Again, this too can be driven by a digital output of the processor so that the chip may be turned off under software control. The MC33298 supports SPI daisy chaining, so multiple devices may be coupled together.

The **SPFD** pin is Short Fault Protect Disable. Sending this pin high allows the internal over-current detection circuitry to be disabled. When switching some loads, such as light bulbs, there is a very high current for a short period of time. This would normally cause the MC33298 to register an over-current fault and shut off that output. The **SPFD** pin allows this protection to be overridden so that such loads may be controlled. Even though the over-current protection is bypassed, the MC33298 is still protected. If the high current lasts long enough, the chip's thermal shutdown circuit will kick in, thereby preventing damage. **SPFD** may be driven by a processor digital output, and should be used with caution! For normal operation (with over-current protection on), this pin should be low.

Now we've finished looking at I/O options for our embedded computers. In the next chapter, we'll look at some processors and see how to design complete embedded systems.

CHAPTER 14

The PIC Microcontrollers

*Where a calculator on the ENIAC is equipped with
18,000 vacuum tubes and weighs 30 tons, computers
in the future may have only 1,000 vacuum tubes and
perhaps weigh 1 ½ tons.*
—*Popular Mechanics*, March 1949

This chapter introduces you to the Microchip PIC. To start our discussion of micro-processor hardware, we'll look at the basics of creating computer hardware by designing a small computer based on a simple 8-pin PIC processor. The same design principles apply to the AVR and many other microcontrollers. This PIC processor is so simple that building a computer based on one of them is trivial, as you will see. From there, we'll look at a mid-range PIC processor and see just what you need to do to design an embedded computer based on one. First, though, let's take a quick tour of the PIC architectures before getting into designing some computers.

A Tale of Two Processors

In the late 1970s, General Instruments had a 16-bit processor known as the CP1600. It has since passed into extinction and is all but forgotten, long ago losing out to the Intel 8086 and the Motorola 68000. One major failing of the CP1600 was that it had limited I/O capability, and so General Instruments designed a tiny companion processor to act as an I/O controller. The idea was that this controller could provide not only the I/O for the CP1600, but being a processor in its own right, it could provide some degree of intelligent control. This processor was called the *Peripheral Interface Controller*, or *PIC*. The CP1600 died a quiet death, passing gently into oblivion, but its little companion lives on. In the mid-80s, the microelectronics division of General Instruments was spun off into Microchip, and the PIC processor was its core product. Today, PICs are widely used. They live in the hand controllers of Sony PlayStations, children's toys, consumer appliances, and industrial systems.

The original PIC architecture has only one accumulator (known as the *working regis-ter*, or *w register*) and 25 to 368 bytes of RAM in the original processors. The pro-gram counter's least significant byte, the status register, and various control registers are mapped into the lowest part of the RAM space and may be accessed by standard memory move operations. The upper part of the RAM space is for data. Microchip refers to the RAM space as "registers," although they have limited functionality as true registers. They are primarily for data storage.

The processor has a stack that is fixed to a depth of between two and eight entries (depending on the particular processor) and is used solely for holding return addresses for subroutine calls and interrupts. There is a single register, known as the *FSR* (*File Select Register*), which can act as an index register into the RAM space. Limited indexed addressing is available using the FSR, and it can be used to imple-ment a pseudostack for user data.

Apart from a few exceptions, the PIC has no external buses and is a self-contained computer within a single chip. Only limited expansion is possible using the proces-sor's peripheral interfaces (SPI and I2C) or digital I/O ports. The PIC excels in appli-cations for which size and power consumption are critical. Being able to drop a tiny computer system into a design is a great bonus, and it is ideal for battery-powered applications, since it can (almost) run off the field of a stray electron.

The PIC is also very robust. It takes a *lot* to kill a PIC. I had one client that inadvert-ently switched power and ground on his PIC-based computer and left it that way for a week. At the end of it, the little processor was still operational (once powered the right way). Another time, one of my PIC-based dataloggers was tested for its long endurance by attaching it to the Indian Pacific express. This is a long-haul passenger train that goes between Sydney and Perth, crossing the deserts of central Australia. Unfortunately, during the trial the Indian Pacific was involved in a serious rail acci-dent. A signaling fault caused a commuter train to impact the rear of the express, completely demolishing the end carriages. The datalogger had been attached (exter-nally) to the rear of the train. It absorbed the full impact of the collision, and, when recovered from the wreckage, the datalogger was still operating normally. PICs are tough little processors!

The PIC is very RISC-like in many respects. The architecture is Harvard, with sepa-rate data and code spaces. The data space is 8 bits wide, while the code spaces are between 12 and 16 bits wide, depending on the particular PIC family. The data space is mapped into multiple banks, including most control registers. With only one accu-mulator, banked memory, and limited addressing modes, a reasonable percentage of a given program can be spent simply shuffling data around, much more so than many other processors. The PIC excels in small-scale, simple applications. However, the lure of its ultra-low power consumption sometimes means that it is pressed into service running some quite involved algorithms. Writing complicated software for the PIC sometimes feels as impossible as trying to solve a *Tower of Hanoi* puzzle that has only a single peg. It can be a challenge! Many a PIC programmer has wished for just a bit more memory, and just a few more accumulators. The new *dsPIC* architecture, which is a significant advance over the standard PIC, has been received with chortles of joy by PIC developers around the world, as is a much more advanced processor.

The Microchip software development environment (MPLAB) provides an assembler, simulator and software for burning code into the processors. MPLAB is freely downloadable from the Microchip web site (*http://www.microchip.com*). A number of commercial C compilers are also available for the PIC, but there is no port of the gnu C compiler for it. (At the time of writing, there are rumors that the gnu compiler will be ported to the new dsPIC architecture.)

For many simple digital applications, a small microprocessor is a better choice than discrete logic, because it is able to execute software. It is therefore able to perform certain tasks with much less hardware complexity. So, let's see just how easy it is to produce a small, embedded computer.

Starting Simple

The PIC12C508 processor is a tiny 8-pin computer with just 512 words of internal program memory and just 25 bytes of internal RAM. It is intended for the simplest of control functions. It can be used in any small application for which you need to monitor digital inputs or turn something on or off. Its I/O pins can be used to synthesize a SPI or I²C interface, or to control a motor using PWM.

Figure 14-1 shows the schematic for a small computer based on the PIC12C508. The digital I/O signals of the PIC are brought out through a 7-pin connector. If the design were implemented using surface-mount components wherever possible, the connector would be the largest component on the PCB!

This particular PIC processor includes an internal RC oscillator that runs at 4 MHz, so we can use it without any external oscillator circuit. The design in Figure 14-2 shows the same PIC-based design, but this time using an external 32 kHz watch crystal for its oscillator. By running off a (slower) 32 kHz crystal, we have the advantage of greatly reducing the processor's power consumption. This is important for battery-powered applications.

Two 15 pF capacitors remove unwanted higher-order harmonics from the crystal's oscillation. The values for the capacitors vary depending on what speed and type of crystal you are using. The processor datasheet has tables showing recommended capacitor values for various crystal frequencies.

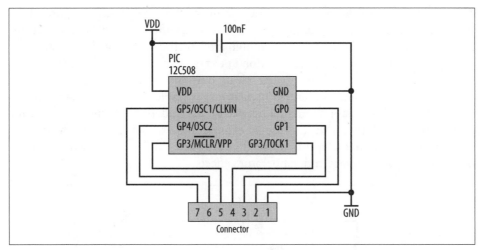

Figure 14-1. Minimal PIC12C805 computer

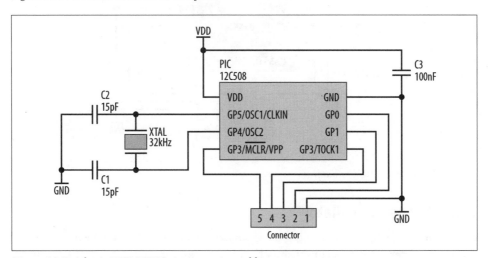

Figure 14-2. A basic PIC12C508 computer; just add power

The PIC processor has to be configured to use the appropriate oscillator source. When using the PIC with a 32 kHz crystal, the chip has to be configured in "LP mode." If you're using the PIC with faster crystals (greater than 455 kHz), the chip has to be in "XT mode." The internal RC oscillator is selected by "INTRC mode," while an external oscillator requires "EXTRC mode." The Microchip development software (MPLAB) allows you to easily set these parameters when burning software into the processor.

The alternative is to use an external RC circuit as the clock source (Figure 14-3). While not the most precise timing option, it is by far the cheapest. The actual frequency of oscillation depends on a combination of the values of the resistor, the capacitor, the supply voltage, the variation in tolerances for the components, and the current operating temperature. To be clear, only an approximate operating frequency can be determined for an RC oscillator. For stable operation, Microchip recommends that the resistor should be between 3 kΩ and 100 kΩ, and the capacitor greater than 20 pF. If you wish to use an external RC oscillator, refer to the processor's datasheet, as Microchip has detailed information on RC component selection, taking into account voltage and temperature effects.

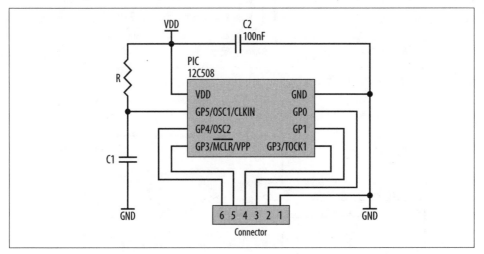

Figure 14-3. External RC oscillator

Variable-Speed Oscillator

One of the neat tricks you can do if using an external RC oscillator is have a variable-speed computer. This is accomplished by adding a pull-up resistor (R1) between the oscillator input and an I/O pin (Figure 14-4). For normal operation, the I/O pin is configured as an input. By configuring the I/O pin as an output and placing it high, the resistor R1 is effectively placed in parallel with the resistor R. The overall resistance is increased by the relationship $R_{TOTAL} = 1 / (1/R + 1/R_1)$, and the oscillator slows accordingly. This is a useful technique to reduce power consumption under software control.

When using an external RC circuit to drive the internal oscillator, an extra PIC I/O line (**GP4**) becomes available for use.

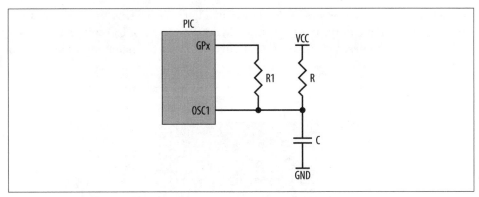

Figure 14-4. Variable-speed RC oscillator

Power-on Reset

No external reset is needed for this PIC. Instead, the design relies on the internal power-up reset circuit of the processor. Further, not even an external resistor is required on the reset input, $\overline{\text{MCLR}}$, since the processor incorporates a weak pull-up resistor for this purpose. When not used as a reset input, $\overline{\text{MCLR}}$ can be utilized as a general-purpose input.

 $\overline{\text{MCLR}}$ on other PIC processors *does* require either a pull-up resistor or direct connection to V_{DD}. Leaving it unconnected will not work, nor can it be used as a general-purpose input. Always check the datasheet!

The power supply (V_{DD}) for the PIC12C805 can range from 2.5 V to 5.5 V.

That covers the basics of a PIC12C805 system, and it's not that much different from the corresponding AVR computer, which we'll look at in the next chapter. The real differences lie in their internal architectures (and instruction sets) and in the subtleties of their operating voltages and interfacing capabilities. As you can see, there's not a lot of hard work involved in putting one of these little machines into your embedded system.

A Bigger PIC

In this section, we'll look at the PIC16C73 processor. For a mid-range PIC, the design is not dissimilar to the simpler PIC we've already seen. The only real difference is that the processor has more pins, more I/O, and more functionality. Designing for PIC17 and PIC18 processors is not dissimilar to creating machines based on the PIC16 family. What you learn here is applicable to many other PICs.

The schematic for this processor is shown in Figure 14-5. This processor has 4K words of program memory, 192 bytes of RAM, and a variety of I/O subsystems, such as three timer modules, SPI, I2C, a UART, five channels of analog input, and up to 22 digital I/O pins.

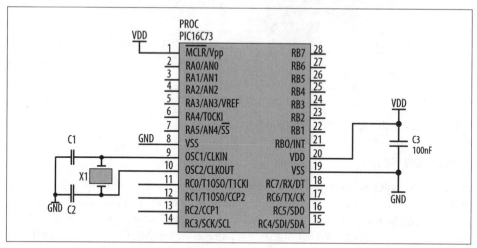

Figure 14-5. PIC16C73 processor and support components

This processor has one power pin (**VDD**) and two ground pins (**VSS**). As always, power is decoupled to ground with a small capacitor (C3). The only other requirements are some form of clock generation—in this case provided by a crystal, X1—and two decoupling capacitors, C1 and C2. The clock could just as easily have been provided using an RC circuit, as we saw with the 12C508 PIC. The reset input, **MCLR**, is tied directly to the power supply, such that it is permanently inactive. In this case, we are relying on the processor's internal power-on reset circuitry and don't need to provide an external reset. It is common practice to use a pull-up resistor to tie an unused input, such as $\overline{\text{MCLR}}$, inactive. However, in this case I have found that a pull-up resistor can affect the activation of the internal power-on reset to the point where it fails to kick in. (The internal capacitance of the pin combines with the resistor to form an RC circuit, which delays $\overline{\text{MCLR}}$ from reaching the appropriate level.) Thus, the resistor can actually cause the processor to never start properly. So in this case, it's better to leave it out.

Port A (**RA0...RA5**) functions as an analog input port or a general-purpose digital port. Port B (**RB0...RB7**) is a general-purpose digital port with weak internal pull-up resistors. Port C (**RC0...RC7**) can act as a digital port or provide timers, PWM, a serial port, a SPI port, or an I2C interface. Depending on your application, you may use some or all of these pins in your design, connecting to other subsystems as appropriate.

This basic design, in combination with the appropriate datasheet, can be adapted to most other PIC processors that you will come across.

PIC-Based Environmental Datalogger

Now let's look at a complete system based on a PIC processor. The design presented here is a simplified version of my DL4 datalogger product. This datalogger is designed for extended recording of data (for at least a year), using a minimum of power. It has 1M of nonvolatile memory, capable of retaining data without power for as much as 20 years. The sensors fitted are light and temperature, but you could easily adapt this design to record any analog sensor you like, from acceleration to magnetic field. It's also small. The entire datalogger fits onto a circuit board smaller than your smallest finger.

The processor is a PIC16LF873A, a variant of the PIC16C73. The "L" means that it is low-power, and the "F" means that it is a flash-based part (rather than EPROM or OTP) that can be reprogrammed in-circuit, making debugging (and life) so much easier. The "8" indicates that the processor includes EEPROM for nonvolatile parameter storage, useful for holding user preferences and machine state. Finally, the "A" tells us that it is a second revision (version) of the silicon. The basic circuit for the processor and its support components is shown in Figure 14-6.

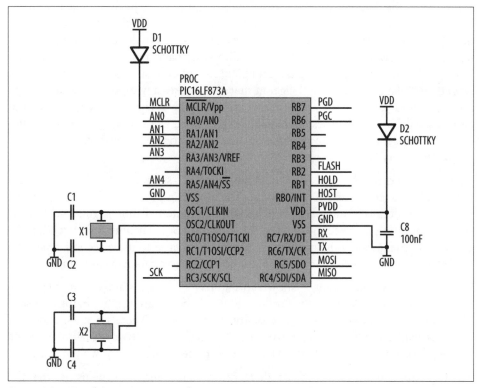

Figure 14-6. Datalogger processor and support components

Note that the processor's power pin is connected to a net labeled **PVDD** rather than the system's **VDD**. Since the processor can be reprogrammed in-circuit, we must consider this in our design. During programming, the burner provides its own supply voltage (+5 V) for the processor. Now the flash chip used in the datalogger requires a nominal supply voltage of 3.3 V, and the 5 V supplied by the burner could potentially damage the chip. Hence, we use a Schottky diode, D2, to isolate the system supply voltage from the processor when it is being reprogrammed. When not being programmed, D2 conducts and supplies the processor with power. During programming, D2 doesn't conduct, and the rest of the datalogger remains unpowered.

In the same way, we use a Schottky diode (D1) to isolate the processor's reset pin from the supply voltage. When not being programmed, D1 conducts and pulls $\overline{\text{MCLR}}$ to **VDD**. However, during programming, D1 isolates $\overline{\text{MCLR}}$ and allows the burner to pull this reset input to a higher voltage as required.

The processor has two crystals, X1 and X2. X1 provides the timing for the processor that drives its internal operation. Depending on our application, X1 could be anything from 32 kHz to 20 MHz. The choice of crystal for X1 affects the power consumption of the datalogger. The faster the crystal, the more juice the machine uses. For ultra-low-power operation, a 32 kHz crystal is the best choice. However, this does have a drawback. Since the internal oscillator is used to drive the UART's transmitter and receiver clocks, a slow crystal limits the baud rate that we can achieve. Using a 32 kHz crystal gives a maximum baud rate of only 300 baud. Downloading a megabyte of data from the datalogger at that speed takes a whopping 7 hours and 42 minutes! (And you thought your Internet connection was slow.) Hence, you need to choose a value of X1 that best suits your needs. If you can live with a 7-hour download and want the maximum possible operating life from your battery, use a 32 kHz crystal. If battery life is not critical, use a faster crystal.

X2 is used to drive the processor's internal TIMER1 subsystem, which we use for timekeeping functions and for scheduling the sampling process. While it is possible to use the processor's main oscillator to drive the internal timers, this oscillator is shut down during the execution of the SLEEP instruction. (The internal watchdog circuit is used to reawaken the processor.) Hence, it is better to use a second crystal on TIMER1 for your timekeeping, as TIMER1 continues to operate even during sleep.

The voltage regulator circuit is shown in Figure 14-7. It's a standard MAX604 circuit, providing a 3.3 V supply voltage on VDD. Since we are using a battery to supply power, we can live without a capacitor on the input. There's a huge choice of batteries available. I like the Energizer EL123 battery. It's relatively small (two-thirds the length of a AA and slightly fatter) and can run the datalogger for well over a year.

The regulator is important in the datalogger for two reasons. First, it ensures that the supply voltage within the datalogger is constant. This is critical, as the supply voltage

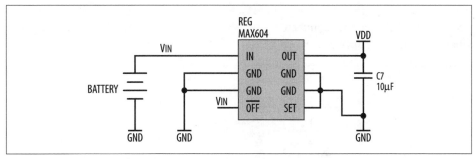

Figure 14-7. Datalogger power supply

is used as a reference for the analog-to-digital converter. While it is perfectly possible to run the processor directly off a battery, as the battery's voltage begins to drop with use, the readings from the sensors will become increasingly meaningless. We'd be recording data quite successfully, but its relevance would be nil.

The second reason for using the regulator is that it is able to operate off a lower voltage than other components in the system and still provide a stable 3.3 V. This means that even as our battery is draining, we can still get the maximum operating life possible.

Figure 14-8 shows the nonvolatile flash (made by ST Electronics), which is used for holding data. The flash uses a simple SPI interface to connect to the host processor. It is selected by the **FLASH** chip select, which is controlled from a processor I/O line (**RB2**). The **HOLD** input to flash acts as a "pause" function during accesses. This allows the processor, until software control, to temporarily suspend its access to the flash and perform SPI transfers with other peripherals. This feature currently isn't used in the datalogger but is included to allow for future functionality, such as the inclusion of digital, SPI-based sensors. Finally, the chip select (**FLASH**) is pulled high to ensure that the flash is not inadvertently selected as the datalogger is powering up.

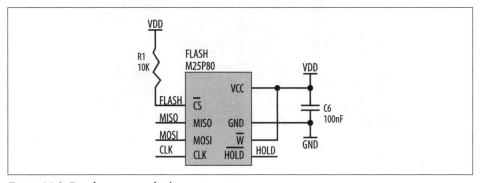

Figure 14-8. Datalogger nonvolatile memory

Figure 14-9 shows the datalogger's interface to the outside world. The DL4 datalogger uses a small Harwin connector, also shown in Figure 14-9, but you could use whatever suits your application, even an IDC header.

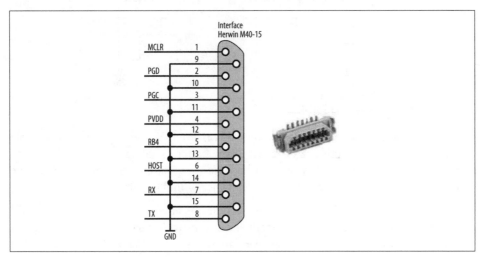

Figure 14-9. Datalogger connector

The connector is used to mate with two separate devices. The first is shown in Figure 14-10. This in-house adaptor allows the datalogger to be plugged into a Microchip PICSTART Plus programmer for burning new code. It simply maps the signals required during programming ($\overline{\text{MCLR}}$, **PGD**, **PGC**, power, and ground) to the equivalent pins for a DIP-based PIC. In essence, it converts the datalogger's connector into the pinout of a DIP-based PIC. The adaptor board has pins underneath that insert into the programmer.

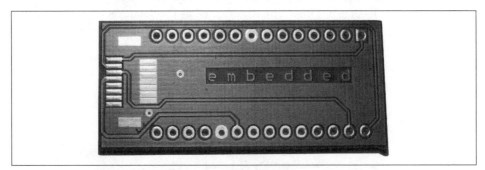

Figure 14-10. Programming adaptor for the DL4 datalogger

The second device into which the datalogger plugs is an RS-232C adaptor module, shown in Figure 14-11.

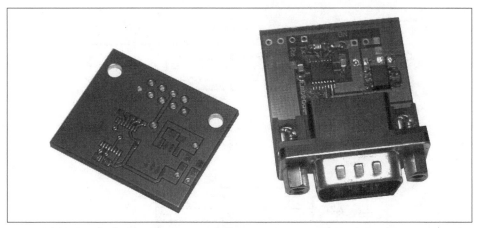

Figure 14-11. Serial adaptor

This module allows the datalogger to connect to a host computer for both configuration setup and data recovery. The adaptor has a Maxim RS-232C level-shifter and a voltage regulator (both fitted to the top side of the circuit board), and a DB-9 connector. It draws its power from the RTS signal of the host computer's serial port and, as such, requires no external power supply. The schematic for this circuit is shown in Figure 14-12. Note that this is an independent circuit from that of the datalogger.

The diode D2 is needed since **RTS** can have negative voltages as well as positive voltages. D2 prevents damage to the regulator when **RTS** is negative. During normal operation, **RTS** is set at +12 V by the host computer under software control, turning on the serial adaptor. The regulator turns this +12 V into +3.3 V, which powers the MAX3232 and illuminates the LED. Note that pin 6 of the Harwin connector on the datalogger is connected to a net called **HOST**. This pin corresponds to pin 3 of the adaptor's Harwin connector and is tied to ground. When the datalogger is plugged into the adaptor module, **HOST** is pulled low, but at all other times it is high due to the internal pull-up resistors inside the PIC. In this simple way, software running on the datalogger can tell whether a host computer is present. This is useful as the datalogger's UART may be disabled to save power until it is required. Further, it can act as a simple switch for the firmware, toggling between "talk to host" mode and "datalogging" mode. It's interesting to note that the Harwin connector is much bigger on the schematic than the DB-9 due to the number of pins. Yet, when placed next to a DB-9, the Harwin connector is physically tiny.

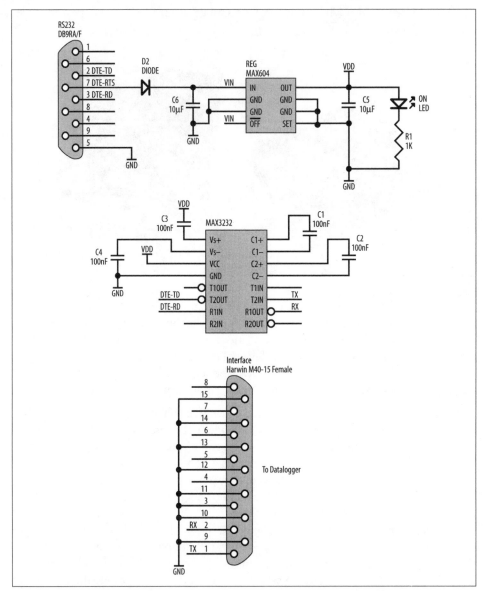

Figure 14-12. Serial adaptor schematic

Finally, Figure 14-13 shows the sensors of the datalogger. These particular sensors are covered in detail in Chapter 13. You could just as easily use other sensors or provide a connector allowing for interfacing to interchangeable sensor modules or external analog subsystems.

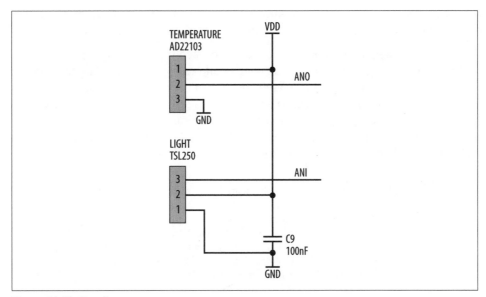

Figure 14-13. Datalogger sensors

Motor Control with a PIC

Now let's look at using a PIC in a completely different sort of application: motor control via user input. While the design presented in this section is targeted at a specific application, it is just as easily adapted to any task where small DC motors need to be controlled, from tools to robotics.

My young nephews are into model trains, and the standard controller that came with the railroad was a fairly simple device. The speed of the locomotives is controlled by simply varying the voltage on the track. Turn up the voltage, and the trains go faster; turn down the voltage, and the trains stall on dirty rails. Fine control and realistic operation just wasn't possible. I decided to solve this problem by throwing a little high-tech at it and designed for them a microprocessor-based controller using a PIC. It's this design that I will share with you.

I've designed literally many dozens of embedded systems over the years, from tiny controllers to small parallel supercomputers, but I have to say that I've never had so much fun debugging as when I was debugging the train controller.

The design uses pulse-width modulation (PWM), discussed in Chapter 13, to control the motors inside the locomotives. As PWM uses pulses of fixed amplitude to drive the motor, the problems of low-voltage stalls disappear. Further, since the PWM is controlled by software, very slow speeds can be achieved, giving very realistic operation. The PIC processor has two PWM generation modules inbuilt. Generating PWM with a PIC is just a matter of writing some simple code.

The hardware design takes the basic concept one step further by adding momentum control and braking. The momentum control allows you to specify the mass of the train under control so that when you open up the throttle, the train gradually builds up speed, and rolls to a halt when the throttle is closed. Braking speeds up the stopping. All this sounds complicated, but the hardware to do it is trivially simple when you use a microcontroller. All the real "work" is done in the software, and you can keep it as simple or as fancy as you want.

 There is a much more sophisticated way of controlling model trains called *Digital Command Control* (DCC), which treats the trackwork as a LAN and sends command packets to the locomotives. This is a published standard and is quite sophisticated. You can read more about it at *http://www.dcc.info*. The design presented here is not as complicated as DCC, nor is it compatible with DCC. However, it's certainly a lot cheaper and easier to implement than DCC.

The processor schematic is shown in Figure 14-14. It's not that different from the one used in the datalogger.

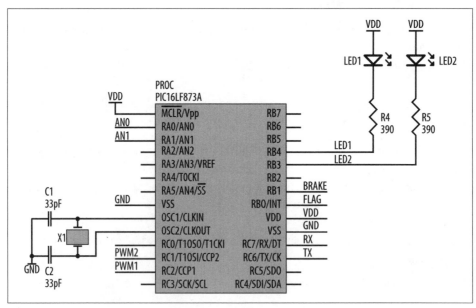

Figure 14-14. Processor

You'll notice that there's only one crystal, since there's no need for timekeeping. Two status LEDs are provided for user feedback by software. As there are several spare pins on Port B (**RB2, RB5..7**), you could add extra LEDs if you feel so inclined. **BRAKE** and **FLAG** are inputs to the processor. **BRAKE** comes from a push-button switch, and **FLAG** is an output from the H-bridge chip that indicates an over-current fault.

You'll also notice that there's no provision for in-circuit programming as was provided in the datalogger design. For this particular project, I used a DIP-based PIC processor that I had lying around, and to reprogram the part it was a simple matter to remove it from its socket on the circuit board and drop it into the burner. If you want to be able to reprogram the chip in-circuit, simply use the same connections as in the datalogger design.

The choice of crystal frequency is up to you, but the choice you make does have an interesting consequence. The frequency of the crystal relates directly to the PWM frequency the processor is able to generate. The clock signal from the crystal circuit is divided by four before being fed into the processor's PWM modules. Registers within the PWM modules can then scale this back further to produce a slower PWM frequency. Commercial train controllers use a PWM frequency of 16,125 Hz. Any slower than this and you will hear noise from the motors; any faster and there is a loss of torque. So to achieve a PWM frequency of 16 kHz, you'll need a crystal with a frequency greater than 64 kHz. As you can't easily obtain crystals of that exact frequency, the best choice would be a 1 MHz crystal, using the PWM modules' registers to scale it back appropriately.

Now, all that is if you don't want to hear the motors of the locomotives. If your model railroad uses diesels, you may want to choose a crystal frequency of 32 kHz (readily available watch crystal) and scale it back so that the PWM frequency is on the order of tens of Hz. At this frequency, the motors do make a noise, a growling, throbbing sound that sounds very much like a real diesel engine. As the locomotive starts up, the motors produce a sound like a diesel idling, and as it picks up speed, the sound echoes a diesel doing real work.

The voltage regulator circuit is shown in Figure 14-15. The regulator chosen is a standard (and cheap) LM7805 that provides a constant +5 V output from an input voltage of between +7 V and +35 V. Since the motors of model locomotives run on a nominal maximum of +12 V, this is the actual supply voltage for the system. Also included in the regulator schematic is a LED to indicate when power is on and extra decoupling capacitors to help eliminate digital noise in the system.

Figure 14-16 shows the controls used to drive the train. The throttle and momentum controls are simply 50 kΩ potentiometers, which are used as voltage dividers. The wipers of these pots provide a voltage of between 0 V and +5 V to the analog inputs of the PIC. Thus, position of the control can easily be read by software. The direction and brake controls are simple push buttons. The direction control connects directly to an input on the H-bridge chip (discussed shortly), and the brake control is used as a digital input to the processor. The direction control has a 100 kΩ pull-up resistor, and the brake control relies on the internal pull-ups of Port B of the processor.

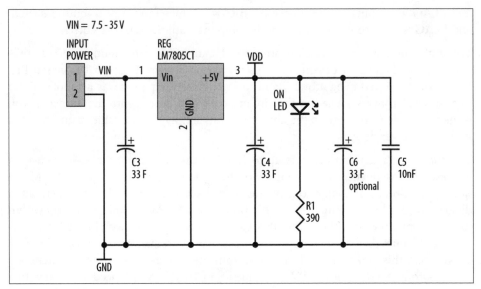

Figure 14-15. Voltage regulator

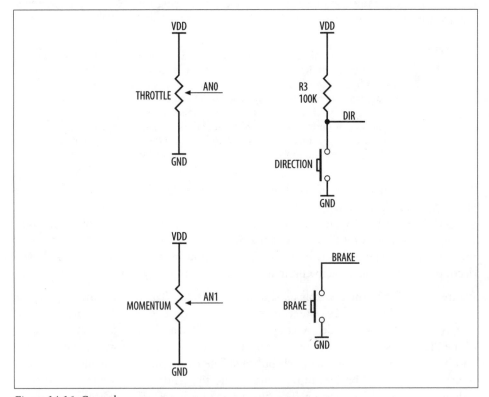

Figure 14-16. Controls

Figure 14-17 shows the H-bridge chip. This converts the PWM output of the processor to voltage levels appropriate for driving the small DC motors found in model locomotives or, for that matter, any sort of small DC motor.

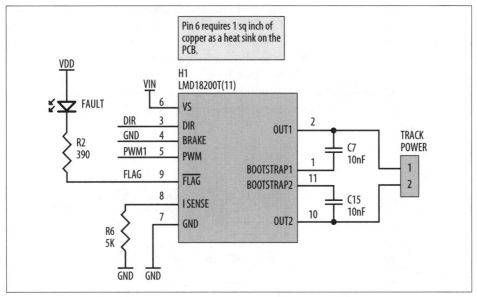

Figure 14-17. H-bridge

The H-bridge uses **VIN** (+12 V) as its power source because it must supply that voltage to the motors. As mentioned, the **DIR** (direction) input comes from a simple push button and determines the polarity of the output. Alternatively, the direction switch could be connected to a spare digital input of the processor, and a digital output could drive **DIR**. Since it would be a simple mapping of input to output by the software, it's easier just to connect it straight through and bypass the PIC.

The output of the PIC's PWM1 module is connected directly to the PWM input of the H-bridge. The H-bridge converts the 5 V amplitude, PWM signal from the PIC to a 12 V amplitude, PWM output whose polarity is determined by **DIR**.

> You may have noticed that the PIC has two PWM modules. If you wish to control a second motor (train or whatever) with the second module, simply replicate the H-bridge circuit and connect it to PWM2. (Don't forget to keep the appropriate nets separate by using different net names in your schematic editor.)

The H-bridge has internal over-current sensing and will shut itself off if its temperature rises too high (as would happen if the outputs were shorted together). The **FAULT** output indicates when this occurs. This active-low output is used to control a LED and is also connected to an input on the processor so that the software can be made aware of the fault condition.

Finally, we can add an optional serial port to the controller, shown in Figure 14-18. This is a standard RS-232C level-shifter circuit and is connected to the **RX** and **TX** pins of the processor's UART. The serial port can be used for software debugging to display status messages to a host computer or terminal. If you wanted to get very fancy, you could use the serial port to allow a host computer to send commands to the train controller. If you're adapting this design for robotics, a serial port would be a very useful addition. However, if you are providing control from an external host, don't forget to connect the **DIR** input of the H-bridge to the PIC and not directly to a push button.

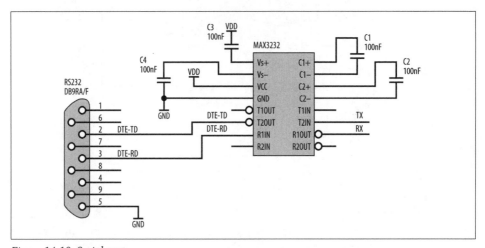

Figure 14-18. Serial port

In the next chapter, we'll take a look at the AVR processor family. These processors are comparable to PICs in terms of I/O and functionality but have a higher through-put and a more versatile architecture.

CHAPTER 15

The AVR Microcontrollers

A really useful engine...
—W.V. Awdry

In this chapter, we'll look at the Atmel AVR processor. Like the PIC, this processor family is a range of completely self-contained computers on chips. They are ideally suited to any sort of small control or monitoring application. They include a range of inbuilt peripherals and also have the capability of being expanded off-chip for additional functionality.

Like the PIC, the AVR is a RISC processor. Of the two architectures, the AVR is the faster in operation and arguably the easier for which to write code, in my personal experience. The PIC and AVR both approach single-cycle instruction execution. However, I find that the AVR has a more versatile internal architecture, and therefore you actually get more throughput with the AVR.

In this chapter, we'll look at the basics of creating computer hardware by designing a small computer based on the AVR *ATtiny15*. We'll also see how you can download code into an AVR-based computer and how it can be reprogrammed in-circuit. From there, we'll go on to look at some larger AVR processors, with a range of capabilities.

Later in the chapter, we're going to look at interfacing memory (and peripherals) to a processor using its address, data, and control buses. For most processors, this is the primary method of interfacing, and, therefore, the range of memory devices and peripherals available is enormous. You name it, it's available with a bus interface. So, knowing how to interface bus-based devices opens up a vast range of possibilities for your embedded computer. You can add RAM, ROM (or flash), serial controllers, parallel ports, disk controllers, audio chips, network interfaces, and a host of other devices.

Most small microcontrollers are completely self-contained and do not "bring out" the bus to the external world. In this chapter, we'll take a look at the Atmel AT90S8515 processor. It is the only processor of the AVR family that allows you access to the CPU's buses. But first, let's take a look at the AVR architecture in general.

The AVR Architecture

The AVR was developed in Norway and is produced by the Atmel Corporation. It is a Harvard-architecture RISC processor designed for fast execution and low-power consumption. It has 32 general-purpose 8-bit registers (r0 to r31), 6 of which can also act as 3 16-bit index registers (X, Y, and Z) (Figure 15-1). With 118 instructions, it has a versatile programming environment.

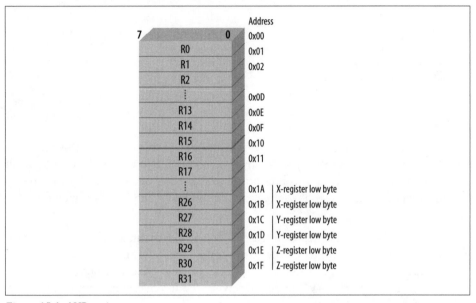

Figure 15-1. AVR registers

In most AVRs, the stack exists in the general memory space. It may therefore be manipulated by instructions and is not limited in size, as is the PIC's stack.

The AVR has separate program and data spaces and supports an address space of up to 8M. As an example, the memory map for an AT90S8515 AVR processor is shown in Figure 15-2.

Atmel provides the following sample C code, which it compiled and ran on several different processors:

```
int max(int *array)
{
  char a;
  int maximum = -32768;

  for (a = 0; a < 16; a++)
    if (array[a] > maximum)
      maximum = array[a];
  return (maximum);
}
```

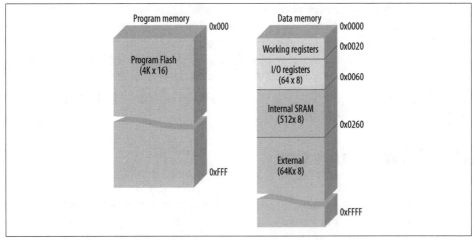

Figure 15-2. Atmel AT90S8515 memory map

The results are interesting (Table 15-1).

Table 15-1. Atmel's comparison of processor speed and efficiency

Processor	Compiled code size	Execution time (cycles)
AVR	46	335
8051	112	9,384
PIC16C74	87	2,492
68HC11	57	5,244

This indicates that, when running at the same clock speed, an AVR is 7 times faster than a PIC16, 15 times faster than a 68HC11, and a whopping 28 times faster than an 8051. Alternatively, you'd have to have an 8051 running at 224 MHz to match the speed of an 8 MHz AVR. Now, Atmel doesn't give specifics of which compiler(s) it used for the tests, and it is certainly possible to tweak results one way or the other with appropriately chosen source code. However, my personal experience is that with the AVR, you certainly do get significantly denser code and much faster execution.

There are three basic families within the AVR architecture. The original family is the *AT90xxxx*. For complex applications, there is the *ATmega* family, and for small-scale use, there's the *ATtiny* family. Atmel also produces large *FPGAs* (*Field-programmable Gate Arrays*), which incorporate an AVR core along with many tens of thousands of gates of programmable logic.

For software development, a port of gcc is available for the AVR, and Atmel provides an assembler, simulator, and software to download programs into the processors. The Atmel software is freely available on its web site. The low-cost Atmel development system is a good way of getting started with the AVR. It provides you with the software and tools you need to begin AVR development.

The AVR processors at which we'll be looking are the small ATtiny15, the AT90S8535/AT90S4434, and the AT90S8515.

The ATtiny15 Processor

For many simple digital applications, a small microprocessor is a better choice than discrete logic, because it is able to execute software. It is therefore able to perform certain tasks with much less hardware complexity. You'll see just how easy it is to produce a small, embedded computer for integration into a larger system using an Atmel ATtiny15 AVR processor. This processor has 512 words of flash for program storage and no RAM! (Think of that the next time you have to install some 100 MB application on your desktop computer!) This tiny processor, unlike its bigger AVR siblings, relies solely on its 32 registers for working variable storage.

Since there is no RAM in which to allocate stack space, the ATtiny15 instead uses a dedicated hardware stack that is a mere *three* entries deep, and this is shared by subroutine calls and interrupts. (That fourth nested function call is a killer!) The program counter is 9 bits wide (addressing 512 words of program space), and therefore the stack is also 9 bits wide. Also, unlike the bigger AVRs, only two of the registers (R30 and R31) may be coupled as a 16-bit index register (called "Z").

The processor also has 64 bytes of EEPROM (for holding system parameters), up to five general-purpose I/O pins, eight internal and external interrupt sources, two 8-bit timer/counters, a four-channel 10-bit analog-to-digital converter, an analog comparator, and the ability to be reprogrammed in-circuit. It comes in a tiny 8-pin package, out of which you can get up to 8 MIPS performance. We're not going to worry about most of its features for the time being. That will all be covered in later chapters when we take a look at the I/O features of some larger AVRs. Instead, we're just going to concentrate on how you use one for simple digital control.

Using a small microcontroller such as the ATtiny15 is very easy. The basic processor needs very little external support for its own operation. Figure 15-3 shows just how simple it is.

Let's take a quick run-through of the design (what there is of it). **VCC** is the power supply. It can be as low as 2.7 V or as high as 5.5 V. **VCC** is decoupled to ground using a 0.1 uF capacitor. The five pins, **PB0** through **PB4**, can act as digital inputs or outputs. They can be used to read the state of switches, turn external devices on or

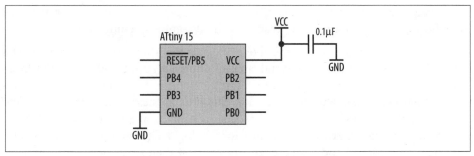

Figure 15-3. A simple AVR computer

off, generate waveforms to control small motors, or even synthesize an interface to simple peripheral chips. The digital I/O lines, **PB0** through **PB4**, get connected to whatever you're using the processor to monitor or control. We'll look at some examples of that later in the chapter.

Finally, one input, **RESET**, is left unconnected. On just about any other processor, this would be fatal. Many processors require an external *power-on reset (POR)* circuit to bring them to a known state and to commence the execution of software. Some processors have an internal power-on reset circuit and require no external support. Such processors still have a reset input, allowing them to be manually reset by a user or external system. Normally, the reset input still requires a pull-up resistor to hold it inactive. But the ATtiny15 processor doesn't require this. It has an internal power-on reset *and* an internal pull-up resistor. So, unlike most (all) other processors, **RESET** on the ATtiny15 may be left unconnected. In fact, on this particular processor, the **RESET** pin may be utilized as a general-purpose input (**PB5**) when an external reset circuit is not required. One important point: the normal input protection against higher-than-normal voltage inputs is not present on **RESET/PB5**, since it may be raised to +12 V during software download by the program burner. Therefore, if you are using **PB5**, you must take great care to ensure that the input never exceeds VCC by more than 1 V. Failing to do so may place the processor into software-download mode and thereby effectively crash your embedded computer.

The AVR processors (and PICs too) include an internal circuit known as a *brownout detector (BOD)*. This detects minor fluctuations on the processor's power supply that may corrupt its operation, and if such a fluctuation is detected, it generates a reset and restarts the processor. There is also an additional reset generator, known as a *watchdog*, used to restart the computer in case of a software crash. It is a small timer whose purpose is to automatically reset the processor once it times out. Under normal operation, the software regularly restarts the watchdog. It's a case of "I'll reset you before you reset me." If the software crashes, the watchdog isn't cleared and thus times out, resetting the computer. Processors that incorporate watchdogs normally give software the ability to distinguish between a power-on reset and a watchdog reset. With a watchdog reset, it may be possible to recover the system's state from memory and resume operation without complete re-initialization.

Now the other curious aspect of the above design is that there is no clock circuit. The ATtiny15 can have an external crystal circuit. (On the ATtiny15, **PB3** and **PB4** function as the crystal inputs, **XTAL1** and **XTAL2**). But our design doesn't have a crystal, or even need one. The reason is that this little processor includes a complete internal oscillator (in this case, an RC oscillator) running at a frequency of 1.6 MHz and so requires no external components for its clock. The catch is that RC oscillators are not that stable and have the tendency to vary their frequency as the temperature changes. (The ATtiny15's oscillator can vary between 800 kHz and 1.6 MHz.) Generally, an RC oscillator is not really suitable for timing-critical applications (in which case, you'd use an external crystal instead). But if your ATtiny15 is just doing simple control functions, timing may not be an issue. You can therefore get by with using the internal RC oscillator and save on complexity. Atmel provides an 8-bit calibration register (OSCCAL) in the ATtiny15 that enables you to tune the internal oscillator, thus making it more accurate.

There we have the basic design for an ATtiny15 machine. In essence, it's a very cheap, very small, versatile computer that requires no work for the core design. The only design effort needed is to ensure that the computer will work correctly with the I/O devices to which it is interfaced. If you're going to power the system off a battery, then the capacitor is optional as well! The only component that *must* be there is the processor itself. (And you thought designing computer hardware was going to be hard!)

So, that's the basic AVR computer hardware with minimal components. We'll look at how you download code to it shortly.

That covers the basics of a ATtiny15 system, and it's not that much different from the corresponding PIC12C805 computer. The real differences lie in their internal architectures (and instruction sets) and in the subtleties of their operating voltages and interfacing capabilities. As you can see, there's not a lot of hard work involved in putting one of these little machines into your embedded system.

So far, our computer isn't interfaced to anything. Let's start with something simple by adding a LED to the AVR. The basic technique applies to all microcontrollers with programmable I/O lines as well.

Adding a Status LED

LEDs produce light when current flows through them. Being a diode, they conduct only if the current is flowing in the right direction, from *anode* (positive) to *cathode* (negative). The cathode end of a LED is denoted on a schematic by a horizontal bar. The anode is a triangle.

The circuit for a status LED is shown in Figure 15-4. It uses an I/O line of the micro-controller to switch the LED on or off. Sending it low will turn on the LED. Sending it high will turn off the LED, as we'll soon see. The resistor (R) is used to limit the current sinking into the I/O line, as we shall also see shortly.

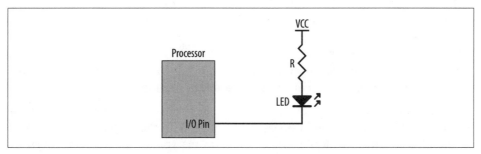

Figure 15-4. Status LED

When conducting (and thereby producing light), LEDs have a *forward voltage drop*, meaning that the voltage present at the cathode will be less than that at the anode. The magnitude of this voltage drop varies between different LED types, so check the datasheet for the particular device you are using.

The output low voltage of an ATtiny15 I/O pin is 0.6 V when the processor is operating on a 5 V supply and 0.5 V when operating on a 3 V supply. Let's assume (for the sake of this example) that we are using a power supply (**VCC**) of 5 V, and the LED has a forward voltage drop of 1.6 V. Now, sending the output low places the LED's cathode at 0.6 V. This means the voltage difference between **VCC** (5 V) and the cathode is 4.4 V. If the LED has a voltage drop of 1.6 V, this means the voltage drop across the resistor is 2.8 V (5 V − 1.6 V − 0.6 V = 2.8 V).

Now, from the datasheet, the digital I/O pins of an AVR can sink up to 20 mA if the processor is running on a 5 V supply. We therefore have to limit the current flow to this amount, and this is the purpose of the resistor. If the resistor has a voltage difference across it of 2.8 V (as we calculated) and a current flow of 20 mA, then from Ohm's Law we can calculate what value resistor we need to use:

```
R = V / I
  = 2.8 V / 20 mA
  = 140 Ω
```

The closest available resistor value to this is 150 Ω, so that's what we'll use. (This will give us an actual current of 18.6 mA, which is fine.)

 The AVR can sink 20 mA per pin when operating on a 5 V supply. However, the amount of current it can sink decreases with supply voltage. When running on a 2.7 V supply, the AVR can sink only 10 mA. As always, it's important to read the datasheets carefully.

The next question is, how much power will the resistor have to dissipate? In other words, how much energy will it use in dropping the voltage by 2.9 V? This is important because if we try to pump too much current through the resistor, we'll burn it out. We thus need to choose a resistor with a power rating greater than that required. Power is calculated by multiplying voltage by current:

```
P = V * I
  = 2.8 V * 20 mA
  = 0.056 Watts = 56 mW
```

That's negligible, so the resistor value we need for R is 150 Ω and 0.0625 W. (0.0625 W is the lowest power rating commonly available in resistors.)

So, what happens when the I/O line is driven high? The AVR I/O pins output a *minimum* of 4.3 V when high (and using a 5 V supply). With the output high, the voltage at the LED's cathode will be at least 4.3 V, so the voltage difference between the cathode and **VCC** will be only 0.7 V (or less). But the forward voltage drop of the LED is 1.6 V. Thus, there is not enough voltage across the LED to turn it on.

In this way, we can turn the LED on or off using a simple digital output of the processor. We have also seen how to calculate voltages and currents. It is very important to do this with every aspect of a design. Ignoring it can result in a nonfunctioning machine or, worse, charred components and that wafting smell of burning silicon.

We've just seen how to use the digital outputs of the AVR to control a LED. This will work with any device that uses less than 20 mA. In fact, for low-power components, such as some sensors, it is possible to use the AVR's output to provide direct power control, just as we provided direct power control for the LED. In battery-powered applications, this can be a useful technique for reducing the system's overall power consumption.

Switching Analog Signals

We can also use the digital I/O lines of the processor to control the flow of analog signals within our system. For example, perhaps our embedded computer is integrated into an audio system and is used to switch between several audio sources. To do this, we use an analog switch such as the MAX4626, one for each signal path. This tiny component (about the size of a grain of rice in the surface-mount version) operates from a single supply voltage (as low as 1.8 V and as high as 5.5 V). It also incorporates inbuilt overload protection to prevent device damage during short circuits. The schematic showing a MAX4626 interfaced to an ATtiny15 AVR is shown in Figure 15-5. Driving the AVR's output (**PB2**) high turns on the MAX4626 and makes a connection between **NO** and **COM**. Sending **PB2** low breaks the connection. In this way, the MAX4626 can be used to connect an output to an input, under software control.

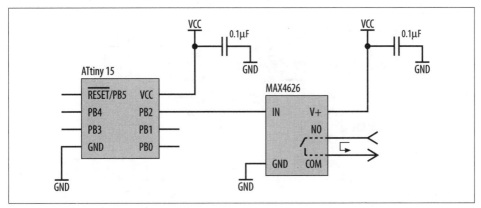

Figure 15-5. Switching an analog signal

The question is: will it work with an AVR? When operating on a 5 V supply, the input to the MAX4626 (pin 4, **IN**) requires a logic-low input of less than 0.8 V and a logic-high input of at least 2.4 V. The AVR's logic-low output is 0.6 V or less, and its logic-high output is a minimum of 4.3 V. So, the AVR's digital output voltages match the requirements of the MAX4626. As for current, the MAX4626 needs to sink or source only a miniscule 1 μA. For an AVR, this is not a problem.

If the MAX4626 doesn't meet your needs, MAXIM and other manufacturers produce a range of similar devices with varying characteristics. There's bound to be something that meets your needs.

The schematic in Figure 15-6 includes a push-button connected to **PB3**, where **PB3** is acting as a digital input. Now, there are a couple of interesting things to note about this simple input circuit. The first is that there is no external pull-up resistor attached to **PB3**. Normally, for such a circuit, an external pull-up resistor is required to place the input into a known state when the button is open (not being pressed). The pull-up resistor takes the input high, except when the button is closed and the input is connected directly to ground. The reason we can get away with not having an external pull-up resistor is that the AVR incorporates internal pull-up resistors, which may be enabled or disabled under software control.

The second interesting thing to note is that there is no *debounce* circuitry between the button and the input. Any sort of mechanical switch (and that includes a keyboard key) acts as a little inductor when pressed. The result is a rapid ringing oscillation on the signal line that quickly decays away (Figure 15-7).

So, instead of a single change of state, the resulting effect is as if the user had been rapidly hammering away on the button. Software written to respond to changes in this input will register the multiple pulses, rather than the single press the user intended. Removing these transients from the signal is therefore important and is known as *debouncing*. Now, there are several different circuits you could include that will cleanly remove the ringing. But here's the thing: you don't always need to!

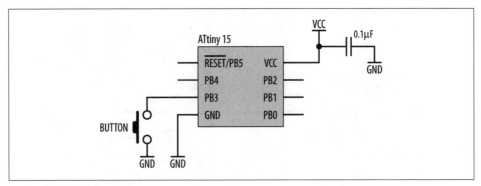

Figure 15-6. Push-button input

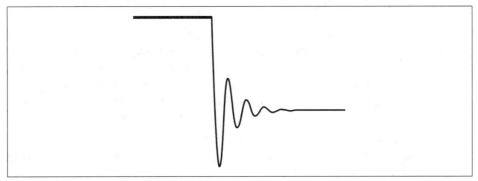

Figure 15-7. Signal bounce

When a user presses a button, he will usually hold that button closed for at least half a second, maybe more, by which time the ringing has died away. The problem can therefore be solved in software. The software, when it first registers a low on the input, waits for a few hundred milliseconds and then samples the input again (perhaps more than once). If it is still low, then it is a valid button press, and the software responds. The software then "re-arms" the input, awaiting the next press. Debouncing hardware does become important, however, if the button is connected to an interrupt line or reset.

So far, we have seen how to use the AVR to control digital outputs and read simple digital inputs. The astute among you may ask, "When looking at the previous two circuits, why do we need the processor?" After all, it is certainly possible to connect the button directly to the input of the MAX4626. Of what use can the processor be? Well, we've already seen one use. The processor can replace debounce circuitry on the input. Since it has internal memory and the ability to execute software, the processor can also keep track of system state (and mode), monitor various inputs in relation to each other, and provide complicated control sequencing on the outputs. In short, the inclusion of a microprocessor can reduce hardware complexity while increasing system functionality. They can be very useful tools. With more advanced processors, and with more diverse I/O, the functionality and usefulness of an embedded computer can be significant.

Downloading Code

The AVR processors use internal flash memory for program storage, and this may be programmed in-circuit or, in the case of socketed components, out of circuit as well. The AVR processors are reprogrammed via a SPI port on the chip. Even AVR processors such as the ATtiny15, which do not have a SPI interface for their own use, still incorporate a SPI port for reprogramming. The pins **PB0**, **PB1**, and **PB2** take on SPI functions (**MOSI**, **MISO**, and **SCK**) during programming.

VCC can be supplied by the external programmer downloading the code. For programming, **VCC** *must* be 5 V. If the embedded system's local supply will provide 5 V, then the connection to the programmer's **VCC** may be left unmade. However, if the embedded system's supply voltage is something other than 5 V, the programmer's **VCC** must be used, and any local power source within the embedded system should be disabled. **RESET** plays an important role in downloading code. Programming begins with **RESET** being asserted (driven low). This disables the CPU within the processor and thus allows access to the internal memory. It also changes the functionality of **PB0**, **PB1**, and **PB2** to a SPI interface. The development software then sends, via the SPI interface, a sequence of codes to "unlock" the program memory and enable software to be downloaded. Once programming is enabled, sequences of write commands are performed, and the software (and other settings) are downloaded byte by byte. The Atmel software takes care of this, so normally you don't need to worry about the specifics. If you need to do it "manually," perhaps from some other type of host computer, the Atmel datasheets give full details of the protocol.

The Atmel development system comes with a special adaptor cable that plugs into the company's development board and allows you to reprogram microprocessors via a PC's parallel port. By including the right connector (with the appropriate connections) in your circuit, it's possible to use the same programming cable on your own embedded system. Depending on the particular development board, there is one of two possible connectors for in-circuit programming. The pinouts for these are shown in Figure 15-8. (**VTG** is the voltage supply for the target system. If the target has its own power source, of the appropriate voltage level for programming (+5 V), then **VTG** may be left unconnected.) Pin 3 is labeled as a nonconnect on some Atmel application notes; however, some development systems use this to drive a LED indicating that a programming cycle is underway.

The schematic showing how to make your computer support this is shown in Figure 15-9. Note that **MOSI** on the connector goes to **MISO** on the processor, and, similarly, **MISO** goes to **MOSI** on the processor. This is because during programming, the processor is a *slave* and not a master.

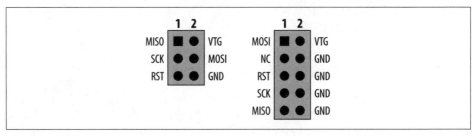

Figure 15-8. In-circuit programming connectors

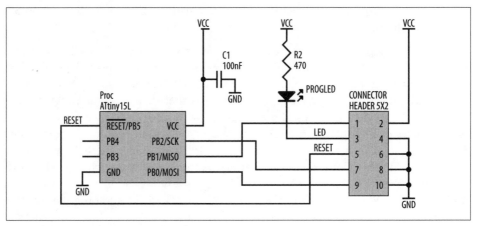

Figure 15-9. In-circuit programming

The connector type is an *IDC* header, and the cable provides all the signals necessary for programming, including one to drive a programming indicator LED. When not being used for programming, the connector may also double as a simple I/O connector for the embedded computer, allowing access to the digital signals. Thus, one piece of hardware can assume dual roles.

There is something important to note, however. If you use **PB0**, **PB1**, or **PB2** to interface to other components within your computer, care must be taken that the activity of programming does not adversely affect them. For example, our circuit with the MAX4626 used **PB2** as the control input. During programming, **PB2** acts as **SCK**, a clock signal. Therefore, the MAX4626 would be rapidly turning on and off as code was downloaded to the processor. If the MAX4626 was controlling something, that device would also rapidly turn on and off, with potentially disastrous effects. Conversely, if there are other components in your system, these must not attempt to drive a signal onto **PB0**, **PB1**, or **PB2** during the programming sequence. To do so would, at the very least, result in a failed download and, at worst, damage both the embedded system *and* the programmer. It's therefore vitally important to consider the implications of in-circuit programming on other components within the system.

So, what's the answer? Well, we could use **PB3** to control the MAX4626 instead, since it doesn't take part in the programming process. Alternatively, if we needed to use **PB2**, we could provide a *buffer* between the processor and the MAX4626, perhaps controlled by $\overline{\text{RESET}}$. When $\overline{\text{RESET}}$ is low (during programming), the buffer is disabled and the MAX4626 is isolated. Another solution may simply be to use a DIP version of the processor, mounted via a socket, and physically remove it for reprogramming. If you're using a surface-mount version of the processor, perhaps the processor could be mounted on a small PCB that plugs into the embedded computer (much like a memory SIMM on a desktop computer) and may be removed for programming. There are plenty of alternatives, and the best one really depends on your application.

Some AVRs (not the ATtiny15) have the capability of modifying their own program memory with the SPM (Store Program Memory) instruction. With such processors, it is possible for your software to download new code via the processor's serial port and write this into the program memory. To do so, you need to have your processor preprogrammed with a *bootloader* program. Normally, you would load all your processors with the bootloader (and Version 1.0 of your application software) during construction. The self-programming can then be used to update the application software when the systems are out in the field. To facilitate this, the program memory is divided into two separate sections: a *boot section* and an *application section*. The memory space is divided into *pages* of either 128 or 256 bytes (depending on the particular processor). Memory must be erased and reprogrammed one page at a time. During programming, the Z register is used as a pointer for the page address, and the r1 and r0 registers together hold the data word to be programmed. The Atmel application note (*AVR109: Self-programming*), available on its web site, gives sample source code for the bootloader and explains the process in detail.

No matter what processor you are using, the technical data from the chip manufacturer will tell you how to go about putting your code into the processor.

A Bigger AVR

So far, we have looked at a small AVR with very limited capabilities. In later chapters, we will look at various forms of input and output commonly found in embedded systems. For this, we will need processors with more functionality. We have exhausted the ATtiny15, so now we need to move on to processors with a bit more "grunt." Before getting into the details of I/O in the later chapters, you'll be introduced to these processors and learn what you need to do to include them in your design.

The first processor is the Atmel AT90S8535. This is a mid-range AVR with lots of inbuilt I/O, such as a UART, SPI, timers, eight channels of analog input, an analog comparator, and internal EEPROM for parameter storage. The processor has 512 bytes of internal RAM and 8K of flash memory for program storage. Its smaller sibling, the AT90S4434, is identical in every other way except that it has smaller memory spaces of 4K for program storage and 256 bytes of RAM. But from a hardware point of view, the AT90S8535 and the AT90S4434 are the same.

The basic schematic for an AT90S8535-based computer, without any extras, is shown in Figure 15-10. It is not that different from the ATtiny15, save that it has a lot more pins. **RESET** has an external pull-up 10k resistor. The processor has an external crystal (X1), and this requires two small decoupling capacitors, C1 and C2. There are four power pins for this processor, and each is decoupled with a 100 nF ceramic capacitor. One of the power inputs (**AVCC**) is the power supply for the analog section of the chip, and this is isolated from the digital power supply by a 100 Ω resistor, R2. This is to provide a small barrier between the analog section and any switching noise that may be present from the digital circuits. The remaining pins are general-purpose digital I/O, as with the ATtiny15. However, unlike the ATtiny15, these pins have dual functionality. They may be configured, under software control, for alternative I/O functions. The processor's datasheet gives full details for configuring the functionality of the processor under software control.

This basic AVR design is applicable to most AVRs that you will find. The pinouts may be different, but the basic support required is the same. As with everything, grab the appropriate datasheet, and it will tell you the specifics for the particular processor that you are using.

AVR-Based Datalogger

In the previous chapter, we saw how to design a datalogger based on a PIC16F873A. A datalogger based on an AVR is not too dissimilar. Figure 15-11 shows the basic schematic.

The connections for interfacing a serial dataflash memory chip to an Atmel 90S4434 AVR processor are simply SPI, as with the PIC processor. The AVR portion of the schematic is no different from the examples we have seen previously. That's the nice thing about simple interfaces such as SPI. They form little subsystem modules that "bolt together" like building blocks. Start with the basic core design and just add peripherals as you need them. The schematic also shows decoupling capacitors for the power supplies, the crystal oscillator for the processor, and a pull-up resistor for **RESET**. Pin 41 (**PB1**) is used as a "manual" (processor-controlled) reset input to the flash.

The analog inputs, **ADC0:ADC7**, can be connected to an IDC header allowing for external sampling, or they can be interfaced directly to sensors, as we saw with the PIC datalogger. The serial port signals, RXD and TXD, connect to a MAX3233 in the same way as we saw in the PIC design.

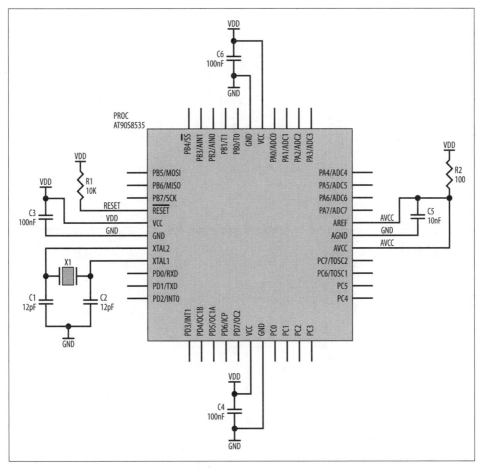

Figure 15-10. AT90S8535 processor and support components

Bus Interfacing

In this section, I'll show you how to expand the capabilities of your processor by interfacing it to bus-based memories and peripherals. Different processor architectures have different signals and different timing, but once you understand one, the basic principles can be applied to all. Since most small microcontrollers don't have external buses, the choice is very limited. We'll look at the one, and only, AVR with an external bus—the AT90S8515. In the PIC world, the PIC17C44 is capable of bus-based interfacing.

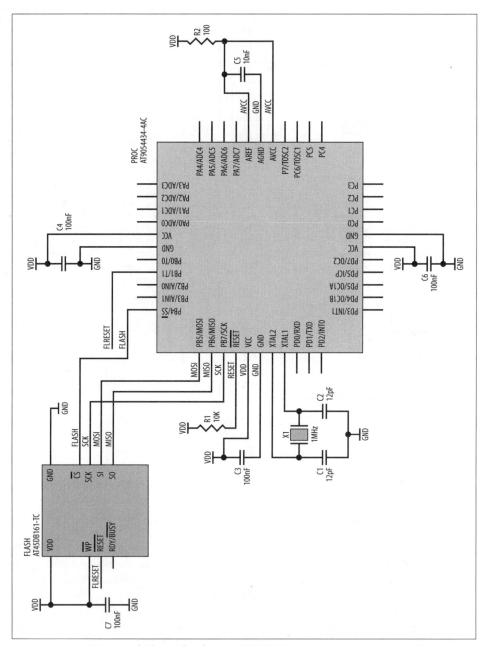

Figure 15-11. A 2M DataFlash interfaced to an AT90S4434

AT90S8515 Memory Cycle

A *memory cycle* (also known as a *machine cycle* or *processor cycle*) is defined as the period of time it takes for a processor to initiate an access to memory (or peripheral), perform the transfer, and terminate the access. The memory cycle generated by a processor is usually of a fixed period of time (or multiples of a given period) and may take several (processor) clock cycles to complete.

Memory cycles usually fall into two categories: the *read cycle* and the *write cycle*. The memory or device that is being accessed requires that the data is held valid for a given period after it has been selected and after a read or write cycle has been identified. This places constraints on the system designer. There is a *limited* amount of time in which any *glue logic* (interface logic between the processor and other devices) must perform its function, such as selecting which external device is being accessed. The setup times *must* be met. If they are not, the computer will not function. The glue logic that monitors the address from the processor and uniquely selects a device is known as an *address decoder*. We'll take a closer look at address decoders shortly.

Timing is probably the most critical aspect of computer design. For example, if a given processor has a 150 ns cycle time and a memory device requires 120 ns from when it is selected until when it has completed the transfer, this leaves only 30 ns at the start of the cycle in which the glue logic can manipulate the processor signals. A 74LS series TTL gate has a typical propagation delay of 10 ns. So, in this example, an address decoder implemented using any more than two 74LS gates (in sequence) is cutting it very fine.

A *synchronous* processor has memory cycles of a fixed duration, and all processor timing is directly related to the clock. It is assumed that all devices in the system are capable of being accessed and responding within the set time of the memory cycle. If a device in the system is slower than that allowed by the memory cycle time, logic is required to pause the processor's access, thus giving the slow device time to respond. Each clock cycle within this pause is known as a *wait state*. Once sufficient time has elapsed (and the device is ready), the processor is released by the logic and continues with the memory cycle. Pausing the processor for slower devices is known as *inserting wait states*. The circuitry that causes a processor to hold is known as a *wait-state generator*. A wait-state generator is easily achieved using a series of flip-flops acting as a simple counter. The generator is enabled by a processor output indicating that a memory cycle is beginning and is normally reset at the end of the memory cycle to return it to a known state. (Some processors come with internal, programmable wait-state generators.)

An *asynchronous* processor (such as a 68000) does not terminate its memory cycle within a given number of clock cycles. Instead, it waits for a transfer acknowledge assertion from the device or support logic to indicate that the device being accessed has had sufficient time to complete its part in the memory cycle. In other words, the processor *automatically* inserts wait states in its memory cycle until the device being accessed is ready. If the processor does not receive an acknowledge, it will wait indefinitely. Many computer systems using asynchronous processors have additional logic to cause the processor to restart if it waits too long for a memory cycle to terminate. An asynchronous processor can be made into a synchronous processor by tying the acknowledge line to its active state. It then assumes that all devices are capable of keeping up with it. This is known as *running with no wait states*.

Most microcontrollers are synchronous, whereas most larger processors are asynchronous. The AT90S8515 is a synchronous processor, and it has an internal wait-state generator capable of inserting a single wait state.

Bus Signals

Figure 15-12 shows an AT90S8515 processor with minimal support components. The AT90S8515 has an address bus, a data bus, and a control bus that it brings to the outside world for interfacing. Since this processor has a limited number of pins, these buses share pins with the digital I/O ports ("port A" and "port C") of the processor. A bit in a control register determines whether these pins are I/O or bus pins. Now, a 16-bit address bus and an 8-bit data bus add up to 24 bits, but ports A and B have only 16 bits between them. So how does the processor fit 24 bits into 16? It multiplexes the lower half of the address bus with the data bus. At the start of a memory access, port A outputs address bits A0:A7. The processor provides a control line, **ALE** (Address Latch Enable), which is used to control a latch, such as a 74HCT573 (shown on the right in Figure 15-12). As **ALE** falls, the latch grabs and holds the lower address bits. At the same time, port B outputs the upper address bits, A8:A15. These are valid for the entire duration of the memory access. Once the latch has acquired the lower address bits, port A then becomes the data bus for information transfer between the processor and an external device. Also shown in Figure 15-12 are the crystal circuit, the In-System Programming port, decoupling capacitors for the processor's power supply, and net labels for other important signals.

The *timing diagrams* for an AT90S8515 are shown in Figure 15-13. The cycle "T3" exists only when the processor's wait-state generator is enabled.

Now, let's look at these signals in more detail. (We'll see later how you actually work with this information. For the moment, we're just going to "take a tour" of the timing diagrams.) The numbers for the timing information can be found in the datasheet, available from Atmel's web site. Figure 15-14 shows the timing information as presented in the Atmel datasheet, complete with timing references.

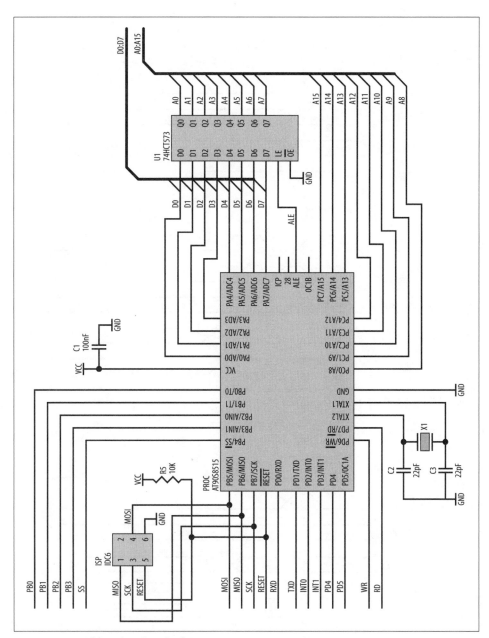

Figure 15-12. Address bus demultiplexing

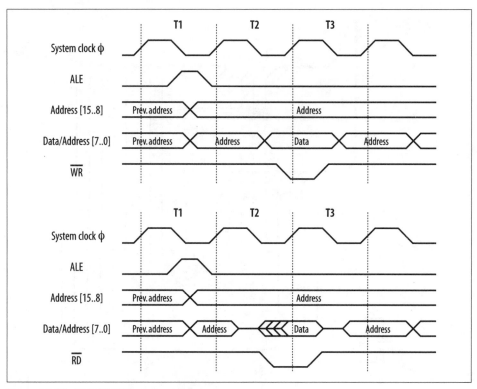

Figure 15-13. AT90S8515 memory cycles

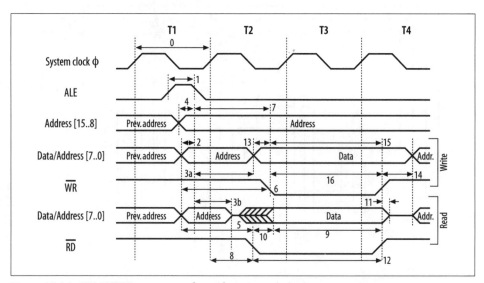

Figure 15-14. AT90S8515 memory cycles with timing parameters

The references are looked up in the appropriate table in the processor's datasheet (Table 15-2).

Table 15-2. Timing parameters

Ref. #	Symbol	Parameter	8 MHz oscillator		Variable oscillator		Unit
			Min	Max	Min	Max	
0	$1/t_{CLCL}$	Oscillator Frequency			0.0	8.0	MHz
1	t_{LHLL}	ALE Pulse Width	32.5		$0.5\,t_{CLCL}-30.0$		ns
2	t_{AVLL}	Address Valid A to ALE Low	22.5		$0.5\,t_{CLCL}-40.0$		ns
3a	$t_{LLAX...ST}$	Address Hold after ALE Low, ST/STD/STS Instructions	67.5		$0.5\,t_{CLCL}+5.0$		ns
3b	$t_{LLAX...LD}$	Address Hold after ALE Low, LD/LDD/LDS Instructions	15.0		15.0		ns
4	t_{AVLLC}	Address Valid C to ALE Low	22.5		$0.5\,t_{CLCL}-40.0$		ns
5	t_{AVRL}	Address Valid to RD Low	95.0		$1.0\,t_{CLCL}-30.0$		ns
6	t_{AVWL}	Address Valid to WR Low	157.5		$1.5\,t_{CLCL}-30.0$		ns
7	t_{LLWL}	ALE Low to WR Low	105.0	145.0	$1.0\,t_{CLCL}-20.0$	$1.0\,t_{CLCL}+20.0$	ns
8	t_{LLRL}	ALE Low to RD Low	42.5	82.5	$0.5\,t_{CLCL}-20.0$	$0.5\,t_{CLCL}+20.0$	ns
9	t_{DVRH}	Data Setup to RD High	60.0		60.0		ns
10	t_{RLDV}	Read Low to Data Valid		70.0		$1.0\,t_{CLCL}-55.0$	ns
11	t_{RHDX}	Data Hold after RD High	0.0		0.0		ns
12	t_{RLRH}	RD Pulse Width	105.0		$1.0\,t_{CLCL}-20.0$		ns
13	t_{DVWL}	Data Setup to WR Low	27.5		$0.5\,t_{CLCL}-35.0$		ns
14	t_{WHDX}	Data Hold after WR High	0.0		0.0		ns
15	t_{DVWH}	Data Valid to WR High	95.0		$1.0\,t_{CLCL}-30.0$		ns
16	t_{WLWH}	WR Pulse Width	42.5		$0.5\,t_{CLCL}-20.0$		ns

The system clock, ϕ, is shown at the top of both diagrams for reference, since all processor activity relates to this clock. The period of the clock is designated in the Atmel datasheet as "t_{CLCL}"* and is equal to 1/frequency. For an 8 MHz clock, this is 125 ns. The width of T1, T2, and T3 are each t_{CLCL}.

No processor cycle exists in isolation. There is always† a preceding cycle and following cycle. We can see this in the timing diagrams. At the start of the cycles, the

---

* Datasheet nomenclature can often be very cryptic. The "CL" comes from "clock." Since Atmel is using four-character subscripts for its timing references, it pads by putting "CL" twice. You don't really need to know what the subscripts actually mean; you just need to know the signals they refer to and the actual numbers involved.

† I'm ignoring coming out of reset, or just before power-off!

address from the previous access is still present on the address bus. On the falling edge of the clock, in cycle T1, the address bus changes to become the valid address required for this cycle. Port A presents address bits A0:A7, and port B presents A8:A15. At the same time, **ALE** goes high, releasing the external address latch in preparation for acquiring the new address from port A. **ALE** stays high for $0.5 \times t_{CLCL}$ - 30 ns. So, for example, with an AT90S8515 running at 8 MHz, **ALE** stays high for 32.5 ns. **ALE** falls, causing the external latch to acquire and hold the lower address bits. Prior to **ALE** falling, the address bits will have been valid for $0.5 \times t_{CLCL}$ - 40 ns or, in other words, 40 ns before the system clock rises at the end of the T1 period. After ALE falls, the lower address bits will be held on port A for $0.5 \times t_{CLCL}$ + 5 ns for a write cycle before changing to data bits. For a read cycle, they are held for a minimum of 15 ns only. The reason this is so much shorter for a read cycle is that the processor wishes to free those signal pins as soon as possible. Since this is a read cycle, an external device is about to respond, which means the processor needs to "get out of the way" as soon as it can.

For a write cycle, t_{CLCL} - 20 ns after **ALE** goes low, the write strobe, $\overline{WR}$, goes low. This indicates to external devices that the processor has output valid data on the data bus. $\overline{WR}$ will be low for $0.5 \times t_{CLCL}$ - 20 ns. This time allows the external device to prepare to read in (latch) the data. On the rising edge of $\overline{WR}$, the external device is expected to latch the data presented on the data bus. At this point, the cycle completes, and the next cycle is about to begin.

For a read cycle, the read strobe, $\overline{RD}$, goes low $0.5 \times tCLCL$ - 20 ns after **ALE** is low. $\overline{RD}$ will be low for $tCLCL$ - 20 ns. During this time, the external device is expected to drive valid data onto the data bus. It can present data anytime after $\overline{RD}$ goes low, so long as data is present and stable at least 60 ns before $\overline{RD}$ goes high again. At this point, the processor latches the data from the external device, and the read cycle terminates. Note that many processors do not have a separate read-enable signal, so this must be generated by external logic, based on the premise that if the cycle is not a write cycle, it must be a read cycle.

So, that is how an AT90S8515 expects to access any external device attached to its buses, whether those devices are memory chips or peripherals. But how does it work in practice? Let's look at designing* a computer based on an AT90S8515 with some external devices. For this example, we will interface the processor to a static RAM and some simple latches that we could use to drive banks of LEDs.

---

* Since we've covered oscillators and in-circuit programming previously, I'll ignore those in this discussion. That doesn't mean you should leave them out of your design!

Memory Maps and Address Decoding

To the processor, its address space is one big, linear region. Although there may be numerous devices within that space, both internal to the processor and external, it makes no distinction between devices. The processor simply performs memory accesses in the address space. It is up to the system designer (that's you) to allocate regions of memory to each device and then provide address-decode logic. The address decoder takes the address provided by the processor during an external access and uniquely selects the appropriate device (Figure 15-15). For example, if we have a RAM occupying a region of memory, any address from the processor corresponding to within that region should select the RAM and *not* select any other device. Similarly, any address outside that region should leave the RAM unselected.

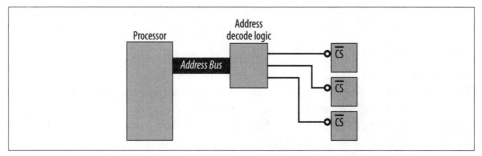

Figure 15-15. An address decoder uses the address to select one of several devices

The allocation of devices within an address space is known as a *memory map* or *address map*. The address spaces for an AT90S8515 processor are shown in Figure 15-16. Any device we interface to the processor must be within the data memory space. Thus, we can ignore the processor's internal program memory. As the processor has Harvard architecture, the program space is a completely separate address space. Within the 64K data space lie the processor's internal resources: the working registers, the I/O registers, and the internal 512 bytes of SRAM. These occupy the lowest addresses within the space. Any address above 0x0260 is ours to play with. (Not all processors have resources that are memory-mapped, and, in those cases, the entire memory space is usable by external devices.)

Now, our first task is to allocate the remaining space to the external devices. Since the RAM is 32K in size, it makes sense to place it within the upper half of the address space (0x8000–0xFFFF). Address decoding becomes much easier if devices are placed on neat boundaries. Placing the RAM between addresses 0x8000 and 0xFFFF leaves the lower half of the address space to be allocated to the latches and the processor's internal resources. Now a latch need only occupy a single byte of memory within the address space. So, if we have three latches, we need only three bytes of the address space to be allocated. This is known as *explicit address decoding*. However, there's a good reason not to be so efficient with our address allocation. Decoding the address

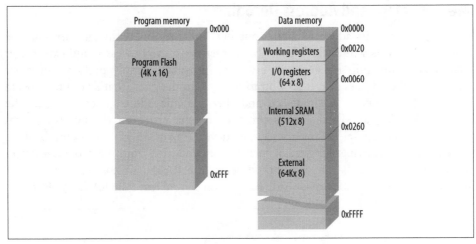

Figure 15-16. Atmel AT90S8515 memory map

down to three bytes would require an address decoder to use 14 bits of the address. That's a lot of (unnecessary) logic to select just three devices. A better way is simply to divide the remaining address space into four, allocating three regions for the latches and leaving the fourth unused (for the processor's internal resources). This is known as *partial address decoding* and is much more efficient. The trick is to use the minimal amount of address information to decode for your devices.

Our address map allocated to our static RAM and three latches is shown in Figure 15-17. Note that the lowest region leaves the addresses in the range 0x0260 to 0x1FFF unused.

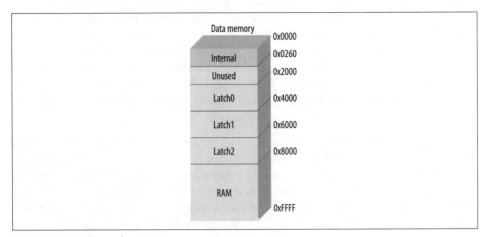

Figure 15-17. Allocated memory map

Any address within the region 0x2000 to 0x3FFF will select Latch0, even though that latch needs only one byte of space. Thus, the device is said to be *mirrored* within that space. For simplicity in programming, you normally just choose an address (0x2000 say) and use that within your code. But you could just as easily use address 0x290F, and that would work too.

We now have our memory map, and we need to design an address decoder. We start by tabling the devices along with their addresses (Table 15-3). We need to look for which address bits are different between the devices, and which address bits are common within a given device's region.

Table 15-3. Address table

Device	Address range	A15 .. A0
Unused	0x0000–0x1FFF	0000 0000 0000 0000 0000 0001 1111 1111 1111 1111
Latch0	0x2000–0x3FFF	0010 0000 0000 0000 0000 0011 1111 1111 1111 1111
Latch1	0x4000–0x5FFF	0100 0000 0000 0000 0000 0101 1111 1111 1111 1111
Latch2	0x6000–0x7FFF	0110 0000 0000 0000 0000 0111 1111 1111 1111 1111
RAM	0x8000–0xFFFF	1000 0000 0000 0000 0000 1111 1111 1111 1111 1111

So, what constitutes a unique address combination for each device? Looking at the table, we can see that for the RAM, address bit (and address signal) **A15** is high, while for every other device it is low. We can therefore use **A15** as the trigger to select the RAM. For the latches, address bits **A15**, **A14**, and **A13** are critical. So we can redraw our table to make it clearer. This is the more common way of doing an address table, as shown in Table 15-4. An "x" means a "don't care" bit.

Table 15-4. Simplified address table

Device	Address range	A15 .. A0
Unused	0x0000–0x1FFF	000x xxxx xxxx xxxx xxxx
Latch0	0x2000–0x3FFF	001x xxxx xxxx xxxx xxxx
Latch1	0x4000–0x5FFF	010x xxxx xxxx xxxx xxxx
Latch2	0x6000–0x7FFF	011x xxxx xxxx xxxx xxxx
RAM	0x8000–0xFFFF	1xxx xxxx xxxx xxxx xxxx

Therefore, to decode the address for the RAM, we simply need to use **A15**. If **A15** is high, the RAM is selected. If **A15** is low, then one of the other devices is selected and the RAM is not. Now, the RAM has a chip select ($\overline{\text{CS}}$) that is active low. So when

A15 is high, $\overline{CS}$ should go low. So, our address decoder for the RAM is simply to invert **A15** using an inverter chip such as a 74HCT04 (Figure 15-18). It is common practice to label the chip-select signal after the device it is selecting. Hence, our chip select to the RAM is labeled $\overline{RAM}$.

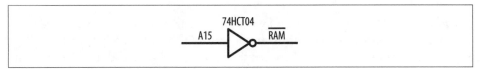

Figure 15-18. Address decode for the RAM

Note that for the RAM to respond, it needs both a chip select and either a read or write strobe from the processor. All other address lines from the processor are connected directly to the corresponding address inputs of the RAM (Figure 15-19).

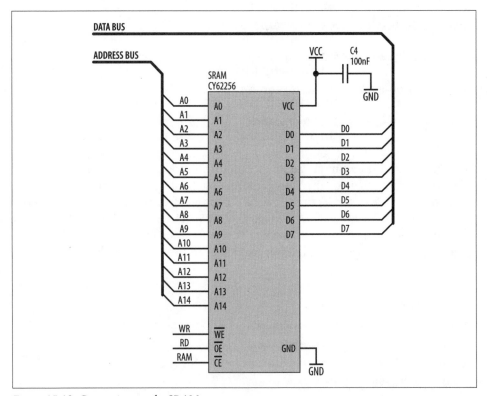

Figure 15-19. Connections to the SRAM

Now for the other four regions, **A15** must be low, and **A14** and **A13** are sufficient to distinguish between the devices. Having our address decoder use discrete logic would require several gates and would be "messy." There's a simpler way. We can use a 74HCT139* decoder, which takes two address inputs (A and B) and gives us four unique, active-low, chip-select outputs (labeled Y0:Y3). Since the latches require active-high enables, we use inverters on the outputs of the 7HCT139. So our complete address decoder for the computer is shown in Figure 15-20.

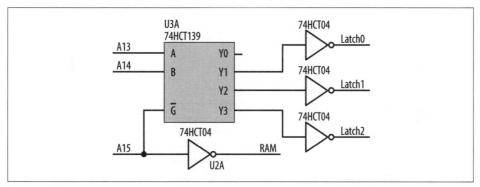

Figure 15-20. Complete address decoder

The 74HCT139 uses **A15** (low) as an enable (input $\overline{\text{G}}$), and, in this way, **A15** is included as part of the address decode. If we needed to decode for eight regions instead of four, we could have used a 74HCT138 decoder, which takes three address inputs and gives us eight chip selects. The interface between the processor and an output latch is simple. We can use the same type of latch (a 74HCT573) that we used to demultiplex the address. Such an output latch could be used in any situation in which we need some extra digital outputs. In the sample circuit shown in Figure 15-21, I'm using the latch to control a bank of eight LEDs.

The output from our 74HCT139 address decoder is used to drive the LE (Latch Enable) input of the 74HCT573. Whenever the processor accesses the region of memory space allocated to this device, the address decoder triggers the latch to acquire whatever is on the database. And so, the processor simply writes a byte to any address in this latch's address region, and that byte is acquired and output to the LEDs. (Writing a "0" to a given bit location will turn on a LED; writing a "1" will turn it off.)

Note that the latch's output enable (**$\overline{\text{OE}}$**) is permanently tied to ground. This means that the latch is always displaying the byte that was last written to it. This is important, as we always want the LEDs to display, and not just transitorily blink on, while the processor is accessing them.

Using the 74HCT139 in preference to discrete logic gates makes our design much simpler, but there's an even better way to implement system glue.

---

* There are actually two separate decoders in each 74HCT139 chip. We'll need only one.

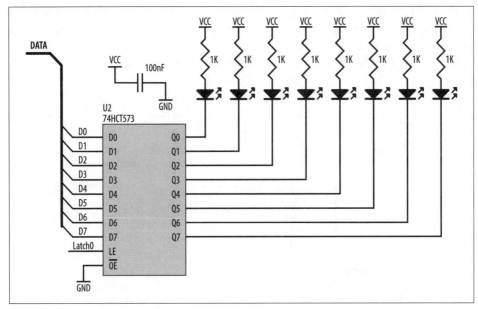

Figure 15-21. Using a 74HCT573 latch to control a bank of LEDs

PALs

It is now rare to see support logic implemented using individual gates. It is more common to use programmable logic (PALs, LCAs, or PLDs)* to implement the miscellaneous "glue" functions that a computer system requires. Such devices are fast, take up relatively little space, have low power consumption, and, as they are *reprogrammable*, make system design much easier and more versatile.

There is a wide range of devices available, from simple chips that can be used to implement glue logic (just as we are about to do) to massive devices with hundreds of thousands of gates. Altera (*http://www.altera.com*), Xilinx (*http://www.xilinx.com*), Lattice Semiconductor (*http://www.latticesemi.com*), and Atmel are some manufacturers to investigate for large-scale programmable logic. These big chips are sophisticated enough to contain entire computer systems. *Soft cores* are processor designs implemented in gates, suitable for incorporating into these logic devices. You can also get serial interfaces, disk controllers, network interfaces, and a range of other peripherals, all for integration into one of these massive devices. Of course, it's also fun to experiment and design your own processor from the ground up.

Each chip family requires its own suite of development tools. These allow you to create your design (either using schematics or some programming language such as

---

* Programmable Array Logic, Logic Cell Arrays, and Programmable Logic Devices, respectively.

VHDL), simulate the system, and finally download your creation into the chip. You can even get C compilers for these chips that will take an algorithm and convert it, not into machine code, but into *gates*. What was software now runs not *on* hardware, but *as* hardware. Sounds cool, but the tools required to play with this stuff can be expensive. If you just want to throw together a small, embedded system, they are probably out of your price range. For what we need to do for our glue logic, such chips are overkill. Since our required logic is simple, we will use a simple (and cheap) PAL that can be programmed using freely available, public-domain software.

PALs are configured using equations to represent the internal logic. "+" represents OR, "*" represents AND, and "/" represents NOT. (These symbols are the original operator symbols that were used in Boolean logic. If you come from a programming background, these symbols may seem strange to you. You will be used to seeing "|", "&", and "!".) The equations are compiled using software such as PALASM, ABEL, or CUPL to produce a *JED* file. This is used by a device known as a *PAL burner* to configure the PAL. In many cases, standard EPROM burners will also program PALs.

PALs have pins for input, pins for output, and pins that can be configured as either input or output. Most of the PAL's pins are available for your use. In your PAL source code file (PDS file), you declare which pins you are using and label them. This is not unlike declaring variables in program source code, except that instead of allocating bytes of RAM, you're allocating physical pins of a chip. You then use those pin labels within equations to specify the internal logic. Our address decoder, implemented in a PAL, would have the following equations to specify the decode logic:

```
RAM = /A15
LATCH0 = (/A15 * /A14 * A13)
LATCH1 = (/A15 * A14 * /A13)
LATCH2 = (/A15 * A14 * A13)
```

I have (deliberately) written the above equations in a form that makes it easier to compare them with the address tables listed previously. You could simplify these equations, but there is no need. Just as an optimizing C compiler will simplify (and speed up) your program code, so too will PALASM rework your equations to optimize them for a PAL.

A PDS file to program a 22V10 PAL for the above address decode might look something like:

```
TITLE decoder.pds        ; name of this file
PATTERN
REVISION 1.0
AUTHOR John Catsoulis
DATE January 2005

CHIP decoder PAL22V10    ; specify which PAL device you
                         ; are using and give it a name ("decoder")

PIN   2   A15            ; pin declarations and allocations
```

```
PIN   3   A14
PIN   12  LATCH0
PIN   13  LATCH1
PIN   14  LATCH2
PIN   15  RAM

EQUATIONS                    ; equations start here

RAM = /A15
LATCH0 = (/A15 * /A14 * A13)
LATCH1 = (/A15 * A14 * /A13)
LATCH2 = (/A15 * A14 * A13)
```

The advantages of using a PAL for system logic are twofold. The PAL equations may be changed to correct for bugs or design changes. The propagation delays through the PAL are of a fixed and small duration (no matter what the equations), which makes analyzing the overall system's timing far simpler. For very simple designs, it probably doesn't make a lot of difference whether you use PALs or individual chips. However, for more complicated designs, programmable logic is the only option. If you can use programmable logic devices instead of discrete logic chips, please do so. They make life much easier.

Timing Analysis

Now that we have finished our logic design, the question is: will it actually work? It's time (pardon the pun) to work through the numbers and analyze the timing. This is the least fun, and most important, part of designing a computer.

We start with the signals (and timing) of the processor, add in the effects of our glue logic, and finally see if this falls within the requirements of the device to which we are interfacing. We'll work through the example for the SRAM. For the other devices, the analysis follows the same method. The timing diagram for a read cycle for the SRAM is shown in Figure 15-22. The RAM I have chosen is a CY62256-70 (32K) SRAM made by Cypress Semiconductor. Most 32K SRAMs follow the JEDEC standard, which means their pinouts and signals are all compatible. So, what works for one 32K SRAM *should* work for them all. But the emphasis is on *should*, and, as always, *check the datasheet* for the individual device you are using.

The "-70" in the part number means that this is a "70 ns SRAM," or, put simply, the access time for the chip is 70 ns. Now, from the CY62256-70 datasheet (available from *http://www.cypress.com*), t_{RC} is a minimum of 70 ns. This means that the chip enable, $\overline{CE}$, can be low for no less than 70 ns. $\overline{CE}$ is just our chip select ($\overline{RAM}$) from our address decoder, so we need to ensure that the address decoder will hold $\overline{RAM}$ low for at least this amount of time. For the SRAM to output data during a read cycle, it needs a valid address, an active chip enable, and an active output enable ($\overline{OE}$). The output enable is just the read strobe ($\overline{RD}$) from the processor. These three conditions must be met before the chip will respond with data. It will take 70 ns

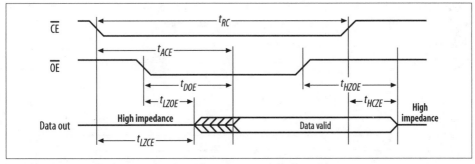

Figure 15-22. Timing for a read cycle to the RAM

from $\overline{CE}$ low (t_{ACE}) *or* 35 ns from $\overline{OE}$ low (t_{DOE}), whichever is the latter, until data is output. Now, $\overline{CE}$ is generated by our address decoder (which in turn uses address information from the processor), and $\overline{OE}$ ($\overline{RD}$) comes from the processor. During a read cycle, the processor will output a read strobe and an address, which in turn will trigger the address decoder. Some time later in the cycle, the processor will expect data from the RAM to be present on the data bus. It is critical that the signals that cause the RAM to output data will do so such that there will be valid data when the processor expects it. Meet this requirement, and you have a processor that can read from external memory. Fail this requirement, and you'll have an intriguing paperweight and a talking piece at parties.

We start with the processor. I'm assuming that the processor's wait-state generator is disabled. For an AT90S8515 processor, everything is referenced to the falling edge of **ALE**. The high-order address bits, which feed our address decoder, become valid 22.5 ns prior to **ALE** going low on an 8 MHz AT90S8515. If we're using a 74HCT139 as an address decoder,* this takes 40 ns to respond to a change in inputs. So, our chip select for the RAM will become valid 17.5 ns after **ALE** has fallen (Figure 15-23).

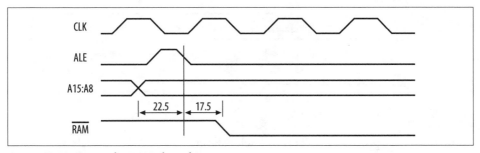

Figure 15-23. Timing for RAM chip select

---

* PALs may respond in 15 ns or less. This is another reason why PALs are a better choice than discrete logic.

Now, $\overline{RD}$ will go low between 42.5 ns and 82.5 ns after **ALE** falls. Since the RAM will not output data until $\overline{RD}$ (**OE**) is low, we take the worst case of 82.5 ns (Figure 15-24).

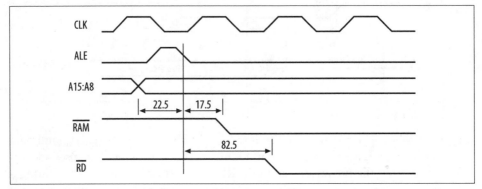

Figure 15-24. Read strobe and chip select for RAM

The RAM will respond 70 ns after $\overline{RAM}$ and 35 ns after $\overline{RD}$, whichever comes last. So, 70 ns from $\overline{RAM}$ low is 87.5 ns after **ALE**, and 35 ns after $\overline{RD}$ is 117.5 ns after **ALE**. Therefore, $\overline{RD}$ is the determining control signal in this case. This means that the SRAM will output valid data 117.5 ns after **ALE** falls (Figure 15-25).

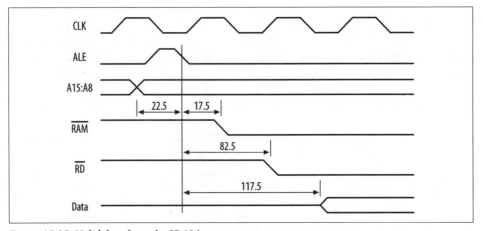

Figure 15-25. Valid data from the SRAM

Now, an 8 MHz processor expects to latch valid data during a read cycle at 147.5 ns after **ALE**. So our SRAM will have valid data ready with 30 ns to spare. So far, so good. But what about at the end of the cycle? Now, the processor expects the data bus to be released and available for the next access at 200 ns after **ALE** falls. The RAM takes 25 ns from when it is released by $\overline{CS}$ until it stops outputting data onto the data bus. This means that the data bus will be released by the RAM at 142.5 ns. So that will work too.

The analysis for a write cycle is done in a similar manner. It is important to do this type of analysis for every device interfaced to your processor, for every type of memory cycle. It can be difficult, because datasheets are notorious for leaving out information or presenting necessary data in a roundabout way. Working through it all can be time-consuming and frustrating, and it's far too easy to make a mistake. However, it is very necessary. Without it, you're relying on blind luck to make your computers run, and that's not good engineering.

Memory Management

In most small-scale embedded applications, the connections between a processor and an external memory chip are straightforward. Sometimes, though, it's advantageous to play with the natural order of things. This is the realm of memory management.

Memory management deals with the translation of logical addresses to physical addresses and vice versa. A *logical address* is the address output by the processor. A *physical address* is the actual address being accessed in memory. In small computer systems, these are often the same. In other words, no address translation takes place, as illustrated in Figure 15-26.

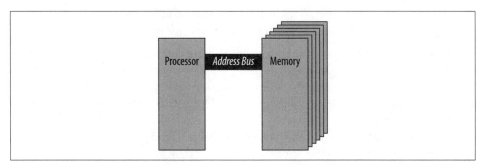

Figure 15-26. No address translation

For small computer systems, this absence of memory management is satisfactory. However, in systems that are more complex, some form of memory management may become necessary. There are four cases where this might be so:

Physical memory > logical memory
> When the logical address space of the processor (determined by the number of address lines) is smaller than the actual physical memory attached to the system, it becomes necessary to *map* the logical space of the processor into the physical memory space of the system. This is sometimes known as *banked memory*. This is not as strange or uncommon as it may sound. Often, it is necessary to choose a particular processor for a given attribute, yet that processor may have a limited address space—too small for the application. By implementing

banked memory, the address space of the processor is expanded beyond the limitation of the logical address range.

Logical memory > physical memory

When the logical address space of the processor is very large, it is not always practical to fill this address space with physical memory. It is possible to use some space on disk as *virtual memory*, thus making it appear that the processor has more physical memory than exists within the chips. Memory management is used to identify whether a memory access is to physical memory or virtual memory and must be capable of swapping the virtual memory on disk with real memory and performing the appropriate address translation.

Memory protection

It is often desirable to prevent some programs from accessing certain sections of memory. Protection can prevent a crashing program from corrupting the operating system and bringing down the computer. It is also a way of channeling all I/O access via the operating system, since protection can be used to prevent all software (save the OS) from accessing the I/O space.

Task isolation

In a multitasking system, tasks should not be able to corrupt each other (by stomping on each other's memory space, for example). In addition, two separate tasks should be able to use the same logical address in memory, with memory management performing the translation to *separate*, physical addresses.

The basic idea behind memory management is quite simple, but the implementation can be complicated, and there are nearly as many memory-management techniques as there are computer systems that employ memory management. Memory management is performed by a *Memory Management Unit (MMU)*. The basic form of this is shown in Figure 15-27. An MMU may be a commercial chip, a custom-designed chip (or logic), or an integrated module within the processor. Most modern, fast processors incorporate MMUs on the same chip as the CPU.

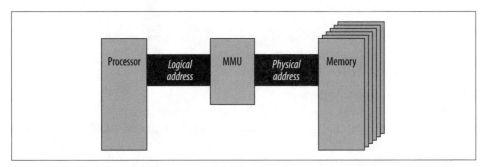

Figure 15-27. Address translation using an MMU

Page mapping

In all practical memory-management systems, words of memory are grouped together to form *pages*, and an address can be considered to consist of a page number and the number of a word within that page. The MMU translates the logical page to a physical page, while the word number is left unchanged (Figure 15-28). In practice, the overall address is just a concatenation of the page number and the word number.

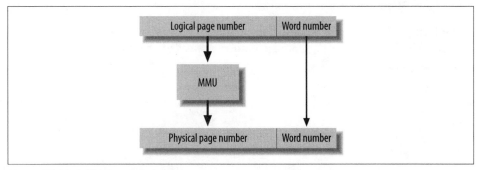

Figure 15-28. Address translation

The logical address from the processor is divided into a page number and a word number. The page number is translated by the MMU and recombined with the word number to form the physical address presented to memory (Figure 15-29).

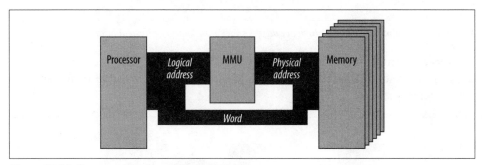

Figure 15-29. System using page address translation

Banked memory

The simplest form of memory management is when the logical address space is smaller than the physical address space. If the system is designed such that the size of a page is equal to the logical address space, then the MMU provides the page number, thus mapping the logical address into the physical address (Figure 15-30).

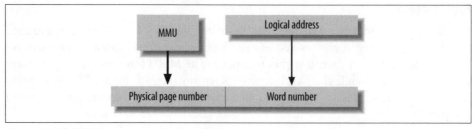

Figure 15-30. MMU generation of page number

The effective address space from this implementation is shown in Figure 15-31. The logical address space can be mapped (and *remapped*) to anywhere in the physical address space.

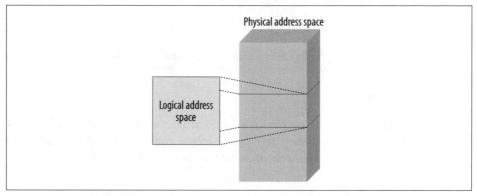

Figure 15-31. Mapping a smaller logical address space into a larger physical address

The system configuration for this is shown in Figure 15-32. This technique is often used in processors with 16-bit addresses (64K logical space) to give them access to larger memory spaces.

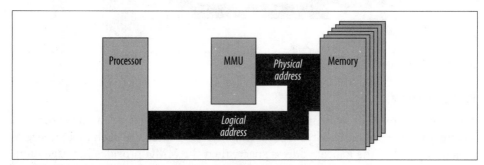

Figure 15-32. Generating a larger physical address

For many small systems, banked memory may be implemented simply by latching (acquiring and holding) the data bus and using this as the additional address bits for the physical memory (Figure 15-33). The latch appears in the processor's logical space as just another I/O device. To select the appropriate bank of memory, the processor stores the bank bits to the latch, where they are held. All subsequent memory accesses in the logical address space take place within the selected bank. In this example, the processor's address space acts as a 64K window into the larger RAM chip. As you can see, while memory management may seem complex, its actual implementation can be quite simple.

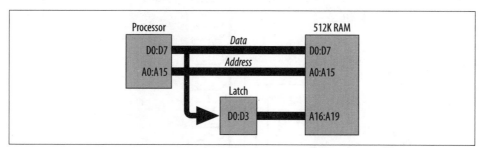

Figure 15-33. Simple banked-memory implementation

 This technique has also been used in desktop systems. The old Apple /// computer came with up to 256K of memory, yet the address space of its 6502 processor was only 64K.

Figure 15-34 shows the actual wiring required for a banked-memory implementation for our AT90S8515 AVR system, replacing the 32K RAM with a 512K RAM.

The RAM used is an HM628511H made by Hitachi. In this implementation, we still have the RAM allocated into the upper 32K of the processor's address space as before. In other words, the upper 32K of the processor's address space is a window into the 512K RAM. The lower 32K of the processor's address space is used for I/O devices, as before. Address bits **A0** to **A14** connect to the RAM as before, and the data bus (**D0** to **D7**) connects to the data pins (**IO1** to **IO8***) of the SRAM.

Now, we also have a 74HCT573 latch, which is mapped into the processor's address space, just as we did with the LEDs latch. The processor can write to this latch, and it will hold the written data on its outputs. The lower nybble of this latch is used to provide the high-order address bits for the RAM.

Let's say the processor wants to access address 0x1C000. In binary, this is %001 1100 0000 0000 0000. The lower 15 address bits (**A0** to **A14**) are provided directly by the processor. The remaining address bits must be latched. So, the processor first stores the byte 0x03 to the latch, and the RAM's address pins **A18**, **A17**, **A16**, and **A15** see

---

* Memory chip manufacturers often label data pins as "IO" pins, since they perform data input and output for the device.

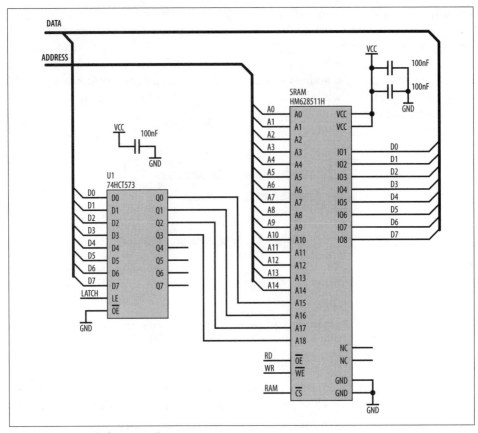

Figure 15-34. Banked memory for an AVR computer

%0011 (0x03), respectively. That region of the RAM is now banked to the processor's 32K window. When the processor accesses address 0xC000, the high-order address bit (**A15**) from the processor is used by the address decoder to select the RAM by sending its $\overline{CS}$ input low. The remaining 15 address bits (**A0** to **A14**) combine with the outputs of the latch to select address 0x1C000.

The **NC** pins are "No Connection" and are left unwired.

Address translation

For processors with larger address spaces, the MMU can provide translation of the upper part of the address bus (Figure 15-35).

The MMU contains a *translation table*, which remaps the input addresses to different output addresses. To change the translation table, the processor must be able to access the MMU. (There is little point in having an MMU if the translation table is unalterable.) Some processors are specifically designed to work with an MMU, while

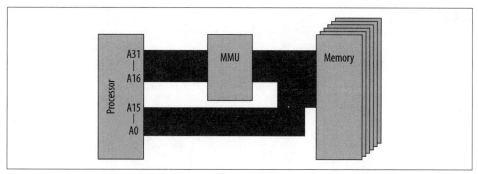

Figure 15-35. Logical page-number translation

other processors have MMUs incorporated. However, if the processor being used was not designed for use with an MMU, it will have no special support. The processor must therefore communicate with the MMU as though it were any other peripheral device using standard read/write cycles. This means the MMU must appear in the processor's address. It may seem that the simplest solution is to map the MMU into the physical address space of the system. In real terms, this is not practical. If the MMU is ever (intentionally or accidentally) mapped out of the current logical address space (such that the physical page on which the MMU is located is not part of the current logical address space), it becomes impossible to access the MMU ever again. This may also happen when the system powers up, because the contents of the MMU's translation table may be unknown.

The solution is to decode the chip select for the MMU directly from the logical address bus of the processor. Hence, the MMU will lie at a constant address in the logical space. This removes the possibility of "losing" the MMU, but it introduces another problem. Since the MMU now lies directly in the logical address space, it is no longer protected from accidental tampering (by a crashing program) or illegal and deliberate tampering in a multitasking system. To solve this problem, many larger processors have two states of operation—*supervisor state* and *user state*—with separate stack pointers for each mode. This provides a barrier between the operating system (and its privileges) and the other tasks running on the system. The state the processor is in is made available to the MMU through special status pins on the processor. The MMU may be modified only when the processor is in supervisor state, thereby preventing modification by user programs. The MMU uses a different logical-to-physical translation table for each state. The supervisor translation table is usually configured on system initialization, then remains unchanged. User tasks (user programs) normally run in user state, whereas the operating system (which performs task swapping and handles I/O) runs in supervisor state. Interrupts also place the processor in supervisor state, so that the vector table and service routines do not have to be part of the user's logical address space. While in user state, tasks may be denied access to particular pages of physical memory by the operating system.

CHAPTER 16

68HC11

You could not step twice into the same river;
for other waters are ever flowing on to you.
—Heraclitus
  On the Universe

In this chapter, we'll look at the Freescale Semiconductor (formerly Motorola) 68HC11, a processor architecture that goes back to the very early days of microprocessors. I have a soft spot for this architecture. I first learned to write assembly language on a machine based on a 6802 processor, and I can still remember many of the opcodes by heart and can "read" raw 6800 machine code as though it were source.

The architecture is far from cutting-edge. But it's easy to program, easy to build, and has been stable for a very long time. It's a good platform to start out on, and it's quick and easy to throw together a simple 8-bit computer using these chips. Let's start by taking a quick overview of the processor architecture.

Architecture of the 68HC11

The MC68HC11 is a member of the 8-bit, 6800 microprocessor family. The 68HC11 is a high-density, HCMOS microcontroller unit (MCU) featuring a fully static design. It is essentially a standard 6800 processor (with some enhancements) combined with inbuilt peripherals, such as an enhanced 16-bit timer with four-stage programmable pre-scaler, a serial peripheral interface (SPI), a serial communications interface (SCI), an 8-bit pulse accumulator, real-time interrupts, onboard static RAM, an eight-channel ADC, and onboard EEROM.

The main registers of the MC68HC11 are shown in Figure 16-1. (Note that this does not include the control registers associated with the various peripherals inside the chip.)

The MC68HC11 has two accumulators, A and B. The accumulators are both eight bits wide, but they may also be treated as a single, 16-bit accumulator, D (Figure 16-2).

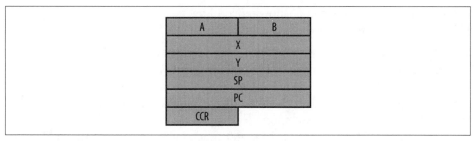

Figure 16-1. MC68HC11 registers

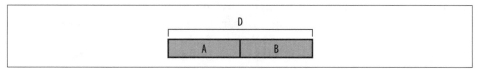

Figure 16-2. MC68HC11 accumulators

The *index registers* (X and Y) are 16-bit registers that are used to hold addresses. As such, they can be used to point to locations in memory. They may also be used as 16-bit counters or temporary storage registers. The *program counter* (PC) is a 16-bit counter that points to the next location in memory from which an instruction is to be fetched. (In other words, it holds the address of the next instruction.) The *condition code register* (CCR) is a special 8-bit register that shows the status of the processor.

The *stack pointer* (SP) is a 16-bit register that points to the next free location on the stack. The stack is an area of memory defined for storage of data or addresses (treated as data). When a value is pushed onto the stack, the value is stored at the location pointed to by the stack pointer. The stack pointer then decrements automatically and points to the next available location. When something is pulled from the stack, the stack pointer is incremented automatically, and the data value is retrieved from that location. As a 68HC11's stack fills, it grows down through memory. When a 16-bit value is pushed onto the stack, the stack pointer is decremented twice (two 8-bit locations).

So that's the basic programmer's model for a 68HC11. While not overly powerful, it's nice and simple, and easy to master. Now let's see how to build a machine based on a 68HC11.

A Simple 68HC11-Based Computer

The computer will have 32K of static RAM, 16K of EPROM, a serial interface (internal to the 68HC11), and a latch controlling a bank of LEDs. While EPROM is old technology, I have chosen it for this system for two reasons. The first is that it is still common for 68HC11 machines to use EPROM, often for historical and legacy reasons. The second reason is that it allows me to show you how to use an EPROM in a design. Following the theme of "showing you how it's done," we'll also do the glue logic for the computer using discrete gates rather than a PAL.

The 68HC11 was designed to be used in a wide range of small applications, many relating to the monitoring or control of external devices. As such, it can run in several modes: *single-chip mode*, *expanded multiplexed mode*, *bootstrap mode*, and *test mode*. This last mode is used by Freescale during manufacturing and is not intended for user applications. In single-chip mode, the processor relies entirely on its internal features (small RAM, small ROM, I/O, and timers) and has no external address or data bus. The majority of pins (known as ports A, B, C, and D in this particular processor) are therefore dedicated to digital I/O functions. In expanded multiplexed mode, the processor behaves like an ordinary, 8-bit processor, with ports B and C assuming the roles of the address and data buses. In bootstrap mode, the processor loads its vectors from the internal 192-byte ROM and initializes the internal serial interface. The processor can change from bootstrap mode to any of the other modes under software control. Two special pins on the processor (**MODA** and **MODB**) determine in which mode the processor will "come up." Table 16-1 shows the settings for **MODA** and **MODB** and how these affect the 68HC11.

Table 16-1. Boot modes for the 68HC11

MODB	MODA	Mode
1	0	Single chip
1	1	Expanded multiplexed
0	0	Special bootstrap
0	1	Special test

Since we wish to add external memory and a latch, the processor must be in expanded multiplexed mode. Hence, **MODA** and **MODB** must be tied high in our design.

To reduce the number of external pins of the 68HC11, Freescale has multiplexed the address and data buses onto the same physical pins. This means the chip is smaller (and therefore cheaper), but it requires the system designer to add external logic to *recover* (separate) the address and data buses from the multiplexed bus. The data bus and the lower half of the address bus share port C, while the upper half of the address bus is on port B and requires no recovery. A special output, **AS** (address strobe), is provided to indicate whether address information or data is present on the bus.

The timing for a memory cycle is shown in Figure 16-3. The address becomes valid after **AS** goes high and remains valid as **AS** falls. **AS** can be used as the control input to a latch to recover the lower half of the address bus. Once latched, the address continues to be output by the latch and hence continues to be valid throughout the cycle. The data appears on the multiplexed bus later in the cycle.

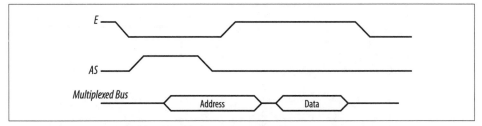

Figure 16-3. Timing of the multiplexed bus on a 68HC11

The upper address bits (**A8:15**) appear on port B 94 ns before **E** goes high (in the middle of the cycle) and remain valid for the whole cycle. No recovery is required for these address lines.

The basic circuit for a 68HC11 processor in expanded multiplexed mode, including the recovery of the lower address bits, is shown in Figure 16-4. Interrupt inputs, $\overline{\text{IRQ}}$ and $\overline{\text{XIRQ}}$, require pull-up resistors as well. Motorola recommends the use of a special chip, MC34064, for generating a power-on reset. This simple three-pin device requires only power and ground, and will output a reset pulse on power up. This reset pulse is of an appropriate duration for a 68HC11. To provide a clock for our processor, we add an 8 MHz crystal to the processor's internal oscillator (pins **XTAL** and **EXTAL**). The crystal needs two bypass capacitors, C1 and C2, and also requires a resistor, R1, parallel.

Port D is used for the internal serial interface, with bit 0 as the receive data input (**Rx**) and bit 1 as the transmit data output (**Tx**). Port D also contains the processor's SPI interface, allowing it to be interfaced easily to a variety of peripherals.

That completes the processor's basic requirements. The next task is to design the rest of the computer, which for our system with its one RAM, one ROM, and a latch is very simple. We start by allocating the memory space and then design the address decoder.

Address Decoding

The MC6800 and MC68HC11 address spaces are shown in Figure 16-5. They are both 64K spaces (16-bit address), but note the additional, internal features of the 68HC11 located in its memory map. The register block is not the accumulators or index registers that were mentioned previously. These do not appear in the memory map. The register block is an array of special registers that control the many internal peripherals this processor has, such as counter/timers, analog-to-digital converters, etc. Note that a 68HC11 has the ability, through software, to relocate the internal I/O registers and the 256-byte RAM to any 4K boundary. This means the designer can place these wherever is most appropriate for the design. The "external" designator in Figure 16-5 means that addresses in this range are available externally for use by memory or other devices.

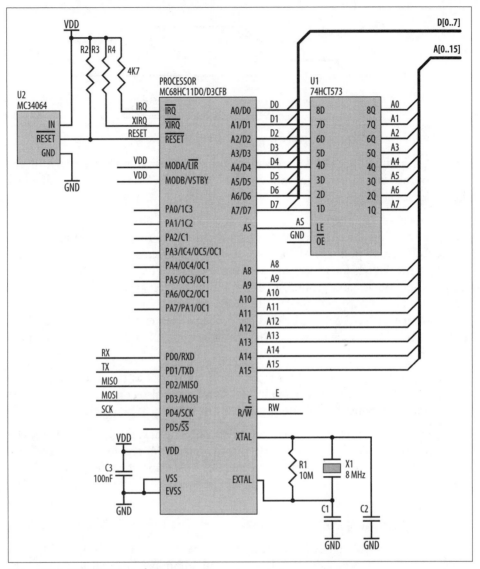

Figure 16-4. MC68HC11 and support components

The vectors are a table of addresses stored externally that point to routines in memory. The most important of these is the 16-bit *RESET* vector starting at address 0xFFFE. This location contains a 16-bit pointer to the location in memory where the initialization code lies. The processor will load this pointer into its program counter after power-on or reset and thereby begin execution of the software. Therefore, since this vector needs to be valid at power-on, it must be nonvolatile (able to survive without power). For this reason, a ROM is usually located in the uppermost region of the address space.

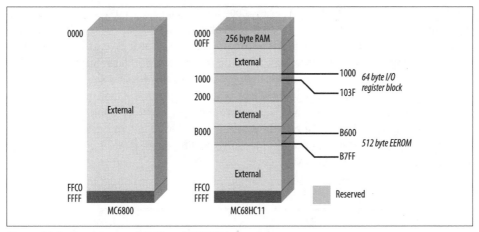

Figure 16-5. Comparison of 6800 and 68HC11 memory maps

Now, the 68HC11 has a 64K address space, so a 32K RAM is going to occupy half of this space. But which half? As mentioned earlier, for the vector table to be preserved during periods of no power, a ROM must be located in the uppermost part of the address space. Thus, our 32K RAM must be put in the lower half of the address space. However, the internal RAM and registers of the internal peripherals are mapped into the lower half of the address space. If we map our 32K RAM into this space, will it cause conflict? (In other words, will we need special logic to accommodate this?) The answer is no. The internal RAM and I/O registers take precedence, and accesses to their locations will not cause activity on the external buses of the processor. In effect, they are overlaid on top of the external RAM. From our point of view, this makes the design simple, as we don't need special logic to exclude those addresses from our memory space. And since the internal peripheral registers can be remapped under software control, these can be shifted elsewhere to an unused part of the address space.

In the case of the 32K RAM, its address size ranges from 0x0000 to 0x7FFF. In binary, this is 0000 0000 0000 0000 to 0111 1111 1111 1111. Any combination of bits between these two addresses lies within the space allocated to the RAM. So address bits **A0** to **A14** relate to memory locations internal to the RAM, and hence they are not used by the address decoder. In other words, the address decoder "doesn't care" what they are since they go directly into the RAM. The address table for the RAM is shown in Table 16-2. The "X" means "don't care."

Table 16-2. Address bit usage for the RAM

	A15	A14	A13	A12	A11	A10	A9	A8	A7	A6	A5	A4	A3	A2	A1	A0
RAM	0	X	X	X	X	X	X	X	X	X	X	X	X	X	X	X

Look at the address range for the RAM: 0000 0000 0000 0000 to 0111 1111 1111 1111. The only bit in common for all those address bits is the "0" at **A15**. As the RAM is 32K in size and this is half of the 64K address space of the processor, the only bit that needs to be taken into account when decoding for the RAM is **A15**. Since the RAM is in the lower half of the address space, the RAM will need to be selected when the most significant address bit is low. When it is high, the RAM will not be selected. The address decode for the RAM is therefore simply a direct connection between **A15** and the RAM's **CS**. What could be easier than that? The circuit for the RAM, in this case a 62256 SRAM, is shown in Figure 16-6. This same generic circuit will work for any standard 32K × 8 SRAM.

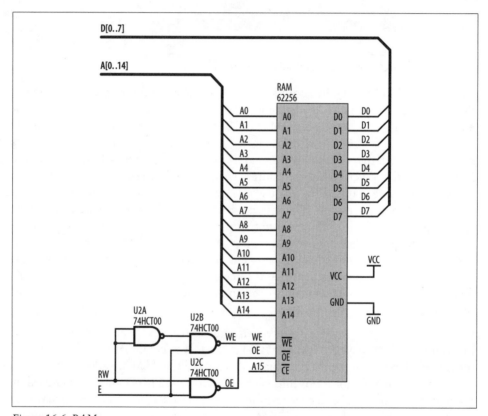

Figure 16-6. RAM

When **A15** is low, the chip enable (**CE**) is pulled low and is therefore asserted (since it is active low). Thus, the RAM is enabled when **A15** is low, and not enabled when **A15** is high.

Note the additional logic (the three NAND gates) in the circuit. The 68HC11 generates a **R/W** strobe indicating whether the cycle is a read cycle (**R/W** high) or a write cycle (R/W̄ low). Now, the RAM has separate inputs to signify whether the access is a read or a write, and, in both cases, these are active low. The logic is used to convert the single R/W̄ strobe into separate W̄Ē (write enable) and ŌĒ (output enable) inputs to the RAM. The R/W̄ strobe is combined with the processor's E clock to ensure that the enables are active only during the valid part of the cycle (when E is high). Otherwise, ŌĒ would be active whenever it *wasn't* a write cycle. The NAND gate U2A is simply acting as an inverter.

The ROM is a 16K device, which is one half of the remaining address space. The only other external device is a latch (which need occupy only one byte). There are two ways of allocating the remaining 32K of memory to these two devices. The first is to use explicit address decoding in which every address line is accounted for. In this scheme, the latch would occupy exactly one byte of memory and no more. So if we decide to locate the latch at address 0x8000, we have the address bits as shown in Table 16-3.

Table 16-3. Address bits to select the latch at 0x8000

	A15	A14	A13	A12	A11	A10	A9	A8	A7	A6	A5	A4	A3	A2	A1	A0
Latch	1	0	0	0	0	0	0	0	0	0	0	0	0	0	0	0

If we are using explicit decoding, we must use all of these bits in our address decoder. Such logic would be both complex and slow.

A better way is to use partial address decoding. With this method, we divide our memory space among the devices, using just enough address bits to distinguish each device. It doesn't matter if the memory space allocated is much greater than that required by the device. Even if we allocate 16K of space to the latch, the latch will still work when we select it. It's true this is somewhat wasteful of address space, but it is a far more efficient method (in terms of logic) than explicit decoding. The logic required is much less, and if you are using discrete logic, the propagation delays are reduced. Timing is the most important consideration when designing any logic for a microprocessor system. If the timing isn't right, it simply won't work.

So our remaining 32K of address space needs to be divided between two devices. The address table for all three devices (RAM, latch, and ROM) is shown in Table 16-4.

Table 16-4. Address bit allocation for all devices

	A15	A14	A13	A12	A11	A10	A9	A8	A7	A6	A5	A4	A3	A2	A1	A0
RAM	0	X	X	X	X	X	X	X	X	X	X	X	X	X	X	X
Latch	1	0	X	X	X	X	X	X	X	X	X	X	X	X	X	X
ROM	1	1	X	X	X	X	X	X	X	X	X	X	X	X	X	X

In this table, I have allocated the latch and the ROM 16K of space each. In other words, I have divided the remaining 32K of space equally between the two devices. This will make the address decoding much simpler. The resulting memory map for the computer (ignoring the internal I/O registers and memory for the moment) is shown in Figure 16-7.

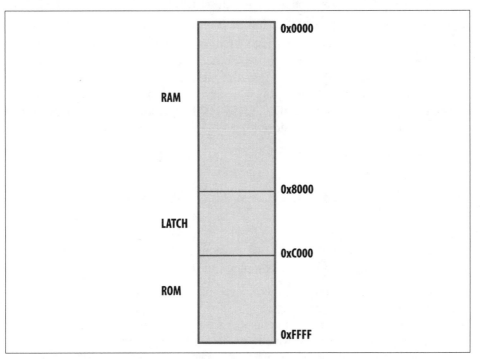

Figure 16-7. Memory map using partial address decoding

Note that because we have used partial decoding, the latch will appear multiple times in its allocated space. The latch represents one byte at address 0x8000, but because we are looking at only **A15** and **A14** for its address decode, it is selected for all addresses in which **A14** is low and **A15** is high. Therefore, the latch appears throughout the address range 0x8000 to 0xBFFF. For instance, if we access location 0x9401, since **A14** is low and **A15** is high for that address, we will select the latch. **A0** to **A13** are not used by the decoder, so their state is irrelevant to the address decode.

The schematic for the LED latch circuit is shown in Figure 16-8 (power and ground connections for U3 are present but are not shown for clarity). The latch has two control lines, **LE** and **OE**. **LE** going from high to low causes the latch to capture and hold the current input data, in this case from the processor's data bus. **OE** controls whether the latch outputs the data. Since we want the LEDs to always show their current state, we want the latch to permanently output the currently latched data. Hence, $\overline{OE}$ must always be asserted (tied low). The address decode for the latch is relatively simple. When the processor is writing data to the latch, **A14** is low and **A15** is high. **A14** is inverted by U5A and ANDed with **A15**. The output of the AND gate (U4A) will be high; therefore, the latch will capture the data that is being written to it. In effect, the latch is acting as a single byte of write-only memory.

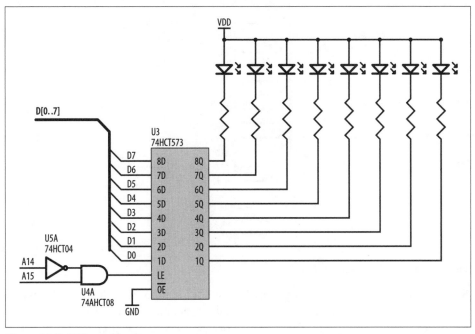

Figure 16-8. LEDs and latch

The address decode for the ROM is shown in Figure 16-9. When both **A14** and **A15** are high, the output from the NAND (U2D) gate will be low; therefore, the ROM will be selected. If either **A14** or **A15** are low, the ROM will not be selected. The ROM shown in the schematic is a 27256 (a 32K part), since these are easier to acquire than 16K devices. Because it is a 32K device, and we're using only half of its internal space, its address input **A14** is tied high. In this way, we permanently select the upper half of the device's space. Note that this **A14** input is not the same as the **A14** address bit from the processor. The $\overline{OE}$ (output enable) input is connected to the same $\overline{OE}$ we generated for the RAM. Finally, the power pin **VPP** is used during programming (out of circuit) to load the chip with data. During normal operation, this pin is tied to **VCC**.

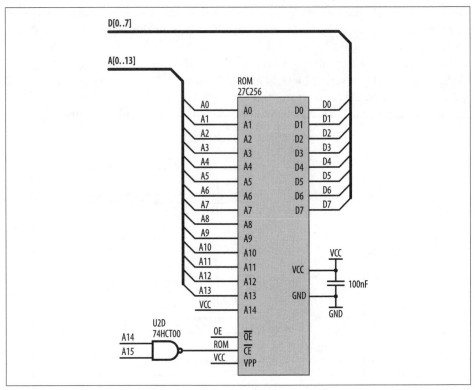

Figure 16-9. Address decode for ROM

So that completes the basic design for the 68HC11 computer. Using the processor's SPI port, we could add a variety of additional peripherals or data-storage memories. Alternatively, we could add additional peripherals using the processor's buses by breaking up the address space allocated to the latch and providing support for more devices. We could also apply the memory-management techniques covered in the AVR chapter to increase the amount of RAM in the computer.

CHAPTER 17

MAXQ

We will find a way, or we will make one.
—Hannibal, 218 B.C.

In this chapter, we'll look at an innovative new processor architecture introduced to the world in 2004. Dallas Semiconductor, a subsidiary of Maxim (*http://www.maxim-ic.com*), developed the 16-bit MAXQ microcontrollers to target the low-cost, low-power embedded applications market. The architecture is aimed directly against Microchip's PIC, Atmel's AVR, Texas Instruments' MSP430, and the 8051 architecture offered by many manufacturers (including Dallas Semiconductor itself). The MAXQ is an interesting contender for top RISC microcontroller. It's fast, has a lot of functionality, and is very low-powered. At the time of writing, the *User's Guide* for the MAXQ is 230 pages long. Obviously, this processor has a lot of features, too many to be thoroughly covered here. Therefore, I'm going to simply concentrate on the basic design for a MAXQ-based system. Let's start by seeing what makes the MAXQ so different and so interesting.

Architectural Overview

The stated design goal for the MAXQ was to achieve a high performance-to-power ratio. In other words, the aim was to maximize the processor's throughput of instructions while minimizing the current draw. Many RISC processors achieve single-cycle execution but do so through the use of an instruction pipeline. In a pipelined architecture, the execution unit is comprised of many stages. At any one time, several instructions will be in the process of being decoded and executed. Thus, with a pipeline, although a given instruction may take several cycles to execute, the processor is able to have an instruction terminate on each cycle (Figure 17-1).

Each cycle moves each instruction further along the pipeline, from fetch to termination (and result). The disadvantage of a pipeline is that a call or jump instruction means that all instructions following in the pipeline are not needed and the pipeline must be reloaded from a new location (where the jump/call was directed). So, while

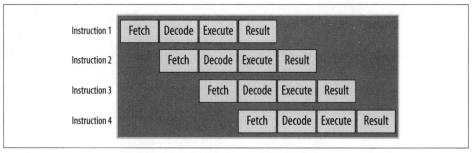

Figure 17-1. Four-stage instruction pipelining

pipelining can achieve single-cycle execution, it falls down in a big way unless the code is linear.

The MAXQ does not have an instruction pipeline, yet it still achieves single-cycle execution, with the exception of long jumps and calls and some extended register accesses. Now, you may say, "So what's the difference?" since pipelined processors have problems with jumps and calls too. The difference is that a pipelined processor executing a jump means that not only is the jump not single-cycle, but it will cause a disruption to the pipeline affecting the following instructions. With the MAXQ, this is not the case. Only the jump or call is not single-cycle, and all subsequent instructions execute without incurring the delay of a pipeline reload.

The MAXQ achieves this by having instruction-decode and execution units that are much simpler than those found on many other processors. How simple? Well, the MAXQ has only *one* instruction (move), but that one instruction has multiple functions, depending on the source and destination operands. By having only one instruction, a classical decode unit is not required. (You already know what the instruction is going to be, so what's there to decode about it?) Hence, the execution of instructions is reduced to determining source and destination, and whether additional hardware operations are triggered as part of the move. The source and destination bits of an instruction merely activate internal data paths, and this happens as the instruction is fetched.

The basic format for a MAXQ instruction is fdd dddd ssss ssss, where f is the format bit, d represents the destination-field bits, and s represents the source-field bits. When the format bit is a 1, the instruction moves data from one index module to another. When the format bit is a 0, an immediate 8-bit value is loaded into an index module (Table 17-1).

Table 17-1. MAXQ instruction format

Format bit	7-bit destination	8-bit source
1	Index module	Index module
0	Index module	Immediate byte data

In the MAXQ architecture, the index modules are not necessarily specific registers, and herein lies the flexibility of the architecture. A given working accumulator may actually be represented by more than one index module. One index module will target the accumulator and perform an *addition* operation, while another index module will target the same accumulator yet perform a *subtraction*. In this way, two different operations are specified by two index modules, even though they both target the same register. Clever, isn't it?

 A few years ago, I designed an experimental *zero-operand processor* (as a soft core) that also implemented single-cycle execution without pipelines. A zero-operand processor has its registers configured as a stack, and all instructions implicitly operate on the stack. An add instruction, for example, takes the top two stack entries (registers r0 and r1), adds them, and stores the result back to the top of the stack (r0). Since the source and destination are always known, operands can be pre-fed to the ALU, which computes all possible operations in parallel. An incoming instruction simply selects an appropriate ALU result or operation. In many ways, this conceptual simplicity is comparable to the MAXQ but is the other side of the same coin. The MAXQ uses one instruction with multiple index modules, whereas the zero-operand processor has many instructions but only one source/destination.

See Chapter 3 for more information about stack-based languages.

Like the PIC and AVR, the MAXQ is a Harvard-architecture processor, with separate code and data spaces. Overall, the MAXQ is a very nice processor, and one that I'm sure will gain market share as time passes.

With that in mind, let's see how simple it is to design a MAXQ-based embedded computer. As you will see, although this is a powerful processor, when it comes to the "hard work" of design, there's not much to it!

Schematics

A major problem common in utilizing a microcontroller in a mixed-signal environment (one that combines both digital and analog components) is the noise the digital subsystem introduces. Higher processor performance normally results in greater noise in the analog section, unless great pains are undertaken to minimize these effects. Thus, achieving high throughput is often contrary to the goal of keeping the analog circuits as noise-free as possible. The MAXQ implements intelligent clock management that reduces noise by enabling clocks only to those subsystems that require them, and only *when* they require them. In this way, the overall digital noise is reduced considerably. The MAXQ processor requires two crystals, a 16 MHz crystal (X1) for the main CPU clock and a 32.768 kHz watch crystal (X2) for the timers. Figure 17-2 shows the MAXQ2000F processor with its support components.

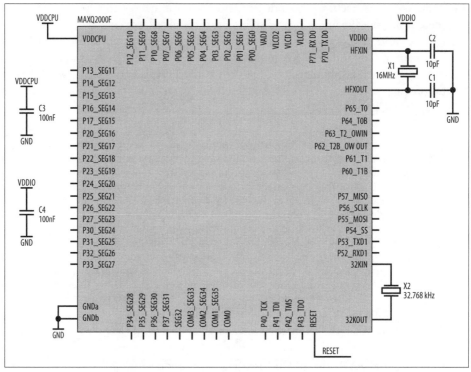

Figure 17-2. MAXQ processor and support components

The MAXQ processor requires two power supplies, **VDDCPU** (2.5 V) and **VDDIO** (3.6 V), each decoupled to ground with 100 nF ceramic capacitors. The 2.5 V supply may be generated using a MAX1658 (Figure 17-3). This is a general-purpose regulator, the output of which is adjustable via bias resistors. These resistors, R1 and R2, set the output to +2.5 V. It is important that these resistors are precise, so choose resistors with 1% tolerance. The input and output of the regulator are each decoupled with 10 uF capacitors. The MAX1658 can operate on an input voltage (**VIN**) of between 2.7 V and 16.5 V, supplying up to 350 mA to the embedded computer system.

A similar circuit is used to generate the 3.6 V supply required by the MAXQ's I/O subsystems (Figure 17-4). Note the different resistor values required to generate 3.6 V rather than 2.5 V.

The MAXQ has an internal power-on reset generator, kicking the processor to life at power-up. No external reset circuit is required. If a manual reset is required, a pushbutton switch may be used to pull the **RESET** line low. However, it is important to note that **RESET** is a bidirectional line. The MAXQ also uses this signal as an output to indicate that a reset condition (possibly generated internally) is being serviced.

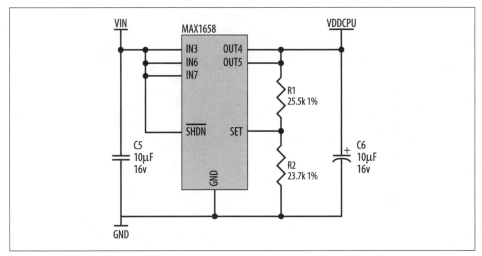

Figure 17-3. Generating 2.5 V for VDDCPU

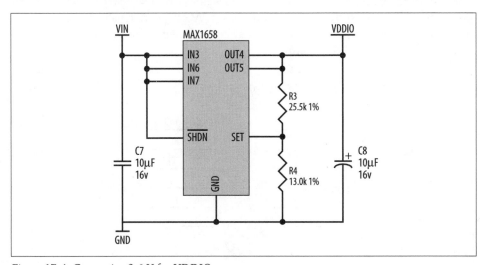

Figure 17-4. Generating 3.6 V for VDDIO

This can be used by the system designer to reset external peripherals as well (if required).

The various ports, labeled Px, provide access to the MAXQ's I/O. As well as providing digital I/O, they also serve dual purposes. Port 5 provides a SPI interface as well as a serial port. The SPI interface may be connected to any SPI-based peripheral. The serial port requires a level shifter such as a MAX3232, as shown in Figure 17-5. The transmitter (TXD1) and receiver (RXD1) of the MAXQ connect to the receiver and transmitter pins on the MAX3232.

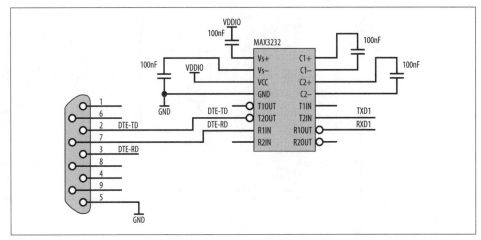

Figure 17-5. Serial port

Port 5 of the MAXQ provides access to JTAG signals for in-system programming and debugging. Figure 17-6 shows the pinout for a JTAG header. This is the same pinout used on the Maxim MAXQ development system, allowing you to use the same environment for your embedded computer.

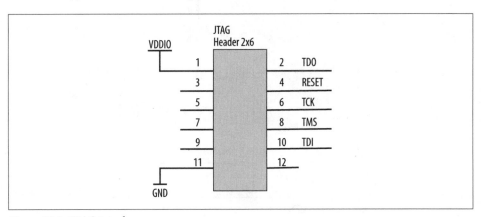

Figure 17-6. JTAG interface

Ports 1, 2, and 3 double as an interface to a 36-segment (numerical) LCD. Figure 17-7 shows the connections to a header for the LCD ribbon cable.

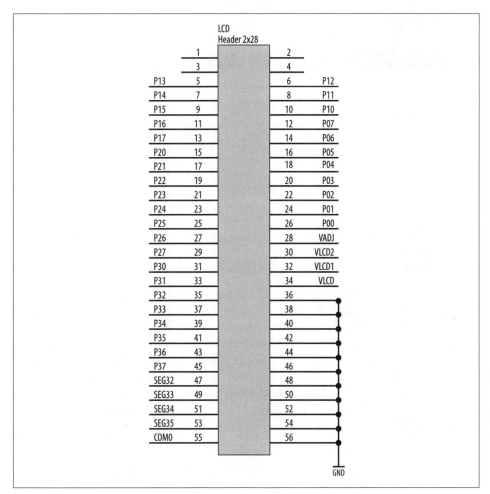

Figure 17-7. Numerical LCD interface

The MAXQ is a versatile and fast 16-bit processor, and the family is due to be expanded by Maxim. If you're looking for a low-powered, yet very capable processor for an embedded application, take a close look at the MAXQ. You'll find it's an impressive little processor.

CHAPTER 18

68000-Series Computers

All is flux, nothing stays still.
—Heraclitus
  Diogenes Laertius' *Lives of Eminent Philosophers*

In this chapter, we'll take a look at a 32-bit processor that has been around for quite some time and has evolved into a plethora of controllers and embedded processors. The 68000 (also known as the "68k") is produced by Freescale Semiconductor and is licensed by several other manufacturers. The range of 68000-based processors is large (check out the manufacturers' web sites for a list of processors and their features). The number of applications that the 68000 has found its way into is enormous. You can even get 68000s as soft cores for FPGAs, which means you place a 68000 CPU in the midst of your programmable logic, all on the one chip.

The Motorola* MC68000 was introduced in 1979 as the successor to its 8-bit 6800 family. It featured a large address space, 32-bit registers, a large number of addressing modes, and an enlarged instruction set with over 1,000 opcodes. It was designed with the intention of running multitasking operating systems, specifically Unix. Its use in Unix machines has now long since passed, having been usurped by more advanced RISC processors. The 68000 processor was also used in the original Macintosh computers, as well as in the Atari ST, the Commodore Amiga, and Jef Raskin's CAT computer, all long extinct.

 For an interesting overview of the CAT, read Jef Raskin's *The Humane Interface* (Addison-Wesley Professional). He discusses the CAT's unique design and has some interesting ideas on user interface design.

The processor's wide range of software and reasonable computing power are now encouraging its extensive use in embedded systems. It now forms the basis of a

---

* Motorola Semiconductor is now known as Freescale Semiconductor.

family of microcontrollers designed for embedded systems, industrial control, networking, and PDAs. The 683xx series is the primary family of microcontrollers, specifically tailored to embedded applications. These processors combine a *CPU32* core (68020-based) with various integrated functions (such as UARTs, SPI, ADCs, etc.). Additional 68000 processors have been developed for specialized applications. The original Palm PDA has a 68EZ328 *DragonBall* processor, also based on a CPU32 core, that incorporates an LCD controller along with many of the common functions found in PDAs. The DragonBall is essentially a PDA on a chip—just add memory. The ucLinux fraternity uses a DragonBall processor in its small embedded controller board.

The 68000 architecture was upgraded to RISC with the *ColdFire* series of processors. These see extensive use in industrial control and network interfaces.

The 68000 series of processors are good general-purpose processors. They have a nice instruction set, are easy (and fun) to write code for, and are relatively easy to build computers around. They have large address spaces and asynchronous operation, allowing them to be interfaced to a wide variety of memory and peripherals of varying operating speeds. They are used in industrial control and monitoring, and also in consumer electronics.

In this chapter, we'll look at the standard 68000 processor. More than likely, this is not the processor you will use in a design. Rather, you will choose a 68000-based integrated controller that better suits your needs. So, why look at a standard 68000 and not one of the derivatives? First, there are far too many diverse 68000-based processors to cover. Second, since these processors are all based on the 68000, understanding the basic 68000 is a great starting point. Finally, all the derivatives are generally easier to use than the original, so if you can design around a standard 68000, then you can design for a derivative processor as well.

Understanding the 68000 gives you access to a wide range of available processors. There are dozens of commercial C compilers and assemblers available for the 68000 family, as well as a number of public-domain compilers as well. The 68000 is fully supported by the gnu development suite. Both Linux and BSD are also available for the 68000, as well as for numerous commercial operating systems.

The 68000 Architecture

The 68000 has eight 32-bit data registers (D0–D7), eight 32-bit address registers (A0–A7), a 32-bit program counter, two 32-bit stack pointers, and a 16-bit status register (Figure 18-1). The processor is capable of handling data as 32-bit long words, 16-bit words, bytes, or bits.

The processor has two modes of operation: *supervisor mode* (operating system) and *user mode* (applications). The mode of operation is made available to external

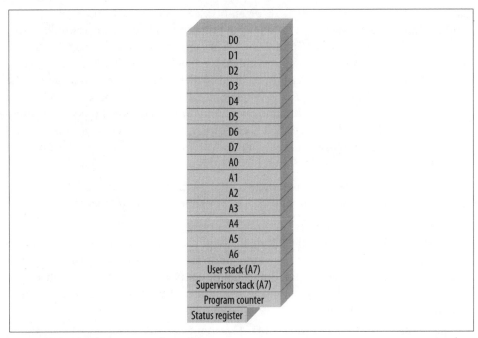

Figure 18-1. 68000 programmer's model

hardware, thereby giving the address decoder the ability to have separate supervisor and user spaces.

The standard 68000 is just a conventional, bus-based processor. A block diagram of a generic 68000-series processor is shown in Figure 18-2. The figure also shows the pins for a sample 68000-series processor. The pins and signals of 68000s can vary from one device to another, but they all have the same core functionality. The embedded controllers add to this basic functionality with additional I/O capability. We'll look at the pins for the MC68EC000 shortly. You can download datasheets, programmers' manuals, and technical references for 68000-series processors from the Freescale Semiconductor web site, *http://www.freescale.com*. While you're there, check out the other Freescale processor families, which range from 8-bit controllers (such as the 68HC05 and 68HC11) to 64-bit PowerPC RISC processors, and everything in between.

The original 68000 has a 23-bit address bus (A1 to A23), giving it access to a memory space of 16M, and a 16-bit data bus. Most other processors based on the 68000 architecture have address and data buses of 32 bits and can therefore access up to 4G of memory.

The processors have an input clock that drives all processor operation. Memory accesses typically take eight input clock cycles, provided that wait states are not introduced. Many processors based on the 68000 incorporate in-built address coding and software-configurable wait-state generation, making interfacing much simpler.

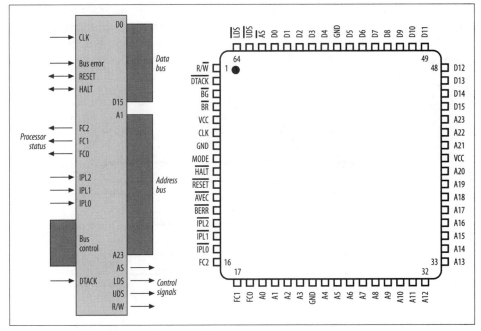

Figure 18-2. MC68000 block diagram and pinout

The processors have an address strobe ($\overline{\text{AS}}$) indicating when a valid address is present on the bus, data strobes ($\overline{\text{LDS}}$, $\overline{\text{UDS}}$) indicating valid data, and a **R/W** line that shows the direction of the transfer. In addition, a Data Transfer Acknowledge input, **DTACK**, is used by external devices to indicate to the processor that it may terminate its current memory cycle. (Some 68000 processors call their Data Transfer Acknowledge **DTACKB**.) The function code outputs (**FC0**, **FC1**, and **FC2**) indicate the current operating mode (supervisor or user) of the processor. Bus Error (**BERR**) is used by an external address decoder to indicate an error condition. This allows the system to trap out accesses to unused regions of memory space, or in combination with the status lines, to detect user access to memory space allocated for supervisor use only. For example, if a program crashes and, in the process of crashing, attempts to access a region of memory to which no device is allocated, the address decoder is able to signal that fault back to the processor. An assertion of **BERR** causes the processor to execute an interrupt and take appropriate action. **HALT** is used to suspend processor operation without generating a reset. Three interrupt inputs (**IPL0**, **IPL1**, and **IPL2**) are used to generate seven levels of external interrupt handling. Bus Grant (**BG**) and Bus Request (**BR**) are DMA control signals by which another processor can arbitrate to acquire the computer's buses. The **MODE** pin, present on only some 68000 processors, determines whether the 68000 uses its data bus as 16 bits or 8 bits. **MODE** is sampled as the processor comes out of reset. **AVEC**, also found in only some 68000 processors, determines whether the processor uses auto-vectoring for its interrupts. If auto-vectoring is enabled, the processor will expect the interrupting peripheral to supply the appropriate vector. This allows a peripheral to specify what type of action the processor needs to take when a given interrupt is generated. Other 68000 processors may have other signals as well, but these are the main ones.

The basic timing diagram for a 68000 memory access is shown in Figure 18-3.

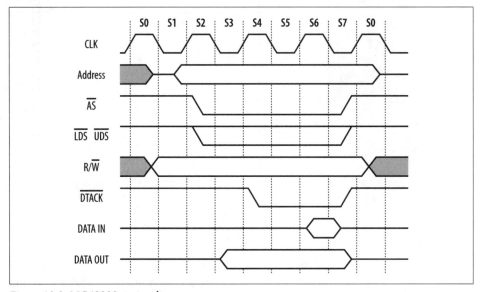

Figure 18-3. MC68000 timing diagram

The memory cycle of a 68000 is divided into a number of clock states, S0 through S7. The cycle begins with state S0. The processor validates **R/W** for the coming cycle, sending it low for a write access, driving it high for a read access. The processor also tristates its address bus from the previous memory access. By S2, the processor has output a valid address and drives the address strobe (**AS**) low, indicating that a valid address is present. The lower and upper data strobes (**LDS** and **UDS**) go low as appropriate and indicate the width of the memory access taking place. For a 16-bit transfer, both **LDS** and **UDS** assert. For an 8-bit transfer, only one of **LDS** or **UDS** asserts, depending on whether the upper byte or lower byte is being transferred. If the current memory access is a write cycle, the processor outputs valid data in state S3. At this point, all outputs from the processor are valid, and the processor waits for the device being accessed to respond.

At the falling edge of the clock in S4, the processor begins checking the state of the **DTACK** input. If **DTACK** is high, the processor inserts wait states and continues to do so until **DTACK** is found to be low on the falling edge of the clock. (You'll learn how to generate wait states in "Wait States," later in the chapter.) When **DTACK** is low, the processor recognizes this as an indication that the device being accessed has had sufficient time to respond and prepares to terminate the cycle. If the cycle is a read cycle, the processor will latch data on the falling edge of the clock in state S6. If it is a write cycle, the device being accessed will latch data as the data strobes go high in S7.

Support for synchronous operation is also provided for, using control signals found in the old 6800 series of processors. Since 6800s have long since passed into history, and 6800-based peripherals are now exceptionally rare, just ignore the 6800 control signals. Most 68000-based derivative processors no longer include support for 6800 peripherals.

A Simple 68000-Based Computer

Let's look now at a small 68000-based computer. For simplicity, we'll give it just a small amount of memory and a single peripheral, an MK68901 MFP (Multi-Function Peripheral) produced by ST Electronics. The MFP gives us a UART, parallel I/O, and interrupt control. A block diagram of the system is shown in Figure 18-4.

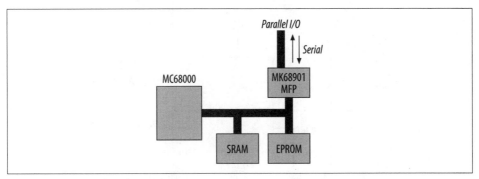

Figure 18-4. 68000-based computer

This system is designed with only a small amount of memory, to keep the design uncomplicated. While this is not much compared to many desktop machines, it is sufficient for many small, control applications. This design could be used for a number of simple applications. The counters of the MK68901 may be used to monitor external event pulses or to generate PWM for motor control. This computer could also be used to accept commands through its serial port and activate (or deactivate) external subsystems using the parallel I/O pins of the MK68901. This basic design could also be adapted to provide a bridge between an RS-232C interface and a parallel port. You could use this to interface a parallel-port printer to a serial-port-only computer. Alternatively, you could use it to put a serial modem on your PC's parallel port. Using the bus-interfacing techniques we learned in the AVR chapter, you could add additional peripherals such as ADCs and DACs, Ethernet, or a whole range of other devices. The list of possible applications is endless. And it all starts with this core design.

So, let's start our tour of a 68000-based computer system. We'll look at the reset circuit, address decoder, I/O, and memory.

Reset Circuit

To reset an MC68000, both **RESET** and **HALT** must be driven low simultaneously. In addition, both of these signal lines may also act as outputs from the processor. Therefore, both must be independently driven by the reset circuit through open-collector gates. The conventional way of doing a 68000 reset circuit is shown in Figure 18-5.

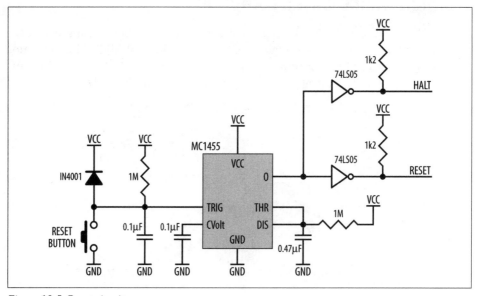

Figure 18-5. Reset circuit

The MC1455 will respond to a disruption on **VCC** by sending its output low. This output is used to drive **RESET** and **HALT** low simultaneously. In normal operation, **RESET** is held high by the pull-up resistor, unless pulled low through the reset switch being pressed. The diode is present to remove any glitches that might send **RESET** above **VCC**.

A better reset circuit is shown in Figure 18-6, using a MAX825 integrated reset controller. Again, both **RESET** and **HALT** need to be driven low.

Address Decoder

Logic to perform address decoding and the generation of separate read and write strobes is implemented in a PAL. In each case, $\overline{\text{AS}}$ (Address Strobe) of the processor

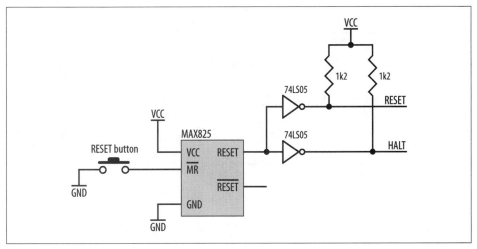

Figure 18-6. MAX825 reset circuit for a 68000

is used as an indication of a valid address present on the bus. The address-decode equations are as follows:

```
ROM  = /(/AS * /A23 * /A22)
RAM0 = /(/AS * /A23 * A22 * /LDS)
RAM1 = /(/AS * /A23 * A22 * /UDS)
MFP  = /(/AS * A23 * /A22)
```

With the exception of the MFP, which generates its own **DTACK**, **DTACK** for all other devices is generated as part of the address decoding. Since **DTACK** from the PAL must be OR-tied with **DTACK** from the MFP, it must be driven from an open-collector gate. Therefore, we generate an active-high acknowledge (which we'll designate **TACK**) from the PAL and invert this through a 74LS05 open-collector inverter.

The PAL equation to generate **TACK** is simply:

```
TACK = (/AS * MFP)
```

Therefore, **TACK** is active (high) whenever the processor accesses its address space, so long as it is not accessing the MFP. If the address strobe is high, or if there is an access to the MFP, then **TACK** is low. The **TACK** output from the PAL is inverted through an open-collector 74LS05 and "OR-tied" (directly connected together) with **DTACK** from the MFP. **DTACK** requires a pull-up 1 kΩ resistor, since this input must have a sharp rise time. A block diagram is shown in Figure 18-7.

No provision for generating a **BERR** is made because our simple address decoding allocates all of the address space. If we had any unused regions of the memory space, we would use our address decoder to generate a **BERR** when accesses to the unused regions were made.

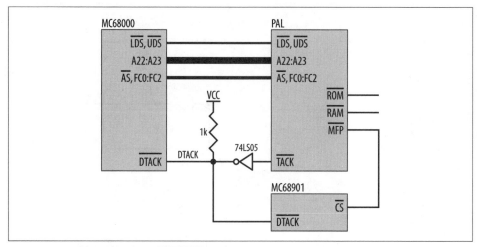

Figure 18-7. Address decode and DTACK generation

The PAL equations to generate separate read and write strobes for the memory chips are:

```
UWE = /(/UDS * RW)
LWE = /(/LDS * RW)
UOE = /(/UDS * /RW)
LOE = /(/LDS * /RW)
```

The connections for the PAL are shown in Figure 18-8. Additional addresses are brought into the PAL to allow for future changes to the memory map. The processor's clock (**CLK**) is used by the PAL to generate the clock for the MFP (**MFPCLK**).

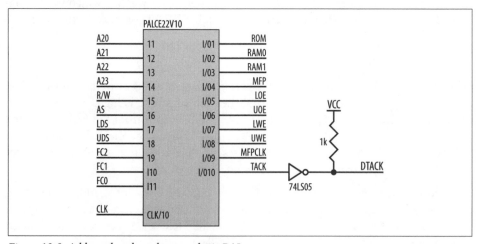

Figure 18-8. Address decode and system-logic PAL

The function code outputs (**FC0–FC2**) can be decoded using a 74LS138 demultiplexer to drive three LEDs (Figure 18-9). These provide a visible indication of processor status. The function codes could also be used by the address decoder if you wanted to have separate user and supervisor address spaces. Many of the more sophisticated peripheral chips (such as the MFP) require the processor to acknowledge when they have generated an interrupt. The 74LS138 also uses the function codes to generate an interrupt acknowledge (**IACK**) for peripherals, since the function codes also indicate an IACK condition.

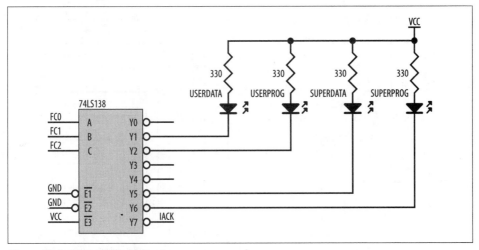

Figure 18-9. Status LEDs indicating processor mode

I/O

The MK68901 Multifunction Peripheral (MFP) provides a serial port, as well as basic parallel I/O functions, a 16-source interrupt controller, and four 8-bit timers. The MK68901 has an internal oscillator that drives the internal timers. A timer output (**TD0**) is fed back into the MFP as the clock for the serial interface. The internal oscillator must therefore run at a frequency appropriate for RS-232C. An external 3.6864 MHz crystal drives the oscillator. This input clock can be divided up by the MFP, providing the appropriate baud rates for the serial port. The serial lines from the MFP are converted to RS-232C voltage levels by a MAX3232 level shifter. A 9-pin, D-type connector provides access to the RS-232C signals. The parallel I/O lines and timer inputs and outputs are also made available through a 26-pin IDC connector.

The schematic for the MFP is shown in Figure 18-10.

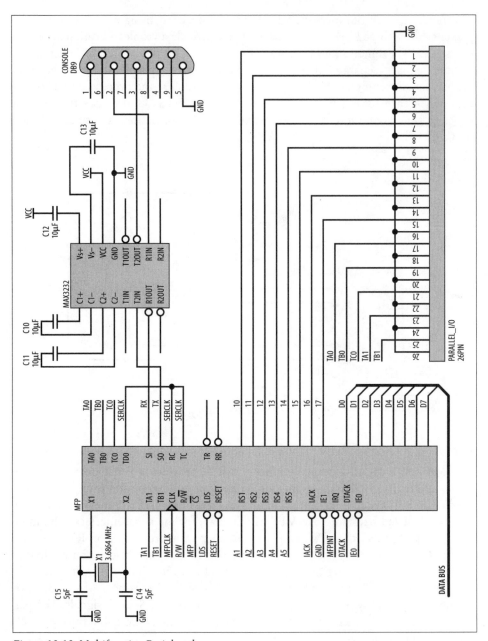

Figure 18-10. Multifunction Peripheral

Memory

The system is designed with 256K of EPROM and 512K of static RAM. The connections to the SRAM are shown in Figure 18-11. Note that since the data bus of a 68000 is 16 bits wide, two SRAMs are required. For 68000-based derivatives with

32-bit external data buses, four memory chips would be required in parallel. Note how half the data bus goes to one chip and the other half goes to the other chip.

Now, note the address lines going to the SRAMs. The lowest address bit from the processor is **A1**, and this is connected to the **A0** inputs of the SRAMs, and so on. Since the processor accesses external memory in 16-bit words, **A1** represents the least significant address bit. In other words, as you move from word to subsequent word in memory, it is **A1** that increments. However, **A0** is the least significant address bit of the SRAMs, but since the two SRAMs together form a 16-bit word of memory, the **A0** of the SRAMs must connect to **A1** of the processor. The other address bits follow on from that starting point.

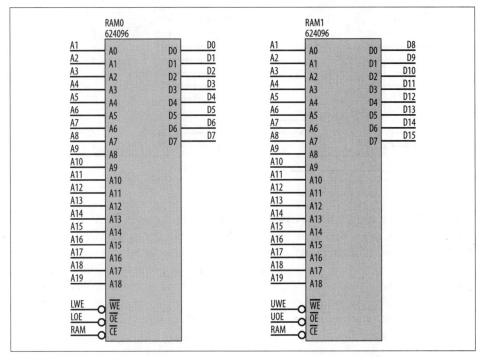

Figure 18-11. Interfacing to SRAM

Similarly, the connections for the ROMs are shown in Figure 18-12.

Wait States

Depending on the speed of your processor and the access times of your memory and peripheral chips, it may be necessary to introduce wait states into the 68000's memory cycle. Wait-state generation follows basically the same principle for processors that support asynchronous memory cycles. The processor will have an input (sometimes more than one) that will cause it to delay the memory cycle, giving slower

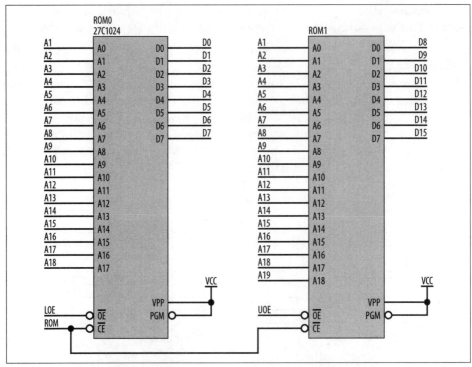

Figure 18-12. Interfacing to EPROMs

devices time to respond. In the case of the 68000, that input is **DTACK**. To insert a wait state for a given device, we need to detect an access to that device and hold **DTACK** inactive for the required additional clock cycles. In other words, we need to use the chip select for a given device to delay **DTACK** going low. The circuit to do this is simple and is best done inside a PAL or other programmable logic device. This facilitates changing the wait-state generator if faster parts are used in the design at a later stage. The wait-state generator consists of a series of D-type flip-flops* (Figure 18-13). Each flip-flop represents an additional clock cycle that the transfer acknowledge is delayed.

Between memory cycles, the address strobe, $\overline{\text{AS}}$, goes high. It is first inverted and then connected to the active-low **SET** input of each of the flip-flops. Thus, the output of each of the flip-flops is driven high between each memory cycle. This resets them from any previous cycle. The address decoder generates a chip select for the particular device, and this is connected to the D input of the first flip-flop. So, on each successive clock pulse, the 0 provided by the chip select is clocked through from

---

* A flip-flop is a logic element that feeds the D input through to the Q output on the changing edge of a clock pulse.

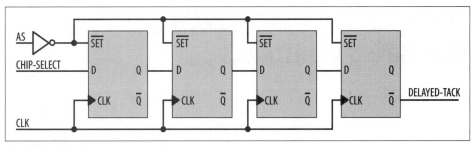

Figure 18-13. Wait-state generator

one flip-flop to the next. After four clock pulses, the 0 has arrived at the Q output of the last flip-flop. The inverted output of this flip-flop, $\overline{Q}$, becomes a 1. This is then output by the PAL to be inverted by the 74LS05 open-collector inverter to provide **DTACK** for the processor. For additional wait states, add more flip-flops. For several devices requiring different numbers of wait states, use their combined chip selects to feed the D input of the first flip-flop; then "tap" into the wait-state generator at different stages for the required delay. Each of these taps is gated with the respective chip select to enable/disable that output before they are all recombined to generate a unified acknowledge for the processor.

Most processors that support wait states now include inbuilt, software-configurable wait-state generators. This makes the task of designing the system logic much simpler.

In the next chapter, we'll take a look at a different sort of embedded processor—one based on a Digital Signal Processing (DSP) architecture.

CHAPTER 19
DSP-Based Controllers

*...the uniformity of the world, that everything which
happens is connected, that the great and the small
things are all encompassed by the same forces of time
... this unity and necessary sequence of all things is
nevertheless broken in one place, through a small gap,
this world of unity is invaded by something alien,
something new...*
—Hermann Hesse
  Siddhartha

In this chapter, we're going to take a look at a different sort of processor. *Digital Signal Processors* (*DSPs*) are special-purpose processors designed for executing mathematically intensive algorithms. They first appeared in the early 1980s, and since then have expanded into a wide range of devices used in a variety of applications. These processors are characterized by their ability to quickly move data in and out of memory (or a peripheral), and their architectures are optimized for mathematical processing of that data.

The basic purpose of a DSP is to rapidly read in some data, perform a complex algorithm on it, and then move out the result. Many DSPs have dual data spaces, known as *X* and *Y*. They are able to access both data spaces simultaneously, retrieving two operands at once for processing. Many DSPs are also Harvard architecture, and so have three separate address spaces, one for code and two for data, all of which can be accessed concurrently. That ability, combined with very sophisticated ALUs, gives DSPs their advanced data-processing prowess.

DSPs are commonly used in audio processing, video or image processing, communications, radar and sonar systems, and biomedical applications. Your cell phone has a DSP in it. So does your DVD player and the surround-sound (AV) amplifier in your home-theater system. The so-called bionic ear, made by Cochlear, uses a DSP.

Some applications of DSPs are:

- Engine control and anti-skid brakes in cars
- Digital radios and TVs
- DVD players and home-theater systems
- Music synthesizers
- GPS navigation
- Radar and sonar processing
- Aircraft navigation and guidance, spacecraft avionics, and missile guidance systems
- Industrial motor control
- Robotics
- Virtual-reality systems
- Image processing, compression, and enhancement
- Pattern recognition and machine vision
- Adaptive filtering, Fast Fourier Transforms (FFTs), and Hilbert transforms
- Scientific data processing
- Medical diagnostic equipment, ultrasound, and medical imaging systems
- Cell phones, pagers, modems, cell-phone base stations, and digital fax machines
- Data encryption
- Digital PABXs and ADSL
- Echo cancellation
- Spread-spectrum processing in communications
- Video-conferencing systems
- Speaker verification
- Speech enhancement and recognition
- Speech synthesis and coding
- Voice-mail systems

And that's just for starters.

The three big manufacturers of DSPs are Texas Instruments (*http://www.ti.com*), with its TMS320 series; Analog Devices (*http://www.analogdevices.com*), with the 21xx and SHARC (21xxx) processors; and Freescale Semiconductor (*http://www. freescale.com*), with the DSP56xxx processors and the high-end MSC8100 *StarCore* processors designed for communications and network processing. Many other manufacturers are starting to add DSP functionality into their embedded controllers. An example of this is the dsPIC processor by Microchip (*http://www.microchip.com*).

TI's DSPs range from small, low-cost units to supercomputers on a chip. Its TMS320C6000 series makes your average PC look like a rusty abacus by comparison. They are 128-bit *VLIW* (*Very Long Instruction Word*) processors and can execute up to *eight instructions every clock cycle*. They can run at up to 2,000 MIPS and 900 MFLOPS, and TI is working to make them even faster. These are processors designed for *serious* number crunching. (And if you want to play with one, you'll need serious dollars too.)

Both the TI and Analog Devices DSPs are designed for use as building blocks in parallel DSP computers. The Analog Devices SHARC supports both message-passing MIMD and shared-memory MIMD in the machine. You can have six SHARCs as a shared-memory parallel computing node, and you can have six of these nodes message-passing with one another.

When you consider that each SHARC has more processing power than a CRAY-1 supercomputer, well, let's just say that a parallel SHARC machine is an awful lot of grunt sitting on your desk. (Before you get too excited, we won't be designing a machine like that. It's far too complex and far too expensive for you to consider, and well and truly out of the context of this book!)

The Freescale Semiconductor DSP56000 series are 24-bit processors, primarily intended for audio applications, although they do see use in other fields as well. The 24-bit architecture is specifically chosen because 24 bits is a common word size in audio processing. Cochlear uses a DSP56000 in its bionic ear.

Now, although DSPs are beautiful in their intended applications of signal processing, they're also pretty good in general control applications too. An embedded system with a DSP is able to execute sophisticated software and perform advanced algorithms far more efficiently than a conventional processor. Early implementations of embedded DSP systems tended to use the DSP for data processing and included a microcontroller for its ubiquitous functionality. While DSPs are ideal for number crunching, they just weren't particularly good at conventional processor stuff. Having two processors in one system is not the most efficient design, and so the logical step was a hybrid processor, combining a DSP core with microcontroller functionality.

To this end, the makers of DSPs have developed variants of their DSP architectures specifically intended for embedded applications. They incorporate a DSP core with the type of subsystems normally found in microcontrollers, such as UARTs, SPIs, ADCs, and so on. Their instruction sets are also a mixture, incorporating both DSP (data movement and arithmetic) instructions and conventional microprocessor instructions. They are ideal for such applications as motor control (especially in robotics), neural networks and fuzzy control, data compression, digital communications, digital cameras, or any application that is mathematically intensive yet requires small (and relatively cheap) hardware.

In this chapter, we're going to look at the Freescale Semiconductor DSP56800 series of DSP controllers, specifically the DSP56805 processor. We'll see how to design and build a computer based on this chip. DSP56800 processors are specifically designed for implementing advanced digital control and processing in small-scale and low-cost embedded systems. Both TI and Analog Devices produce comparable processors, and while their architectures may vary, the basic techniques involved in building a computer based on them are fundamentally the same.

The DSP56800

Unlike the conventional DSP56000 with its 24-bit architecture, the DSP56800 series has a 16-bit architecture better suited to small-scale control applications. It is *fixed-point* (integer) only, which is fine for most control applications. If necessary, floating-point arithmetic can be synthesized in software.

The architecture is based on four functional units, each with their own registers, operating independently and in parallel with the other units. These functional units are the *program controller*, which is responsible for software execution; the *Address Generation Unit* (AGU), which handles bus accesses; the *Data ALU*, which performs the arithmetic operations; and the *bit-manipulation unit* for efficient and rapid bit-based operations.

The independent operation of these units allows for very efficient and fast software execution. While the Data ALU or bit-manipulation unit are performing an operation specified by an instruction, the AGU can be generating addresses for the execution of another instruction, while the program controller can be fetching yet another instruction for execution. The instruction set directly supports this parallelism. To accomplish this high internal throughput, the processor has not one but *three* internal address buses and *four* internal data buses (three data buses for the core and one for peripherals). Two operands may be sourced from the internal memory and operated on in a single instruction. The result is that the architecture achieves a throughput of 40 MIPS on an 80 MHz clock. That's RISC-like performance with a CISC-like instruction set. In other words, that's a lot of punch.

It has hardware looping using the DO and REP instructions. DO allows you to specify a block of code (of any size) and have the processor execute it as a loop *in hardware*. You don't need a counter test and conditional branch instruction at each iteration, saving processor execution overhead. REP allows the repetition of a single instruction, and REPs can be nested inside DO loops. As such, you have very versatile looping capability with no overhead. Loops on a DSP are *fast*.

The programmer's model for the DSP56800 core is shown in Figure 19-1.

The processor has two 36-bit accumulators, a 16×16-bit *Multiply and Accumulate* (*MAC*) unit, and a 16-bit barrel shifter. The MAC allows you to multiply two numbers and then add the result to a growing total, all with a single instruction. MACs allow for efficient execution of many signal-processing algorithms, as well as neuro-fuzzy code.

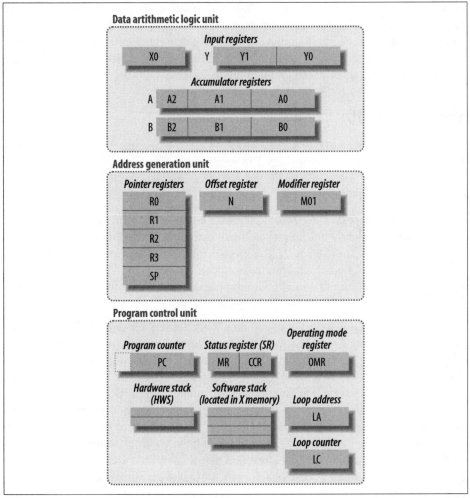

Figure 19-1. DSP56800 programmer's model

The barrel shifter allows you to shift up to 16 bits in either direction *in a single cycle*. So, if you want to shift an operand 15 bits to the left, a conventional processor would require 15 separate shift-left instructions (or one shift-left, a loop, a counter variable, and a conditional test for the loop). The DSP56800, like many DSPs, can perform this operation in just one cycle.

In short, the DSP56800 has very tight and efficient code with high functionality that it executes exceptionally quickly. It is a fast processor around which it is easy to design a powerful embedded computer system.

We'll look at how you design a system based on the DSP56805 processor, a member of the DSP56800 family specifically designed for industrial control. The DSP56805 has an internal 1K program RAM, 4K of bootstrap ROM (for loading boot software from an external memory or peripheral, 63K of program flash, 8K of data flash, and 4K of data RAM. The processors also have external data and address buses, so the processor's memory can be expanded well beyond its internal resources. It has a 64K × 16-bit address space, giving access to 128K (bytes) of external memory.

 There are DSP568xx processors with significantly larger address spaces than this. The DSP5685x series can support up to 2M of program memory and up to 8M of data memory.

The DSP56800 processors also provide the ability to separate data and program spaces, thereby doubling the external address space. The processor also has a programmable wait-state generator, simplifying interfacing to external devices. The generator may be programmed to provide 0, 4, 8, or 12 wait states for accesses to a given device.

DSP56800s in general come with a range of inbuilt peripherals, including SPI ports (sometimes two), several 16-bit general-purpose timers, a watchdog timer (called a *Computer Operating Properly*, or *COP*, timer by Freescale Semiconductor), a timer for real-time operation, a *Synchronous Serial Interface* (*SSI*) for accessing audio *codecs* (combined ADCs and DACs) and other DSPs, and general-purpose I/O lines. The DSP56805 adds two 6-channel *Pulse Width Modulation* (*PWM*) units for motor control and other uses, two 4-channel ADCs at a resolution of 12 bits per channel, and two *quadrature decoders* for measuring motor positions. It also has a *CAN* networking module, two serial ports (called *Serial Communication Interfaces*, or *SCIs*, by Freescale Semiconductor), and 14 dedicated and 18 shared I/O lines.

The processors operate from a supply voltage of between 3.0 V and 3.6 V but have 5 V–tolerant inputs, making interfacing to a wide variety of devices easy. (Other DSP56800s may operate on a supply voltage of between 4.57 V and 5.5 V, depending on the particular chip.) The processor has several low-power and sleep modes, making it ideal for battery-powered systems.

All DSP56800 processors incorporate a *JTAG* (*Joint Test Action Group*) port for interfacing to specialized debugging instruments. The JTAG port also allows direct access to the processor's onboard flash program memory, making the job of downloading new code simple and fast.

A block diagram of the DSP56805 is shown in Figure 19-2.

All in all, quite a nice processor. So, let's look at how you build a system based on one. For simplicity, I'll look at each subsystem in turn.

A DSP56805-Based Computer

The DSP56805 has nine power pins. Each of these must be decoupled to ground using 100 nF ceramic capacitors. Each capacitor should be placed as close as possible

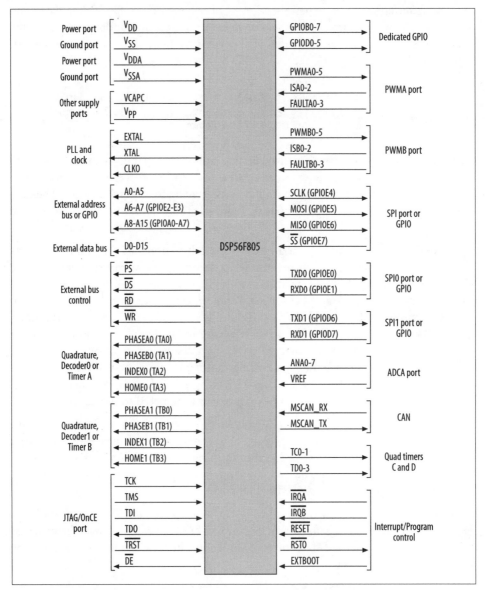

Figure 19-2. DSP56805 block diagram

to its respective power pin. Since this processor can operate at a relatively high speed, and can therefore generate a lot of noise, a four-layer circuit board is the preferred option for construction. (See Chapter 6 for more information). As with any design, any unused inputs must be tied inactive.

Oscillator

Like all processors, the DSP56805 requires a clock signal. The processor can operate from an oscillator frequency of up to 80 MHz (giving 40 MIPS) or as slow as a few MHz to save power. The processor may even have its clock completely stopped (so-called "DC operation," meaning the clock is no longer an AC signal) to further save power. (This processor's sibling, the DSP56801, has a complete internal oscillator and so requires no external clock-generation circuit.)

The processor has an inbuilt oscillator circuit, requiring only an external crystal in the range of 4 MHz to 8 MHz and support components (Figure 19-3). From this low crystal frequency, the processor internally synthesizes a clock speed of between 40 MHz and 110 MHz under software control. Note that while the clock-generation circuit is able to produce 110 MHz, the processor isn't able to operate at that speed. So keep the speed below 80 MHz, and the processor, your software, and you will all be happy.

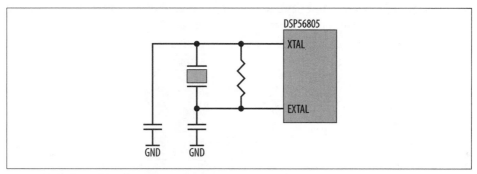

Figure 19-3. Crystal oscillator circuit

In a typical application, the crystal frequency is 8 MHz, with a resistor value of 10 MΩ. Decoupling capacitors are approximately 15 pF or so. However, the values of the resistor and capacitors required can vary, so make sure you check the technical data from the crystal manufacturer. It will tell you specifically what values to use for a particular crystal.

Alternatively, you could use an external oscillator module to generate the processor's clock (Figure 19-4). The module's output is connected to the **XTAL** input of the processor. When operating in this configuration, **EXTAL** must be connected to ground.

Reset and Interrupts

The DSP56805 has an internal power-on circuit to correctly start up the processor. It also has a watchdog reset circuit, driven by an internal timer, to recover the processor from a software crash. So, all we need to do is to provide our system with an

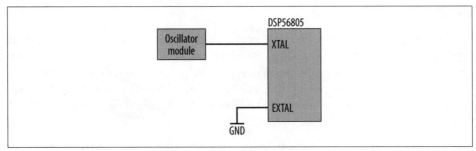

Figure 19-4. Oscillator module

external reset so we can manually restart the machine by pressing a button. Normally, such a reset circuit would need to debounce the button press and also ensure that the reset state was held for a minimum period of time. On the DSP56805, life is much simpler. The processor incorporates internal debounce circuitry on its **RESET** input. Further, it has circuitry that ensures that a reset is held for the appropriate duration. So, our external reset circuit is simply a push-button and a pull-up resistor (Figure 19-5). What could be simpler?

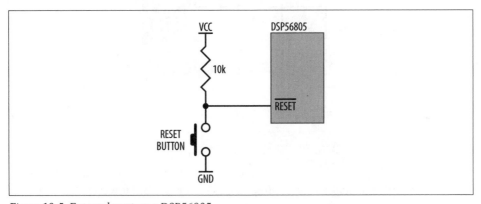

Figure 19-5. External reset on a DSP56805

The DSP56805 can boot from external memory or from its internal ROM for single-chip operation. An input pin, **EXTBOOT**, is sampled as the processor comes out of reset. If **EXTBOOT** is pulled low, the processor executes code from the internal ROM. This is known as Mode 0 operation. There are two forms of Mode 0. Mode 0A maps all memory as internal, whereas Mode 0B maps the lower 32K words (64K bytes) of the address space as internal and the upper 32K words as external. Mode 0A is the default mode, and Mode 0B may be entered only under software control.

If the **EXTBOOT** pin is high upon exiting reset, then the processor boots from external memory. This is known as Mode 3 operation. (There is no Mode 1 or Mode 2, as these are reserved for ROM-based DSP56800 processors.) Once operational, the processor can toggle from one mode to the other under software control.

Other DSP56800 processors have variations of the operating modes and memory maps, so, as always, check the datasheet for the particular processor you are using.

Aside from numerous internal sources of interrupts (from the onboard peripherals), the DSP56805 has two external interrupt sources, **IRQA** and **IRQB**. These may be used by external-interface peripherals (or even external systems) to gain the processor's attention. Whether they are connected to an external interrupt source or not, they require an external pull-up resistor. In the example given (Figure 19-6), **IRQA** has an interrupt source from a peripheral, while **IRQB** is unused.

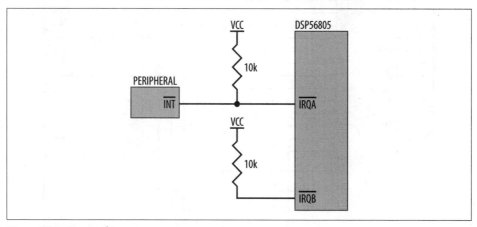

Figure 19-6. External interrupt sources

External Memory

The processor has an external 16-bit data bus that serves for accesses to both external program memory and external data memory. Data and program memory can exist within the same memory chips, or separate data and program address spaces may be implemented. The processor has two outputs, $\overline{\text{PS}}$ (Program Strobe) and $\overline{\text{DS}}$ (Data Strobe), which indicate the type of memory access.

The timing for a DSP56805 write cycle followed by a read cycle is shown in Figure 19-7. Since the processor has a programmable wait-state generator, external memory devices or peripherals of varying response times may be accommodated.

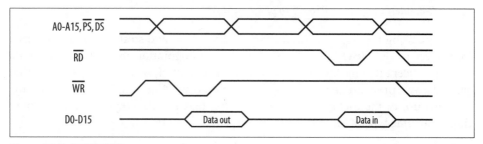

Figure 19-7. DSP56805 memory cycle

The DSP56805 may be connected to memory using a "glueless" interface. This means no external logic is required. The connections for interfacing a DSP56805 to two 64K program SRAMs are shown in Figure 19-8.

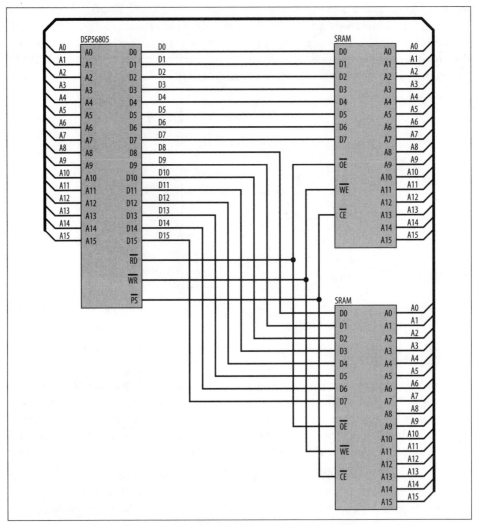

Figure 19-8. Interfacing the DSP56805 to program SRAM

When accessing the program address space, $\overline{PS}$ is low, and so this may be used as a chip select to the SRAMs. Similarly, the same configuration may be used for data memory, except that in this case, $\overline{DS}$ becomes the chip select (Figure 19-9). Note that when I say "program memory" or "data memory," I'm simply referring to the intended use of these chips, not distinguishing between different types of memory chip. The same type of SRAM chips will suffice for both regions.

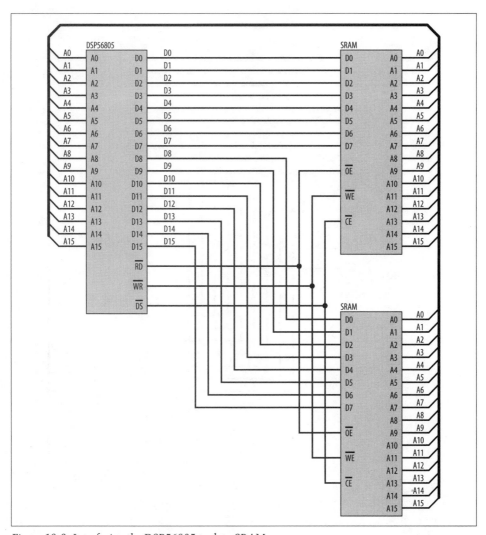

Figure 19-9. Interfacing the DSP56805 to data SRAM

So, our DSP56805 computer has four SRAM chips in total, evenly divided between program memory and data memory. Each region has 64K×16 bytes (two 19-bit memory chips), giving a total of 128K bytes of program space and 128K bytes of data memory. The total memory for our system is therefore 256K bytes. If more data memory is required, memory banking may be used to increase the available space, as we saw with the AT90S8515 in Chapter 15.

Note that you do not necessarily have to have separate program and data spaces. You can just as easily have two SRAMs total, with the program and data spaces coexisting in the same chips (Figure 19-10).

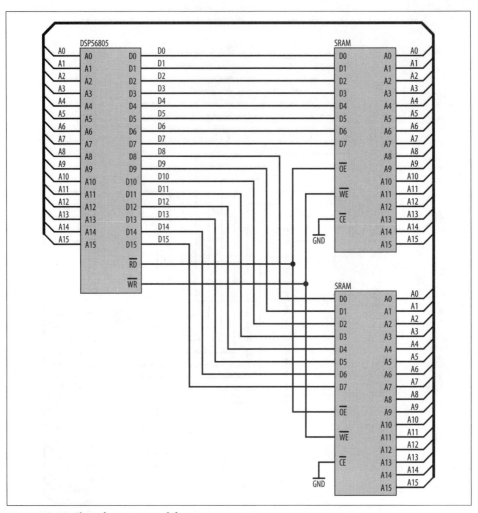

Figure 19-10. Shared program and data memory

In this case, both $\overline{PS}$ and $\overline{DS}$ are ignored, since we are no longer distinguishing between data and program spaces. The chip enable ($\overline{CE}$) inputs of the SRAMs are simply tied to ground, so that these devices are permanently enabled. This will work because an SRAM will respond only if $\overline{CE}$ is low *and* either the output enable ($\overline{OE}$) or the write enable ($\overline{WE}$) go low as well. So in this example, it is the output enable or write enable that will activate the SRAMs. Note that permanently enabling an SRAM will increase its power consumption. Of course, we could just as easily combine $\overline{DS}$ and $\overline{PS}$ such that either going low will enable the SRAMs, but this requires extra logic, and it really isn't necessary.

If you have different types of devices within your memory space, such as a smaller data SRAM and some peripherals, then you must include $\overline{DS}$ as part of the chip enable for the SRAMs and peripherals. The most logical way to do this is to use $\overline{DS}$ as the enable to your address decoder, which in turn selects the appropriate device. Note that it must be $\overline{DS}$ for accessing peripherals, since you can't execute code directly out of a peripheral!

A sample address decoder is shown in Figure 19-11. This will select either two 32K SRAMs or one of eight peripherals within the data space.

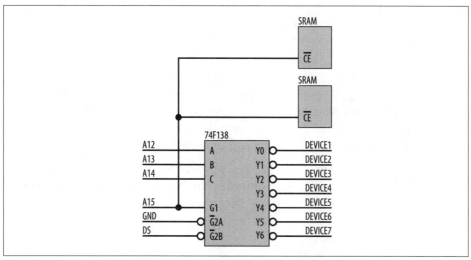

Figure 19-11. Address decoder for two 32K SRAMs and eight peripherals

When **A15** is low, the SRAMs are selected. When **A15** is high and $\overline{DS}$ is low, the address decoder is enabled and one of the eight peripherals is selected, depending on the state of **A12**, **A13**, and **A14**.

Using this address-decode scheme, you can add up to eight bus-based peripherals. The processor also has a SPI interface, so that opens up another avenue for expansion. Using SPI, you can add extra ADCs, DACs, real-time clock calendars, nonvolatile data memories, as well as a host of other devices. Of course, the DSP56805 has a range of inbuilt peripherals already. Its SPI, parallel I/O, and serial port interfaces are used just as we saw with the smaller microcontrollers. The DSP56805 has a wide variety of onboard peripherals, making this an exceptionally capable processor.

JTAG

The DSP56805 has a JTAG port to aid system debugging. A JTAG port consists of four dedicated signals (Table 19-1).

Table 19-1. JTAG signals

Signal name	Function
TDI	Test data input
TDO	Test data output
TMS	Test mode select
TCK	Test clock

Freescale Semiconductor adds additional signals to the standard JTAG set. Specifically, it adds **TRST** (Test Reset) to reset the JTAG state machine and $\overline{\text{DE}}$ (Debug Event), which is equivalent to an interrupt output, indicating that an event (such as a breakpoint) has happened in the *OnCE* (*On-Chip Emulation*) module.

JTAG is principally intended for debugging purposes, but since it gives you complete control of the processor's internals, it can also be used for reprogramming the internal program flash. The Freescale Semiconductor application note (AN1935/D) *Programming On-Chip Flash Memories of DSP56F80x DSPs Using the JTAG/OnCE Interface*, available from the Freescale Semiconductor web site, contains full details on the process involved, as well as sample source code and examples.

The Freescale Semiconductor Software Development Kit, based on the CodeWarrior C compiler, for the DSP56800 series provides both software and hardware tools for programming these processors.

Index

Numbers

We'd like to hear your suggestions for improving our indexes. Send email to *index@oreilly.com*.

C

caches, 17
CAD libraries and PCBs, 144
CAN (Controller Area Network), 215–219
    Bosch, 216
    driver, 217
    DSP56805, 217, 218–219
    packets, 217
    standard, 218
capacitive coupling, 121
capacitors, 80–82
    blocking, 86
    ceramic, 81
    decoupling, 121, 122
    decoupling AC and DC components of
        voltage source, 81
    electrolytics, 82
    regulators and, 113
    tantalum, 82
CAT computer, 334
CCR (Condition Code Register), 32, 41
cell phones, 348
ceramic capacitors, 81
charge pumps, 113, 114
chip enable, 70
chip select, 70
Chip/smart card interface devices (CCID)
        class (USB), 206
circuit, 66
Cirrus Logic, 220
CISC processors, 12–15
    versus RISC processors, 15
clock phase one/zero, 162
clock speed, 95
clocks, 95–97, 297
coarsely grained machine, 23
codec (COder DECoder), 229
CodeWarrior C compiler, 362
cold weld, 139
ColdFire series of processors, 335
Commodore Amiga, 334
Common class (CCS) class (USB), 206
common-mode rejection, 190
Common-Mode Rejection Ratio
        (CMRR), 229
Communications device class (USB), 206
Complex Instruction Set Computer (see CISC
        processors)
computer architecture, 1–29
    concepts, 2–4
    embedded (see embedded computer
        architecture)

conductors, 66
Connection Machine (CM-1), 23
control bus, 8
control registers, 32
Controller Area Network (see CAN)
conversion from parallel to serial format, 182
coupling
    capacitive, 121
CP1600 processor, 258
CPU (Central Processing Unit), 5
CRC algorithm, 183
crossbar switch, 26
crosstalk, 121
Crystal Semiconductor, 220
crystals, 93
CS8900A, 220–225
    block diagram of implementation, 221
    chip-select input, 224
    crystal connections for, 221
    default setting for, 224
    EEPROM support, 224
    interrupt, 223
    RESET, 222
    when used in 16-bit mode, 223
CTS (Clear To Send), 186
current, 65, 66
    minimizing current loop area, 120
    sinking, 98
    sourcing, 98
Cyclic Redundancy Check (CRC)
        algorithm, 183

D

DAC, 230
DACs (Digital to Analog
        Converter), 245–247
data bus, 8
data-chaining transfers (DMA), 21
DC component of analog signal, 68
DC electrical characteristics, 102–104
    input capacitance, 102, 104
    input high voltage, 102
    input low voltage, 102
    output high voltage, 102
    output low voltage, 102, 103
    sleep current, 102, 103
    supply current, 102, 103
    supply voltage, 102
DC operation, 95
DC voltage, 74
DC-DC converters, 113
debounce circuitry, 285

About the Author

John Catsoulis lives under the tropical sun in Brisbane, Australia. He has a Bachelor of Science with Honors (Griffith University) with a triple major in quantum physics, electronics, and mathematics, and a Master of Engineering (La Trobe University) in specialized computer architectures. He has been responsible for the design of more computer systems than he can remember, from tiny finger-sized machines to multi-processor compute engines. Corporations and government bodies around the world have used his designs and software. John has also taught the dark arts of computer architecture and design at several universities. He is currently conducting research at the University of Queensland into fault-tolerant reconfigurable computers for space-craft avionics.

When not slaving over a hot microprocessor, John enjoys hiking and camping, wild-life and landscape photography, fishing, dabbling in permaculture, cooking Indian and Mediterranean food, and playing model trains with his nephews, Andrew and James.

Colophon

Our look is the result of reader comments, our own experimentation, and feedback from distribution channels. Distinctive covers complement our distinctive approach to technical topics, breathing personality and life into potentially dry subjects.

The animal on the cover of *Designing Embedded Hardware*, Second Edition is a porce-lain crab. These tiny invertebrates are common in tide pools along the coast of the Pacific Ocean. They are an orangy brown color, and are only five millimeters long. Porcelain crabs have six pairs of legs, with one tiny pair tucked in across the base of the tail. Although they can swim, sharply pointed spines on the ends of their walking legs make it easier for them to cling to the hard surfaces of submerged rocks. Hair on their legs collects mud from the ocean floor and helps camouflage the crab from pred-ators. Additional protection is provided by mussel beds, sponges, and algae. Once concealed in these preferred habitats, the porcelain crab sweeps its feathery arms through the water, capturing plankton and other tiny plants and animals. When threatened by a predator, these crabs can detach a leg or claw to distract an attacker. The tricky crab scurries away, and its lost appendage eventually grows back.

Sanders Kleinfeld was the production editor and copyeditor for *Designing Embedded Hardware*, Second Edition. Matt Hutchinson proofread the book. Genevieve d'Entremont and Colleen Gorman provided quality control. Julie Hawks wrote the index.

Emma Colby designed the cover of this book, based on a series design by Edie Freedman. The cover image is a 19th-century engraving from *Cuvier's Animals*. Karen Montgomery produced the cover layout with Adobe InDesign CS using Adobe's ITC Garamond font.

David Futato designed the interior layout. This book was converted by Joe Wizda to FrameMaker 5.5.6 with a format conversion tool created by Erik Ray, Jason McIntosh, Neil Walls, and Mike Sierra that uses Perl and XML technologies. The text font is Linotype Birka; the heading font is Adobe Myriad Condensed; and the code font is LucasFont's TheSans Mono Condensed. The illustrations that appear in the book were produced by Robert Romano, Jessamyn Read, and Lesley Borash using Macromedia FreeHand MX and Adobe Photoshop CS. The tip and warning icons were drawn by Christopher Bing. This colophon was written by Philip Dangler.

Better than e-books

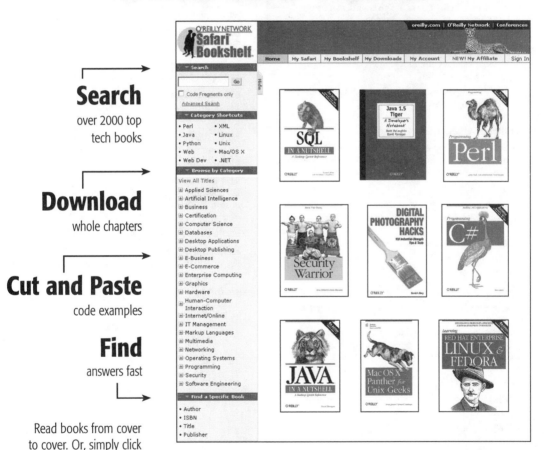

Search
over 2000 top
tech books

Download
whole chapters

Cut and Paste
code examples

Find
answers fast

Read books from cover
to cover. Or, simply click
to the page you need.

Search Safari! The premier electronic reference
library for programmers and IT professionals

Keep in touch with O'Reilly

1. Download examples from our books

To find example files for a book, go to:

www.oreilly.com/catalog

select the book, and follow the "Examples" link.

2. Register your O'Reilly books

Register your book at *register.oreilly.com*

Why register your books?
Once you've registered your O'Reilly books you can:

- Win O'Reilly books, T-shirts or discount coupons in our monthly drawing.

- Get special offers available only to registered O'Reilly customers.

- Get catalogs announcing new books (US and UK only).

- Get email notification of new editions of the O'Reilly books you own.

3. Join our email lists

Sign up to get topic-specific email announcements of new books and conferences, special offers, and O'Reilly Network technology newsletters at:

elists.oreilly.com

It's easy to customize your free elists subscription so you'll get exactly the O'Reilly news you want.

4. Get the latest news, tips, and tools

www.oreilly.com

- "Top 100 Sites on the Web"—PC Magazine
- CIO Magazine's Web Business 50 Awards

Our web site contains a library of comprehensive product information (including book excerpts and tables of contents), downloadable software, background articles, interviews with technology leaders, links to relevant sites, book cover art, and more.

5. Work for O'Reilly

Check out our web site for current employment opportunities:

jobs.oreilly.com

6. Contact us

O'Reilly & Associates
1005 Gravenstein Hwy North
Sebastopol, CA 95472 USA

TEL: 707-827-7000 or 800-998-9938
        (6am to 5pm PST)

FAX: 707-829-0104

order@oreilly.com
For answers to problems regarding your order or our products. To place a book order online, visit:

www.oreilly.com/order_new

catalog@oreilly.com
To request a copy of our latest catalog.

booktech@oreilly.com
For book content technical questions or corrections.

corporate@oreilly.com
For educational, library, government, and corporate sales.

proposals@oreilly.com
To submit new book proposals to our editors and product managers.

international@oreilly.com
For information about our international distributors or translation queries. For a list of our distributors outside of North America check out:

international.oreilly.com/distributors.html

adoption@oreilly.com
For information about academic use of O'Reilly books, visit:

academic.oreilly.com

O'REILLY®

Our books are available at most retail and online bookstores.
To order direct: 1-800-998-9938 • *order@oreilly.com* • *www.oreilly.com*
Online editions of most O'Reilly titles are available by subscription at *safari.oreilly.com*

PackingSlip : Your order has been filled by Page One Bookstore.

102276

mazon Marketplace Item: Designing Embedded Hardware [Illustrated] [Paperback] by Catsoulis, John
Listing ID: 1111J518652
SKU: 2632000-596-00755-844.95
Quantity: 1

Purchased on: 15-Jan-2007
Shipped by: amazon@page1book.com
Shipping address:

Ship to: Drew M. Zimmer
Address Line 1: 504 Winston Dr
Address Line 2:
City: Norman
State/Province/Region: OK
Zip/Postal Code: 73072-3817
Country: United States

Buyer Name: Drew M. Zimmer